CULINARY CULTURES
OF THE MIDDLE EAST

Culinary Cultures
of the
Middle East

edited by

SAMI ZUBAIDA
and
RICHARD TAPPER

I.B.TAURIS PUBLISHERS
LONDON · NEW YORK

In association with
CENTRE OF NEAR AND MIDDLE EASTERN STUDIES
SCHOOL OF ORIENTAL AND AFRICAN STUDIES
UNIVERSITY OF LONDON

Published in 1994 by
I.B. Tauris & Co Ltd
45 Bloomsbury Square
London WC1A 2HY
Reprinted in paperback 1996

175 Fifth Avenue
New York
NY 10010

In the United States of America
and Canada distributed by
St Martin's Press
175 Fifth Avenue
New York
NY 10010

A full CIP record for this book is available from the British Library

Library of Congress catalog card number: 95–62328
A full CIP record for this book is available from the Library of Congress

ISBN 1–86064–035–4

Typeset by Philip Armstrong
Printed and bound in Great Britain by
WBC Ltd, Bridgend, Mid Glamorgan

Contents

Preface

This volume is based on a conference organized by the Centre of Near and Middle Eastern Studies, School of Oriental and African Studies, in April 1992. Most of the chapters are revised versions of papers presented at the conference, but the introduction, one of the chapters by Fragner ('From the Caucasus to the roof of the world') and one of those by Zubaida ('Rice in the culinary cultures of the Middle East') are new, and that by Charles Perry replaces the paper he delivered at the conference.

We would like to record our gratitude to the Trustees of the Nuffield Foundation and to the SOAS Research and Publications Committee for contributing to the funding of the conference. Our thanks are also due to Pauline Rose, then Organizer of the Centre, who administered the preparations for the conference with enthusiasm and good humour. The manuscript was prepared with the assistance of Diana Gur, Publications Editor at the Centre, and also of Simonetta Calderini. George Joffé very kindly helped with the translation of the chapter by Abdelhai Diouri. We are also indebted to all the participants in the conference, including those whose contributions unfortunately could not be printed here, as well as to those who acted as discussants at the panels, to numerous friends and colleagues who have read and commented on the various drafts of these papers, and to several Middle Eastern restaurants in London which assisted with catering arrangements.

Note on Transliteration

Consistency in transliteration is notoriously difficult to achieve in collective volumes on Middle Eastern topics. Authors, publishers and readers have different priorities. The problem is compounded here, where not only are the authors from different academic traditions and nationalities, but their subjects are a combination of literary sources and vernacular speakers in a range of different Middle Eastern languages. The result is inevitably a compromise. In this case, it has been decided to follow a modified version of the system adopted by the *International Journal of Middle East Studies*, omitting all diacritical marks from the main text but including a differentiation (where appropriate) of the Arabic *'ain* and *hamzeh*, and allowing for individual vernacular transliteration where appropriate. In the bibliography, a fuller transliteration has been attempted.

Notes on Contributors

Tony Allan, Professor of Geography at the School of Oriental and African Studies, publishes and researches on the renewable resources of the Middle East, particularly its water, land and vegetation resources. He is interested in the environmental and economic features of these resources and also takes a close interest in the political, international relations and legal aspects of monitoring and managing renewable natural resources. He has published widely on the Middle East and has recently edited books on Water in the Middle East and on the Nile. He also advises governments and international agencies on the use of remote sensing techniques as well as on water policy.

Françoise Aubaile-Sallenave is a Researcher in Cultural Anthropology attached to the Laboratory of Ethnobiology of the Musée National d'Histoire Naturelle of Paris, where she was the scientific commissioner, and edited the catalogues, for the exhibition *Parfums de plantes*. She obtained her PhD at the Sorbonne, Paris. She has done field research in Morocco and published several papers on anthropology and the ethnoscience of Muslim culture. She has edited a volume on *Sucre et sel*.

Christian Bromberger teaches ethnology at the University of Provence at Aix-en-Provence where he is Director of the Laboratoire d'éthnologie méditerranée et comparative (C.N.R.S.). He is also member of the research team 'Sciences sociales du monde iranien contemporain' (C.N.R.S., Paris). His main interest is the study of collective identities through different themes. He has carried out field research in Gilân, Iran, on which he has written numerous articles and two books, most recently *Habitat, architecture and the rural society in the Gilân plain* (Bonn, Ferd Dümmlers Verlag, 1989). At the same time he is completing a book on the passion for football in some cities of the north-west Mediterranean.

Holly Chase writes and lectures on the arts and cuisines of countries that lie between Portugal and India. A specialist in Islamic textiles and ethnographia, she has lived in Turkey. Recent work advising non-profit international agencies on handicraft preservation and development has taken her to Hungary, Bahrain, and Uganda. She is the author of *Turkish Tapestry, A Traveller's Portrait of Turkey* (Bosphorus Books, 1993). She lives in Groton Long Point, Connecticut, USA.

Abdelhai Diouri is Maître-Assistant at the Institut Universitaire de la Recherche Scientifique, Université Mohammad V, Rabat. He studied Philosophy and Sociology in Paris, writing a thesis (with Roland Barthes) on 'La Trans au Maroc'. Since 1989 he has conducted a multidisciplinary research seminar on 'Le Symbolique' at IURS. His current field of research is traditional medicine: mental health, bio-medicine, food, cult and ritual. He has published many articles, in Arabic and in French, in Moroccan and international reviews. He has two books in the press: ed. *Les puissances du symbole*, Horizons Mediterranéens, Casablanca; and *Ananké: rencontre autour de la mort*, Les Editions du CNRS, Paris.

Bert Fragner is Professor of Iranian Studies at the University of Bamberg, Germany. He studied at the Universities of Vienna (1959–1965 and 1969–1970; PhD in Iranian Studies, Turcology and Islamic Studies), Tehran (1964–1965) and Freiburg (1977). He has taught in Germany (Universities of Freiburg and Freie Universität, Berlin), Austria (University of Vienna), Switzerland (University of Bern) and Iran (Tehran). His research interests are the economic and social history of premodern Iran and Central Asia; history of administration and institutions in Iran; Persian diplomats; early Soviet Tajikistan and Central Asia; anthropological aspects of history (e.g. food and other aspects of everyday culture in historical perspective).

Sabry Hafez is Professor of Modern Arabic at the School of Oriental and African Studies. He studied sociology and drama in Egypt and obtained his PhD in Arabic literature from the University of London with a thesis on *The Rise and Development of the Egyptian Short Story*. He has published extensively in Arabic and English with several books and numerous articles on the Arabic novel, the short story and drama to his name. His most recent books in English are *The Genesis of Narrative Discourse: A Study in the Sociology of Modern Arabic Literature* (Al-Saqi Books, 1993) and *Arabic*

Cinema (BFI Publications, forthcoming 1994).

Peter Heine is Acting Director of the Forschungszentrum Moderner Orient in Berlin, having studied oriental languages, anthropology and philosophy in Münster, Germany and Baghdad, Iraq. His main research interests are the cultural history of the Middle East and cultural change. His publications include *Weinstudien, Untersuchungen zu Anbau, Produktion und Konsum des Weins im arabisch islamischen Mittelalter* (Wiesbaden, 1982), and *Kulinarische Studien. Untersuchungen zur Kochkunst im arabisch islamischen Mittelalter* (Wiesbaden, 1988).

Ianthe Maclagan recently completed a PhD based on twenty months' fieldwork in the then Yemen Arab Republic in 1982–3. Living in a small highland town in Mahwit Province, she looked at the lives of women, their constraints and room to manoeuvre, and the effects of male migration and economic change. She is currently working as a researcher for the charity Youthaid.

Manuela Marín is a researcher in the Department of Arabic Studies at the Consejo Superior de Investigaciones Científicas in Madrid. She is the editor of the journal *Al-Qanflara*. Her current research interests are the social and cultural history of al-Andalus, and food in Islamic societies. Her most recent book is *Individuo y sociedad en al-Andalus* (Madrid, 1992).

Charles Perry is a journalist living in Los Angeles. He studied Near Eastern languages at Princeton University (1959–61) and the University of California at Berkeley (1961–62 and 1963–64) and spent a year at the Middle East Centre for Arabic Studies at Shemlan, Lebanon (1962–63). After eight years as an editor at *Rolling Stone* magazine, he spent twelve as a freelance food writer. Since 1990 he has been a Staff Writer at the *Los Angeles Times*. He has written numerous articles for *Petits Propos Culinaires* and seven papers for the Oxford Symposium.

Claudia Roden was born in Egypt. She writes about food, and has published several cookery books and travelled around the world as a journalist. She has also taught Middle Eastern cooking. Her *A New Book of Middle Eastern Food* is the expanded edition of a book first published in 1968. She has worked on the BBC Television series *Mediterranean Cookery* and has written the accompanying book.

Richard Tapper is Reader in Anthropology at the School of Oriental and African Studies. He has carried out field research in Iran, Afghanistan and Turkey; his monographs include *Pasture and Politics* (Academic Press, 1979) and the forthcoming *The King's Friends: A Social and Political History of the Shahsevan*, and he has edited volumes on *The Conflict of Tribe and State in Iran and Afghanistan* (Croom Helm, 1983), *Islam in Modern Turkey* (I B Tauris, 1991), *Some Minorities in the Middle East* (SOAS CNMES, 1992), and *The Nomads of Iran* (forthcoming).

Mai Yamani, a Saudi Arabian, was born in Cairo. She was educated in Switzerland, the United States and Oxford. She became a member of the board of the Centre for Contemporary Arab Studies at Georgetown University. She has written and lectured extensively on many aspects of the contemporary Middle East, especially Saudi Arabia. Her main interests include social identity and ethnicity and she has several papers and articles in international journals and other publications.

Sami Zubaida is Reader in Politics and Sociology at Birkbeck College, London. His main area of research and writing has been on religion, culture and politics in the Middle East. He has published many articles on the subject and a book, *Islam, the People and the State*. A gourmet and an amateur cook, he has also been active in the study of food and culture, on which he has contributed articles, lectures and conference papers.

CULINARY CULTURES OF THE MIDDLE EAST

Introduction

Richard Tapper and Sami Zubaida

The culinary cultures of the contemporary Middle East are formed by a number of geographical and historical parameters. On one side the region borders the Mediterranean, and participates in the material civilization generated in that basin. On the other it faces the Central Asian plateau, and has been host to many migrations and dynasties originating to the east of it. The region is heir to a succession of urban, agriculturally based civilizations from the earliest times, at the same time profoundly influenced by nomadic, pastoralist peoples and cultures. In the present century this varied heritage is being overlaid and transformed by the global processes of world markets and the revolutions in transport and communications. Are there any coherent patterns to be discerned in this variety and flux?

The chapters of this book, written by geographers, historians, ethnographers and sociologists, have the cumulative effect of an affirmative answer to this question: there are coherent patterns, both historical and contemporary. This coherence is less the product of some cultural essence of Islam or ancient Near Eastern civilizations or '*the* Mediterranean', continuous over historical time, and much more to do with successions and articulations of political and cultural hegemonies established by successive dynasties and elites.

This introduction briefly surveys the growing field of studies of the cultural and social aspects of food and cookery, and shows how the themes discussed in the contributions to the book relate to that field. The previous relegation of this field to the margins of history and the social sciences is now being reversed, with growing signs of serious interest in the form of conferences and symposia offering outlets to the growing body of research and writing. In particular, the annual Oxford Symposium on Food and Cookery, started by Alan Davidson and Theodore Zeldin, has offered a forum, a stimulus and an example for efforts in these directions.

There are various books on the history of food, some general, some concerning particular ingredients or regions. We single out here histories by and in the style of the Annales School (after the journal *Annales: économies, sociétés, civilisations*), because it sets up a model for the integration of history, geography and sociology/anthropology in the study of cultures and civilizations over time. There are a few major works in this school directly concerned with food, most notably Louis Stouff's *Revitaillement et alimentation en Provence aux XIVe et XVe siècles*. However, there is a wealth of material on food, diet, feasts, rituals and so on, in the many works of social history, notably Fernand Braudel's voluminous work on the Mediterranean in the 16th century, and especially the chapters on food and drink in his *The Structures of Everyday Life*, and E. Le Roy Ladurie's *The Peasants of the Languedoc*. More recently, Jean-Louis Flandrin, distinguished for his work on the history of the family and sexuality, has made exciting contributions to food history. His book *Chronique de platine* (1992) is subtitled 'Pour une gastronomie historique', which indicates his interest in exploring the historical vicissitudes of gastronomic sensibilities. Eugene Weber's *Peasants into Frenchmen* contains much important information on the diet of the French peasant in the latter half of the 19th century.

Braudel's chapters on 'Daily bread' and 'Food and drink' survey the broad developments in world patterns, particularly over the period 1400–1800. He remarks: 'From now on [after the neolithic/agricultural revolution] history records two opposing species of humanity: the few who ate meat and the many who fed on bread, gruel, roots and cooked tubers' (1981: 106). Until the 18th century, Europe was much more profligate than the rest of the world in eating flesh. However, argues Braudel, it did not develop sophisticated food cultures until the 16th century. China and the Near East came first in this respect. In all regions of civilization, however, accounts of food and cookery are overwhelmingly biased towards the 'few who ate meat'. We shall see that this is certainly the case when it comes to the Middle East.

In anthropology, classic debates have focused on systems of classification of edible and inedible animals and plants, the nature and logic of food taboos, the sacrifice of animals and plants, and the social role of food in exchange and commensality. There are vast literatures on these themes, to which writers such as Claude Lévi-Strauss (1964, 1966) and Mary Douglas (1966) have made significant contributions. The titles of many of Lévi-Strauss's works include food terms: *The Raw and the Cooked*, *From Honey to Ashes*, *The Origin of Table Manners*. But it has been argued that there is actually very little on food as such in these works, and that they are much more concerned with detecting 'structures' in myths and cultural categories and their homologies with other spheres of culture, and ultimately with revealing the structure of the human mind. It is undeniable, however, that Lévi-Strauss's structuralist approach has inspired many substantive and stimulating analyses of food cultures, including Diouri's contribution in this volume. Douglas (1975) and others such as Marshall Sahlins (1976), influenced by the structuralism of Lévi-Strauss and the semiology of Roland Barthes (e.g. 1961), have focused on topics such as the structure of meals, table manners, and the role of food as a marker of ethnic difference; topics which are discussed in a number of chapters in this volume.[1]

In the sociology of food, after major contributions from the 1970s by Pierre Bourdieu (1977 and 1984), two books of the 1980s stand out: Stephen Mennell's *All Manners of Food* (1985) and Jack Goody's *Cooking, Cuisine and Class* (1982). Both, in different ways, have broad historical and comparative ambitions. Goody's terms of comparison are of particular interest to our studies. He contrasts the relatively undifferentiated cooking cultures of Black Africa to those of the class-differentiated historical civilizations of China, India, the Near East and Europe. In the former, where a limited and localized range of ingredients were used, there was little cultural differentiation between rich and poor. The rich just ate more of the same. (Would Braudel's characterization put medieval Europe into this category?) Specific forms of 'high cooking' for the upper classes, distinct from the staples of the common people, develop under conditions of diversity of ingredients (based on more advanced agriculture and trade), and a sizeable class of relatively prosperous and adventurous eaters, who adopt an aesthetic attitude to food. Writing facilitates the recording, transmission, and ultimately the cumulative refinement of recipes and menus. These were precisely the conditions under which food cultures flourished in the Muslim Middle Ages.

MATERIALS FOR THE HISTORY OF FOOD IN THE MIDDLE EAST

Historical studies of food in the Middle East have centred primarily on writing: recipe books and medical treatises written by and for court personalities, scribes and savants. There are also books of belles lettres, essays, stories and poems which feature episodes on food. Maxime Rodinson is the pioneer and doyen of these studies. His 'Recherches sur les documents arabes relatifs à la cuisine' (1949) surveyed this literature. Two manuscripts from the Abbasid period, both entitled *Kitab al-Tabikh*, one by Muhammad b. Hasan al-Baghdadi (d 1239; 1934), the second by Ibn Sayyar al-Warraq (10th century; 1987), and a later one (in several variant versions), *Kitab al-Wusla ila 'l-Habib*, of uncertain authorship, but probably by a 13th-century Ayyubid prince in Syria, form the extant canon of cookery literature for the medieval Eastern Muslim world. These works refer to a wide range of other sources which have been lost. Rodinson concentrated on these works, with a detailed summary of the last. The recipes are generally of great complexity, calling for a wide range of ingredients, spices, herbs and aromatics.

These works, in addition to a few other medieval manuscripts from the Maghreb and Spain, and some treatises on medicine, have formed the subject of continuing scholarly investigations, notably in the work of Charles Perry, Peter Heine, Manuela Marín and David Waines. In recent books, Heine (1988) and Waines (1989) have systematically reviewed the available materials on medieval Arabic culinary arts, and compiled a number of recipes, principally from the two works entitled *Kitab al-Tabikh*, with (in Waine's case) adaptations for the modern kitchen. Marín also draws on this literature for her contribution to the present volume, in which she examines the ways in which food was prepared and presented so as to stimulate other senses than that of taste: notably visual appeal through artificial colouring, and olfactory stimulation with perfumes.

This literature, as well as the belles lettres of *maqamat* and *aghani* (narratives and anecdotes, often in rhymed prose), which include descriptions of food, were clearly directed to a readership of court aristocracy and other literate and prosperous strata. Literary quotations and references and versified recipes abound. Like all the literature in this genre, it is predominantly masculine, with few and exceptional references to a court lady or a slave girl who excelled in one or other of the cooking genres. Unlike the European historical literature, it tells us very little about the food of the peasants, of the lower classes, of the markets and the streets. Some material on these subjects may be found in essays and stories, notably in the remarkable *Kitab al-Bukhala'* (The Book of Misers), by the Basri writer al-Jahiz (775–868), which contains a wealth of details on social life, including food and drink, told in the context of humorous narrations about misers. There are many references to food and drink in the tales of *The Thousand and One Nights*. These, however, still await detailed study from the food and drink angle.

There is no equivalent cluster of scholarly work on the food of early modern and modern periods in Middle East history. Rodinson devotes a few pages of his survey to cookbooks appearing in Turkey, Egypt and

Syria in the 19th and early 20th centuries. Some of these are particularly interesting, partly because they respond to the European cultural impact by defining and defending their native food cultures, and partly because they give accounts and adaptations of European foods. The health and hygiene angles become prominent in the later books.

A rather different approach is that adopted by Sabry Hafez in his chapter on 'culinary semiology', where he examines various kinds of modern Arabic literature, not for information on food and food habits (the job of the ethnographer) but to analyse how the authors use food, both in descriptions of its preparation and consumption, and metaphorically, to convey many-layered social and cultural meanings.

There is much information on food and foodways in historical and travel accounts, on Iran and the Ottoman lands, but these have not been systematically researched from the food angle. We should mention, in particular, the diaries of the 17th-century Ottoman traveller, Evliya Chelebi, published under the title of *Siyahetname* (Dankoff 1990; see also Zubaida's chapter on rice in this volume). There is also a remarkable ethnography of early 19th-century Egypt, Edward Lane's *Account of the Manners and Customs of the Modern Egyptians*, which includes a wealth of detail on all aspects of social life, including food and drink, table manners, feasts and fasts and so on. Historical studies of courts, embassies, religious institutions and markets have also yielded information on food and foodways. One especially interesting work in this respect is Suraiya Faroqhi's excellent *Towns and Townsmen of Ottoman Anatolia*, which contains information and analysis on social and economic life in the 17th century, including material on trade and markets in food, and the curious organization of butchers and the meat trade in Istanbul. There is considerable scholarly interest in these fields among some Turkish historians writing in Turkish, notably Gunay and Turgut Kut.

Among historians of Iran, Afghanistan and Central Asia, Bert Fragner's seminal article on Safavid and Qajar cookbooks (1984) appears to be rare in its specific reference to food, and his chapters in this volume do much to extend our knowledge. A number of recent ethnographic studies, by Pierre Centlivres (1972, 1985) and Richard Tapper and Nancy Tapper (1986) on northern Afghanistan, and by Christian Bromberger (1985, and see this volume) on northern Iran, focus on food practices in rural areas, with a stress on systems of classification (especially the hot–cold dimension) and discourses of evaluation. An interesting article by Farhad Khos-rokhavar (1989) analyses radical changes in *mentalité* in modern urban Iran as reflected in eating habits. He notes the increase in consumption of exotic fruits and other imported foods, even under the xenophobic Islamic Republic. Meat, despite its escalating cost, has become the expected base of most household dishes, at the expense of traditional vegetable-based soups and stews as well as local varieties of cheese and other products. His discussion of the fast-food lunch in Tehran complements Holly Chase's description (this volume) of contemporary Istanbul, but where she finds that 'the presence of establishments like McDonald's may actually be contributing to a revival of old-fashioned foods which have been in danger of disappearing', he sees only culinary loss, and the desire, common in Third World countries, to escape daily reality through dreams of a transnational, consumerist modernity.

CONTINUITY, DIFFUSION AND TRANSFORMATION

Tony Allan's chapter reviews the regional background in terms of the natural resources, agricultural practices and the production of food, patterns of consumption in the Middle East and the more or less general problem of water supply. He argues strongly that Middle Eastern governments must radically alter national priorities which have hitherto aimed at the impossible target of food self-sufficiency, making un-sustainable allocations of water to agriculture, and must recognize the need for substantial food imports. As he points out, most of the people of the region have long accepted ingredients and dishes from elsewhere in their cuisines, and the other chapters provide further evidence of this.

Many of the contributions to this volume deal with food and drink in modern contemporary settings. The chapters by Diouri, Bromberger, Maclagan and Yamani have an ethnographic focus, analysing the place of food and drink in terms of social relations and cultural expressions in specific bounded social contexts. Yamani's chapter shares with those of Chase, Heine and Zubaida the themes of movement and diffusion of food and food cultures as part of the play of global processes of production, trade, migrations, tourism and communications.

Diffusions are not, of course, peculiar to modernity. On a different scale they are at the basis of formations and transformations of food cultures throughout the history of the region. The theme of historical diffusions and adaptations is prominent in the contributions by Aubaile-Sallenave, Fragner, Perry and Roden. What do we learn from these contributions regarding continuities and transformations of food cultures (of ingredients, dishes, meals, cuisines) and the factors which determine the process and direction of diffusion? What are the traces of the past in what is eaten and drunk at present?

It is paradoxical that we who inhabit the modern (or post-modern) world, one so spectacularly discontinuous with its past, are nevertheless transfixed by history. We constantly search for the origins and essences of our personality, our culture, our nationality in the remote past. This tendency is nowhere more apparent than in the nationalist ideological project to construct a long and continuous history for a nation conceived of only in recent times. This search for origins, however, is by no means confined to nationalist ideologues. Many cosmopolitan observers of culture seem to be drawn to explanations in terms of origin, and to assumptions of cultural continuity in the history of a people or a region. Writers on food are no exception.

Claudia Roden, the doyenne of food writers on the Middle East and the Mediterranean, starts the second edition of her famous *A Book of Middle Eastern Food* with a long introduction setting out the background of Middle Eastern food, mostly in terms of history. She gives a fascinating account of the formation of the food cultures of the region from the inputs of the different peoples and dynasties. The overall impression created by this account is one of cumulative continuity. At one point she remarks:

Some of al-Baghdadi's recipes for stews could be word for word instructions for an Iranian *khoresh* or a Moroccan *tagine* of today; and we still make in my family many of the dishes described in the *Wusla*. As for the methods, grinding fine, rolling into balls or oblongs, pounding in the mortar, simmering long in broth, cutting up in lozenges, bathing in syrup – every touch and movement required are those employed today (1986: 39).

This is true as far as it goes. Our perceptions of the past as origins predispose us to an emphasis on similarity and continuity.

If we examine the recipes carefully, however, we can equally discern crucial differences. Modern cookery almost invariably starts with frying the meats with onions, tomatoes and aromatics before adding liquids, which then form a sauce. Some of the medieval recipes follow a similar pattern (but with the crucial absence of the now ubiquitous tomato); in many, however, the meats are boiled with vegetables and spices until dry, then further dressed and seasoned. In one or two, the meat is boiled dry then finished suspended in the *tannur* (earthenware oven). Some medieval recipes require the meat to be first boiled then fried and stewed. These procedures may be found in modern practice, but are unusual (though more common in Indian recipes).

The widest differences are in spicing and seasoning. Medieval cuisine (in common with its contemporary European counterpart) used a great many spices: pepper, ginger, saffron, cinnamon, galingale, cumin, coriander and mastic (but no garlic), often all in the same dish, in addition to that most characteristic flavouring of the period, *murri*, a condiment made from rotted cereals or bread (see Perry 1988), which seems to have been the equivalent of the Roman *garum*. A regular feature was sweet and sour flavouring using honey or *dibs* (date syrup) and vinegar, another element shared with the European Middle Ages, but not with the modern Middle East. Souring agents commonly used were vinegar, verjuice and sumac, rarely lemon and lime. The ubiquitous lemon in the modern cookery of the region was then all but absent. In recent and modern cookery of the region, spicing has been very restrained, often confined to sparing use of aromatic mixtures, *baharat* or *ras al-hanut* in addition to salt and pepper. Istanbuli cuisine, which claims the Ottoman heritage, prides itself on restraint in the use of flavourings, implying that their overuse further south is a sign of vulgarity and lack of refinement.

Some of the similarities noted by Roden are not specific to the region but common items of complex cookery everywhere, such as pounding, mincing, shaping into balls or pretty patterns, bathing in syrup, and one may add, stuffing animals with meats, nuts, fruits and other exotic ingredients (though not the more recent rice) especially in banquet food. Many of these procedures are to be found in European antiquity and in China. Complex cookery for exalted households and their banquets in the ancient and medieval world would seem to have shared many common features distinct from those of modern times.

Fragner (in his chapter 'From the Caucasus') traces the likely routes of diffusion of food products and practices into Iran from the East, and argues that politics is the major determining factor:

The character and density of the transmission and adoption of foodstuffs also depend very much and intensely on political structures. Thus it is evident that traditions and fashions in nutrition and cooking are influenced by politics; to a historian, the diffusion of certain culinary customs may even indicate the distribution of political power within certain social strata in a given territory.

History – compilations ranging from Roden's introduction to the massive surveys by Braudel and others – gives countless examples of how politically dominant elites adopt ingredients and dishes liberally from neighbours and subject peoples, and how the resultant cuisines are imitated by weaker, dependent classes.

Politics, in the form of the nationalist project, is also a major shaper of modern cuisines. Peter Heine's chapter in this volume surveys recent cookery books in the Arab world, and he notes the implicit and sometimes explicit claims to a national cuisine, Kuwaiti or Saudi or Iraqi. 'Food nationalism' is also discussed in Zubaida's contribution. Like all nationalisms this manifestation is deeply concerned with history: the national culture must be shown to have had a continuous existence over the centuries. In addition, it has a tendency to claim the original introduction of the now common items. This kind of claim is illustrated in the dispute over the origin of baklava discussed by Perry (this volume), who casts doubt on the case for the Byzantine invention of such layered breads and pastries and argues convincingly for their origin among the Turks in Central Asia.

Discussing modern cookbooks which describe the cuisines of Iran and Central Asia, Fragner (in his chapter 'Social Reality') points out their fictional quality, in some cases as highly idealized ethnographic records, in others as expressions of cultural sentiments of nostalgia, so that these books tell us less about actual culinary conditions than about 'collective imaginations, symbolic values, dreams and expectations'. He also argues that the fictional nature of Persian cookbooks is not a new phenomenon, but can be traced to the literary tradition of which they formed part.

Most modern cookery books have an introduction which alludes to history, where the claims for antiquity and originality are made. Books on Persian food have claimed almost the totality of the Middle Eastern repertoire as originally Persian, supporting the claim by reference to current food vocabulary and some speculative etymology. Furthermore, the Persian culinary tradition is traced to Sassanian or more ancient beginnings, to Khosrow and his banquets in the 7th century (again a familiar starting point for many historical introductions). Of course, Persian culture has been an important source of Middle Eastern civilizations. But like all cultures it is subject to many diffusions and mutations. Some items survive, some words survive but change their meanings, many things mutate, and other items (like the curious *murri*) disappear without trace. Al-Jahiz's Book of Misers (9th century), already mentioned, contains many Persian food words which have now disappeared. Much of the modern food vocabulary, including the ubiquitous *kufta*, does not appear there. Current food vocabulary in the region was most probably developed and generalized in later Ottoman times.

The patterns of Middle Eastern food cultures we discern do not depend on historical continuity. History is made up of movement and trans-formations of societies, dynasties, populations, diffusions and innovations. In this flux, cultures, too, are transformed, though they continue to refer back to their past. Culture, historically considered, appears as variations and play of interwoven themes, which shift their weave and patterns but remain recognizable. Françoise Aubaile-Sallenave's chapter on *kashk* is perhaps the best illustration of this point. *Kashk* (and its cognates) refers to a variety of foods found in many parts of the Middle East over many centuries, mainly involving either a soured-milk product, or fermented barley, or some complex preparation; through detailed analysis of the etymology and semantics of the term, and examination of historical and contemporary evidence relating to the preparations it has designated, she is able to unravel its complex history and the links between its different referents.

So many things eaten now in the region are of relatively recent origins. New World foods – the tomato, the potato, maize, peppers, fasolia beans – are all taken for granted as items of contemporary Middle Eastern cookery, but date back at the earliest to the 18th century, and mostly to the 19th. Rice, the pride of Persian cuisine, has a longer ancestry, but is by no means ancient (see chapters by Zubaida, Fragner and Bromberger). While known from ancient times, it was little used until Safavid times, when it acquired pride of place on the highest tables. Earlier, its use was limited to the small areas where it was cultivated, where it was cooked in puddings and porridges, mostly in milk, or ground and baked in cheap bread. On the tables of the rich, it featured, when it did, as puddings.

Two further examples illustrate the transformation of dishes over time and space, and the shifting referents of common words. *Sikbaj* is a dish attributed by Abbasid writers to Sassanian Iran.[2] In these writings it is a stew made from fatty meat, flavoured with vinegar and date syrup, a sweet and sour effect common in medieval foods in the Middle East and Europe, as we have seen. In recent times it is unknown in the region. It surfaces, however, in Spain as *escabeche*, this time a dish of fish fried and marinated in vinegar, typically eaten cold. And from there to South America, where the same word designates a dish of raw fish slices marinated in lime juice and chillis. The only element left from the Abbasid usage is that of a soured meat.

Or consider the appellation *korma* or *qormeh* in present-day Indian and Persian cookery (Zubaida 1989). The word stems from the Turkish *qavurma*, from the verb to fry. Indeed, one version of it in modern Turkey consists of fried slices of meat (served typically on 'Id al-Adha when a sheep is slaughtered). Another derived meaning in Turkey and Syria is meat preserved in its own fat with salt and spices. It can also mean that in western Iran. However, *sabzi qormeh* in modern Iran consists of a stew of meat in butterfat with a large quantity of chopped green herbs and whole dried limes. In northern India it is a meat stew with yoghurt or cream. The only element in common to all these usages is meat cooked in fat in a rich dish. In both the examples of *sikbaj* and *korma*, the words are diffused over time and place, but with shifting referents, retaining only elements of common allusion to sourness and richness respectively.

The greatest transformations are those of modernity. But part of modernity, as we have tried to show, is the obsession with history. Many of the chapters in this collection are on the theme of the modern search for origins and traditions, and the 'discovery' and construction of these traditions. Is this search for tradition part of the 'post-modern condition'?

FOOD AND THE SOCIAL ORDER

Food is essential to the subsistence and survival of individual human beings, who can prepare and consume it alone. Almost universally, however, the jobs involved in food preparation (from the production or procurement of ingredients to the cooking of meals) are allocated to specific categories of people, commonly by gender; and equally universally people prefer to eat with others. This specialization and sharing mark a wide range of social distinctions and relationships.

As we have noted earlier, several chapters in this book, and specifically Zubaida's, analyse the modern tendency to mark boundaries through the creation of distinctive national cuisines. The model for this is the age-old association of social and cultural difference with different food customs. At the most obvious level, the wealthy and poor in a society, different ethnic groups, city and village dwellers (cf Centlivres-Demont 1985), men and women, adults and children, eat differently. Food is a marker of social status; not surprisingly, since 'we are what we eat', status differences are often also held to imply differences in essence, personality and worth: hence, ethnic and national stereotypes which focus on food habits (cf Bromberger's chapter).

The chapters by Ianthe Maclagan (on rural Yemen) and Mai Yamani (on the wealthy elite of Mecca) show in fascinating detail how the preparation and serving of food, and the ingredients used, differentiate the participants according to kinship and affinity, gender and status. So also, shared consumption – commensality – whether between two or in a feast, conveys cultural and social meanings, some of which lie in the act of sharing, its forms and conventions, others in the nature of the food that is shared and the structure of the meals.

Commensal occasions range from normal family meals to the entertainment of visitors and invited guests, to life-cycle and other ceremonial meals, to religious occasions. At all these, commensality is a demonstration of social solidarity among participants, bearing moral implications of mutual support in the future. Those who eat together implicitly mark their common identity and equality, particularly on religious occasions. In a Muslim context, these range from family occasions such as *iftar* in Ramadan (see Diouri's chapter for Ramadan foods in Morocco, Yamani's for Mecca, and Hafez's for Arabic literary examples) or sacrificial meals where guests are invited, to feasts or distributions of food at mosques, shrines, *imaret* or other religious foundations.[3]

But at the same time, commensal occasions can also reinforce structures of authority, between men and women, old and young, powerful and weak, between classes and ethnic groups, both in the family context and also in feasts, since these are usually sponsored, or organized and financed, by someone in authority. Some feasts (at marriages, for example) are occasions for a would-be leader to make claims to authority or status, and those who eat the food he (or she) provides implicitly accept these claims. A host always takes a risk – issues a challenge – when offering food. Though often playing the humble servant of his guests, and doing his best to honour them, he is honoured by their presence and acceptance of his food. Refusal to eat another's food may be seen as an explicit challenge to honour; in some cases, it might be a tactical move by a rebel against authority, or a plaintiff in a dispute (Tapper and Tapper 1986: 69).

The institution of hospitality – feeding the stranger, entertaining invited guests, and accepting food when it is offered – is a cultural and religious obligation (see Pitt-Rivers 1977): Yamani describes how in old Mecca the guest should literally be 'fed' by the host's own hand. Throughout the Middle East, both giving food (feeding) and receiving food (being fed) have complex implications of status and honour, which are further complicated by the type and amount of food, drink and other substances (and services) involved, and often, for example, whether the food given and received is cooked or uncooked. The potlatch of western Canada, familiar to generations of anthropology students as the extravagant competitive giving and destruction of food and other items, has its parallels in many Middle Eastern contexts of hospitality, where conspicuous consumption, as so often, finds its rationale not in household economics but in informal politics.

The political themes of honour and challenge, which are pervasive in the language and conduct of occasions of hospitality, are elaborated in the details of seating patterns in the guest room, in the order of precedence in serving, and in the manners expected of guests and host generally, as described in numerous accounts, both by foreign travellers and ethnographers, and in local manuals of etiquette.

Adding to the uncertainty and risk incurred by the host, in each area, certain foods tend to be expected at feasts and on occasions of hospitality, and they should be prepared and served according to ritualized patterns. The resulting anxiety and tension for the host and the cooks (will they get it right, will their culinary efforts be judged 'proper' and adequate by the guests?) reflect – or deflect? – the political and ritual 'danger' and uncertainty of the occasion (cf Douglas 1966).

Commensality implies shared understandings and evaluations of what constitutes 'proper' food. But when we entertain guests from other traditions, we expect them – challenge them – to approve and applaud our food. Every culture and community is proud of its own food traditions and tends to be ambivalent or contemptuous about those of others (see, for example, Maclagan on *baladi* foods in rural Yemen, Yamani on the re-invention of 'Meccan' cuisine). Stereotypes of other ethnic and religious groups frequently refer to food customs (as Bromberger documents for northern Iran and Zubaida for Iraq). Alternatively, a cosmopolitan orientation may be demonstrated by those who consume 'ethnic' foods, though dishes served in 'ethnic' restaurants are often adjusted radically to suit the perceived tastes of the local consumers, just as native cuisine may be almost unrecognizable when served to international tourists (Zubaida).

THE LANGUAGE OF FOOD

The complex language of food evaluations is evident in many chapters of this volume. The language operates at several levels. First and most obvious, perhaps, is the aesthetics of taste, notoriously subjective and liable to changes of fashion, in the world of food as in those of dress and other cultural phenomena. Second is the realm of etiquette associated with eating, particularly on occasions of feasting or hospitality: the proper manners and pace of eating; whether conversation and conviviality are appropriate at the time (matters on which Yamani and Maclagan, for example, comment in detail). Many religious treatises, particularly those of recent Iranian Shi'ite divines, prescribe in minute detail all the manners proper to eating and related actions. Third is the language of metaphor, in which, for example, the personality of individuals and groups is summarized in terms of categories from the realm of food (see the chapters by Bromberger, Marín and Hafez). Food, being the focus of the major festive and communal occasions in most communities, may also be used metonymically to describe those festivities, as when Afghan tribespeople evaluate weddings according to the number of cauldrons of rice cooked (N. Tapper 1991: 172ff). At the other extreme, 'bread' is very commonly the metonym for 'food' in general.

Food evaluations, Richard Tapper and Nancy Tapper have suggested, may be analysed in terms of a number of different domains of discourse: the religious, the political, the medical and the magical. Their analysis is applied specifically to the context of Durrani tribespeople in northern Afghanistan, but it may well have wider applicability in Middle Eastern contexts: 'Analytically, these domains are distinct: each refers to a discrete social context in which [people] evaluate and use food in quite different ways: the contexts, respectively, of formal religious belief and action, political and economic competition, personal health and nutrition, and coping with misfortunes caused by occult powers' (1986: 62–3).

Religious discourse includes rules of purity and pollution; marks out certain substances as taboo (in Islam: pork, blood, alcohol) and others as specially blessed, as God's gift (bread) or as favourites of the Prophet (dates: see Diouri); and prescribes sacrifices, especially of meat. Political discourse marks certain foods (usually the more expensive – with bread the notable exception) as having better taste, more prestige and honour in contexts of competitive hospitality, and often reserves some of these foods to elites or to men rather than women. In medical discourse, which may have religious connotations, the nutritive and therapeutic values of food come to the fore. In the magical discourse, finally, substances sometimes gain therapeutic – or harmful – value by being devalued or tabooed in one of the other domains, particularly the religious: blood, for example. The domains exist 'as alternative frames of reference between which [people] can switch according to context'. These semantic switches are facilitated by the use of certain broad and ambiguous value scales – such as 'goodness' or 'power' – and by reference to certain dominant symbols, such as blood, and associated rituals, such as sacrifice.

FOOD AND OTHER CULTURAL SYSTEMS

A further semantic problem is fundamental to the analysis of the language of food: how far do our major categories ('food', 'drinking', 'eating') translate indigenous Middle Eastern categories and conceptions? How far do the latter either assimilate 'drinking' to 'eating' or associate these with other actions such as 'smoking'? What are the common linguistic – and customary – associations of food and drink in different Middle Eastern cultural contexts? What can be learned from the answers to these questions?

Richard Tapper attempts some answers in his survey of 'drink' and 'drinking' in the Middle East. The current climate of opinion about the Middle East fosters the view, among the uninitiated, that wine and alcohol in general are taboo, and as such do not feature in the cultures of that region. Nothing could be further from the truth. Drink has always featured prominently in urban settings, and in sophisticated literate and prosperous circles whole cultures and etiquettes were generated around drink. Classical poetry and belles lettres abound in celebrations of the stuff. The fact that it was not religiously approved merely added to the piquancy. Medical treatises also dealt with the medicinal properties of wine, and many of them recommended its intake in moderation. Peter Heine has elsewhere written at length about this in the medieval context (1982), while Tapper's chapter elaborates on the theme of drink (not only alcoholic) and its ritual and symbolic meanings in the present day.

Other chapters also refer to different types and contexts of drink: Chase to the consumption of *boza* and *sahlep* in modern Istanbul, Aubaile-Sallenave to liquid forms of *kashk*, Maclagan (like Tapper) to the social role of tea and coffee. Hafez describes the association, in Naguib Mahfuz's work, of alcohol (and the consumption of *mezze*) with the context of conviviality, conversation, poetry, leisure – and illicit sex.

It is an anthropological and psychological commonplace, referred to in several chapters, that food and sex (as well as gender, but that is another issue, alluded to earlier) are linked in many ways: as basic drives (for survival, through production and reproduction) but also as basic sources of pleasure, and as focuses, beyond the satisfaction of the drives, for elaborate codes of manners relating to commensality and conjugality. Food and sex are also subject to more or less strict regulation by society and the state. Almost universally linked in imagery and metaphor, they are less explicitly linked in conversation and practice, where they are separated by a firm allocation of food to the public and sex to the private sphere.

Drink on the other hand, especially alcohol, is much more explicitly associated with sex in practice, particularly (and not only in the Middle East) in the context of illicitness. Alcohol and other sources of potential intoxication (i.e. abandonment of self-control) – drugs (coffee? tobacco?), music and dancing – are viewed with ambivalence by Islam, and often subject to state control in the Muslim Middle East, as commonly elsewhere.[4]

In a structuralist analysis, we would here be dealing with a series of linked systems. With food, the ingredients in a dish, the dishes in a meal, the meals and dishes in a cuisine, would be seen to form structured systems, in which the elements are relationships between qualities, tastes, smells, textures; some of these elements would link these food systems to other systems – those perhaps evident in drink, sexual regulations, magic and medicine, music and so forth. These systems might be analysed as structural transformations of each other. Certain substances – typically and classically blood, semen, milk, magical plants – would recur and might be analysed as 'operators' by means of which people make sense of their daily experience of these different cultural systems.

Some suggestions as to this form of analysis are evident in the chapters by Diouri and Tapper. However, whether we adopt a formal structural analysis, or the more fashionable post-modern recognition of a chaotic lack of structure in cultural forms, it is undeniable that the various spheres of food, sex, music and dance are certainly closely linked in practice in the Middle East, notably in the context of wedding feasts.[5] And here is a comparative study yet to be undertaken for the region: weddings are constituted of rich layers of shared symbolism and meaning, together with crucial details – of food, music, dance – which act as markers of difference between religious groups, ethnic groups, classes, genders, and local communities. Weddings, it may be suggested, are not just among the most colourful occasions in Middle Eastern cultural life, but arenas where the most important elements in the social fabric of each locality are culturally expressed in a complex and subtle code, to which the language of food is an important key.

This book is offered as a richly varied menu of both approaches and contents, which will satisfy readers' appetites for both information and stimulation, but at the same time provoke further investigation of this fascinating new field of study.

Notes

1. Of less concern to our contributors has been the recent renewed interest, in the context of anthropological studies of social and economic development, in the social basis of nutrition, following earlier classic work by Audrey Richards (1932, 1939); see Thompson (1993) and Fiddes (1992).
2. See Waines (1989), who gives a recipe.
3. See Roden's chapter for religious and other commensal occasions among the Sephardi Jews. Apart from Roden, and Zubaida in his chapter on culinary nationalism, discussions in this book relate mainly to Muslim cultures of the

Middle East. There is little specific discussion of food among Christians, and none of Zoroastrians and other minorities. It should be noted that the major religious cultures are differentiated from each other by culinary markers, most notably perhaps their attitudes to or treatment of items such as pork, blood and alcohol (see Tapper's chapter).

4. It would be worth comparing the processes of diffusion of food practices around the Middle East, and between the region and beyond to Europe, Central Asia and India, with those of musical traditions, genres, instruments, popular numbers; see, for example, Stokes (1992).

5. We should perhaps include annual festivals at local shrines, which are frequently referred to by the same term as weddings – 'urs.

1. Food Production in the Middle East

Tony Allan

The peoples of the Middle East have played an important role in the history of the cultivation of plants and the domestication of animals in nomadic and sedentary society. The developments of these techniques and inter-species relationships were very significant stages in the development of human political economies, providing the economic foundations of the first civilizations.

The region has always had the reputation of being environmentally harsh, being over 90 per cent desert, but until the late 20th century there was never any question that its natural resources of water, land and natural vegetation would be sufficient to feed its population. The historically rapid increase in population since the beginning of the 20th century, and especially in the past four decades, is one major reason for the Middle East being one of the major food-importing regions of the world. The other is the presence of the oil-exporting countries which transformed their food consumption patterns, especially in the 1960s and 1970s. Some Middle Eastern countries still export food, especially high-value horticultural products, including vegetables, potatoes and fruit produced in the winter both for the prosperous markets outside the region as well as for the oil-rich Gulf. But the agricultural options are being seriously restricted by the rapidly developing water gaps in such countries as Egypt and Jordan. And all the countries of the region except Turkey are finding that their capacity to maintain the past level of water allocation to agriculture is being impaired.

NATURAL RESOURCES OF THE MIDDLE EAST

Food production in the Middle East has been achieved in a generally harsh natural environment. Over 90 per cent of the Middle East is desert and most of the remaining 10 per cent receives poor and unreliable rains. Less than 1 per cent of the Arab Middle East receives reliable rainfall of over 500 millimetres a year and even the relatively well-watered Turkey and those parts of Iran which receive reliable rains are usually high and broken so that they do not provide extensive tracts of well-watered cultivable land. There are two important river systems in the region which have a long history of agricultural significance – the Nile and the Tigris-Euphrates. Another river, the Jordan, has great cultural significance but was not harnessed for significant agricultural use until the late 20th century. Only the Jordan is located in the heart of the region. The Nile receives its water from Ethiopia and East Africa and the waters of the Tigris-Euphrates come from rains which fall in Turkey and to a lesser extent those which feed the tributaries of the Tigris rising in Iran.

An important feature of the renewable water of the Middle East is that it comes in the form of seasonal rain. The major centres of population, which lie in the northern part of the region, enjoy winter rains resulting from the Atlantic weather systems which pass eastwards through Mediterranean latitudes between October and April each year. The advantage of receiving winter rains is that the meagre rainfall is effective, since temperatures are not high in the Mediterranean latitudes and crop production can be effective in regions which receive over 300 millimetres of rainfall in the season. Grain crops such as barley and wheat can be raised without supplementary irrigation and valuable tree crops such as the olive and the almond will survive. Other fruit crops need supplementary irrigation in winter unless they are raised on the better-watered uplands of Lebanon and Syria and, of course, Turkey.

In arid countries which lack alternative natural resources or a developed industrial sector, the availability of reliable water is crucial for sustaining viable agricultural livelihoods. The surface water of the region, flowing in the major river systems, has historically been important agriculturally, and remains so. Unfortunately these water resources are not substantial. In the past they have been more than sufficient to sustain the populations who were attracted to settle in the river lowlands. But with the increase in population since the beginning of the 20th century, all the Arab countries of the region and Israel face incipient, or very serious, water gaps. Only Turkey and, for the moment, the Sudan enjoy water surpluses.

Groundwater has always been an important water resource for agriculture in the region, and throughout the history of the Middle East it has been cleverly managed locally by means of water-lifting systems; groundwater has also been moved over long distances by sophisticated traditional systems such as the *qanat* in Iran and the Gulf (Bonine et al.

1989). Modern technology has enabled access to much deeper and very remote groundwater resources. In both Libya (Allan 1989b) and the Arabian Peninsula, fossil groundwater has been developed to support crop production without much regard to the economic or ecological viability of such practices.

The other natural resource which has been the basis of an important part of the regional economy is vegetation. In the millennia before the establishment of agriculture 6000 years ago, the tracts which then (as now) received rainfall over 500 millimetres a year were covered by forests. The tracts receiving between 200 and 500 millimetres annually supported rich seasonal pastures. The forests were almost completely removed during the classical era when insensitive Roman environmental exploitation led to the denudation of the northern Middle East, especially Turkey. The impairment of the region's grazing resources has been more recent and is still in train. The steady increase in livestock numbers during the past two decades beyond the carrying capacity of the vegetation resources in almost all countries of the region has led to severe degradation of rangelands (Thalen 1979; Yotopoulus 1983; Jaubert 1983; Gurdon 1985; Allan 1988; Murray 1990).

AGRICULTURAL TRADITIONS: IRRIGATED FARMING AND LIVESTOCK REARING
The Middle East has a long tradition of adopting the cultivation of crops and the domestication of animals. Its peoples devised systems of resource management which both stimulated the development of civilized societies and sustained them for millennia. The creation of agricultural economies in the major river basins over six millennia ago provided security and ultimately economic surpluses which could be converted into political power, exerted first at home and then within the region. The two systems on which survival and ultimately region-wide influence depended were the food-production systems of irrigated farming in the river lowlands and livestock rearing in the regions of low and generally unreliable rainfall.

The use of low-rainfall marginal tracts required a very different system from the intensive land and water management of the river lowlands. A low-intensity system of resource management – livestock rearing – was developed, requiring that livestock managed by communities of herders respond to the availability of natural feed, by moving from place to place and by the opportunistic raising of supplementary fodder. Nomadic and transhumant systems enabled a significant proportion of the population of the region to sustain livelihoods. For most of the history of the region, up to a quarter of the population was nomadic. The marginal character of the tracts on which these communities depended made it necessary for the grazing communities to have occasional access to substantial tracts of reliable grazing, and the rights to raise fodder, or at least to enter into arrangements for the use of grazing, in seasons of poor rains. When this symbiotic relationship between the settled and nomadic communities was stable, and not affected by food shortages caused by protracted drought or demographic pressures in the dry areas, there were long periods of accord and economic reciprocity in resource use and trade.

FOOD-CROP PRODUCTION IN THE MIDDLE EAST

The traditional staple food products of the Middle East have been determined by the environmental circumstances of the region and the capacity of its peoples to deploy technology to overcome the constraints which climate would otherwise impose. The high temperatures which prevail in the summer months mean that annual field crops of the tropics can be produced, provided reliable water supplies are available or can be engineered. Staple tropical grains such as rice and maize can be cultivated, as well as the essential food staples of barley and wheat which grow well in the cooler but more humid winter months. Wheat and barley can also be raised on land which receives no rainfall, provided that water can be brought to the crop from a surface or groundwater source. The yields of rain-fed and irrigated crops differ widely. Yields of rain-fed grain depend on the rainfall of a particular growing season and range from 1.5 tonnes to less than 200 kilograms per hectare – when it is preferable to feed both the straw and the grain to livestock without harvesting them. Yields of irrigated wheat and barley can reach five tonnes per hectare, but less where water management is poor. Rice and maize are always irrigated except in the northern parts of Turkey and Iran; some of the finest rice in the world, especially in appearance, comes from the Caspian region of Iran.

High-quality vegetables of all types are grown throughout the southern two-thirds of the region continuously in all seasons, as well as the condiments which enrich meals based on both vegetable and meat dishes. The continuity of vegetables through the year is a feature of Middle Eastern domestic life not found in other latitudes where temperatures rise too high or fall too low for crop production and divide the year into two wholly separate farming regimes. The climatic regime of northern and western Turkey, northern Iran and parts of Afghanistan is, however, so seasonal that vegetables are only grown in the rainy season. A common pattern is the raising of grain in winter and fruit and vegetables in summer. And seasonality does everywhere affect many field crops in addition to the staple grains already discussed. One of the most wonderful gifts of agriculture in the Middle East is the melon. At the height of the summer throughout history it provided unique and precious refreshment both at meals and throughout the waking day. Not only were the juices of the melon cool and refreshing, but they could also be a connoisseur's delight, as the flavours of some varieties were very particular. Iran is most famous for the range and quality of its melons, but they play an important part in the culture of all the countries of the region and they are traded widely internationally.

Tree crops are especially seasonal. The citrus season is an enjoyable one, occurring during the late winter months, but it has been extended by judicious breeding and the adoption of varieties from outside the region, so that fresh oranges are available from early December to April.

Dates are ready to harvest in late summer, and they are mightily enjoyed at that hot season as a cool, fresh and delicious fruit, but they are also much enjoyed later in the year as their sugar content preserves them into a wonderfully durable sweet. The date is one of the most widely raised foods in the whole region, in that the date-palm grows in the secure irrigated environments of the river lowlands as well as in the most extreme desert conditions of the Sahara and the Arabian Peninsula, where its deep rooting system can reach water which other crops cannot utilize. The geography of the date makes it historically one of the most extensively cultivated crops in the region, and as a result the date is probably more central than any other food crop in the culture of the Middle East. Although the better-watered and cooler tracts of Turkey, Iran and Afghanistan are not favourable for the cultivation of the date and it plays only a minor part in the cultures of these areas, elsewhere it is integral to the lives of both the nomadic and the settled peoples. It is just as famous in Morocco in the far west as it is in Baluchistan in the east. For the nomads it was always a staple as well as an insurance against the insecurity of periodic drought. For the settled peoples the fruit of the date-palm was and remains a great enrichment of their more secure diet. The appreciation of the uniqueness of the different varieties of the date is a feature of this fruit in the region's culture. In Basra it was claimed that there were over 350 different varieties, reflecting the importance of the date in the lives and food culture of the peoples of Iraq and the Gulf.

Other seasonal tree crops have an important place in the livelihoods and cultures of the region. The olive is a crop with an ancient tradition, grown on the southern shore of the Mediterranean wherever annual rainfall exceeds 300 millimetres. It is also widely grown in the Levant, Syria and

Turkey in similar frost-free rainfall zones. The role of olive oil in enhancing the food prepared in the homes of Middle Eastern families cannot be over-estimated. It is a superior oil against which other cooking oils are measured. And the fruit itself is a delicious and easily preserved delicacy.

Associated with the olive, and often raised in the same fields, is the almond. Both olive and almond can survive in poor soils and on broken land, and the flavour of their fruits is not impaired by the stress of growing in difficult circumstances. Both bear fruit in the summer, and the picking is extremely labour-intensive if the fruit or the trees are not to be damaged. Olive and almond have been grown in large plantations since the colonial period in northern Africa, and, after a period in the 1960s when harvesting and distribution encountered difficulties, these important tree crops have gained in value and significance as the premiums which the international market is prepared to bear for high-quality fruit have increased. Such is the international demand for high-quality fruit, both olives and almonds, and for high-quality oil, that these products have for the past two decades been priced beyond the purchasing power of the ordinary Middle Eastern family except in the oil-rich countries.

The vine, another seasonal crop, has been grown throughout the agricultural history of the Middle East – like the olive and the almond it can be raised on poor soils and in areas where rainfall is low. The fruit has always had a high place in the consumption of the peoples of the region, and the vines of some areas are particularly famous; for example, those from the gardens around Damascus. The production of wine has had, and still has, a less continuous record of acceptability in Muslim provinces and countries. As in neighbouring Mediterranean countries, the flavour of both grape and wine seems to be improved where irrigation is not used.

Environmental stress has been noted as a significant element in the raising of some of the best varieties of olives and grapes. Some of the most preferred dates are grown in remote and stressful desert oases. Other fruits, most notably the pistachio nut, grow naturally in areas of low and unreliable rainfall, where no plants other than grazeable shrubs and seasonal herbs can survive. Iran is the most famous source of pistachio nuts, but they have also been widely harvested in Turkey and in north-western Afghanistan. The market for this wonderfully flavoured nut has long been far beyond the tracts where it grows, and the demand for it has far outstripped the capacity of the rangelands of Iran to supply it. The demand has come from all the urban populations of the region and especially in the past three decades from the oil-rich states, but there is also a very strong and growing international demand stemmed only by the dramatic rise in the price of the pistachio on the world market. So strong has been the demand for this Middle Eastern delicacy that it has been planted in similar environments in the south-western United States.

LIVESTOCK PRODUCTION IN THE MIDDLE EAST

In the past the only food products which rivalled the date and olive in range and even the degree to which they were integrated into the diet of the region, were livestock products. Since the beginning of the 20th century, the technological and economic capacity for trading bulky food products such as grain throughout the region has increased the volume as well as the range of the foods used, but livestock products have retained their position as prime items in demand, latent if not immediate, in all communities in the region.

It is not so easy to generalize about livestock as it is about some of the vegetable products. Not only do different livestock occupy different niches in the natural and the agro-ecological environments, but they have taken up different cultural niches in the societies of the region. In the deserts the camel and the goat can survive deprivations of water and grazing better than, for example, the sheep. In less arid conditions the sheep and the goat are commonly raised together by both settled and nomadic communities. Cattle are the least durable of the livestock raised in the region and are associated with the settled farming areas where water and fodder are more reliable. Cattle, however, like the camel of the desert, perform a number of functions in addition to the conversion of natural and cultivated fodder into livestock products.

But the pattern of production and consumption of livestock products shows clear regional differences and is also evolving rapidly. Livestock production is the extreme form of low-intensity natural resource management and use. As a resource-using practice it is the least intensive and most appropriate means of utilizing the poor shrubs and herbage of low-rainfall (less than 200 millimetres annually) tracts. Herds and flocks move according to season as well as to drought cycles and, provided that livestock numbers do not exceed the carrying capacity of the range, and the extent of the grazing areas is not diminished by other communities introducing new economic systems such as settled farming based on supplementary irrigation or fenced pastures, then the environmentally sustainable traditional systems are the best way to utilize the scarce vegetation of the marginal rangelands.

The practice of nomadic livestock rearing is a deeply entrenched culture in the Middle East, but it is not one which will survive the economic and social changes in train in the region. The practice has declined significantly in the past four decades. In the middle of the 20th century the proportion of nomads in the population approached 30 per cent in some North African and Arabian Peninsula countries, but by 1990 had fallen to less than 5 per cent. Meanwhile, in the past three decades, livestock production has grown steadily in all the countries of the Middle East, driven partly by the overall growth in demand for food, but especially by the increased purchasing power of the oil-rich states since the mid-1960s (Allan 1989a; Murray 1990). Growth in production has been achieved by increasing livestock numbers in the settled areas and in the best-watered tracts to unsustainable levels. Fodder deficits have been filled by feed imports, which have become a very significant element in regional food imports, especially to the oil-rich countries (Khaldi 1984: 53).

Traditional livestock rearing in marginal areas was a practice which existed alongside settled communities. Both settled and nomadic communities raised livestock, depending on the better grazing areas close to the settlements for feed, either regularly but not intensively on the part of the settled farmers, or during periods of drought on the part of the nomadic livestock communities. Increases in livestock numbers have been achieved by more intensive production at all points on the continuum from the least productive low-rainfall areas to the intensive irrigated farms located in the river lowlands or on tracts where groundwater is accessible. The ecological consequences of these unsustainable practices are becoming evident in the form of degraded rangelands (Thalen 1979; Allan 1989a; Murray 1990) or irreversibly damaged groundwater (Allan 1981 and 1989b), together with the economic effects of misallocating scarce water to fodder production when the livestock products derived from this scarce water could be more economically imported.

The demand for livestock products has been driven partly by the population increase throughout the region, but mainly by two developments in the urban centres of the Middle East. The rapid urbanization of the oil-rich countries was associated with rapid change in the food-consumption patterns of the indigenous population, together with the immigration of large numbers of people to promote all sorts of economic and institutional development, who also acquired higher expectations with respect to diet, including the consumption of livestock products.

In non-oil-rich countries, such as Egypt, demand for meat and other livestock products also rose steadily from the 1960s. When Egypt was a mainly rural economy, with over 80 per cent of the population living in the villages of the delta and the river lowlands, livestock played an integral part in the livelihoods of the farming families. The animals were needed for draught purposes as well as for the production of milk and its derivatives. In these ways livestock were integral to the Egyptian economy, and the cow or buffalo was revered in the individual farm economy and given a privileged place in the household. But it was the non-meat livestock products which were important; meat, other than occasional chicken, was not a significant part of the rural diet, and in the towns and cities only the prosperous consumed meat regularly.

The demand for meat has increased rapidly everywhere in the region and especially since the 1970s in Egypt, a change in culinary culture in the most populous country of the region which has had profound and irreversible ecological consequences as well as distorting economic effects. Current levels of demand for livestock products are unsustainable from local renewable natural resources in Egypt and in all countries of the region, apart from Turkey.

Possibly the most important revolution in the Middle East in the provision of animal protein in the past three decades has been in the extraordinary increase in the numbers of poultry raised for meat and egg production. Increases were recorded in all countries of the region, and especially in the oil-rich countries. In order to feed this new livestock, it was necessary to import almost all the feed in such countries; even in the major food-producing countries such as Egypt, part of the grain imports were for livestock feed. In terms of food conversion, poultry are relatively efficient compared with other livestock. But those who care about the quality of food rather than its mere availability have not been impressed by industrially produced chicken meat.

A final note on a feature of livestock production which makes this sector particularly difficult to manage. Locally raised meat, especially mutton, is very highly prized. It can command a market price more than twice that of imported meat, and the premiums that consumers are prepared to pay for locally produced mutton are such that no farmer who can gain access to this burgeoning local market, whether legitimately or even illegally, will do other than try to raise more sheep. The pressure generated by this demand is greater than any market or other sanctions which might control it. Prices for locally raised meat have risen steeply and governments have attempted to regulate livestock numbers. In neither case has there been a reduction in livestock populations. As yet, since the ecological and economic consequences of the increase in livestock numbers are not recognized by farmers or consumers, the damage caused by the process is increasing.

MODERN FOOD PRODUCTION AND THE WATER GAP

The water-management policies of all the countries of the region were devised during periods when there was no evident water shortage affecting agriculture, or where, as in Egypt, shortages had been foreseen but it was believed that appropriate investments had been made in such structures as the High Dam to ensure an adequate supply of water for the foreseeable future. The primacy of the agricultural sector in national water budgets was everywhere taken as an irreversible starting point. A second factor which determines water-management policies in the region is the notion that food self-sufficiency is an essential national strategy. That food self-sufficiency is economically and ecologically unachievable for all countries of the Middle East, with the possible exception of Turkey, makes the pursuit of self-sufficiency a dangerous policy option. That it is the basis of much agricultural policy in the region means that the descendants of the present leaderships and the present generation of government officials will look back on the late 20th century as a period when irreversible damage was perpetrated on the region's very fragile resource base.

The Middle East is a region of deserts and high rates of evaporation and evapo-transpiration. If water is stored in open reservoirs such as Lake Nasser/Nubia, then three metres' depth of water a year is lost to evaporation. It is assumed that on average 10 cubic kilometres of water are lost in this way each year from the storage impounded by the Aswan Dam; in the late 1970s, when the lake stood at what has proved to be an unusually high level, the rate of loss reached as much as 13 cubic kilometres a year. Secondly it means that, where crops are grown throughout the year, over two metres' depth of water for every irrigated hectare will be required from the national water budget to raise crops effectively. This rate of use is so high compared with any other use that, in all countries of the region where it has been decided to maintain or enhance the agricultural sector, agriculture takes at least 80 per cent, and in some cases over 90 per cent, of the national water budget.

With the needs of agriculture being so dominant in national water budgets, the first place that governments should look for means to improve the efficiency of use of scarce water is in the agricultural sector. Initially, existing practices of cropping and water management should be examined to ensure that maximum returns to water are being achieved. Technology has some role to play in the improvement of returns to water, but much more important is the allocation of water within the agricultural sector to those crops which maximize economic returns to water – crops where the farmers of the region have a comparative advantage. At the sectoral level, the principle of returns to water points to the reallocation of water from agricultural to municipal and industrial uses. But this is a politically difficult policy to adopt, and in the region so far only Israel has identified the policy as the unavoidable option.

A more balanced view of the value of water in the various sectors of the national economies of the region would reveal that, while agriculture is an important element in many of the national economies, it always forms a shrinking proportion of the national GDP and employs a decreasing share of the working population. In Jordan, for example, agriculture contributes about 7 per cent of GDP, compared with 30 per cent two decades ago, while the proportion of the population employed in the industrial sector had risen to over 30 per cent by 1990. The challenge facing those responsible for striking a balance between the different sectors is, however, highly politically charged. Those involved in agriculture can and do mobilize strong political pressure based on popularly conceived (though misguided) economic imperatives and on the long agricultural tradition of the region's rural populations. The emotional power of arguments based on the traditional role of agriculture cannot be underestimated, and certainly has not been underestimated in practice by the current govern-ments of the region. At the same time professional groups, especially the engineers responsible for extending and maintaining the irrigation systems, who include some of the most talented and highly educated members of society, are deeply entrenched and align themselves with the emotional arguments mobilized by the farming communities.

The validity of the argument that food production is an integral part of national history and culture is easily established in such countries as Egypt, but even in Israel food production has a vastly inflated significance in the national psyche as a result of the comparatively recent settlement experience of the early immigrants before the creation of the state. The governing elite of Israel has been dangerously identified with the importance of agriculture, despite the progressive adjustment of water-using policies to the need for increased efficiency through the inten-sification of water use in agriculture and the shift to high-value products (Weinbaum 1982: 3). National recognition that the significance of Israeli agriculture was emotional and symbolic, rather than economic, came in early 1991 when the advice of the water technocrats was heeded publicly and it was announced that Israel would cut its annual water allocation to agriculture by 50 per cent. It was recognized that Israel could no longer export scarce water, which is what it was doing when it exported irrigated agricultural products such as citrus and avocados.

Unavoidable options in the Middle East's food future

Since the water resources of the Middle East are insufficient to meet the needs of the region's rising population, the kitchens of the region will have to accommodate increasingly to food produced in other, mainly temperate, countries, where water comes free or almost free to farmers, and where exporting water in food products is a sound economic proposition. The peoples of the Middle East are already at an advanced stage of accommodation to this situation, in that the environmental resource endowment is such that food self-sufficiency is not a policy option. Compared with other regions of the world, however, where food deficits manifest themselves in famine and extreme human hardship (Weinbaum 1982: 3), the governments and peoples of the Middle East have made a number of the major economic and political adjustments necessary to maintain a flow of resources sufficient to enable food purchases from outside the region.

According to Sen's important analysis of food availability in poor countries, the governments of such countries and their international sponsors have dealt with the 'acquisition problem', understood as the 'right to food' being reflected in the management of normal resources, augmented by international assistance, to ensure the provision of basic needs. In other words there has been an implicit recognition in the policies of the United Nations and other international bodies that both the urban and the rural poor have an 'entitlement' to staple foods (Sen 1981 and 1985). Other important adjustments have been made by Middle East consumers; for example they have shifted to a diet of imported food, both products based on staple commodities such as wheat flour and products with a high value-added content through processing and packing. These adjustments have been made with as little apparent discomfort as that undergone in earlier decades by consumers in the industrialized world, where a continuity of supply of exotic foods has come to be seen as a material and social enrichment by the majority of those involved in such consumption.

A green minority raises valid environmental objections to the trend in the world trade in food, and such ideas are likely to be in tune with those who value traditional modes of food preparation. It is likely too that those attempting to record and maintain the culinary traditions of the Middle East will find common cause with those who campaign for a strengthening of the agricultural sector, in so far as it enhances the availability of traditional food products.

The consumers of the oil-rich states already consume large quantities per capita of much that is best of manufactured and processed food on the world market. In all of these countries food imports increased by between 15 and 20 per cent a year from the date of the flow of oil revenues. Although the rate of increase slowed considerably during the 1980s, which were difficult years for the oil exporters, their demand for imported food remains strong. The major food importer of the region, Egypt, is not a major oil producer. Over 80 per cent of the food staple, wheat grain and flour for bread, is imported, and other staples such as sugar are also imported. All other countries in the region, apart from Turkey, will become progressively greater food importers.

The challenge for the political leaders and legislators, as well as for the international community, is to devise means of earning foreign exchange so that these food-deficit economies can operate effectively in the international market. It is essential that major economies such as that of Egypt are strengthened so that they replace political dependence with economic competence. At the same time, potentially important economic entities of regional significance, such as Iraq, must also become positive elements in the Middle Eastern economy, so that their wealth generates demand for the production and labour of other countries of the region. Iraq is also a major potential importer of food; before August 1990, 75 per cent of Iraq's food needs were imported. In this case, food imports have a positive impact in regional politics, since they lessen pressure on the waters of the Euphrates by reducing the need to produce food from this increasingly hard-pressed resource.

The last decade of the 20th century will be one during which those who make policy on the basis of the symbolic significance of agriculture will have to yield to the arguments of those who argue for the unavoidable adoption of principles of economic returns to water within systems which are ecologically sustainable (Allan 1985; 1991). In the way of politics, the struggle will not be one in which the misguided renounce the current economically and environmentally unsustainable policies; they will gradually adopt sustainable policies, and make a virtue out of their adoption. Meanwhile water is being misallocated and mismanaged, and in some cases environments are being irrevocably impaired. In due course, principles relating to the equitable international use of water (Waterbury 1979; Allan 1992) and the management of minimum standards of water quality will also appear on the international agenda and, when implemented, will enhance the stability of the region.

2. National, Communal and Global Dimensions in Middle Eastern Food Cultures

Sami Zubaida

The map of the modern world is one of nation-states. This is compulsory on all 'sovereign' political entities, whether multi-national megaliths like the USA or family emirates like Kuwait. Apart from having a flag and a seat in the UN, nation-states are usually engaged in creating and maintaining constructions of national culture. Increasingly, they must have a 'cuisine'. I put inverted commas around 'sovereign' because these states and their societies are subject to global processes beyond their control. These processes are important influences on food as they are on other spheres of culture. At the same time 'the nation' in most countries comprises communal stratification or even fragmentation which defies national constructions. In this chapter, I shall explore some of these factors in relation to Middle East culinary cultures.

The nations, regions and communities of the Middle East share a common set of cultural idioms. This is not to assert a cultural homogeneity, but that differences and boundaries are drawn and redrawn, negotiated and altered, within vocabularies and idioms often comprehensible if not familiar to the socially diverse parties.

The idioms of food and drink fit into these patterns. Localities and communities have their own distinctive food styles, including some highly specific dishes, but mostly describable in a common vocabulary within which the differences are marked. A Baghdadi will say, 'No, we do not flavour grilled meat with garlic, it is in Mosul that they put garlic with everything'; a Muslim Baghdadi may have found it surprising that his Jewish neighbour ate *dolma* with a sweet-and-sour flavouring, and may even remark that this is a Persian practice. Thus the regional and communal boundaries are drawn, but within a field of common cultural knowledge.

Common food vocabularies seem to cross language barriers. Varieties of kebab, *dolma* and pastries are variously designated in polyglot vocabularies, drawing mostly on Turkish and Persian, but widely used in the Arab lands. Food vocabularies, like place names, seem to survive the process of national linguistic homogenization; witness the survival of Arabic designations in Spanish food, as in *albóndigas* (meatballs) and *mujabana* (a cheese dessert).

NATIONAL BOUNDARIES

Some modern nation-states in the region are built on long pre-existing cultural and territorial entities, such as Egypt, Iran and Turkey. Even there, however, regional and communal variations are considerable. The axes of these variations differ in the three countries. Egypt, perhaps the most culturally and linguistically homogeneous of the three, displays its greatest cleavages along class and rural–urban lines. Unlike greater Syria (Syria, Lebanon and Palestine, 'Syria' in what follows), Ottoman food themes do not seem to have penetrated below the prosperous urban bourgeoisie, who in this century were in turn converted to European styles. The common people, urban and rural, maintained what seem to be long-standing food traditions based on the basic staples: *ta'miya* and *ful*, notable items of this tradition, both based on the fava bean, and Egypt's contribution to the emergent Middle Eastern food repertoire.

The major divide in Turkey is, perhaps, between the Istanbul and Izmir regions on the one side and the rest of Anatolia on the other. Certain ingredients and styles distinguish the more cosmopolitan regions of the capital and the Aegean: seafoods, mostly mussels (shunned further south), more widespread use of rice (as against *burghul*), restraint in the use of spices, special sauces and sweets. Anatolia is in turn regionally diverse. Distinctive Black Sea coast foods feature the extensive use of fish, especially the popular *hamsi* (a kind of anchovy), itself the basis of many dishes, and Balkan and Slavonic influences. The south, in the regions of Antep, Mardin and Adana, shares many culinary themes with Syrian cities, especially Aleppo: more robust spicing (the delicious flaked red pepper of Antep), the *kofteh/kebbe* genre, and characteristic salads and *mezzeler*.

Iran, historically the least politically centralized of the three, never-theless shows strong common and distinctive themes in its culinary cultures, particularly in the Persian-speaking centre: distinctive and elaborate rice cookery, specific varieties of kebab, fruit and meat, sweet-and-sour, sweet-and-savoury combinations, distinctive spices, especially the use of fenugreek and tarragon. Of the non-Persian-speaking regions, Azarbayjan and, particularly, Tabriz enjoy a high reputation for food. Distinctive foods include the unique *kofteh tabrizi*, a large parcel whose outer cover consists of a paste of meat and rice stuffed with chicken, prunes and eggs. The Caspian provinces feature special styles in fish cookery, in turn quite distinct from the fish cookery of the Gulf province of Khuzestan.

Of the Arab countries resulting from the break-up of the Ottoman Empire, the cities of the three countries into which Syria was divided display a degree of cultural homogeneity, sharing food ingredients and styles. In Ottoman times, Aleppo was commercially and culturally the centre of a region comprising southern Anatolia and north-west Iraq (the Mosul province). Their food is to the present day distinguished by common themes. One of these is the *kebbe/kofteh* genre: typically pastes of ground meat and bulgur stuffed with seasoned minced meat with various additions, including pine nuts. We find examples and varieties of this genre all over Syria and parts of Iraq, sometimes made with rice and not bulgur. This is also an area of prominent Christian communities, with a strong culture of drink and *mezze* in homes as well as cafés and restaurants. Urban Muslims share this culture, but perhaps a little more discreetly. Distinctive *mezzes* have characterized this culture, including the now ubiquitous *homus be-tehine*, popularized in the United Kingdom by Greek Cypriot caterers, and as such thought to be Greek. Also the now familiar repertoire of the Lebanese restaurant *mezze* tray of *tabbuleh*, *mutabbal* and so on are mostly parts of the general Syrian repertoire, some of it shared with Anatolia.

Iraq is the receptacle of the greatest diversity of communities and cultures. Persian and Turkish influences are evident in the foods of different communities and the common vocabularies of food. Mosul, as we have seen, was historically part of the Aleppo–southern Anatolia commercial and cultural circuit. Baghdad, historically an open and cosmopolitan city, comprised many traditions: the Sunni notables followed Ottoman styles, Shiʻi merchants showed Persian influences, Jews had distinctive foods but also showed Persian influences, Christians were mainly from the north and maintained Mosuli and montagnard traditions, and so on. Old Arabian foods centring on dates and milk and butter, as well as boiled meats as in *tharid* or *tashrib*, are part of the common background. Basra, the nearest thing to a seaport in Iraq, features fish cookery, which it shares with other Gulf regions and Khuzestan. Indian dishes and spicing are also to be discerned in these areas.

Two other nations must be mentioned, Armenians and Kurds. Armenians enjoy a reputation throughout the region as distinguished cooks, both in domestic food and in professional catering. They are particularly renowned for their pastry cooking and for fine *basturma*. They share in the cooking traditions of their original homelands in Anatolia. I have no knowledge of the foods of the former Soviet state of Armenia.

The Kurds are renowned for their cheeses and yoghurts, no doubt the products of rich mountain pasture. They also use yoghurt in cooking, notably a *kebbe/kofteh* in yoghurt sauce. Otherwise, they share in the cooking traditions of their various neighbours.

THE NATION–STATE AND THE CONSTRUCTION OF NATIONAL CULTURE

The borders of the nation–states resulting from the demise of the Ottoman Empire are thought by many to be arbitrary. Relatively homogeneous Syria is broken up into three states, while diverse elements are included in Iraq. Tribal family-ruled emirates of the Gulf have to pretend to be nation-states. Even the old entities of Iran and Turkey are ethnically diverse. What start as arbitrary entities, however, acquire some homogeneity and coherence over time. Borders are not just lines drawn on a map and frontier posts with soldiers. They are drawn much more firmly by institutions, techniques and forms of control. National economies, money, fiscal measures, trade barriers and protections, grants and subsidies, all create powerful economic boundaries. Official educational systems typically impose a common language and national curricula, producing generations of children who have read the same passages and recited the same poems and songs, learned the same historical constructions of the nation and the world and so on. When they graduate, the nation-state is by far the largest single employer, some employing a majority of all workers. Education and employment are bound together by national qualifications and diplomas. The state makes the nation, and the state with petroleum resources is particularly well placed to do that. This is not to say that the state necessarily enjoys the loyalty of its citizens, for this is manifestly not the case in most instances. However, it does create for its citizens a common life world of social knowledge, language and communications. An educated Iraqi Kurd, though usually politically alienated from the national state, is nevertheless discernibly Iraqi in many aspects of culture and education, in the same way as his counterparts in Iran and Turkey are products of national educational and cultural systems. Common educational systems, media of communication, social and geographical mobility within the national boundaries, military conscription, all these are factors which work towards cultural standardization, or at least to facilitate knowledge by each sector of citizens of the culture of other sectors. This must affect food cultures as much as others. Istanbul, as much as Paris, features regional ingredients and restaurants, so that migrants as well as natives will have knowledge and taste of these elements.

Cookery books and broadcasts further this familiarity as well as helping to create the itinerary of national cuisines. One of the most remarkable phenomena in this respect is the Egyptian book *Usul al-Tahi* (Principles of Cookery) by Nazira Nikola and Bahiya Othman, affectionately known to most Egyptians as the book of *Abla Nazira* (*abla* being a Turkish term meaning older sister). I have the 18th edition, published in 1988, which does not indicate the date of first publication. It has, however, been a regular item in domestic education for many generations and, I am told, an item in the dowry of every bride. The authors are both graduates from British colleges in domestic science and home economics, who became government school inspectors in Egypt. The book is a grand compendium of recipes and techniques, ranging over Egyptian and Middle Eastern foods as well as British and European recipes. *Al-hisa' al-iskotlandi* (Scotch broth) and *buding al-khubz bi'l-zebd* (bread-and-butter pudding) feature alongside numerous recipes for *molukhiya* and *bamya*. So it helps to create a national repertoire, but at the same time includes in it a process of globalization of food (to be discussed in what follows). The introduction to the book (undated) proclaims it as a contribution to the national renaissance by educating girls in the essential task of nourishing bodies.

Other important effects of the nation-state include 'police' (in the sense of regulation and discipline) of social life and culture. These relate to food through regimes of hygiene, public health and family welfare. Trade and agricultural policies can also have crucial effects on domestic economies and diets. Without the benefits of research on these aspects, there is little to say at this stage.

COMMUNAL SENTIMENTS

Food is a cultural 'marker' of social boundaries. Before nationalism, these boundaries were between communities differentiated by ethnicity, religion or region (distinctions which have, of course, survived in the nation-state). There is, however, a subtle difference between 'boasting with food' in communal discourses and the nationalisms of food.

Communities were always proud of their own food while denigrating that of their opponents or rivals, often in terms of stereotypes. We have already noted the example in which Mosulis are ridiculed by Baghdadis for allegedly putting garlic in everything. Another common traditional theme is that of generosity versus meanness. I have heard, in the old days, Baghdadi women and cooks jeer at Syrians (in this instance, Syrian neighbours in Baghdad) for being very economical with meat: all those salads and pastes that were just being introduced in Iraq, *tabbuleh*, *homus*, *baba-ghanush*, were only means of saving on meat. In contrast, 'we' cooked lots of meat in grills and stews. The other side of the coin was the belief that Iraqi men preferred Syrian wives, precisely because they were economical with the household budget. Examples of this boasting and stereotyping are many: the others may eat foods similar to ours, but they don't cook it half so well, use too much or too little spice, 'greasy' fats, smelly oils and so on.

The food markers of religious communities are interesting in this regard. Christian and Jewish communities shared, for the most part, the culinary themes of their Muslim neighbours, but with specific variations. These could come from past migrations, as in the case of Armenian or Sephardic communities, or Baghdadi Christians, most of whom hailed from Mosul and Kurdistan. The Jews of Baghdad, native for centuries and Arabic-speaking, showed distinctive food patterns, with some notable Persian influences. This could have been the result of their relative insulation in the previous century from the mainstream of urban life, thus retaining older customs forgotten by others. A major source of differentiation, however, concerns the ritual food requirements. Each Jewish community, for instance, had its distinctive Saturday meal. The ritual imperative was the prohibition on cooking on the sabbath. If a hot meal was to be had, it had to be cooked overnight from Friday and kept warm. The *dafina* of Morocco and the *tebit* of Iraq are outcomes of these imperatives. Other ritual imperatives determine the use of fats and oils. Jews cannot use butterfats or yoghurt in cooking meat; Christians also forgo butter for Lent cookery. Butterfat is the favoured medium for cooking meat and rice in most Middle Eastern regions. In the olive regions, Jews and Christians used olive oil. In Egypt and Iraq it was *siraj*, sesame oil, one with a distinctive and powerful smell. This smell featured in the negative stereotypes of Jews in both countries. Edward Lane reported on 19th-century Egypt that the Jews were thought to have bloated complexions and sore eyes, the result of immoderate consumption of this oil (1978: 545). Iraqis related that they could smell Jewish houses and streets miles away. The Jews had apparently internalized their disgrace on that score, for as soon as factories were established to produce tasteless, odourless vegetable oils, they switched immediately, thus sacrificing a delicious taste to prejudice.

On the positive side, under conditions of social stability and harmony, people were genuinely curious about the foods of others, and experimented with them. Neighbours and friends from different communities exchanged gifts of cooked food, and would try each other's recipes. As I have indicated,

Armenians are widely admired as cooks, especially for their pastries and sausages, notably *pasturma*. Jewish *tebit* and *dafina* are admired in their respective countries, and the latter features in books on Moroccan cookery, as an item of 'national' cuisine. Positive or negative evaluations, however, are functions of prevalent conditions, and can change or alternate rapidly depending on who is talking and for what purpose.

FOOD IN THE NATIONALIST PROJECT

An essential element of every national project is to construct a history of the nation. In a polyglot region like the Middle East this construction involves disentangling Arab from Turk from Kurd from Persian, and, within the Arab world, the subtle and not so subtle utilization of the pre-Islamic past to construct country histories: Pharaonic Egypt and Babylonian Iraq. Each of these histories then claims as much as is possibly credible of the common Middle Eastern heritage as its own, and heaps the undesirable elements on the other. The supposed corruptions and accretions in Islam were blamed by Arab thinkers on the Turks and Persians; Kurds claimed Saladin (Salah al-Din) as their own; Arabs and Persians disputed the identity of the illustrious scientists and philosophers of Islamic history, and so on. Food comes into these disputations at a less formalized level: it does not rank with the exalted spheres of religion, philosophy and statecraft. It is the frame of mind which claims all good things as 'ours', which operates at various levels to include food.

Let us be clear first how this nationalist pride in food differs from the communalist attitudes discussed above. Communalist attitudes are ahistorical. They are not concerned with origins, but with the insistence that their foods are best. The nationalist attitude, in contrast, is eminently historical. Aware that similar genres of food are shared by other nations, it is concerned to claim that these are originally 'ours'.

The Turks, being the most recent imperial masters of the region, come in for attacks along the lines of cultural nationalism from the Arabs and Greeks alike. The argument runs as follows: Turks were savage peoples from the steppes (Arabs here conveniently forget their own past) without the props of civilization or material culture; how could they have developed all these elaborate and sophisticated dishes like baklava, *dolma*, and so on? As the prior civilization which they conquered, these things must be 'ours'. Witness 'our' glorious past of the Abbasid Caliphate or Byzantium (as the case may be), where civilization, including brilliant culinary feats, flourished. There then follow excursions into speculative etymology and folk history to prove the point. The logic behind these narratives is one of national-historical essentialism: national essences and their attributes are fixed in history, and some of these attributes may be falsely appropriated by barbarian conquerors, but in truth they remain the property of the original nation. The facts of historical transformations and syntheses are excluded from this logic.

Reports of a recent conference on Greek food held in Salonika in 1991 ('The Foods and Wines of Greece: an International Symposium'), organized by American-Greek business interests for media personnel and food writers, illustrate this point very well. Apparently, the papers and the discussions were almost entirely about ancient Greece, Byzantium and village foods. Grand pageants of banquets were organized along these themes, and 'street food' scenes were constructed from these elements. The only mention of the Ottoman period (presumably the most directly relevant to modern Greece) was apparently made by a Greek-Jewish speaker who remarked on the historical amnesia of the participants. The reaction was uniformly hostile, and his intervention was brushed aside.

At another conference, this time in Turkey (International Food Congress, 1988), one of a series of international congresses on food, Turks were delighted by a paper from Charles Perry on the origins of baklava (a version of which is included in this book). It was an ingenious hypothesis based on information on nomadic Turks in old Arabic sources. Perry concluded that the pastry could have originated from the attempts of the nomads to produce thick bread (like the bread they encountered in the cities) from their native *yuvka* by layering many sheets of it. That is to say, it was a product of the very nomadic conditions which Arabs and Greeks cite as an inhibition on the possibilities of sophisticated foods. Whenever I have tried this account on Arab or Greek friends it has been greeted with derision and disbelief.

The national and nationalist claims and constructions of food are evident in many cookery books. Peter Heine, in his chapter in this book, notes examples of this trend in recent Arabic cookery books. It is also evident in books on Middle East national cuisines in European languages. I found a particularly interesting example of this trend in the publisher's news release for *New Food of Life: Ancient Persian and Modern Iranian Cooking and Ceremonies*, by Najmieh Batmanglij (1993).[1] It reproduces a picture of an Assyrian clay tablet containing four kitchen and food scenes, with the caption 'A three thousand year old kitchen scene'. The implicit claim of Assyria for Persian history, while it may not be approved by an Iraqi nationalist, is nevertheless correct in so far as the heritage of early Mesopotamia has entered into *all* the civilizations of the ancient world.

However, the logic of cultural nationalism is to claim for one modern national entity a thoroughly mixed historical heritage. It also implies a historical continuity of a fixed national entity and its culture from that ancient point of origin to the present day. This supposed historical antiquity and continuity are cited as, somehow, a confirmation of the authenticity and the superiority of the present-day national cuisine. History, then, becomes the measure of national virtue, including food.

MIDDLE EASTERN FOOD IN THE GLOBAL CONTEXT

'Globalization', a problematic concept, conjures up images of cultural invasions and the spread of standardized cultural forms to all corners of the earth. The effects of international trade, migrations, mass communications and tourism, however, have been diverse, some in the direction of homogenization, but sometimes in favour of revivals of threatened or obscured regional traditions. An example of the former is the emerging pattern of grain consumption in the Middle East. Until the 1950s, grain staples used to vary greatly by region; maize and millet in upper Egypt, barley bread in much of rural Iraq and Iran, maize in the Black Sea regions of Turkey, a preponderance of rice in the marsh areas of southern Iraq and some of the Caspian regions of Iran, and so on. International markets have brought relatively cheap and plentiful supplies of wheat and rice, and the consumption of these staples has risen to replace the regional diversity. It is as if everyone had been waiting for white wheat bread and *pilav* with every meal.

Processes of diffusion between different parts of the world have been going on for a long time. A good example of imperceptible diffusion is the Cairo *kushuri*, an ever-popular street food, a dish of rice and lentils, often bulked up with the even cheaper macaroni, served with a garnish of fried onion and spicy sauces. I have not been able to find any satisfactory accounts of the origins of this dish in Egypt. I can only assume that it is the Indian *kitchri*, also made from rice and lentils and spices. And it must have reached Cairo through the British forces. Long before the hamburger and the fried chicken, colonial circulation spawned a popular staple which Cairo made its own. Here, international diffusion and economic pressures have led to greater diversity.

Fats and oils. Processes of global influence are well illustrated with regard to oils and fats as cooking media, and as dressings.

The most common and preferred cooking fat by far was (and is?) butterfat or *samn*. Meat was fried and stewed in this fat and it was added in plenty to rice at various stages of cooking. It is used in pastries of the baklava/*kunafa* genre.

One of the main preoccupations of the Ottoman administration was the provisioning of Istanbul, and clarified butter supplies were among the most jealously regulated and guarded. Suraiya Faroqhi gives accounts of these provisions in the 17th century. Kefe (Feodosiya) in the Crimea, across the Black Sea, provided much of this commodity for Istanbul, and the Sultan's palace was an enormous consumer.

In fact, at the beginning of the seventeenth century a number of taxes collected in Kefe were specifically set aside to pay for large quantities of clarified butter that the Sultan's household consumed every year ... Moreover, references to shipwrecked boats carrying edible fats were frequently made in the *muhimme* registers ... and the concern with which the central administration attempted to salvage as much of the cargo as possible, demonstrates the importance of Crimean edible fats in the food economy of Istanbul (Faroqhi 1984: 92).

At another point in this book we have an account of the foods consumed at the *imaret* (public kitchen funded from charitable foundations producing food for specified personnel of mosques and Sufi orders) of Sultan Selim II in Konya. There, all cooking was done with clarified butter, and although the supplies included olive oil and sheep's-tail fat, these do not seem to feature in the cooking, and were probably used for lighting. Two to four tons of clarified butter were consumed every year. The author's conclusion on this count is interesting and worth quoting.

Thus the dietary regime emerging fron the Konya *imaret* accounts differed considerably from what we have become accustomed to regard as the standard Mediterranean diet. Even southern Spanish diets, in which the impact of Muslim dietary preferences could still be discerned during the sixteenth century, appear to have been markedly different. A preference for clarified butter as opposed to olive oil, even when the latter was available, reflects an environment in which pastoral activities were strongly represented (Faroqhi 1984: 215).

The author is wrong about 'Muslim dietary preferences', if she meant by that the preferences of Middle Eastern cultures. But hers is a very interesting mistake which reflects some modern attitudes and beliefs. The idea of the 'standard Mediterranean diet' (which is here somehow mixed up with 'Muslim dietary preferences') is a modern construction of food writers and publicists in Western Europe and North America earnestly preaching what is now thought to be a healthy diet to their audiences by invoking a stereotype of the healthy other on the shores of the Mediterranean. Their colleagues in Mediterranean countries are only too willing to perpetuate this myth. The fact of the matter is that the Mediterranean contains varied cultures, and that Spain is in a minority of regions (the others are Greece and southern Italy) which use olive oil as a predominant medium of cooking. Whether in Spain this is due to Muslim influence or not I do not know. One thing which is certain, however, is that this preference does not extend to the Middle East. As Faroqhi shows earlier, butterfats were highly favoured in the Sultan's palace and in Istanbul in general. This picture is general for the whole region: meat, rice and pastry are always cooked in butter (at least for those who can afford it). The alternative is not olive oil but meat fat, preferably that rendered from sheep tails. Oil (whether olive or other) was confined largely to vegetable cookery (though not when cooked with meat). It was sometimes used as a flavouring or a dressing added to complex dishes which were started with animal fats. Poor people who ate little meat would also use animal fats, in so far as they were available, in cooking pulses (lentils and chick-peas) and porridges of meat and cereals (such as *harisa* and *keshkek*, which, according to Faroqhi's researches, were cooked in the palace kitchens with sheep's-tail fat and in the Konya *imaret* with butterfat).

It is only in recent years that cooking habits with respect to fats have changed. These changes are the product of global influences in technology and trade as well as in health ideologies. Tasteless, odourless vegetable oils, cheaply produced in factories, have become predominant throughout the region. Hydrogenated solid vegetable fats are now substituted for butter. This is understandable in terms of economics, but even prosperous people are now wary of animal fats because of the cholesterol scare. So Mazola rules.

What about olive oil? Few regions seem to use it in any significant quantities: parts of Greater Syria, where it is produced in some abundance, and parts of Tunisia. Elsewhere it is a luxury product reserved for salad dressings. Turkey, a major producer, poses a puzzle. It is difficult to find olive oil used in cooking or dressing in restaurants, even on the Mediterranean and Aegean coasts. Replies to inquiry always plead its high cost. But butter and meat are also expensive, and widely used. My guess is that cost factors have combined with earlier Western stereotypes of Turkish food as being 'greasy' to effect a shift to other cheaper oils. The new Western vogue for olive oil has not yet penetrated, but it will. This is another indication of the influences in the ups and downs of international fashions.

THE GLOBAL PRESSURES FOR NATIONAL AND REGIONAL 'CUISINES'
National cuisines are constructed not only by the 'nationalist project', but also by global expectations, which, in turn, feed into that project. Countries are nations and are expected to have things national, including a cuisine. International migrations, tourism and the associated travel and food writing are among the important factors generating these demands.

International tourism has rightly been associated with the banalization of resort foods: the fish and chips, veal escalope and flambé and chips of the costas are well known. Equally bland concoctions are produced in Turkish and Tunisian resorts for the package tourist seeking sea and sun and undemanding food. However, more recently there is a different kind of tourism: one which seeks the exotic and knowledge of the other. Food is an important part of this tourism, and responses to it have occurred at the higher levels of the market. Some of the Hiltons and Sheratons in Cairo and Istanbul have led the trend, with menus of 'Ottoman' food in Istanbul, and bubbling cauldrons of *ful* and *belila* on the breakfast tables of Cairo international hotels. At a recent meal in one Cairo hotel, I was offered (alongside veal escalopes and roast turkey) a broth of oxtail and vegetables, which even had a native name (*akawi*). This was a surprise to my Egyptian companions, who had not encountered it before and certainly wanted nothing to do with it. Who knows, they may try tripe and trotters next! *Belila*, a porridge of wheat grains in milk with sweet garnishes, was until recently seen only at a few pastry shops in popular quarters of Cairo. Drinks like *sahlab* are being served in more cafés and restaurants.

In effect, Egyptians and Turks and others are being asked: show us your national cuisine. Entrepreneurial caterers respond to this demand, and in the process educated natives are rediscovering what they had previously abandoned as elements of popular backwardness: 'heavy', unhealthy and labour-intensive food. Like all 'revivals' of tradition, however, this one is bound to be a modern construction.

In another sphere, 'ethnic' restaurants run by migrant communities in northern European and American cities also have to respond to this search for exoticism and national cuisines. Discerning eaters who have read cookery and travel books and columns are seeking authentic national and regional cuisines, beyond kebab, *homus* and *tandoori*. Restaurants with signs proclaiming 'Indian cuisine', 'Peking cuisine' or whatever offer what is by now a familiar repertory, specific to restaurant catering. There are signs, however, that these repertories are being enlarged in certain enterprising establishments, to cater for seekers of authenticity and exoticism. The Hong Kong restaurants of Soho's China Town are the leaders in this field. In relation to Middle Eastern food, London now boasts an 'İstanbul İşkembecisi', serving tripe and head soups as well as kebabs and stews. *Kalleh-pacheh* (a broth of heads and feet) is now available in a number of Iranian and Turkish restaurants in London. Is this a portent of future trends?

The recent trend in television series on national foods and their regions (and the much larger field of travel and cookery books on these subjects) may very well come round to Middle Eastern countries, when it has done Italy and Spain and 'the Mediterranean'. Here is one more source in the construction of national cuisines and their regions.

Note

1. I have not been able, at the time of writing, to get hold of a copy of this book. Bert Fragner, in 'Social Reality and Culinary Fiction' in this volume, refers to an earlier book by the same author, entitled *Food for Life*, an earlier edition, perhaps, of *New Food for Life*. He comments: 'This cookbook conjures up an idealized, almost ahistorical Iranian cultural setting, represented by a culinarily refined community of eaters, thus creating the image of an unbroken continuity of Iranian civilization, practised as far away as Los Angeles or Vancouver.'

Part I

Cuisines, Dishes, Ingredients

3. From the Caucasus to the Roof of the World: a culinary adventure

Bert Fragner

Europeans, and perhaps also Americans, were recently informed that the French minister of education wanted the schoolchildren of his country to be regularly instructed in what the French call *bon goût*, good taste, or, more appropriately, *culinaires*. The younger generation, spoiled by the culture of fast food, should be motivated to renew their acquaintance with the mysteries of olive oil, *herbes de Provence* and truffles. 'They teach children music,' he said, 'sports, and how to read and to write, but they never teach them the essentials of taste!'

This criticism has some interest beyond the education of children. It has very much to do with a general feature of occidental civilization: the treatment of the culinary art in our culture, especially since the 19th century, is very unbalanced. Discussion of culinary matters is largely restricted to ceremonial aspects of manners, life-style and so on, and often neglects the more immediate aspects of eating such as the taste and texture of food. Discussion of the latter is usually considered to be rather plebeian. In this respect, there is no doubt that northern Europeans, especially Germanic peoples, still have something to learn from their Latin and Mediterranean neighbours.

A very cautious, not to say reluctant, attitude towards the art of preparing and eating food as a permanent temptation to sensuality is far from limited to general aspects of social life. It is also to be found in various traditions of scholarly learning, including oriental studies. Despite the fact that there are numerous oriental texts concerning various aspects of food and cooking, this subject is much less discussed by philologists than, for instance, history of science and technology, theory of medicine and music, pharmacology or mathematics, even though all these subjects may be far more limited in their contemporary and practical use than traditional and historical cookbooks.

We owe a great deal to social scientists, especially social and cultural anthropologists, for showing us during recent decades that preparing and eating food is a very essential and basic element of human culture all over the world, and therefore should be treated as one of the more respected and dignified categories of cultural behaviour, like listening to symphonies, visiting art galleries or reading classical literature.

About a decade ago I began to treat historical Persian cookbooks philologically, just like the literary texts we are used to dealing with (see Fragner 1984). My earlier personal and practical experience with Middle Eastern, and especially Iranian, cuisine stimulated me to investigate the role of food in social and cultural history. In this essay, I present some of my observations, hypotheses and findings resulting from my dealings with oriental food.

THE POLITICS OF CULINARY TRADITION

First, some general remarks on culinary research. Whenever we want to analyse any question connected with the art of preparing and consuming food, it will immediately turn out that the problem is in fact a whole complex of heterogeneous problems, each one of which must be seen through a special perspective and analysed by a special set of methods.

Let us concentrate first on problems connected with raw materials. Clearly, any local tradition of cookery depends on the availability of plants and animals in that locality, and we must deal with botanical and zoological aspects whenever we want to focus on this problem. Further, it is evident that the transmission of breeding stock and cultivated plants has been one of the central and essential elements of human cultural activities from early antiquity. Traces of this kind of transmission indicate cultural and social contact, even in cases when the historian, the archaeologist or the folklorist is unable to provide reliable data. As an example, I suggest that a reconstruction of the path taken by the domestic fowl from the Malayan peninsula and the Sunda Islands throughout the ancient world would tell us much about the possibilities of early human contact in areas between ancient Egypt and Babylonia, China and India; perhaps more than a single isolated coin or a piece of clay. The distribution of plants and breeding animals, since time immemorial, has required a certain degree of intensity in exchange activities, much more than the occasional trade eventually documented by isolated findings of artefacts.

The character and density of the transmission and adoption of foodstuffs also depend very much and intensely on political structures. Thus it is evident that traditions and fashions in nutrition and cooking are influenced by politics; to a historian, the diffusion of certain culinary customs may even indicate the distribution of political power within certain social strata in a given territory. Those who do not believe that food customs are closely connected with politics may compare the recent customs of cooking and eating in the two parts of the country I come from, Germany. The nostalgic background shaped by memories of grandmother's cooking is more or less the same in former West and East Germany. Nevertheless, the actual culinary practices are astonishingly different in these two regions, solely as a result of political conditions. To the historian, this means that signs of culinary difference may also indicate political splits and rifts not evident from other sources.

For example, in the 18th century Prussia's ruling elite used its political power to transform the potato from a sign of extravagance and luxury into the most popular item of basic nutrition in northern Germany. The subsequent process of distribution of the potato to nearby countries and principalities represents the degree of actual political permeability and potential intensity of contacts, maybe even more than contemporary protagonists were aware. This means that careful observation of potato cultivation and consumption in Poland, Russia and Bohemia is obviously a category of sources, complementary to the historian's archival studies of diplomatic relations between Prussia, the Habsburgs and the Romanovs.

An even better example, much closer to our region, is the history of the adoption of animals, plants and fruits from the New World in the Mediterranean area in the 16th and 17th centuries. Tomatoes, sunflowers, Indian corn, paprikas and chillis, not forgetting the amazing turkey, found their way within an astonishingly short time via Spain straight to the areas of the Ottoman Empire along the eastern Mediterranean shores, arriving in Italy only some decades later. At a first, superficial glance one might be inclined to see climatic reasons as responsible for this process of diffusion. Closer examination makes it clear that it was shaped exclusively by the political climate of the period.

To elaborate: in early modern times, European politics were very much characterized by the political axis between Madrid and Constantinople, the Mediterranean scheme resembling the continental relationship of Vienna and Constantinople, comparable to the Moscow–Washington axis of the past 45 years. Apart from the political animosity which pervaded political relations between the Spanish and Austrian Habsburgs and the Ottomans, there also existed a special network of hegemony within which these two superpowers were rivals and partners at the same time. This means that new commercial and consumer goods brought by the Spaniards from the American continents to the European sphere found their immediate way into the Ottoman Empire, even earlier than to other European regions. Therefore, the 'Indian chicken', then recently imported from Mexico, was directly transported from Spain to the Ottomans, who took over its denomination as Hindi or Hindi Tavuq (*tawuq hindi* in Syrian Arabic until today). The term for this bird in Austrian German, *Indian*, indicates that Habsburg subjects in central Europe became acquainted with it through Ottoman help! So strong was Ottoman hegemony that, as far away as England, the notion of that crisp and tasty poultry as Turkish must have been more deeply ingrained than any awareness of its 'Indian' (i.e. American) origin; in English – and in English-speaking America – it is called 'turkey'.

Similar migrations are to be observed in connection with other foods: tomatoes, paprika, green peas, beans, maize (Indian corn) and sunflowers (together with American silver) all found their way from Catholic Spain via the North African coast and Egypt straight to the Muslim and enemy Ottoman Empire, much earlier than to their immediate Christian hinterlands, France and Italy, to say nothing of the delay in transmission to central Europe.

There is no doubt that Constantinople played a unique role as a capital, famous throughout the territories under Ottoman rule for its incomparably metropolitan urban life. There is also no doubt that culinary trends and fashions in the Ottoman Empire were very much shaped by Constantinople's metropolitan elites, often based on regional or local cuisine from various parts of the empire, but homogeneously shaped by the prestigious and refined taste of fashionable urban dandies in the vicinity of the Saray. To them we owe the fact that, despite the disintegration of the Ottoman political empire, we can still see the survival of a large region which could be called the Ottoman culinary empire. The Balkans, Greece, Anatolia and the Fertile Crescent are today the homelands of partly hostile peoples, but there is no doubt that, beyond their consciousness, they are common heirs to what was once the Ottoman life-style, and their cuisines offer treacherous circumstantial evidence of this fact. Of course, they represent at the same time a good deal of local or regional culinary traditions. Besides, one should not forget that it is typical of any great cuisine in the world to be based on local varieties and on mutual exchange and enrichment among them, but at the same time to be homogenized and harmonized by a metropolitan tradition of refined taste. Turks and Greeks may seem as hostile as could be imagined, and they themselves may even be deeply convinced of their mutual animosity, but nevertheless their culinary traditions show, on a very trivial if not materialist level of their cultures, that they have much more in common than many of them believe.

It is a matter of mere speculation whether the origins of this imperial culinary legacy are to be traced back to Greek antiquity, the Byzantine heritage, or the ingenuity of the glorious Turkish and Arab nations, not forgetting Phoenician and Jewish traditions; nowadays you may find support for any of these claims in various countries in the Balkans and the Near East. What we can seriously maintain is the following: there still exists a large area shaped culinarily by Ottoman traditions. This culinary macro-region consists of a number of micro-regions, each characterized by local traditions of cuisine. This clandestine survival of an element of the otherwise defunct Ottoman Empire belongs to an even larger area, defined as that of Mediterranean cuisine. But one should not believe that these Mediterranean traditions are mainly based on what is supplied by Mediterranean nature and climate. The main features of this common culinary area have been shaped by two important political superstructures, the ancient Roman Empire and the period of Spanish–Ottoman hegemony. To the latter, contemporary Mediterranean cuisine owes its astonishingly uniform use of American imports like tomatoes, pepper and maize. Between these two, we should not refrain from mentioning another important political movement, the expansion of the early Muslim caliphate, by means of which several important plants from the east, from China and India via Iran, found their way to the Mediterranean shores. In due course, Spain turned out to be a kind of turntable between medieval Muslim (Arab) cuisine and the Christian coasts: so the French and subsequently other peoples of Western Europe had their chance to become acquainted with tasty things like aubergines, spinach and rice.

One could argue that traditional Ottoman cuisine might have much more in common with the traditional medieval cuisine of the Muslim Arabs, at least their upper classes. Thanks to Peter Heine, we have excellent documentation of cooking customs among 11th- and 12th-century Muslim Arabs; it turns out that their traditions were highly uniform from al-Andalus to al-Iraq, but clearly different from Ottoman traditions three or four centuries later. There can be no doubt that Ottoman and Spanish cuisine of the 16th and 17th centuries, and subsequently Mediterranean cookery in general, were characterized by an incomparably high degree of 'Americanization' and, at the same rate, by creative assimilation of these American factors which were brand-new, fascinating and absolutely fashionable at that time. Taking all this into consideration, our conclusion must be that around the year 1600 Ottoman cookery might have been the most modern, fashionable and creatively developed cuisine in a European or Mediterranean perspective. I think that this is an important argument in discussions and debates over the supposed stagnation and lack of cultural and societal change in the pre-modern Middle East. The development of material culture, especially culinary culture, clearly refutes this theory of extra-European stagnation.

CUISINE EAST OF THE OTTOMANS

What about the geographical borders of this area of Ottoman cuisine, especially towards the east? As we trace back relevant conditions in the Middle East and even further into Central Asia, there seems not the slightest doubt that Ottoman culinary frontiers were by and large identical with political frontiers, and moreover that these culinary frontiers still exist.

The eastern borderlands of the former Ottoman Empire were the Caucasian regions of Georgia and Armenia, but mainly the Iranian plateau: The Ottoman–Iranian frontier led from Transcaucasian Azarbayjan through Kurdistan into the present Iran–Iraq borderlands. In this connection, it might be of interest to note that the borders between Iran on the one side and Turkey and Iraq on the other are not based on post-First World War treaties and decisions, but represent a relatively old and stable frontier of pre-modern, mainly Safavid origin.

Until the late 1970s, every traveller passing through Turkey and entering Iran through Doğu-Bayazit and Bazargan was confronted by a major experience on entering Iranian soil: those who travelled through this region for the first time used to be surprised to notice that gastronomic institutions and the character of food differed totally from what they were used to throughout Turkey. Despite the linguistic affinities of the Azarbayjanis with the Turks, in terms of food they turn out clearly to be Iranians.

Let me trace these culinary peculiarities of the Iranians historically. As far as we can judge, the general features of food in medieval Iran, that is to say up to the 13th or 14th century, had much in common with culinary traditions of southern Central Asia, or more precisely with Transoxiana, including Khorazm. This whole region, at that time from eastern Anatolia through the Iranian plateau to the Hindu Kush, Khorazm and Sogdiana, perhaps even up to the Tarim basin in the east, was virtually untouched by Mediterranean influences. Migrations of culinary trends and traditions, whether they originated in India or China, followed an east–west course far more than one in the opposite direction. Much earlier than the above deadline of the 14th century, aubergines and melons from India, various tasty fruits (among them Seville oranges and mandarins, peaches and quince), rhubarb and spinach, not forgetting wheat, rice from China or India, and many other goods, migrated from eastern areas through Iran to the Mediterranean. Evidence of transmission in the other direction is rather negative. Olives and olive oil remained largely alien beyond the eastern borders of Ottoman cuisine. Centuries later, when American plants were quickly distributed throughout the Mediterranean area, including the Ottoman Empire, the Iranians and their eastern neighbours refused to adopt them until the 19th century. Iranians still show very limited usage of tomatoes or paprika in their traditional cuisine in comparison with their western neighbours.

What were the main features of Iranian cuisine in medieval times? First of all: wheat. Old-fashioned soups, mainly of local origin, still represent very much that sort of mushy spoon food that must have been so common throughout the Iranian deserts and the Central Asian steppes. *Haute cuisine* in traditional Iranian culture had a very strong tradition of using meat together with fruits and fruity ingredients, including walnut, rhubarb and *kangar*, a special sort of thistle similar to artichoke. These fruit/meat combinations can be traced back even to pre-Islamic times, not only for the highlands of Iran proper, but also for ancient Central Asia and the Caucasian civilizations. Rather archaic remnants of this tradition are still to be found among the Armenians and especially among the Georgians and related peoples in the Caucasus. In Iran we can find traces of these obviously ancient traditions, particularly in regional cuisine. An example is the famous dish *fesenjan/fesenjun*, originating from the province of Gilan on the south-western shores of the Caspian Sea. In its present-day version, pieces of poultry are cooked in a sauce prepared from ground walnut and pomegranate syrup. The Gilanis, living in the Caspian swamps, have always preferred to combine this sauce with wild duck, which is rather uncommon among other Iranians, who have nevertheless discovered *fesenjan* as one of their favourite dishes, especially during the past 30 years, but who usually prepare it with chicken.[1]

Although *fesenjan* is regarded as being 'typically Iranian', its relatives are mainly to be found in the Caucasus, but rarely if ever prepared with such refinement. The basic idea, since ancient times, was the combination of first frying ground walnut in a pan and then cooking the meat in this sauce.

Typical Iranian uses of various sorts of dairy products point clearly to Central Asia as their region of origin. Fresh yoghurt, the famous white cheese, dried yoghurt shaped into balls (*qurut*) and powdered dry yoghurt (*kashk*) represent a wide range of long-lasting products of high nutritive value.[2] The Iranians and the Afghans share them with Central Asian tribal peoples, not only those of Turkic origin but even Mongols and Tungus. It was obviously the great heritage of the horse-riding shepherds from the Central Asian steppes, dating back at least to early antiquity. Possibly another Central Asian tradition is a special way of preparing meat, called *yakhni kardan* in late medieval Persian cookbooks and recipes. The meat is first cooked in various kinds of liquid mixed with fat, thus partly producing a kind of bouillon; the liquid, if not used partly for other purposes, evaporates and the meat, already well cooked, is then roasted or fried in the remaining shortening. This procedure is the reverse of usual practice in the Mediterranean region, but similar or identical to methods used everywhere in Central Asia, even in Tibet and High Tartary.

RICE CUISINE IN IRAN

Of course, the main category of dishes which are typically Iranian, and equally point to close relations with eastern Asia, is well known to anyone who has had the opportunity of visiting the land of Iran itself, or at least an Iranian restaurant. It is rice that easily produces analogies between Iranian food and that of the Far East or India. More detailed and critical observation shows some peculiarities which distinguish Iranian customs of eating rice from those of other 'rice civilizations'.

Especially in the Far East and South-East Asia, and to a very high degree also in India, rice is one of the commonest and most basic elements of nutrition. It is the famous 'bowl of rice' that has for centuries saved the ordinary Chinese peasant from starvation. Even in India, rice is considered a very popular foodstuff, its lower grades at least being cheaply obtainable.

The Iranian attitude towards rice is quite different: rice is traditionally regarded as a relatively expensive dish, not to be compared with wheat or millet. Rice obtained such a high degree of prestige among Iranians that they never allowed it to be substituted by cheaper stuff like *burgul* (cracked wheat), as the Arabs or the Mediterranean Turks do. This means that Iranian rice dishes will never be prepared with any sort of cheap substitute for expensive rice; if rice is not available to poor people, then they will decide to prepare something entirely different.

The rice varieties valued in Iran are those of long-grain rice lacking gluten and producing a very distinctive flavour. Next comes Indian basmati rice, equal to an acceptable yet not outstanding variety called in Iran *dom-siah* (black-tailed). The rice varieties cultivated and favoured by the

Iranians do not, in general, yield well. They even show a decline in productivity through consecutive generations. As Iranian varieties of rice are without exception of Indian origin, regular seed imports from India turned out to be inevitable down to the beginning of our century. Even today, outstanding qualities like *sadri* sometimes need some rejuvenation by importing seed from the Indus valley.

In other rice-eating civilizations, mainly in East and South-East Asia, rice is supposed to be a very basic foodstuff and is therefore usually prepared in the simplest manner. Culinary refinement does not concentrate on the rice itself, but rather on the dishes it accompanies. This is not the case in Iranian cuisine where the usual preparation of rice is complex, not to say complicated, and takes the cook a fair amount of time. The rice must first be washed, then soaked for a couple of hours, then carefully rinsed and boiled in plenty of water until the grains are *al dente*. Then, well strained, the rice is put into a large pot in which a good quantity of shortening has been heated first, then covered with a special lid made of raffia. Now the rice must, as the Persians say, 'steam' (*dam keshidan*) for another half-hour or more, the whole procedure resulting in an absolutely unique taste.

There are two main categories of rice dishes prepared by this method: *chelow* and *polow*. The former, typically *chelow-khoresht*, is plain boiled and steamed rice, afterwards combined with various stews or ragouts. *Polow* is rice with tasty ingredients mixed with the boiled rice *before* the second part of the procedure, the *damkeshi* (steaming). Both kinds of preparation need two steps – first boiling, then *damkeshi*, a combination which is unique in rice-eating civilizations.

The main and basic aspect of *all* Iranian *polows* is that boiled rice is combined with other ingredients and *then* finally cooked by the procedure called *damkeshi*. Contemporary Iranian cuisine offers remarkable and mouth-watering combinations of rice with highly refined ingredients within the category of *polow*. One of my personal favourites is *baqali-polow*, a fantastic mixture of rice and already roasted pieces of mutton, together with fava beans and fresh dill leaves, combined with the fragrant taste of saffron or turmeric. Further *polow* possibilities include *sabzi polow* (boiled rice steamed with chopped fresh herbs and roast mutton), *albalu polow* (a combination of mutton and sour cherries, offering a very distinctive taste), and so on.

RICE TRADITIONS IN IRAN AND ITS EASTERN NEIGHBOURS

The question is now: what can we learn from comparisons, on the one hand, between historical and contemporary recipes and cookbooks within the Iranian tradition, and, on the other, between Iran and neighbouring rice-eating countries belonging to the same, non-Mediterranean culinary region, this is to say, the former Soviet Transoxiana (Uzbekistan and Tajikistan), Afghanistan and the Indo-Pakistani subcontinent? Such comparisons have often been made, for instance in Claudia Roden's well-known and classic Middle Eastern cookbook, to which we are much indebted for stimulation to scholarly research in oriental cuisine. But let me now introduce a historical perspective searching for traces of cultural transmission, perceived as interrelated with political, demographic and social dynamics in history. Historical investigation usually relies on sources, and whenever the sources are limited, a certain degree of speculation enters, based on plausibility rather than strict evidence.

What might this mean in concrete terms in connection with the preparation of rice in Iranian, Indian, Afghan, and Central Asian kitchens? I shall try to answer this question.

The earliest Persian cookbook I know dates back to 1520/21, the second decade of Safavid rule in Iran, written by a certain Mohammad 'Ali Ba'urchi-Baghdadi, a professional cook in the service of a Safavid prince, he himself being possibly of Turkic origin. His recipes largely represent a tradition of cooking dating back to the 15th century, that is to say, the Timurid period. Furthermore, since his text (see Afshar 1981) obviously offers the culinary traditions of the upper class if not the elite, we may conclude that Ba'urchi-Baghdadi's recipes document late Timurid or Turkoman and early Safavid princely cuisine. In connection with rice, it is striking that he does not use the word *polow* in the contemporary Iranian sense discussed above, but still in the sense of 'rice with something', which might be stews or pieces of meat or anything mixed with the rice. Even a stuffing called *gipa* (poultry or lamb stuffed with spicy rice) is registered as *polow*. This very much represents the present-day usage of the word *polow* (or *pulaw* or *pullaw* or *plow*) in India, Afghanistan and Central Asia.

Another Persian collection of recipes, compiled by one Ostad Nurollah some 70 years later, in Shah 'Abbas's reign at the end of the 16th century, contains a highly differentiated range of rice dishes, including *polows* and *chelow-khoreshts*, in exactly the same senses as we should find in today's Iran. This shows clearly that the modern Iranian conception of *polow* came into existence during the first century of Safavid rule. Since the two authors seem to have been related to each other, and the second was not only a princely but even a royal cook, it is clear that both refer to a continuous chain of culinary tradition. There can be no doubt that the modern Iranian conception of *polow* was invented in the vicinity of the Safavid court during the 16th century and then survived at least until our day. Despite the fact that the Safavid court repeatedly influenced cultural fashions among its neighbours, the new and very sophisticated method of preparing *polow* did not cross the frontiers to the Uzbek khanates of Central Asia, nor to Mughal India. Methods of cooking rice in India, Afghanistan and Central Asia are very similar, the main differences being in the usage of spices. They form a uniform area of rice cooking distinct from Iran, or rather from *contemporary Iran*, because still in about 1500 the Iranians themselves obviously did not yet differ from their neighbours to the south-east and north-east in their principal methods of preparing rice.

Iranians thus share with Afghans, Indians, Uzbeks and Tajiks their love for rice dishes, and equally esteem rice as a highly prestigious food; and they use a widely shared professional terminology in rice cooking, based on Persian but heavily enriched by mostly eastern Turkic expressions. But only the Iranians stepped forward to a refined, even sophisticated method for preparing rice, taking much more time than all the others, but being rewarded by the most delicious rice dishes anywhere in the world.

Origins of Iranian rice traditions

We have established a common rice-eating region, to be traced back at least to the 15th century, comprising Central Asia, the Iranian plateau and Muslim north India, an area congruent with the Persian-speaking area which was politically and culturally dominated by the Timurid courts during the 15th century. In our case, culinary boundaries turn out to have coincided with those of linguistic, cultural and political influence and hegemony. These observations confirm my earlier hypothesis that culinary factors may serve the historian as complementary evidence for the strength and intensity of political influences on societal conditions, at least in pre-modern times and in the absence of written sources.

What were the origins of this rice-eating tradition in those regions of the Middle East and Central Asia in late medieval times? There is no doubt that rice offered the Indians a means of basic nutrition, but this is just what we are *not* discussing now: our subject is rice as an aspect of the refined culinary entertainment of upper classes.

According to Bertold Spuler's study of early Islamic Iran (1952), actually referring to the period from the Arab invasion of the Iranian plateau until at least Seljuq rule, rice was not at all common among the Iranian peoples at that time. There has even been discussion of whether the Iranians in the Sassanian era were acquainted with rice at all; it seems probable that they did use rice, thanks to the mediation of the Indians.

The Mongol invasions of China, Central Asia, Russia, Eastern Europe and Iran in the 13th century were followed by a series of waves of East Asian, mostly Chinese, cultural influence towards areas along the western part of the Silk Road; it seems plausible that these included culinary influences. One, dating back to the 14th or 15th century in Central Asia, was then brought from there to Anatolia, probably by migrating Turks: a special kind of large stuffed ravioli of definite Chinese origin, still called in Central Asian languages and Turkish by the Chinese name *mantu*, and still prepared, at least in Central Asia and in northern Afghanistan, according to the Chinese method of steaming instead of boiling. There cannot be any doubt that the migration of *mantu* from Imperial China to the ancestors of the Uzbeks and Tajiks must have taken place during the Chingizid–Timurid periods. As long as no other evidence disproves my hypothesis, I am very much inclined to conjecture that the fashion for eating rice found its way to them, and consequently to the Iranians, more or less at the same time.

India might be an example of 'non-genetic' convergence. Of course, the custom of eating rice dates back to antiquity, but obviously not as a prestigious dish. In India, rice seems to have owed its career to Iranian influence, and indirectly to Sino–Mongol traditions originating in the post-Chingizid periods. No doubt, during Mughal rule cultural borrowing from Iran and Transoxiana, where the Mughal rulers and their vassals originated, increased dramatically.

CHANGES IN IRANIAN *POLOW* PREPARATION

It might be interesting to find out how the art of preparing Iranian *polow* developed from the end of the 16th century to the present day. Cookbooks again tell us much. In a 70- or 80-year period during the 16th century, 70 or more different recipes for preparing *polow* were invented. It is clear that, at the start of this culinary fashion, the degree of innovation was strongly developed. To us, some of these recipes may seem to be rather bizarre. In one, we find the prescription that the rice should be coloured with indigo, so that the whole *polow* was served in a strong bluish colour! Another *polow* recipe, dating straight back to Shah 'Abbas's times, was for *morassa' polow*: *polow* decorated with jewels.

Another cookbook, written by a 19th-century royal cook from Qajar Tehran, presented his readers with 29 recipes for *polow*. In quantity, this constitutes only some 40 per cent of what his Safavid forerunner from

'Abbas's court had offered. About 30 per cent[3] of these 29 recipes were already to be found in the recipe collection of 'Abbas the Great's cook; the remaining 70 per cent (roughly 20 recipes) were new, that is, the degree of innovation in the 250 years between 1600 and 1850 was still some 25 per cent. Within the same period, about 60 per cent of recipes were forgotten: they obviously fell out of use when they lost their attractiveness in terms of fashion in the course of history. What originally was a more or less sophisticated fashion among the elite of the Safavid empire turned into a limited range of dishes belonging to what had gradually become an item of classical Iranian cuisine.

And in our day, what has happened to this classical cultural heritage of the Iranians? Cookbooks again can offer us an answer. I have compared Iranian cookbooks from the 20th century, especially more recent ones, some of them even published during the last 10 or 15 years. Each contains a certain number of unique *polow* recipes. So I counted those recipes to be found in at least 10 or 12 of the 25 or 26 Iranian cookbooks at my disposal. This calculation resulted in some 12 to 14 recipes, roughly representing the average range of *polow* recipes practised in an average Iranian middle class household, leaving aside customs belonging to micro-regional or local cuisines. Every single one of these common recipes was already to be found in the cookbook from the middle of the 19th century.

This means that the balance between innovation and loss of tradition, still to be observed in 19th-century conditions, has vanished in our modern times. Again, the general trend of political and cultural development in societies and civilizations is reflected in culinary affairs: Iranian culture, in our days, has become a defensive culture, scarcely developing within its traditional parameters, but just defending its internal cultural values against irresistible waves of Western civilization with mainly Americanizing features. In comparison with other elements of everyday culture, such as dress, furniture or architecture, traditional cuisine has even resisted well and relatively successfully. Iranian culinary conservatism, at least in private and family spheres, turns out to be an effective weapon for warding off the total victory of a faceless and tasteless junk-food culture that endangers mankind almost as much as the destruction of the rain forests or the drying out of the Aral Sea. Let us hope that the successful survival of culinary traditions in Iran and its neighbouring countries may be an indication of the limited power of present-day hegemonies and dominant superpowers, whether political, technical or economic.

Notes

1. See Bromberger's chapter (this volume). Heine, in his chapter, notes that Iraqis claim *fesenjan* as theirs.
2. See Aubaile-Sallenave (this volume).
3. Precision is impossible, as the names of recipes and sometimes the details of their preparation changed.

4. Social Reality and Culinary Fiction: the perspective of cookbooks from Iran and Central Asia

Bert Fragner

Cookbooks, being usually read for instructions on how to prepare this or that dish, may be considered as a category of literature which is limited to practical purposes. However, closer investigation and consideration make us quickly understand that there are many more fictional elements found in cookbooks than is commonly supposed.

Let me begin with a rather trivial example. Suppose that an author is engaged in compiling a cookbook containing about 400 recipes. Trying out one single recipe will take the author, on average, some 45 minutes. If he intends to check every single recipe in his book by personal experience, this will take him at least 300 hours. Working in his experimental kitchen for five hours a day testing his recipes will take a total of 75 days, or 15 weeks, of cooking before he writes a single sentence.

This rather simple-minded example may make clear what I want to explain: writing cookbooks is not so much a matter of describing personal, practical culinary experience; perhaps, to a far greater extent, it is a matter of literary borrowing and appropriation from others. Reliable professional authors have developed serious critical methods for practising such appropriation. Mostly, they combine receptiveness with personal and practical experience and control. Less reliable, but perhaps none the less professional and even successful, writers of cookbooks confine themselves to reproducing the texts of recipes found elsewhere, in many cases without giving any information on their sources.

If we follow this line, we may get the impression that writing cookbooks is, to a certain extent, structurally related to the well-known, highly respected science recognized in Islamic culture as *'ilm al-hadith*. Appropriating a recipe is in most cases closely connected with transmission and borrowing, but not necessarily with culinary practice and experience at the same rate. This is a simple statement and I intend no offence to authors of cookbooks. There cannot be the slightest doubt that such authors have to be primarily receptive, not creative, or at least not to the same extent. The author of a cookbook is, first of all, a collector of transmitted recipes. In addition, he may also practise control of these transmitted recipes, mainly by his own personal experience. In fewer cases, authors of cookbooks may behave as creative inventors.

With these considerations it should be easy to regard cookbooks not only as collections of instructions for practice, as usually seems to happen, but also as a special category of texts. Cookbooks thus contain more information and perhaps even messages from their authors than instructions on how a certain dish is prepared.

This chapter is concerned with just these less visible aspects of cookbooks, in a geographical area covering the Iranian plateau, including Afghanistan, Transcaucasian Azarbayjan and Transoxiana, that is, today's independent Central Asian republics of Tajikistan and Uzbekistan.

EARLY PERSIAN COOKBOOKS

What do these countries and areas culinarily have in common? In the previous chapter I argued the hypothesis that historically they formed a homogeneous culinary region. Research on early Persian recipes from the beginning of the 16th century leads to the conclusion that, perhaps as part of the Timurid heritage, there was a widespread consensus, from Azarbayjan to the Pamirs, on how to prepare some representative foods, mainly dishes consisting of rice. The habit of rice eating was imported to this region from China following Mongol rule in Eurasia. In China, and to a certain extent in India, rice has always been regarded as a basic means of nutrition, whereas in the area described above rice is traditionally an extraordinary and highly prestigious kind of food. The earliest Persian recipes from western Iran refer to the preparation of rice by methods resembling those we can still find in Afghanistan and Central Asia. Subsequently, under the influence of Safavid court life in the 16th and 17th centuries, special techniques for cooking rice were developed in Iran proper which are still unknown, or at least unusual, in Afghanistan and Transoxiana.

To avoid misunderstanding, I should stress that, within what I call a culinary region, beyond the general characteristics typical of the whole region, a wide variety of different local and sometimes entirely original culinary traditions and elements can be observed; but at least for a given historical period they seem embedded in traditions of wider range, which make local customs mutually compatible within the culinary region.

In our region – that is between the Ottoman Empire, India and China – until the 19th century the most commonly used language for any literary purposes, including the transmission of recipes, was Persian. Cookbooks and recipe texts in Turkic languages belong clearly to modern times. Until the end of the 19th century, none of the Persian cookbooks we now know were written for housewives, who obviously had their own methods of transmitting recipes from one generation to another. Early, pre-modern cookbooks were, as far as we know, written by men, prominent masters of the art of cookery, mostly employed at princely courts. On the one hand, they sought to present a wide if not total documentation of the 'state of their art'; that is, a large collection of recipes. On the other, they intended to produce a substantially literary text according to the general rules of *adab* literature. Already in the 19th century there existed clear stylistic regulations and ordinances as to how a cookbook should be written.

The authors of the two earliest known Persian cookbooks, Ba'urchi-Baghdadi and Ostad Nurollah (see previous chapter), were professional, princely cooks. Ostad Nurollah especially must have been prominent during his lifetime, since he was Shah 'Abbas's personal chef. He followed a clearly structured, systematic arrangement of recipes, very much reminding us of the structures of various *adab* books. Later generations of authors accepted this structure as classic. A 19th-century author named Mirza 'Ali Akbar Khan, who was himself the *ashpaz-bashi* (head cook) at the court of Naser al-Din Shah Qajar, wrote a cookbook for *Monsieur le docteur* Désiré Tholozan, the shah's personal French physician, in about 1883 or 1884, some 300 years later than Ostad Nurollah. Nevertheless, the way he arranged his material is in perfect accordance with his forerunner.

These early, pre-modern cookbooks contain a number of cross-references to the experience of other, obviously famous masters of the kitchen. All of them were restricted to large kitchens, mostly to socially high-ranking individuals. These kitchens combined a capacity for large-scale catering with the ability to prepare a wide range of luxurious dishes. Cookbooks by authors like these professional masters were clearly not written in order to offer detailed instructions to housewives who had to take culinary care of individual average households. They were used to maintain their very own, gender-specific methods of transmitting recipes among themselves, both horizontally within generations as well as from one generation to the next.

For whom did the Ostad Nurollahs and Ba'urchi-Baghdadis write their cookbooks? Not for housewives, as I have said; nor for keepers of average restaurants, because these did not exist in Iran or Central Asia until the beginning of the 20th century. What did exist, though only in cities, were simple cookshops offering only a very restricted number of invariable dishes like *ash* (porridge-like soups), *ab-gusht* (meat broth), *kalleh-pacheh* (a variety of dishes prepared from sheep's feet and heads), and more recently the famous *chelow-kabab*, the serving of which is still mostly limited to the traditional institution of cookshops. There is no doubt that the keepers of these cookshops were professionals too, but their profession clearly differed from that of the master of a princely kitchen. We may therefore conclude that neither keepers of cookshops nor masters of large kitchens located in traditional *karvansarays*, *khanqahs* or *bimarestans* were the addressees of the prominent masters' cookbooks. If these cookbooks were indeed part of *adab* literature, it is very likely that they wrote them for one another, and maybe sometimes also for prominent personalities. Even the above-named 19th-century Mirza 'Ali Akbar Khan (1974) followed the same style and structure in the arrangement of his recipes, despite the fact that he wrote his text as a personal gift for Monsieur Tholozan.

MODERN PERSIAN COOKBOOKS

From the conditions which prevailed in the Ottoman Empire, we learn that early cookbooks for housewives were written under the influence of European modernist traditions. One example is the famous Ottoman cookbook *Ev Kadını* (House-woman) written by Ayşe Fahriye (1882–3).

The oldest modern cookbook in Persian that I could find is the *Tabbakhi-ye Nashat*, the date of which is uncertain but must be about 1920. Its author was a lady bearing a typically Qajar honorary title (*laqab*), Nashat al-Dowleh. Her short foreword, introduced by the *bismillah*, gives some interesting information. Curiously enough, her original name was French, Joséphine Richard. How did she gain her Qajar *laqab*? Biographical research reveals that she was the granddaughter of a French renegade named Jules Richard (1816–91) who entered Qajar court service at Tehran in about 1870, subsequently converted to Islam, and was decorated by Naser al-Din with the honorary title Reza Khan. Nevertheless, his contemporaries used to call him Rishar Khan. His son Joseph (Yusof) Mo'addeb al-Molk, father of Joséphine, had a great reputation; he kept one of Tehran's most cultured households around 1900 and was well known as a connoisseur and collector of Iranian fine arts and numismatics.

In 1903, Yusof Rishar Khan Mo'addeb al-Molk published his *Resaleh-ye Tabbakhi*, obviously the first Persian *bonne femme* cookbook, which contained a number of Iranian recipes as well as an introduction to French cuisine. Despite various efforts, I have been unable to examine a copy personally, but there cannot be the slightest doubt that his daughter Joséphine Nashat al-Dowleh wrote her own cookbook about 20 years later by drawing heavily on her father's work, which must have been quite rare by the early 1920s. She not only took over her father's collection of Iranian recipes, but she also reproduced his chapter on French dishes. In comparison with later Iranian cookbooks, her description of how to prepare Western food seems extremely accurate. In her introduction she dedicated her book to Iranian women, to whom she wanted to teach modern methods of housekeeping, including not only basic principles of hygiene but also the mysteries of French cuisine. It was another 15 years or more before further cookbooks were published in Iran. More recent cookbooks in Persian are heavily influenced by Joséphine Richard's bestseller, which was published in numerous impressions (I use the 39th, which I acquired in the late 1970s).

I should like to stress the close relationship of dependence between more or less all recent Persian cookbooks and the *Tabbakhi-ye Nashat*. Until the end of the 1970s, immediately before the Islamic Revolution, it was rather unusual in Iranian households, even the more westernized and modern, for housewives to do their daily cooking according to cookbooks instead of following traditional instructions received from their mothers. Even more unusual at the time was preparing non-Iranian food at home.

The question must be asked: why did all the authors of cookbooks during the Pahlavi period continue to follow Joséphine Richard's model by offering a large section on *ashpazi-ye farangi*, a section which gradually grew in size until ultimately in many cases it far exceeded the chapters on Iranian food? There is a contradiction between this phenomenon and the fact that, at least until the 1970s, there was a clear preference in Iranian middle- and upper-class households for Iranian food at home, not for any Western stuff. The consumption of European food, among westernized strata of urban Iranian society, was strictly limited to European-style restaurants; home was usually a culinary refuge for indigenous cuisine. Most of the so-called 'Western' recipes in Iranian cookbooks of the time were definitely not practised by those who bought them. Closer examination offers much evidence that a fair number of those ostensibly 'Western' dishes had little or nothing in common with what they pretended to be, just like the 'oriental' or 'Indian' recipes in many European cookbooks which are sometimes based entirely on fantasy.

These 'Western' chapters in 20th-century Persian cookbooks represent by and large a fictional conception in cookbook writing, obviously serving a theoretical interest in Western cuisine, which probably consisted of talking about it much more than preparing or eating it. In many Iranian cookbooks *ashpazi-ye farangi* seems to feed what we may call a culinary 'cargo cult' rather than having any practical effects, at least as far as the period from the 1950s to the 1970s is concerned. *Gharbzadegi* seems to have pervaded even the world of cookbooks!

'ETHNOGRAPHIC' COOKBOOKS

Another category of Iranian cookbooks is that of recipe collections whose authors want to introduce and to explain the character and the highlights of Iranian cuisine to Westerners. They are usually written in Western languages, mostly in English. Some contain a message similar to that of Nashat al-Dowleh at the beginning of our century: a mixture of didactic intentions and nostalgia motivated that lady to introduce French cuisine to Iranians. In many cases, Iranian women living abroad do the same with similar intentions, though in the opposite direction. Besides, the fact cannot be ignored that Iranian cookbooks in Western languages are part of a widespread and very fashionable category of culinary literature on 'ethnic food' from all over the world. Most such cookbooks have a clearly ethnographic character; that is, their author's intention is to present a homogeneous Iranian culture through the perspective of the cookbook genre.

This fascinating mixture of nostalgia and ethnography gains striking lucidity in the case of cookbooks written by Iranians who left their country, perhaps for good, after the Islamic Revolution of 1978/9. For instance, Najmieh Batmanglij's *Food of Life* (1986), written entirely in English, is allegedly conceived for a younger generation of American Iranians who may feel alienated from their national language but should still maintain strong ties with their ancestral culture. This cookbook conjures up an idealized, almost ahistorical Iranian cultural setting, represented by a culinarily refined community of eaters, creating the image of an unbroken continuity of Iranian civilization, practised as far away as Los Angeles or Vancouver.

Motivated by similar intentions, but shaped by the high standards of scholarly methodology, the well-known scholar Mohammad Reza Ghanoonparvar has produced possibly the best ethnographic inventory of collected Iranian recipes (1984). A fair number seem to have fallen into oblivion some time ago, but nevertheless the author has still presented them all. His book has a similar effect to that of Najmieh Batmanglij: the culinary richness and abundance it projects has almost nothing to do with culinary reality, whether within Iran or among Iranians abroad. These 'ethnographic' cookbooks, besides their valuable documentation of recipes, offer the creative cook a great variety of suggestions, enabling him or her substantially to enlarge their practised culinary repertory, disregarding whether or not they are of Iranian origin.[1]

One of the most impressive examples of explicitly 'ethnographic' compilations of recipes ever written in Persian came into existence in the 1920s, not in Iran but in Afghanistan. By order of Mahmud Sami', one of the prominent generals in the Afghan army during Amir Amanullah's reign, a huge collection of recipes from every region and corner of Afghanistan was published under the title *Tabkh-e ta'am bara-ye maktab-e fonun-e harbiyeh* (Military High School Cookbook) (Sami' 1928–9). Unfortunately, General Sami' was sentenced to death and executed as a political example during Bacheh Saqaw's uprising in 1929. His compilation of dishes, partly refined and partly rural but mostly traditional, is a marvellous source for the culinary traditions of the Afghan and Central Asian upper classes; but there is not the slightest evidence that the dishes were ever prepared for the Afghan soldiery, who in the 1920s and 1930s were unlikely to have spent a luxurious life during their army service. Nevertheless, the enlightened general, who obviously had a deep interest in folklore research concerning his country, rendered Afghan culture a great service. Since the army recruited from even the remotest areas of the country, Mahmud Sami' obviously took advantage of this opportunity and collected every single traditional recipe told and transmitted by the soldiers themselves. In contrast to what had happened in Iran, it was not until the 1970s that cookbooks were published in Afghanistan which were definitely aimed at Afghan housewives.

MODERN COOKBOOKS FROM AZARBAYJAN AND CENTRAL ASIA

At first glance, native cookbooks from Central Asia and Azarbayjan give the impression of being quite distinct from those we have so far discussed. Embedded in general Soviet socio-cultural conditions that have prevailed from Lvov and Riga to Erevan, Tashkent, Irkutsk and Vladivostok, cookbooks in these areas followed a mainly Russian pattern when describing the preparation of various foods. This refers, first of all, to the arrangement of dishes. In particular, a comparison of cookbooks from former Soviet Azarbayjan with cookbooks from Iran is revealing, since Azarbayjani and Iranian cuisines are very similar, differing only in some regional peculiarities.

Soviet cookbooks have in common an almost encyclopaedic approach, which brings them close to the 'ethnographic' style of cookbook writing, but still with some striking differences. Since the publication of cookbooks, just like any other cultural, economic or social project in the Soviet Union, was expected to be well planned, government publishing houses could not accept just anybody to write a cookbook worth publication. Most writers of Soviet cookbooks therefore were, and still are, professional cooks. If we take account of the utter poverty of average Soviet gastronomy, it is easy to understand the great interest of professional cooks in the rare occasions for preparing official ceremonial receptions and dinners. Many Soviet cookbooks represent the almost magical dream of opulent banquets and festive ceremonies in a land of milk and honey for so long exclusively reserved for the members of *nomenklatura*.

This is a sound account of the situation in which Soviet readers of cookbooks would have found themselves. Therefore, the two Azarbayjani cookbooks I was able to analyse show the broad but nevertheless limited range of what might have been prepared on rare and special occasions at Baku's best restaurants. The selection of recipes within various categories (soups, salads, kebabs, pilaffs and sweets, for instance) gives the superficial impression of being entirely arbitrary and random. Closer investigation makes clear that this selection bears a close resemblance to the contents of an Azarbayjani menu card, including all the fictional items permanently cancelled and crossed out. Fantastic imaginations lead to fantasy denominations: many dishes carry names with the French *à la mode de* ... converted into Russian by expressions starting with *po-* ... A mixed salad made from finely chopped tomatoes and cucumbers is named *Shäki salatı – salat po-shekinskii* (salad *à la* Sheki); a rolled cake stuffed with walnuts is *gözlü Ordubad dürmäji – rulet orekhovyi ordubadskii*, and so on.

The most detailed cookbooks from former Soviet Islamic areas are to be found in Uzbekistan. Professional Uzbek cooks were, it seems, regularly aided by scholarly folklorists or ethnographers, as for instance Karim Mahmudov's (1986) excellent collection of recipes, *Uzbak tansiq taomlari* (Rare Uzbek Dishes), which actually transcends my above comments. This also goes for D. Sidiqov's *Lazzatli taomlar* (Tasty Dishes) (1981). Nevertheless, in a short foreword to this publication we may read: 'This book meets the needs and interests of a broad public, but mainly professional cooks, cookery apprentices and people who want to get acquainted with professional cooking, and [note the order] housewives.'

Curiously, most regional cookbooks in Central Asia, with the exception of Azarbayjan and Uzbekistan, are published in Russian instead of the native languages. In the case of Tajikistan, I tried hard to find a cookbook in Tajik, originally in order to study Tajik culinary terminology for comparison with the Persian of Iran and Afghanistan. It turned out to be extremely difficult to find one; the only one I could discover, *Taomhoi tojiki* (Tajik Dishes) (Aminov 1959), was published when Dushanbe was still Stalinabad. Even this collection of recipes was compiled by two professionals named Orifov and the obviously non-Tajik Tsuckerman.

There is a special mention of the fact that the compilation was approved by the Council of Professional Cooks at the Tajik Ministry of Commerce (*az tarafi Soveti oshpazoni Vazorati Savdoi RSS Tojikiston tasdiq karda shuda ast*). The book is incredibly bad! If there is any value in my hypothesis that Soviet cookbooks in particular resemble expectation far more than culinary reality, Orifov and Tsuckerman offer clear evidence that at the end of the 1950s even expectations and dreams of high life in Tajikistan must have been extremely impoverished, to say nothing of everyday reality.

In clear contrast to this statement, it should be stressed that books on Central Asian cookery written in Russian (again with the exception of Uzbekistan) are much more detailed. Russian accounts are comparable with the books on Iranian cuisine in English, French or German mentioned above. Clearly, this category of books served first of all the interests and curiosity of Soviet Europeans who wanted more information on, and closer acquaintance with, what for them has been for the past 100 years the main location of exoticism within their own realm.[2]

There is no doubt that, where recipes are correctly transmitted, foreign, not to say exotic, cookbooks offer plenty to enrich the culinary repertory of readers and users. As a reflection of actual culinary conditions in a country or rather a region, the value of cookbooks as a category of research sources is rather limited. Rather, they tell us more about a people's collective imaginations, symbolic values, dreams and expectations, in so far as these are connected with the art of eating and drinking.

Notes

1. Special reference should be made to two recently published cookbooks, mainly for Anglophone readers and users: Simmons (1988) offers not only a wide range of often sophisticated, mouthwatering recipes, but also detailed descriptions of Jewish, Zoroastrian and Muslim (and even Christian!) Iranian festivities in some way connected with food. Similar in some ways is Batmanglij (1986).
2. Pokhlebkin (1978) contains an overview of various types of local culinary traditions in the ex-USSR and pays special attention to the cuisine of the Caucasian and Central Asian republics. Seemingly, English, French and German translations exist.

5. The *Meyhane* or McDonald's? Changes in eating habits and the evolution of fast food in Istanbul

Holly Chase

Food consumption in Istanbul today reflects many facets of an evolving Middle Eastern society: mounting urban pressures, newly opened channels of communication, expanding international trade, economic exigencies, and increased social and physical mobility.

Multi-national fast-food restaurants amid the gastronomic wealth of Turkey usually provoke a negative reaction from those who champion the country's traditional cuisines. However, there is evidence that the presence of establishments like McDonald's may actually be contributing to a revival of old-fashioned foods which have been in danger of disappearing.

This chapter raises questions on the nature of fast food and suggests an expanded definition of Turkish fast food. Consumer preferences, along with modes of cooking, consuming, and merchandising food, are discussed in detail.

'*Istanbul'da yok yok*,' the Turks say. 'You can find anything in Istanbul'; or more literally: 'In Istanbul, non-existence doesn't exist.'

But when McDonald's opened its first Turkish franchise within 100 metres of Taksim Square, the commercial hub of modern Istanbul, I was sure its mass-produced hamburgers foreboded the eventual non-existence of much that I had come to know and appreciate in Turkey. My lack of optimism was based on two decades of intimate involvement with Turks. I had found them fiercely proud of their dual Asiatic and Mediterranean heritage and, at the same time, ambivalent about preserving their culture as they strove for economic integration in the European Community.

Pleased that Istanbul's historic preservation commission had apparently refused McDonald's permission to erect its signature golden arches, I none the less wondered how long it would take American-style fast food to eclipse the abundant, distinctive fare of Turkey's cheap restaurants and street vendors.

Dining in both restaurants and private homes, I had eaten the cold vegetable dishes known collectively as *zeytinyağlı*, 'with olive oil', long enough to find them (by the mid-1980s) rarely dressed with any oil other than sunflower (so as not to offend the palates of northern European tourists or Turks who had learned the northern prejudice against olive oil's 'heavy' taste).[1]

In a country where grocers still fashion old newspapers into bags for their produce, I had experienced the introduction of industrial packaging and the subsequent tidal wave of plastic water bottles littering Mediterranean beaches. Thus my pessimism stemmed not only from knowing the flavours of American fast food but also from having seen discarded styrofoam burger boxes swirling on the sidewalks of New York. I could anticipate no positive effects from the Istanbul McDonald's and steeled myself to watch Turkey make yet another compromise in its quest for modernity.

To be fair, it must be said that McDonald's hardly introduced the hamburger to Turkey. In the early 1960s, the Bab Café, which served fried meat patties in round buns, was, in the opinion of one American resident, 'Istanbul's very first fast-food restaurant'. But burgers made in Turkey somehow always seemed Turkish – not necessarily a bad thing. Describing the cheeseburger he had ordered in a five-star hotel, an American Turcophile asserted that it had been a giant *köfte*[2] topped with melted *kaşar*, a ewe's-milk cheese! However, two generations of Turkish-American exchange students, as well as resident American military personnel attached to NATO, have ensured that reasonably American (that is, suitably bland) beefburgers and Coca-Cola are to be found in bilingual settings in Istanbul, Izmir, Ankara, and even Adana, a south-eastern city known more for its peppery grilled lamb than for its large American military base.

Upon seeing the Istanbul McDonald's, only one of my concerns was that it again pitted kebabs against burgers. Indeed, Turkish food seemed to have been holding its own against that challenge for close to 30 years. Widespread as they were, even before McDonald's, hamburgers had not become a major element in urban Turkish diets. Far more worrisome was the juggernaut name: McDonald's. McDonald's, of course, sell more than their menu of hamburgers, french fried potatoes, and soft drinks. Especially when McDonald's establishments are outside the United States, they constitute all-enveloping American environments which themselves are 'consumed' as avidly as the food. Serving dependably edible, inoffensive food in clean, colourful, brightly lit, modern surroundings has proved profitable for McDonald's, Burger King, and other American fast-food firms operating outside North America. What long ago became prosaic to the American or European still retains its allure for the Middle Eastern consumer. Exoticism is relative.

Thus it appeared that as Turkish entrepreneurs viewed Turks' enthusiastic reception of fast food within the genuine McDonald's ambience, the inducement to imitate not only the style of service and decor, but *the food itself* would be greater than ever before. It followed that this imitation would be at the expense of traditional Turkish foods and ingredients, doomed to go the way of olive oil as a dressing for rice-stuffed vine leaves.

In Istanbul, McDonald's and Pizza Hut have now enjoyed a couple of years of great commercial success and show no signs of declining in popularity. But as for their contributing to the demise of what Turks ate before Big Macs, I can report that a recent visit to Istanbul has laid my apprehensions to rest. In February 1992, as Turkey suffered from the world-wide recession, loss of trade with neighbouring Iraq, and 70 per cent inflation per annum, fast food was flourishing in Istanbul. But whose fast food?

Beside the Taksim Square McDonald's is another new (and equally well patronized) glass-fronted restaurant with decor so similar to McDonald's that it seems to be merely an annex of the latter. Each restaurant has colourful menu boards with lettering large enough to be legible from the sidewalk. Except for the the addition of the chilled yoghurt drink known as *ayran*, McDonald's menu makes no concession to its location.[3] But next door the apparent McDonald's clone, actually a branch of the venerable Istanbul cafeteria and caterer Borsa, serves not hamburgers but a selection of kebabs, soups, and stews; fried aubergine with yoghurt; cheese *börek*; and baklava!

For centuries Istanbul has fed on such foods. Moreover, no one watching the noon-time refuelling of an Istanbul taxi-driver, gnawing through half a loaf of bread and gulping lentil soup, would deny these foods the label 'fast'.

What do we mean by the term 'fast food'? Food that can be both quickly procured and quickly eaten? Food that is eaten while one is standing up? Or sitting down at a table to which one has carried one's own meal? Does the term 'fast' have anything to do with preparation? Lentil soup may be quickly eaten, but it is not quickly made. Yet the quintessential fast-food item, the McDonald's hamburger, though rapidly cooked and eaten, is the product of far more intricate manufacturing and merchandising processes than is a bowl of Turkish lentil soup.

And what about price? Is fast food necessarily inexpensive? What is the status of fast food and what are the social implications of its consumption? Is there such a thing as high-class fast food? These are but some of the questions that arise.

Within this chapter, I shall use 'fast food' in the context of consumption. Istanbul fast food is always quickly served and *may* be quickly eaten. As for the purveyors and sites of this food, I include food pedlars; kitchen stalls with little more than a counter for take-away orders; cafeterias where diners with trays choose individual plates from a counter and then seat themselves at tables; and restaurants with anything from a couple of tables and chairs (indoors, and often outdoors) to seating for as many as 200. To qualify, by my broad definition, as a fast-food restaurant, an eatery or *lokanta*[4] in the last category must concentrate on ready-cooked dishes (*hazır yemek*) or items, like kebabs, that are quickly cooked on demand.

In all these situations, waiter service is non-existent or limited to refilling water jugs, replenishing bread baskets, and delivering plates of food from the kitchen (or, more commonly, the steam tray where various stews and pilaf are kept in view of patrons). Tips, usually not associated with fast food, might be left in *lokantas* where waiters actually bring food to the table, though such gratuities are more a matter of loose change than a calculated percentage of the bill.

In any of these circumstances, one can select, eat, and pay for one's choices in as little time as one would expend lunching at a McDonald's – and in many cases for even less money. Currently, Istanbul's cheapest food that includes meat is *lahmacun*, a baked circle of dough thinly spread with a paste of ground lamb, green pepper, onion,[5] parsley and spices. *Lahmacun* is served in all sorts of restaurants, where it is often an appetizer. But it is cheapest (about 30 pence for a 25 cm round) as sold by pedlars in the streets and covered bazaars, where it may constitute a meal for an errand boy or a rushed commuter. This is less than half the price of the basic McDonald's burger or a slice of Pizza Hut pizza, whose taste, no self-respecting *İstanbullu* would dispute, is vastly inferior to the average *lahmacun*.

In the past few years, living costs in Istanbul have soared. Yet until quite recently a generous sit-down fast-food meal of kebab, bread, salad and *ayran* maintained a price (when converted into currencies more stable than the ever-inflating Turkish lira) of about £1.75. However, for Turks living on their own currency (and not all do; many have earned wages in

Western Europe), the lira price of that kebab meal has been doubling yearly.

I had feared that gleaming temples of American fast-food merchandising in Istanbul would encourage only slavish emulation. What I never imagined was that wildfire inflation, genuine economic hardship, and choking traffic jams would boost the variety and quality of fast food in the city. But this is what has occurred. No longer do the majority of workers return home for a midday meal. Increasing numbers opt to save time and transportation costs by eating close to their work. And in Istanbul, wherever there are people there is always someone selling something to eat.

Amid the ferries and commercial water traffic of the Golden Horn, cooks in wooden rowing-boats fry fish in pans of sizzling oil precariously balanced amidships. Hungry rush-hour passengers reach from the bus windows to buy *simit*, the ubiquitous sesame-covered bread rings. (One wonders whether it was the *simit*'s shape or its sustaining qualities that inspired someone to give Turkish marine life-preservers the same name!) In the population-swollen city of Istanbul, the demand for cheap, filling food is greater than ever before, and many traditional foods, some scarce to the point of becoming gastronomic curiosities, are making a vigorous return. Let us examine a few items previously on the 'endangered' list:

BOZA

A slightly tart beverage of fermented millet, *boza* is served with a liberal sprinkling of cinnamon and roasted chick-peas. Long extolled in Turkish literature as a healthful drink, especially recommended for lactating mothers, it is decidedly odd in both taste and consistency, thick enough to be eaten with a spoon. In the mid-1970s I encountered an anachronistic *boza* pedlar whose *basso profundo* bellowed out of the dark winter night, 'BOHzaaaa!' Back then, not one of my Turkish friends had ever drunk it and, as far as I knew, its only fixed point of sale was a single stand-up counter outside the Spice Bazaar. But now there is a small, self-service *boza* parlour (with marble tables) on the chic Bağdat Caddesi. (On the city's Asian side, this avenue of glittering shops occupies a stretch of the ancient route to Baghdad.)

SAHLEB

In winter, the Bağdat Caddesi *bozacı* gives pride of place to a bulging brass urn that holds *sahleb*, a hot drink of sweetened milk thickened with the scarce and costly root of an orchid (*Orchis masculis*), which grows wild in eastern Anatolia. Back in the 1980s, the sight, anywhere in Turkey, of a hand-lettered sign proclaiming that a 'breakfast' restaurant (serving tea, bread, cheese, honey and olives) also featured *sahleb* was cause for rejoicing. But today *sahleb* has become widespread in Istanbul. At 40 pence, a cinnamon-dusted cup of *sahleb* costs more than a Turkish coffee, a large glass of tea, or a Coca-Cola. Nutritious and more filling than the other drinks, it can be considered a relatively costly beverage – or a cheap liquid meal. In the latter category, *sahleb* has found favour with fashionably thin young women, whom it serves as a breakfast or as an afternoon shopper's pick-me-up.

PICKLES

Like the old *boza* parlour on the European side, the new Asian shop also sells other products of fermentation: pickled vegetables and pickle brine. In Istanbul, as in most Middle Eastern cities, pickles are popular not only as a condiment but as a snack food by themselves. Particularly in hot weather, their brine is a refreshing drink.

A cluster of pickle shops in the district of Çemberlitaş survived into the mid-1980s as one of the city's most enticing food displays. Huge blown-glass jars artfully packed with stuffed red peppers, tiny aubergines, beet-dyed turnips, and shredded cabbage layered with whole green tomatoes and carrots rivalled the jewellers' windows of the nearby Covered Bazaar. Now displaced by a restaurant billing itself as a steak house, the pickle-sellers have migrated to the ferry-boat landing on the south side of the Galata Bridge, where they sell their provender from push-carts.

As their city becomes more congested, *İstanbullus* are reluctant to battle against the traffic of many traditional shopping areas. This attitude has encouraged the replication, on both sides of the Bosphorus, of food shops and services that were once unique to particular commercial quarters.

Kokoreç

Labour-intensive in its preparation, *kokoreç*, lamb intestine stuffed with an oregano-seasoned assortment of organ meats, might not immediately strike one as fast food. It differs from a sausage in that pieces of innards are marinated, skewered and tightly bound, bandage fashion, in several lengths of empty intestine. The whole packet is then basted and slowly grilled over charcoal on a horizontal spit. Thin slices are served in a quarter loaf of bread moistened with drippings.

A legacy of the Greeks, who call it *kokoretsi*, the snack is known today only in coastal Turkey, and especially in Istanbul, where there is still a considerable Greek population. Particularly associated with summer, *kokoreç* used to be a popular beach food in the outlying resort districts along the Sea of Marmara. But when single-family seaside houses were replaced by multi-storey apartment buildings and once-sleepy lanes became clogged with private cars, the street-food vendors faded into memory. In recent years the only place where one could be sure of finding *kokoreç* was the Çiçek Pasajı, the Passage of Flowers in the European quarter of Beyoğlu, to which we shall eventually turn.

But like an old chanteuse after a successful face-lift, *kokoreç* has staged a comeback. Butchers now sell ready-to-grill *kokoreç* packets and pre-sliced *kokoreç* (which can be fried and served more quickly) to small restaurants that have never before had the item on their menus. With someone else doing the work (culinary labour is still cheap in Turkey), *kokoreç* is a very inexpensive and delicious way to offer meat – again, cheaper than a McDonald's burger.

Kokoreç is but one item from the elaborately prepared offal and variety-meat repertoire of the Middle East. Economic inducements to use every part of a slaughtered animal are historical as well as contemporary. Ottoman accounts of the chronic financial straits of Istanbul's butchers reveal that profit margins were once so narrow that the government had to conscript wealthy men into the profession (Faroqhi 1984: 221–41)

Probably because intestines, tripe, heads and feet require tedious cleaning procedures, they never played prominent roles in most Istanbul home kitchens. Instead, certain cookshops came to specialize in these items. Often grouped around markets, the source of their ingredients, stalls dispensing soup and boiled sheep's heads continue to provide quick, cheap and fortifying pre-dawn breakfasts to market vendors. But a tripe soup salon, or *işkembeci*, frequently serves an entirely different clientele, the *akşamcıs*, late-night carousers, who, like fellow-drinkers from Iberia to India, swear by the sobering properties of garlicky tripe soup well laced with lemon or vinegar.[6]

The combination of modern economic pressures and increased public alcohol consumption among middle- and upper-class Turks can be credited with bringing tripe and foot soups out of the city's poorer, socially conservative market quarters into affluent, cosmopolitan neighbourhoods.

Manti

In contrast to foods highlighted thus far, all of which are made and consumed outside the home, the pasta called *mantı* has long resided in a thoroughly domestic niche. *Mantı* lies geographically and culinarily between Italian ravioli and the Asiatic expanse of Russian *pelemeni*, Afghan *ashak*, and Chinese wontons. Thin squares of wheat-flour dough folded or pinched to encase minute dollops of seasoned minced lamb, Istanbul *mantı* are usually boiled, drained, and then sauced with warmed yoghurt and a drizzle of garlic-paprika butter.

In Turkey, women gather to make huge quantities of *mantı* for large celebrations, or, as home freezers become more common, simply to have on hand. Among urban families whose women work outside the home and thus spend less time in the kitchen, *mantı* are often considered the speciality of a particular relative, someone with both the knack and the patience to make them. In such households, they are a rare treat, enjoyed only when, say, Aunt Fikriye comes on her annual visit from distant Kayseri (famed for its *mantı*- makers).

Turkic and Mongol horsemen on the move are supposed to have carried frozen or dried *mantı*, which could be quickly boiled over a camp-fire. Lately, the nomadic staple that had settled into comfortable domesticity has wandered out of the house. Can we ask for a better example of fast food than this freeze-dried pasta from the steppes of Central Asia? Almost everyone likes *mantı*; its ingredients are inexpensive; and once the pasta has been filled with meat, it can be frozen for long periods, yet rapidly thawed and cooked to order. In fashionable neighbourhoods on both sides of the Bosphorus, restaurants specializing in *mantı* have mushroomed. The Bağdat Caddesi's slick, white and green-tiled 7-Up Mantı Restaurant looks more like a Swiss clinic than a cosy encampment, but it does ease the wait until Aunt Fikriye's next visit.[7]

The following commentaries are included to illuminate other aspects of Istanbul's current culinary complexity.

CHICKEN

Though I have yet to see low-fat yoghurt offered as an alternative topping for *mantı*, Istanbul Turks, who watch Cable News Network television and read foreign magazines, are increasingly aware of the American and Western European preoccupation with cholesterol. Many home cooks have switched from butter to margarine and buy high-priced 'diet chicken', skinless raw chicken breasts, from their local delicatessens.

Because of the capitalization and technical sophistication needed to raise poultry on a large scale, the availability or absence of inexpensive chicken can be a useful indicator of a country's economic development. During the 1970s, when most Turks had never heard of cholesterol, lamb meat in Turkey was half the price of chicken. At that time I was working with a non-profit Turkish foundation whose primary activity was the establishment of poultry farms in rural Anatolia. In less than a decade, chicken prices fell to the point where chicken became an everyday commodity. Previously, grilled chicken had been one of Istanbul's costlier fast foods. Special shops, whose windows would feature a dozen golden chickens slowly roasting on spits, would advertise that they provided home delivery. Long before Pizza Hut's motorbikes with heated pizza-carrying compartments, roast chickens were delivered by car. That lamb kebab deliveries were still made on foot reflected everyone's proximity to at least one kebab shop, whereas chicken shops were few and far between.

Available since the mid-1980s, and making ever more frequent appearances alongside lamb *döner kebab*, is the comparably priced *tavuk döner*, seasoned white chicken meat and fat layered on a vertical, rotating spit. Vendors relate that *tavuk döner* was invented in Saudi Arabia,[8] where it was first made with Danish chicken.

PORTRAIT OF A GROCERY STORE

In the realm of food, we have seen Istanbul as a city which, in its fascination with the foreign, is both imitative and adaptive. An excellent manifestation of this talent for synthesis is the new Seven-Eleven convenience store[9] on the European side, in the expensive shopping and residential district of Nişantaşı. On one of the city's most desirable pieces of commercial real estate (the equivalent of a corner in Knightsbridge or mid-town Manhattan), sits a store whose United States counterparts are currently relegated to declining suburban shopping strips and crime-ridden urban ghettos.

Taking advantage of American suburbanites' reliance on their cars, the original Seven-Eleven stores were conceived as convenient locations where one would drive to pick up soft drinks, snack foods, small packages of staples (sugar, flour, macaroni), milk, cigarettes, basic toiletries, and magazines. At no time has Seven-Eleven (or any of its imitators) ever had an up-market image *in the United States*, although its food prices have always been considerably higher than those of a large supermarket. (The customer pays for the convenience of longer hours, that is, increased access to what he wants.)

But the Nişantaşı Seven-Eleven is something else. If, like the American outlets, it sells expensive, over-packaged snack foods along with the rest of the aforementioned inventory, it also carries realistically priced one-kilogram bags of Turkish staples – bulgur, chick-peas, lentils, rice. In Turkey, rosewater is an everyday flavouring and cosmetic; Seven-Eleven stocks it. There are foil packets of instant *sahleb* and Knorr versions of traditional soups that most middle-class women no longer bother to make, such as *tarhana*, with dried nuggets of yoghurt and flour, and *ezo gelin*, a richly spiced lentil soup. Such instant comestibles and 24-hour-a-day shopping possibilities present additional aspects of fast food. Along with changes in food consumption, Istanbul is beginning to experience changes in food merchandising.

In a retail location where one could expect easily to sell a suit or a dress costing £200, the costliest single item is probably a kilogram of pistachios priced at under £5. In the United States, one is fortunate to find a convenience-store clerk willing to do more than take a customer's money; stores are totally self-service, so 'if you don't see it, don't ask'. In Istanbul, there is a uniformed Seven-Eleven attendant to help shoppers locate goods ... But the western consumer knows he is in another land (a secular Muslim country with ever-changing ideas of what constitutes status) when he enters the wine section. (US Seven-Elevens are dry.) Here are recognized wines from one of Turkey's most reputable vineyards, and they bear labels that read 'Bottled for Seven-Eleven'. To anyone familiar with an American Seven-Eleven, this is the equivalent of discovering a Coca-Cola can with the legend *mis en boîte au château*!

THE ÇIÇEK PASAJI

Leaving the world of bar-coded packaging behind us, we now descend to the multi-national sector of Beyoğlu, on the north side of the Golden Horn. In the waning days of the Ottoman Empire, this neighbourhood teemed with Greek furriers, Armenian pâtissiers, Jewish shopkeepers and Christian clerics. Merchants, diplomats and spies from every nation in Europe had set themselves up here. One of the last and most extravagant flowerings of that hot-house atmosphere bloomed in a raucous alley behind a wrought-iron art nouveau gate. The Çiçek Pasajı, the Passage of Flowers, named for the adjacent market, was – and is – a collection of tiny restaurants, each a *meyhane*[10] serving alcohol and small plates of *meze*. With the police regularly intervening in drunken brawls, the place was always considered, at least by night, to be very much a male milieu. By the 1970s, however, women could lunch there without raising many eyebrows. After a fire in 1978 and a decade of closure, the refurbished (some might say emasculated) Çiçek Pasajı reopened, taking only a couple of years to regain its former clientele and spirit.

Served without delay, by waiters too busy to be obsequious, *meyhane* meals are consumed in an informal setting. Today, seating is at tables flanked by benches; before the fire, there were many chest-high marble-topped barrels, and few chairs. Among the numerous *meze*, mussels – batter-fried or stuffed with spicy rice pilaf – are a Çiçek Pasajı speciality. Small portions of mixed grilled meats, including liver kebabs and *kokoreç*, are popular, as are *börek*, salads, spreads, olives, salted nuts, cheese, and a variety of cold stuffed *zeytinyağlı* vegetables. All these items are rapidly prepared or ready to eat. But do they constitute fast food?

Everywhere but Beyoğlu, we have been sampling food apart from alcoholic beverages. Because of the types of food offered and the speed of service, one *could* eat quickly in the Çiçek Pasajı, but in practice this is not what one does. There are too many reasons to linger into the night, too much going on among the incidental cast of characters (card-gamblers, fortune-telling gypsy flower-sellers, prostitutes, and itinerant musicians that include an Armenian lady accordion player in a purple plaid dress). Drinking deeply from half-litre beer glasses known as Argentines or sipping lemon vodka, gin, or ice-clouded *rakı*, changes the equation.

This is not McDonald's, where management hope for a rapid turnover of customers. *Meyhane* food, by complementing liquor and increasing thirst, is meant to prolong a patron's stay.

> The *meyhane* became my dwelling place.
> Fate became my friend –
> She emptied my bottle and filled up my eyes
> With the tears that I weep for my very last home...
> The *meyhane* has consumed my Life.[11]

Before he totters home, many a *meyhane* client, or *akşamcı*, will revert to consuming food fast. He will 'drink', as the Turks say, a bowl of tripe soup in a biliously illuminated, unadorned cookshop where the absence of both alcohol and conversation ensures that his stay will be brief. But should we, slightly hung-over despite our tripe soup, return to the Çiçek Pasajı at noon the following day, we will catch no anise scent of the previous evening's *rakı*. Rushed, stand-up crowds of clerks and students will be washing down fried mussel sandwiches and *kokoreç* with *ayran*, and Coca-Cola.

Like Istanbul herself, the Çiçek Pasajı has two sides.

TAILPIECE

Modern Saudi Arabian chicken *shwarma/tavuk döner* has established itself in Istanbul while Turkish-style grilled meats, which Arabs call *meshwiyyat turkiyya*, enjoy increasing popularity in the cosmopolitan world of Arabian Gulf fast food. In Manamah, Bahrain, a bustling Bahraini-owned restaurant proclaims itself a 'Turkish Grill' in both English and Arabic, the languages of its printed menu. Dishes fall under the headings: Arabic (Lebanese and Gulf items), Chinese, Indian, pizza and hamburgers, and grills. Staff are Filipino. Music is taverna-style Greek. The equally international clientele may choose to be seated in the mixed-sexes section, the upstairs family section, or the ladies' section, which features pink curtains drawn to enclose each six-person seating area completely. However, much of the restaurant's volume is in drive-in/take-away orders, primarily kebabs. With advance notice, whole roast baby lamb can also be had. This raises the question of whether take-away food that requires advance notice and costs £58 an order is still fast food.

One of the restaurant's cooks is Bangladeshi and two are Turkish – one of these makes only *pide* bread, the other specializes in kebabs. It appears that, at least in Bahrain, a Turk presides, not over a melting pot, but over a sort of global grill.

Notes

1. When asked why they have shifted to sunflower oil, restaurant chefs usually cite this reason, as well as the fact that olive oil costs more. 'But butter's expensive,' I sometimes counter, 'so why haven't you switched to margarine?' They usually shrug in reply. As for sunflower oil, although I find it virtually unscented and tasteless, I know Turks who detest its 'strong odour'.

2. In Turkey, a small, grilled oval of minced lamb, often seasoned with oregano, coriander seed, black pepper, and sometimes cumin.

3. However, friends returning from Athens report that the local Wendy's (another American burger installation) boasts a salad bar that includes marinated artichoke hearts and Greek olives.

4. The Turkish adoption of the Italian *locanda*, or inn. Most *lokantas* do not serve alcohol.

5. One kebab restaurant in an expensive shopping area currently advertises that it features 'onionless *lahmacun*'. When preparing food for large parties, some restaurants consider it a point of refinement to eliminate raw garlic from certain dishes.

6. Here we have another aspect of fast food's appeal: the expanded hours during which one may have it. As for nocturnal service, the parents of adolescent boys and girls (for whom fast food is also a pretext for socializing) are surely more comfortable knowing that, at 10 pm, their offspring are within a neon-lit Pizza Hut rather than among the reputedly dubious characters of the local tripe-soup kitchen.

7. For *mantı/mantu* in Saudi Arabia, see Yamani (this volume) [Eds].

8. *Shwarma* in Arabic, thus 'chicken *shwarma*' in the polyglot Arabian Gulf;

see Tailpiece.
 9. Though most shops in this American franchise operation are now open 24 hours a day, their name is derived from the chain's original hours of 7 am until 11 pm.
10. Modern Turkish use of the Persian term for 'wine-house'.
11. My translation of the Turkish 'Meyhane Benim Meskinim', contemporary Arabesk song with lyrics and music by Mehmet Ataç; sung by Zekeriya Ünlü.

6. The Taste for Layered Bread among the Nomadic Turks and the Central Asian Origins of Baklava

Charles Perry

The invention of layered pastries such as baklava and strudel, which are so characteristic of the eastern Mediterranean and central Europe today, has been claimed by both Greeks and Turks. One piece of evidence for the Greek claim is the mention of a layered sweetmeat called *gastris* in the second-century *The Deipnosophists* of Athenaeus of Naucratis, but examination of the text shows that *gastris* was not a pastry at all. The Turkish claim, by contrast, can produce very suggestive evidence that the nomadic Turks were making layered dough products as early as the 11th century. It is argued that baklava was the first layered pastry baked in an oven, but that the practice of making the layers of dough paper-thin was probably an innovation of the royal kitchens at the Topkapı Sarayı in the century or so after the Ottoman conquest of Constantinople.

Puff pastry and *filo* (also known as strudel dough) are rather similar: paper-thin sheets of dough, separated by a film of butter, which separate when cooked because of steam from the dough and produce a pastry of thin layers. They are made by totally different techniques, however. For puff pastry, the cook repeatedly folds a slab of buttered dough, forming the layers within the dough; for *filo*, the layers are made separately, then buttered and stacked to make the pastry. The texture resulting from the former process is soft and rich, with somewhat indistinct layers, while the latter process produces distinct, fairly crisp layers.

The basic folding procedure that makes puff pastry is widely known outside Europe, though not used so systematically that it produces the hundreds of layers of a French *pâte feuilletée*. An Indian *waraki paratha* or a Chinese green-onion pancake is greased and folded once or twice, producing only rudimentary layering. The more 'analytical' *filo* process is, or was until its recent discovery by Western European and American cooks, found primarily in the territories of the old Austro-Hungarian Empire and those of its long rival, the Ottoman Empire. It would be natural to seek its origin in the latter.

However, Westerners sometimes resist the idea of seeing the Turks – that is, the Central Asian nomads speaking Turkish dialects who began invading Anatolia in the 11th century – as having anything to do with the creation of this elegant, sophisticated product of the kitchen. They tend to look instead to the ancient settled populations of the eastern Mediterranean as the originators of *filo*.

In his book *The Decline of Medieval Hellenism in Asia Minor*, Professor Speros Vryonis claims that there is evidence of layered pastry in second-century Greece. In the chapter 'The Byzantine Residue in Turkish Anatolia', he dwells on the fact that ancient Greek pastries and modern Turkish pastries favour the same ingredients, such as honey and nuts (a taste which both traditions have in common with Iranian pastry-making, incidentally; it should not be forgotten that the cuisine of the Turks, as of all Islamic peoples, has been decisively influenced by Persian cookery). Then he boldly states, 'Another Byzantine favorite was the so-called *kopte* or *kopton* (*koptoplakous*), which was the same as the Turkish *baklava*' (1971: 482).

He footnotes two sources for this claim. The first is the second-century book *The Deipnosophists* by Athenaeus of Naucratis. However, an examination of the passage in question (XIV: 647) does not bear him out. It should be noted that in the text of *The Deipnosophists*, the word *koptoplakous* actually stands alone, not forming part of a sentence, and is followed by a description of a Cretan sweet called *gastris* or *gastrion*. Most editors assume that *gastris* was merely another name for *koptoplakous*, however. The literal meaning of *koptoplakous* is 'cake made of *kopte*' – that is, of pounded sesame. As we shall see, this would be a very exact name for the Cretan sweet *gastris*.

To be sure, the passage describes a sweet with a filling of nuts (walnuts, filberts, almonds and poppy-seed) mixed with honey, which readily reminds us of baklava, but if we examine the rest of the recipe we find that no dough is called for. Instead, one crushes sesame and mixes it with boiled honey (*sesamon leukon tripsas, malaxon meliti hepsemeno*), exactly as one did with the ground nuts, and draws this paste out into two sheets (*helkyson lagania dyo*). The dark nut filling goes between the two layers of sesame-sweet, producing a result that was evidently felt to resemble a filled paunch (*gastris*). In any case, it was a sweetmeat not a pastry, and there is no reason to see any connection between *gastris* and baklava.

Professor Vryonis also footnotes *Vyzantinon Vios kai Politismos* by Professor Phedon Koukoules, which seems to be the source of his error. In interpreting the passage from *The Deipnosophists*, Professor Koukoules (1952, V: 116) had described *koptoplakous* as made 'from two sheets of dough' (*ek dyo phyllon zymes*), which, as we have seen, are not to be found. Koukoules's 'sheets of dough' are evidently a hasty misreading of the *lagania* ('cakes') of the recipe, which were in fact layers of sesame paste.

Elsewhere in his book, Professor Vryonis dismisses the culinary tradition of the nomadic Turks as an impoverished one, since they lived off their flocks, whatever fruits and vegetables they could gather, and simple griddle breads. It is true that the Turks had to cook their breads on the plain griddle known as *sach*, but ironically it is quite possible that this 'impoverishment' is the very reason for the Turks' invention of layered breads.

It is clear that the ancient Turks were fascinated by the idea of achieving layers in their breads and cakes. Lacking ovens, they were unable to make thick breads of the sort that settled people often make. Perhaps for this very reason, they felt the necessity for creating variety in the thickness of their breads.

Several of these ancient layered breads survive among the Turkish nations of modern Central Asia. The Uzbeks make a cake called *poshkal* from ten or 12 thinly rolled sheets of dough. The first layer is fried on one side and then turned over to fry on the other. While it cooks, a thin layer of sour cream is spread on the cooked surface, and this is covered with a second sheet of raw dough. When the first sheet is cooked on the bottom, this 'sandwich' is turned over and smeared with sour cream, and the process is repeated with more dough until a thick cake is built up (Makhmudov 1962: 48–9).

The Uzbeks make a similar product called *yupqa* with a filling of ground meat fried with onions in place of sour cream. The same word is used in Tatarstan on the Middle Volga (where it is pronounced *yoka*) for a sort of cake served with tea (*Tatarskaia Kulinariia* 1981: 220). For a Tatar *yoka*, ten or 12 sheets of dough are fried and buttered and stacked up. And the same word is used in Turkey (where it is pronounced *yufka*) in the sense of a single sheet of *filo*.

I have speculated that the nomadic Turkish nations experimented with layering in order to vary a boring diet of thin breads, but it may be that they loved layering for its own sake. A pastry called *qatlama* is known among the Uzbeks, Kazakhs, Tatars, Bashkirs, Azarbayjanis and Turkmens, and the Uyghurs of Xinjiang Province, China. It is usually made by rolling up a greased sheet of dough and cutting it into discs, which are flattened by hand and perhaps rolled out with a pin also. This produces a (rather stiff) layering.

The ancient Turkish word *yubqa*, which is ancestral to *yupqa*, *yoka* and *yufka*, meant 'thin, frail', and specifically referred to a thin, flat bread. It still often has that meaning; however, there is evidence that the sense of a layered bread goes back many centuries. In the *Kitab Diwan Lughat al-Turk*, the 11th-century dictionary of Turkish dialects compiled by Mahmud of Kashghar, two forms of the word (*yuvgha* and *yupqa*) are defined as 'thin bread'. However, Mahmud also recorded the expression *qatma yuvgha*, and translated it into Arabic as *khubz mughaddan*, which means 'folded' (or perhaps 'wrinkled' or 'pleated') bread (al-Kashghari 1915–17, III: 20, 27). *Qatma* contains the same root *qat*, 'layer', that is found in *qatlama*, so it is virtually certain that *qatma yuvgha* was layered in some way.

Still, it is a long way from folded or pleated bread cooked on a *sach* over a fire of twigs in the steppes of Central Asia, to a pan of baklava with 100 paper-thin layers of dough sandwiching a layer of ground nuts, all baked in an oven and drenched with syrup. It would strengthen the case for the Turkish origin of baklava if we could find a 'missing link' between these two extremes.

We may very well have the 'missing link' in the peculiar Azarbayjani sweet known as *Baki pakhlavası*, or Baku-style baklava. This is not made with 50 or 100 sheets of dough stretched paper-thin, but with eight sheets of dough rolled no thinner than for noodle paste, alternating with seven layers of nuts.[1] (The Tatars have adopted this dish from the Azarbayjanis; in Tatarstan it is known as *päkhläwä*.)

Azarbayjan was on the nomads' path from Central Asia to Anatolia. A simple way to account for this peculiar pastry is to see it as a first fruit of the contact between nomadic Turks and the settled Iranians of the region. It seems to combine the Iranian tradition of pastries with nut fillings baked in ovens with the layered bread of the Turks.

In this view, the vastly more refined baklava familiar to the world today, made with paper-thin sheets of dough, would be a later elaboration, suited to the wealthy and sophisticated society of Istanbul after the Ottoman conquest. The likely place for the innovation would be the many kitchens of the Topkapı Palace. In fact, the palace had a particular association with baklava. Every year, on the 15th day of Ramazan, the Janissaries of Istanbul assembled at the palace, and each regiment was given two big trays of baklava, which they slung from poles in sheets of cloth and carried through the streets of the city in a celebration called the *Baklava Alayı*, or Baklava Procession.

Note

1. Mustafaev (1971: 59): 'Baku baklava consists of 15 layers, of which 8 are dough, 7 filling' (*Baki pakhlavası 15 qatdan ibarät olur. Bunun 8-ni khämir qati, 7-ni iç qati täşkil edir*). According to the text, each layer of nut filling weighs 285 grams and each layer of dough (apart from the heavier top and bottom layers) weighs 220 grams.

7. Rice in the Culinary Cultures of the Middle East

Sami Zubaida[1]

'What do the people of paradise eat?' – 'Rice in butter'
(old Arab saying)
'izz bi'l-rizz, wu'l-burghul yeshni' nafsu – 'Good living is with rice,
and let the burghul hang itself'(Syrian folk saying)

Rice is a staple only in limited rice-growing regions of the Middle East, parts of the Egyptian delta (Damietta and Rosetta), parts of the Caspian provinces of Iran and the southern marshlands of Iraq being the most notable. Until recent times, rice was considered a luxury food, for the tables of the rich and for special occasions in most parts of the region. Staples were, and remain, other grains: wheat, barley and maize. Wheat, too, was relatively expensive in most areas. Most people in Iraq and Iran ate barley bread, a symbol of poverty and hardship in the popular mind, and in the Black Sea provinces of Turkey, maize bread was the most common, more recently changed to a mixture of wheat and maize. This latter was the staple for Upper and Middle Egypt. The most notable shift in food distribution and consumption in the region since the 1940s has been the shift to wheat and, to a lesser extent, to rice (FAO 1965: 25–8). This results partly from changing production patterns and the reclamation and irrigation of new lands, but most importantly from the vast acceleration of world trade in these commodities and the subsidized exports of large quantities of wheat from North America and western Europe. Rice, too, is exported to the Middle East from America and the Far East, making it more readily and cheaply available in many markets and altering consumption patterns. Rice, however, has not supplanted wheat as the staple. In most places, it is not served at every meal, and when served it constitutes the main dish, or one of the main dishes, while bread is present at every meal as an auxiliary to whatever else is eaten, including rice. To most, a meal without bread is unthinkable. Contrast this to, say, Japan, where a meal (including breakfast) is unthinkable without a bowl of rice.

Until recent times country people generally ate what they produced and what was locally available and cheap. In regions where rice was not produced on any scale (such as most of Greater Syria and Anatolia), its consumption was restricted to the better-off urban households who could afford imported rice.[2] Rice, however, remained an important item for celebrations and banquets. Unless the celebrants were very poor, a wedding banquet would be unthinkable without several platters or trays of rice combined with different ingredients in colourful displays.

An interesting phenomenon is that of *substitution*. In Greater Syria, Anatolia and northern Iraq, wheat in the form of *burghul* (Arabic) or *bulgur* (Turkish), which is wheat parboiled, then dried and cracked, is one of the staples. It is used in a great variety of ways, but one of the most regular is to cook it as a *pilav* (Turkish) or *burghul mufalfil* (Arabic), both terms being derived from rice cookery. It is boiled in water or stock with oil or butter, combined with cooked meats or vegetables, or served plain with yoghurt or stew, just like rice. Burghul in this form was considered a cheaper and inferior substitute for rice, hence the Syrian saying quoted above. We shall consider other instances of substitution in what follows.

RICE VARIETIES

As far as I can ascertain, there is no general system of classification of rice varieties which applies throughout the region. In Iran certain rare and highly esteemed varieties are distinguished: *'ambar-bu*, amber-scented, *darbari*, imperial court, and *dom-siah*, black-tailed. These are all long grains and aromatic (Shaida 1992: 62). More regular varieties are designated *sadri*, *gerdeh* (meaning 'fat') and *champa*, in descending order of value, each of these having sub-categories (Mojtahedi 1980: 8). The *sadri* is a slender, longer grain, while the *gerdeh* is a fatter, shorter grain, and the *champa* a mixed category of varieties considered inferior and only suitable for soups and puddings. In Iraq, the most esteemed variety is called *'ambar* (I am not certain whether it is the same as the Iranian *'ambar*), a slender grain much valued for its aromatic quality, rare in recent years and overshadowed by imported varieties. In Egypt and Syria, *rashidi* rice (after Rosetta) was much esteemed. The term came to be applied to a type of rice harvested while still slightly green, some of which came from Upper Egypt.

In general, the distinctions relate to shape of grain, whether long or round, and its texture when cooked, whether it remains whole and separate, or sticks in a mass. The aesthetic preference throughout the region is for the former. In Egypt, most of the native varieties are round-grained, like Italian and some Spanish rice. This, in turn, comes in different qualities, and the best makes perfectly good *ruz mufalfil*,[3] that is separate grains, contrary to the belief that all round-grained rice is inferior and only good for puddings and soups. In Iran and Iraq, the general preference is for the long, slender grains, which are believed to cook better into distinct grains, the rounder-grained rice being reserved for puddings and soups, as well as making cold rice-balls in some parts of Iran. In Turkey, the most esteemed varieties (such as the one called *baldo*) are long-grained but more boat-shaped than slender.

In recent years, imported Indian rice, especially the basmati variety, has found great favour at the upper end of the market, mostly in the rich Gulf countries. It attains the aesthetic ideal of long, separate grains, with distinct aromatic qualities, better than any of the readily available native varieties, or the imported American rice. This latter, especially the parboiled 'Uncle Ben' variety, has also been extensively used for its convenience, but is disdained by the connoisseurs of rice.

RICE COOKERY

Rice is cooked in a variety of ways in the region, but we can distinguish two primary paradigms, one identified with Iran, the other with Turkey. We shall learn, however, that no rule or generalization about cookery in the region can hold uniformly; there are always exceptions and variations.

Iran features the most elaborate culture of rice cookery,[4] which seems to go back in history at least to Safavid times in the 16th century. The paradigm of rice cookery consists of the following operations. Rice is first washed thoroughly in water, rubbing the grains with the fingers under the water, with several changes of water. It is then soaked in salted water for a minimum of half an hour, but preferably for several hours. The rice is next drained and added to a pan with plenty of salted boiling water. Within a few minutes, the rice grains are nearly tender and the rice is drained. Butter is melted in the pan so that it covers the bottom and comes up to the sides, and sometimes a little water or stock is added to the butter. The drained rice is returned to the pan, the pan covered first with a cloth then with the lid, placed on a medium flame for about ten minutes, then the flame reduced to a minimum and allowed to cook for at least half an hour. This is plain or *chelow* rice, served with a pat of butter on top, as an accompaniment to grilled meat (as in *chelow-kebab*) or to meat/vegetable stews, *khoresht*. A variation (less typical in Iran itself, but more common in parts of Iraq) is to add quantities of melted butter, oil or rendered tail fat to the cooked rice at the end, sometimes with chopped onions fried in the fat.

Polow is the term applied to dishes of rice combined with other ingredients. The same procedure as for *chelow* is followed until the point at which the boiled, drained rice is returned to the pan. At this point, other cooked ingredients are introduced in combination with the rice. Cooked meat, chicken or fish, with a little of the juices and fats of their cooking, are layered with the rice. Aromatics, notably saffron, are also added at this juncture. Vegetables, fruit and pulses also feature in *polows*. In some of these, the vegetable is boiled with the rice, as in the case of *baqali polow*, with broad beans (fava) and dill, or *lubya polow*, with green haricot beans and dill. These often feature meat and chicken in addition to the vegetables. Orange and candied orange peel as well as sugar feature in *shirin* (sweet) *polow*, which also contains chicken and is flavoured with saffron. Other fruits which feature in *polow* are sour cherries (*albalu*). Of the pulses, lentil is the most common in combination with rice in *adas polow*. We shall see that this great variety of *polow* is the very stuff of banquets and feasts.

The aesthetic value sought in *polow* and *chelow* is distinct and separate grains which are soft and fluffy but not mushy. This value is shared throughout the region. In addition, the Iranian cook aims for a splendid *tah-dig*, a crispy crust or cake at the bottom of the pan, dripping with the butter and other juices of the cooking, which tops the platter on which the rice is served, and is often appreciated separately from the rest of the dish. This is the reason why the pan is covered with a cloth under the lid, to absorb the steam so that it does not condense off the lid and drip back into the rice, so making the bottom soggy.

Turkey is, perhaps, more culturally diverse than Iran. Historically, there is a divide between Istanbul and the cities of the north-west (notably Izmir and Bursa) on the one hand, and the great Anatolian hinterland on the other. The first represent Ottoman court culture, with greater sophistication and restraint (especially with regard to spices and flavourings), whereas Anatolia retained the substance of the many regional folk cultures. As such, there is considerable continuity in culinary matters between south-west Anatolia and Syria. Until the collapse and fragmentation of the Ottoman Empire at the beginning of this century, Aleppo was the cultural and commercial centre for that part of Anatolia (Marcus 1989). The culinary repertoire of Gaziantep (the old 'Ain Tab), much celebrated in present-day Turkey, is basically that of Aleppo. We must remind ourselves in this regard that cultural frontiers do not coincide with national ones, not even after many decades of nation-states moving towards greater uniformity within their boundaries. Certainly with regard to culinary matters we cannot speak of 'the Arab world' as a homogeneous domain distinct from Turkey or Iran. The connections are not merely regional, but also relate to class, religion and forms of habitation (i.e. urban/rural and settled/nomadic divides). For instance, in matters of life-style, including that of culinary matters, the upper classes in Egypt followed Ottoman aristocratic fashions, and only abandoned them to follow European styles. The urban Shi'is of Iraq (not all Shi'is, it should be emphasized, most of whom are peasants and tribesmen), as well as the Jews of that country, feature many Persian influences in their cooking and eating, while the Sunni notables (again not provincial or poor Sunnis) traditionally followed Ottoman Turkish fashions. With few exceptions, they all spoke Arabic.

It is possible, however, to distinguish a Turkish paradigm of rice cookery, which spans Istanbul and Anatolia, in common with Egypt and Syria, and distinct from the Iranian paradigm which also includes many Iraqi communities. This involves washing the rice (but not as ritually as the Iranians) often under running water in a colander. Some would also soak it, but this is not essential. The basic method is then to combine the rice with enough water or stock to cook, together with some butter or oil and aromatics, to bring this mixture to the boil, then cover, lower the flame, and allow to cook slowly until all the liquid is absorbed and the rice cooked. This is plain rice. To make more elaborate pilafs, there are two methods. First, the cooked plain rice is combined with cooked meats and vegetables, the whole allowed to cook together and intermingle. Second, to fry the uncooked rice (after washing and draining) in oil or butter, sometimes with meat, chicken and/or vegetables for a few minutes, then add water or stock, bring to the boil, lower the flame, cover and allow to cook until the liquid is absorbed. This method produces a variety of pilafs, also the pride of banquets and feasts.

The Iranian method of cooking rice is known, at least in some quarters, in Turkey, but is used, if at all, only as a curiosity. The term *çilav* is used in Anatolia to designate rice cooked by the Iranian method. *Çilav* seems to have a long ancestry in the region, as it is mentioned by Evliya Chelebi (17th century) in his *Siyahetname*. It occurs in his account of a banquet in Bitlis, near Lake Van (Dankoff 1990: 116–17). This could not have been only on account of its nearness to the Iranian frontiers, because Evliya lists it alongside other dishes without any special explanation. The Iranian method is also known under other names. Turabi Efendi, a Turkish gentleman in the entourage of Said Pasha, Viceroy of Egypt, on his visit to England in 1862, compiled, in English, a Turkish cookery book for the distinguished personages present at a banquet given by the viceroy on board his yacht at Woolwich (Turabi 1987). This includes a section on 'Pilaw'. The instructions for cooking follow the Turkish paradigm as outlined here, including the one he called *'Ajam-pilawi* (i.e. Persian). The only exception is one called *Mevlevi pilawi* (a reference to the Mawlawi or Mevlevi order of dervishes), which is cooked by the Iranian method. A modern cookery book by Nevin Halıcı, who is very well versed in the ethnography of regional Anatolian cooking, lists three ways of cooking rice: *salma*, boiled rice in the Turkish method, *kavurma*, fried rice in the Turkish method, and *suzme*, in which rice is boiled then strained as in the Iranian method, but when it is returned to the pan boiling fat is poured over it. None of her recipes, however, uses this latter method, and she expresses a clear preference for *kavurma* as the method which achieves best results (1989: 119).

The Iranians are proud of their rice cookery and consider their method the only one to get the quality of texture and separation of grains which they value, as well as the esteemed *tah-dig*. It would seem that this culture of rice cookery goes back a long way in Iran. Cookery manuals written by court cooks from the Safavid period (16th century) contain a wide variety of *polows*. The art of rice cookery becomes even more elaborate and refined in the Qajar period in the 19th century. The process of washing, soaking, boiling and steaming or baking, familiar in modern Iranian cookery as outlined above, is apparently described in detail in *Sofreh-ye At'ameh*, the manual written by Mirza 'Ali Akbar Khan, *ashpaz-bashi* or cook to Naser al-Din Shah Qajar.[5]

Iranians who are aware of the Turkish method of cooking rice dismiss it as inferior. Inferior round-grained rice is cooked by this method (called *kateh*, see below) in some regions, but only to form sticky rice-balls which can be stored and eaten cold.

RICE IN THE MEAL STRUCTURE

The place of rice in the meal, as much as methods of cooking it, defines social occasions and boundaries.

As we have seen, banquets and feasts almost everywhere in the region (Arabs, Iranians and Turks) are marked by the variety of rice dishes which occupy the place of honour on the *sofreh* (the spread). Evliya Chelebi describes the feast given by the local Khan of Bitlis for Melek Ahmed Pasha, in the *meydan* of the city: 'Two hundred silver platters, full of culinary delights, ornamented the meydan, their delicate odours perfuming the brains of those attending. There were numerous kinds of pilavs and soups, but the pilavs of partridge and pomegranate and various juicy and well cooked kebabs were incredible' (1976: 117). The pilafs listed comprise a great variety, including saffron, 'chelow pilav' (presumably plain rice), mulberry, pomegranate, aloes, 'amber' (does this refer to a specially aromatic variety, as in present-day Iraq and Iran?), meatball, pistachio, crushed almonds and raisin. It must have made a very colourful spread. The fact that the pilafs are central to the description of the spread underlines their significance for celebrations.

Similar descriptions occur in other sources. *The Adventures of Hajji Baba of Ispahan*, a satire on early-19th-century Persian society by James Morier, an English diplomat, is generally reckoned to be documentary of the period, with only thinly masked real persons and events. In the story, Mirza Ahmak, the shah's physician (the real one was Mirza Ahmed, changed to Ahmak, meaning a fool, as part of the satire), gives a banquet for the shah and his entourage. Here is the description of the dinner:

> The dinner was then brought in trays, which, as a precaution against poison, had been sealed with the signet of the head steward before they left the kitchen, and were broken open by him again in the presence of the Shah. Here were displayed all the refinements of cookery. Rice [note how it tops the list], in various shapes, smoked [steamed] upon the board; first, the *chelau*, as white as snow; then, the *pilau*, with a piece of boiled lamb smothered in the rice; then another *pilau*, with a baked fowl in it; a fourth, coloured with saffron, mixed up with dried peas; and, at length, the king of Persian dishes, the *naranj pilau*, made with slips of orange-peel, spices of all sorts, almonds, and sugar [similar to what now is called *shirin polow*, but this latter also contains chicken and saffron] (Morier 1895: 150).

There follows a description of the meats, game, stuffed vegetables and other delicacies. At one stage, 'a cup full of the essence of meat, mixed up with rags of lamb, almonds, prunes, and tamarinds ... was poured upon the top of the chilau'. Again, the description of a banquet, now in Iran, features rice as the primary marker of festivity and luxury. Examples from all over the region, as well as from Mughal India, can be multiplied. This includes even bedouin desert feasts, where the central item is roast or boiled lamb over a mound of rice.

So much for banquets. What about everyday meals? This is where variation by group and region is most marked. We should keep in mind that for the majority of groups and regions in the area, most meals are eaten without rice, at least until recently.

The main distinction is whether rice is eaten with the stew of meat and/or vegetables, variations of which are found throughout the region, or whether it is eaten separately or subsequently. For Iranians and most Arabs it is always 'with' or 'over' rice; in the Ottoman meal sequence, however, rice comes at the end. This practice, together with other Ottoman styles, was also characteristic of the upper classes in Egypt and other countries, and persists to the present day in Istanbul and other parts of Turkey.

In Iran, as we have seen, rice is the preferred accompaniment to grilled meats as well as to *khoresht*, a stew of meat and vegetables and sometimes fruit. Those with regular access to rice will always eat it at every major meal. This does not exclude bread, which, apart from the rice provinces of the north, is also eaten at every meal. The semantics or aesthetics of the meal allow grilled meats, salads and boiled vegetables and pulses to be eaten with bread alone. *Khoresht*, however, is inconceivable without rice. The exception is *ab-gusht*, a broth made with pieces of mutton on the bone (often mostly bone), with vegetables and pulses boiled together in a panful of water, with dried (Omani) limes as the main flavouring. This is typically eaten with bread dunked into the soup. Often, the cooked meat and pulses (chick-peas, split peas or lentils) are removed from the soup and pounded together to make small cakes or croquettes, also eaten with bread, alongside the soup. This is clearly defined as a genre akin to soups (such as the ones made from sheep's heads, feet and tripe) not usually eaten with rice, rather than to *khoresht*.

This preference for rice with meat stews is also found in Iraq, though in its absence stews are eaten with bread. In Egypt, there is also a preference for rice with stews. This preference, however, becomes almost an aesthetic rule when it comes to *mulukhiya*, a stew of chicken, rabbit or other meat with the chopped leaves of that name which give the sauce a distinctive glutinous texture. Egyptians proudly regard *mulukhiya* as one of their national dishes. It is preferred with rice. The *mulukhiya* is typically served in a soup bowl with an accompanying plate of plain rice for each person: the sauce is spooned over the rice, or spoonfuls of rice dipped into the sauce.

Rice, by itself or with little else coming at the end of the meal, is a practice which seems to characterize meal structures at the upper end of the social hierarchy in China, Japan and Turkey. We have a clear description of it in 19th-century Egypt in Edward Lane's remarkable ethnography, *Manners and Customs of the Modern Egyptians*. He describes a typical meal in an upper-class household, featuring a succession of dishes of meat stews, stuffed fowl, stuffed vegetables, fruit, sweets, and:

> A dish of boiled rice (called 'ruzz mufelfel', the 'pilav' of the Turks), mixed with a little butter, and seasoned with salt and pepper, is generally that from which the last morsels are taken; but in the houses of the wealthy this is often followed by 'khushaf', a sweet drink, commonly consisting of water with raisins boiled in it, and then sugar: when cool a little rose-water is dropped into it. The water-melon frequently supplies the place of this (Lane 1860/1987: 151–2).

In recent years, I have seen customers at traditional Istanbul restaurants eating their meat and vegetable stews with bread, then being served pilaf with a bowl of *khushaf* (similar to the one described by Lane, only with other dried fruit besides raisins, more like a compote than a drink) on the side. Diners would often spoon the *khushaf* liquid over the plain rice. This practice of eating plain rice at the end of the meal, after the meat/ vegetables, is clearly a living tradition in Istanbul and other parts of Turkey. In many places in Anatolia it seems to be optional whether you eat your pilaf with the meat stew or after, depending on personal preference. Here, when plain rice is served on its own it is often moistened with a spoonful of *yakhni* (stew or broth), usually of *fasulia* (white beans) or chick-peas, poured over the pilaf.

Finally, among the common people of the rice-growing areas, rice features much more regularly and prominently in meals. In the marsh region of southern Iraq, some 'bread' is made from rice flour in the form of pancakes cooked on a *saj*, a concave metal pan, and called *siyah*. Plain rice, cooked like the *chelow* in the Iranian method, but with fat added over the rice at the end of the cooking, is served at most meals, at the same time as the other elements of the meal (mostly fish, stewed or fried).

The custom of eating rice at every main meal is also found in the Gulf region at the present time, so much so that rice is called '*aysh* (living), a word reserved for bread in Egypt and Syria.

Another rice area is the coastal plain of the Caspian provinces (Gilan and Mazandaran) of Iran. Here, the most common form of rice cooking is *kateh*, sticky boiled rice made from cheaper inferior varieties, the finer rice being reserved for *chelow* and *polow* on special occasions (see Bazin and Bromberger 1979). *Kateh* is made by boiling the rice (without previous soaking) in enough water to be absorbed. Fat is included if the rice is to be eaten immediately, but not if it is to be stored cold. The cold rice forms a sticky mass which can be cut with a knife and formed into balls. These can be reheated in fat in a frying-pan. In some households, these balls, cold or hot, are eaten for breakfast with cheese and jam, washed down with sugared hot milk or tea. It is also carried by travellers to eat on their journeys. Hajji Baba encountered such a traveller and shared his meal:

> He [the traveller] then groped up, from the deep folds of his riding trowsers, a pocket-handkerchief, in which were wrapped several lumps of cold boiled rice, and three or four flaps of bread, which he spread before us, and then added some sour curds, which he poured from a small bag that hung at his saddle-bow. From these same trowsers ... he drew half-a-dozen raw onions, which he added to the feast; and we ate with such appetite, that very soon we were reduced to the melancholy dessert of sucking our fingers (Morier 1895: 75).

Bazin and Bromberger record that the people of this region are proud of their rice diet, and contemptuous of neighbours who eat other grains, believing such a diet to be harmful. An angry husband would snap at his wife: 'Go eat bread and burst!' and a parent would threaten an errant child with being sent to Araq (in the interior), where he would have to eat bread.[6]

DUMPLINGS, STUFFING AND PUDDINGS

There is a genre of meat dumplings known as *kibbeh* or *kubba* in Arabic, and as *iç köfte* in Turkish. Typically, this consists of a paste made from ground meat and burghul/bulgur, which is then stuffed with further minced meat with onions, herbs, spices and sometimes pine nuts or almonds. The resulting dumpling is then fried or, less typically, cooked in a vegetable stew or broth or a yoghurt sauce. Variations of this genre are common in Syria, northern Iraq, Anatolia and Kurdistan. In Baghdad and southern Iraq, and in Azarbayjan, there are variants made with rice instead of wheat. Some communities in Iraq cook a *kubba* with a crust made of meat or chicken and rice pounded together to a smooth paste then stuffed with mincemeat, onions and parsley with seasonings. The dumpling (walnut-sized) is then cooked in a vegetable stew, typically turnips or bamia, flavoured with lemon or lime, and in some instances sweetened with sugar to a sweet-and-sour effect.

Another rice variant is the *kofteh Tabrizi* of Azarbayjan, in which grains of rice are stuck together with ground meat, made into a large dumpling stuffed with meat, chicken, boiled eggs and/or prunes, then baked or steamed. Iraqi Jews (and perhaps some other Iraqi communities) cook a variant of this *kofteh* which they call *'uruq*. These are smaller dumplings shaped into flat round discs, made with whole grains of rice stuck together with ground meat or fish, and stuffed with further ground meat or fish with seasoning and herbs (parsley for meat, coriander for fish), poached in water to cook the rice, then fried to crisp the outside.

These rice dumplings are another instance of substitution between rice and wheat, depending on availability and cultural preferences. Now the *burghul kibbeh* has been widely diffused in the region and abroad through migrant Lebanese and Cypriot restaurateurs and caterers. But the rice variants are still unknown outside the regions in which they are cooked.

Rice stuffings for vegetables and leaves (vine, spinach, chard or cabbage), as well as for fowl and whole lamb, are common throughout the region. Often inferior rice is used because the separation of the grains is not so important in the stuffing. Other ingredients include minced meat, pine nuts or almonds, raisins, herbs and seasoning. In Turkey, *iç pilavi* is stuffing rice, but has become a separate dish in its own right. The rice is fried with onions, chopped liver, nuts and aromatics (cinnamon and/or allspice), then boiling water or stock is added to cook the rice. The cooked rice is sometimes then baked in the oven, covered with fat.

Finally, sweet rice puddings are so common and varied throughout the region, and have such a multiplicity of cultural and ritual significances, that they should constitute the subject of another paper.

Notes

1. A version of this paper was presented at the seminar 'Food and Society in Islamic Culture' held in Xativa, Spain, 12–15 November 1991, organized by Manuela Marín and David Waines. I am grateful to the organizers for permission to include the paper in this volume.

2. It would seem that in 18th-century Aleppo the price of rice was almost double that of wheat (see Marcus 1989). In the 1960s this price ratio still held in Syria and Iraq, and in Iran rice was three times the price of bread, but in Egypt the prices were almost equivalent. Consumption patterns reflected this price relationship: in Iran rice consumption was less than one-sixth that of wheat, in Iraq one-third, in Turkey a small fraction, but in Egypt, despite the relative cheapness of rice, its consumption remained one-third of that of wheat (FAO 1965: Table 2, p 10, and Table 22, p 47).

3. Many western writers on Middle Eastern food have translated *ruz mufalfil* as 'peppered rice'. This could be the literal translation (from *fulful*, pepper).

In fact it refers to rice cooked with the grains separate, not stuck together. *Muhit al-Muhit*, a 19th-century dictionary, gives this meaning and suggests that it is derived from the analogy with whole pepper grains. Another possible derivation is from the verb *falla*, to break or to defeat, but which also has a vulgar usage to indicate loosening or separating

4. Bert Fragner, 'From the Caucasus to the Roof of the World' in this volume, contains an enlightening discussion of the historical background and the likely routes and patterns of diffusion and innovation of Iranian rice cookery.

5. See Bert Fragner, 'From the Caucasus to the Roof of the World' in this volume.

6. Most Iranian households now have electric rice-cookers (*polow-paz*, made in Japan), which they use both for family meals and for preparing food for guests; the method is strictly that of *kateh*, though the type of rice used is usually fine and the result is close to *chelow*. One attraction of the cooker method is that it can be used to produce 'proper' (*saf*) *chelow*, i.e. by including the draining part of the process, and in addition it produces an even, all-round *tah-dig* crust.

8. *Al-Kishk*: the past and present of a complex culinary practice

Françoise Aubaile-Sallenave

Kashk/kishik refers to certain dishes that were, and remain, popular in Iran, Turkey and parts of the Arab world. However, the exact definition of the term raises problems for ethnologists, linguists and historians of the different regions of the Middle East. Behind an apparently trivial recipe lies a complex history of diffusion which throws remarkable light on the past of these regions. Though the product has been of great interest to many – especially dieticians who have studied it for some time – until now, it seems, there have been no general studies of the word and the complexity of the preparations it designates.

Confusion is created by the facts that the term *kashk/kishik* is present in different language families and cultural areas, dispersed over a large geographical area; and that the substances designated are extremely variable according the different regions: it is a preserved food all over the Middle East, but Persian *kashk* is quite different from the Arab *kishik*; among the Armenians of Turkey and generally in Anatolia it is a dish like *herissa* (pounded meat and cereal); in Egypt it is a sweetmeat. The complexity of today reflects the larger complexity of the past.

I shall offer two levels of analysis: first, on the linguistic level, I shall survey the distribution of the words, and classify usages by linguistic families. This necessary etymological study will bear on the different borrowings in four language families, identify the original language and trace the most ancient sources of the word. Secondly, on the semantic level, I shall classify the products according to the principal ingredients. This will lead to the ethno-technological question of the borrowing of technique. The wide distribution of word and product means borrowings at least of the word alone, but maybe also of the technique, or both of them.[1]

Kashk, *keshk*, *kishk*, the three vocalizations of the same word, occur in several cultural areas – Iran, Iraq, Greater Syria, Egypt, south Caucasia and Turkey – and represent very different language families: Indo-European, Semitic, Altaic, Caucasic.

Indo-European languages

The word *kashk* is not found in earlier Iranian texts, the *Avesta*, the *Vendidad*, nor is it found in Pahlavi or Pazand. But a derived term *k'ashken* appears in an Armenian author of the 5th–6th century, Elishe, certainly borrowed from Pahlavi *kashkin.[2] This is the very first appearance of the word. It meant then 'barley bread'.

The word *kashk* appears abruptly in New Persian in Ferdowsi's 10th-century epic *Shahnameh* (Book of Kings, 1866–78). It is mentioned several times during the reigns of Bahram V Gur (d 438–9), Khosrow II Parviz (early 7th century), and Yazdgerd III, the last king (d. 651–2). Other words meaning 'barley bread' appear in this text: *kashkin* (the suffix -*in* meant originally 'of the colour of', and means today 'in the manner of, as') under Kings Kai Khosrow, Bahram V Gur, Khosrow II Parviz and Yazdgerd III, *nan-e kashk* (*nan* 'bread') under kings Khosrow II Parviz and Yazdgerd III, *nan-e kashkin* under kings Kai Khosrow, Bahram V Gur, Khosrow II Parviz and Yazdgerd III, and *nan kashkinah*. Neither of the latter two composite terms seems to be used later, when *kashkin* and *kashkinah* alone come to designate 'bread made of barley'.

Zamakhshari, a 12th-century Persian lexicographer (1963), quotes three preparations from *kashk*: *kashkba* (suffix -*ba* = 'gruel'), *ab kashk* (*ab* = 'water'), *ash kashk* (*ash* = 'broth').

In Classical Persian (from the 16th century) *kashk* is cooked in the kitchens of the Mughals, while in Iran *kashkak* (diminutive) is a complex dish, *kashkab* 'barley water' is a medicinal infusion and *kashku* is 'barley broth'. *Kashkin* and *kashkina* designate breads and different kinds of dry preserves. Composite terms indicate varieties according to the colour, *kashk siyah* 'black', *kashk sefid* 'white'.

In contemporary Iranian, the word *kashk* on its own is used, meaning dry yoghurt (*mast*). It enters into many composite terms, such as *kashk badamjan* (*kashk* with egg-plants).

Among pastoralists speaking Iranian languages, *keshk* or *kashk* are all milk products: Talesh (dialects of Jowkandan and Siyah Chal), some Gilanis, Kurds; the Bakhtyari know *kashk* and *aw kashk*. Tatis should have it, but I could not find it. And curiously it seems to be unknown among Baluch today (the north-western group of Iranian languages) whose tribes have, in recent history, migrated back to the south-west, to present-day Baluchestan. Perhaps they lost *kashk* to borrow *qurut* from people living around them, mainly Pashtuns, who use this Turkish term. The Afghan Pashtun *kashk*, according to Aslanov (1966), designates a cereal broth or a bread soup. In Urdu, influenced by the Mughals, *kashk* in the 19th century roughly keeps all the meanings of the Classical Persian.

In the 5th to 6th centuries, the Armenians knew the derived term *k'ashken*, 'barley bread', as employed by Elishe, when he speaks of the captivity of two Christian priests to whom their Persian jailers bring two barley loaves (1957: 144). We saw the importance of the testimony of this author, who was the first to use the word, as an *apax legomenon*. *K'ashken* is borrowed from New Persian *kashkin*. Adjarian (1979, IV: 554) traces it to Pahlavi **k'ashken*; I would look rather to Pahlavi **kashkin*, as the phonetic correspondences between Armenian *-k'-* and Iranian *-k-* exist, and the passage *-in>en-* exists too.[3] The word is not known today, but Armenians know the complex dish *keshkeg*, whose present phonetic variants in the different dialects *k'eashkak*, *k'eashkèak*, show that the word has been borrowed from the Turkish *keshkek/keshkak* (the palatalization indicates the borrowing). The word is only known to Armenians who lived in Turkey, not to their brethren in the east. *Kishk* is used among the present Lebanese Armenians as a borrowing. Among the Greeks of Macedonia, *quacheq*, a Turkish loan word, designates cheese.

Semitic languages

The word *kishk* is present in the Arabic of the eastern Arab world, in Syriac and neo-Aramaic. It is a well-attested loan-word from the Persian *kashk* (cf Dozy 1957).

In Arabic, the word *kishk* varies little in form but greatly in meaning. In Iraq at the end of the Abbasid period,[4] we find numerous composite terms in use, with one derived term, *kishkiyye*. The diversity of preparations are then classified according the staple (*al-hinta*, wheat), the flavour (*hamid*, sour), and by region according to the speciality: *kishk shami*, 'Syrian', *kishk mosuli*, 'of Mosul' (al-Warraq 1987), *kishk babli*, 'of Babylon' (Ibn Baytar 1874). The medical books speak of preparations such as *kashkab*, a Persian loan-word referring to an infusion. In Iraq today it is *kishik*.

In Syria, Lebanon and Palestine, *kishik* was well known in the 10th century, as attested by *kishk shami* ('Syrian') in al-Warraq (1987). It is continuously present from that period until now and mentioned in medical books and cookbooks as well as in literary works (*The Thousand and One Nights*) and dictionaries. Other dishes are present, such as *kishkak* (Damascus manuscript of 1503) and *kishkiyye*, from the 10th century to the present.

The composite terms *kishk khamar* (with 'leaven'), and *kishk laban* (with 'curd milk') testify to the extension of both preparations to 13th-century Aleppo (Ibn al-'Adim 1976), as in the 19th-century Hauran (Burckhardt 1822).

In Egypt, a dish called *kishk musbba'un* was cooked in the kitchens of the Mamluk sultans of the 14th to 15th centuries, but there is no indication of its composition. *Kishk* dishes are still cooked today, as in *kishk sa'idi* (from upper Egypt), a chicken *kishk* (Benghiat 1985: 19), one of many preparations.

The modern Syriac *kishk* (in Assyrian dialects of north-western Iran, the plain of Mosul and Kurdistan), seems to be a borrowing from Arabic for a barley gruel (Elias Nisibé in P. de Lagarde 1879: 35). In dialects of the eastern Assyrians of Kurdistan, *kashka*, designating a complex dish, is an Azari-Turkish loan-word, and *kashkina* seems to be related to the Turkmen *kashkina* (MacLean 1901).

The 19th-century neo-Aramaic *kashka* (dialect of Kurdistan) is a Kurdish loan-word (Krotkoff 1982). In Tunisia, *kashkar* 'coarse bran' is probably a borrowing from Turkish. In 9th-century al-Andalus, *kishk* is the first and furthest west extension of the word.

Altaic languages

The 16th-century Turkish *kesh* comes from the Persian *keshk*, as does *keshkek* (from the Persian *keshkak*, diminutive of *keshk*), referring to a complex Turkish dish, and *keshkina*, 'barley bread'.[5]

In Azarbayjani/Azari *kashk* is very common and *kashka* is identified as an Azari-Turkish loan-word in a 19th-century Syriac dialect (MacLean 1901: 141).

The Turkmen in the 19th century seemed to know only the derived terms *keshkina* and *keshkin*. The word does not appear in modern Turkmen dictionaries (Baskakova and Khamzaeva 1956).

Caucasic languages

The 18th-century Georgian *kashi* raises an etymological problem. It means 'cereals cooked with milk', very similar to the Persian *kashk* or *keshk*. But according to the first Georgian lexicographer, the 17th-century Orbeliani

(1685–1716), the Georgian word is a borrowing from the Persian *kashi* or *kaji*, designating a dish similar to *bulmaj*, meaning a sweet liquid preparation or a milk pottage (after Shakespeare in Vullers 1855, sv *kaji*). The Georgian *kashi*, though similar to the Persian *kashi*, has a meaning similar to the Persian *kashk*, and is probably derived from it.[6]

The Circassians of southern Turkey and northern Syria know neither the word nor the product.

Summary

We can be sure that *kashk* is a Persian word which passed to Arabic at an early stage, with vocalic but not consonantic modification: *kashk →kishk*, *kishik*. Later it passed into Turkish as *kashk →keshk*. All the derived terms in Arabic are taken from the Persian: *kishkiyye, kashkab, kishkak, kishkek, keshkin, keshkina*. However, composite terms were formed in Arabic: *kishk khamr, kishk laban, kishk shami, kishk mosuli, kishk hamid, kishk babki, kishk bushul, kishk babli, kishk al-hintah, kashk al-sha'ir, kishk musbba'un*.

The word makes its first written appearance in a 5th- to 6th-century Armenian text as a derived term. It first appears in Persian in 1010 in the *Shahnameh*. The word must, however, predate its textual appearance; we know this to be especially true of popular culinary terms, which can jump 2000 kilometres apparently without relay station. In Arabic *kashk* appears a century and a half earlier, in a medical text from al-Andalus by Ibn Habib (d 853), then in the texts of Persian or Arabo-Persian writers living in Baghdad: al-Warraq (10th century) with his *Kitab Tabikh*; Ibn Sina (980–1037) with his *Qanun fi'l-tibb* (contemporary with the *Shahnameh*).

Some have related *kashk* to the Indian word *kashaya* (Spiegel 1887: 81) and Sanskrit *kashaya* 'medicinal drink' (Monier-Williams 1981: 265).[7] This is close to its meaning as 'barley water', also medicinal. Other possible relations are with the Persian *kesht*, 'sown, cultivated field', which could be related to barley (one of the meanings of *kashk*), and the Khotanese *kalsta* 'sown field' (Emmerick and Skjærvo 1982: 32). As these languages function by derivation, we can postulate the root **kash* at the origin of all those words, constituting a large semantic field around the idea of agriculture and cereals.

The word is diffused over a large but continuous geographical area: Iran, Azarbayjan, Armenia, Kurdistan, Iraq, Syria, Lebanon, Israel, Arabia Petraea, Turkey, Egypt; but it was known at the other end of the Arabic area in medieval Spain. In the 16th century, Da'ud al-Antaki (1979) quotes a scholar who says that there are many kinds of *kishk* extending as far as the country of Herat (Afghanistan). Today, it is not found in Afghanistan, nor in central and southern Arabia, nor in North Africa, save for a trace in Tunisia.

The fact that the word is found in several language families implies relations of contact and borrowing, not tradition. Therefore we can speak of an areal diffusion, since all those populations have long had economic, social and cultural contact with each other. In effect it is not easy to separate a word from its referent: it is what it represents. The word circulates simultaneously with the object or technique that it designates. If, in the borrowing language, the object designated is slightly different, this may imply a modification at the moment of acquisition. If the word passes with the normal phonetic correspondence, it means congruence between the two cultures concerned as regards the object or technique. Since we have differences between *kashk*, a simple product, in Persian, and *kishk*, a complex product, in languages to the west, the question arises whether the technique was known before in the latter. If so, then what was it called? Let us now examine the different meanings of the word and see if, as a consequence, we can solve the problem of the borrowing of the technique.

CLASSIFICATION OF THE DIFFERENT PRODUCTS NAMED *KASHK* OR *KISHK* ACCORDING TO THEIR COMPONENTS

The polysemy of the word

As we have seen, in Iran the word appears in the *Shahnameh* (end of the 10th century). It occurs several times and in different forms and meanings. *Kashk* would mean 'curdled milk'. Composite words have meanings involving barley: *kashkin*, 'something made of barley' (suffix -*in*), and *nan kashkin*, *nan kashkinah*, 'bread made of barley'. The context always evokes a situation of poverty or of a popular use.

In this respect, we should consider some methodological questions. The older sources, whether dictionaries or texts, are, until the 19th century, very imprecise about the real meaning. In contrast, modern sources may be very precise, thus exposing the complexity of the situation. In those cultures where milk is the object of transformations in a chain, each by-product, being a stage in the various operations, has a special name, and *kashk* is no more than one of them. But what is puzzling for the researcher is the inconsistency of naming between the old sources and modern usages. For example *tarf* in Turan today (Martin 1980) is different from *kashk*, while for Zamakhshari in the 12th century they were the same thing.

The polysemy of *kashk* is disconcerting, and each meaning would be worth a study in itself. So it is important to establish the value of the word

Table 8.1 By-products from milk

	Dried yoghurt	Residue of buttermilk dried in balls	Black sour milk dried	Soft cheese	Cheese	Curd sour milk	Whey
Persian 10th–12th C	*kashk*	*kashk*	*kashk siyah*				
Persian 20th C	*kashk*						
Talish		*kashk*					
Gilan		*kashk* (rare)					
Bakhtyari		*kashk, aw kashk*					
Kurd		*kashk, keshk*		*keshk*	*kesk*		
Greek of Macedonia 20th C				*quacheq*	*quacheq*		
Urdu 19th–20th C	*kishk*						
Turkish	*kesh*	*keshk, kesh*					
Azari		*kashk*				*kesh*	
Arab 11th C							*kishk*
(Syria, Lebanon, Palestine)	*kishk*						
Neo-Aramaic		*kashka*					

in a fixed culture, at a given time, in a given place. Three criteria have been employed in this classification according to the main ingredient: milk, cereal, or a mixture – of both, or of one of them – with another ingredient. Pre-eminent here is not the chronological order but the cultural order, and the order of the terms (simple, derived, composite).

By-products from curd milk
These are, generally, preserved foods.

Dried yoghurt or sour milk, known in Iran, Pakistan, Turkey and the Arab world (Ramazani 1974).

In Iran today, *kashk* is made from *mast*, 'yoghurt', rolled into small balls and kept for winter use (Ramazani 1974: 70).

In 19th-century Panjab, *kashk* is dried sour milk (Platts 1982: 837).

In Turkish, *kesh* is dry yoghurt, dry curdled milk (= Persian *keshk* = Turkish *qurut*; Zenker 1866).

In 20th-century Syria, Lebanon and Palestine, *kishk* is 'boulette de lait caillé et séchée au soleil' (Dalman 1928–39, VI: 295, 28, in Denizeau 1960: 454).

A dried product obtained from buttermilk, in Iran, Kurdistan, Azarbayjan.

In Iran *kashk*, 'petit lait condensé, caillebotte', is equivalent to *qurut* (Moallem 1926).

Kashk is made by the Bakhtyari with the casein taken from buttermilk: salted, then boiled, then strained, the paste is formed into small balls which are dried in the sun. In autumn and winter, the balls are stirred into water to give the basic milk food (Digard 1981).

Kashk is rare among the Gilani living in the mountains (Bazin and Bromberger 1982: 35). It is only prepared by the Talesh from Jowkandan and Siyah Chal, who dry in the sun the *showreh* or *shur* obtained from buttermilk (Bazin 1980, II: 49).

Keshk or *kashk* is the residue of buttermilk dried in balls among the Kurds of the Hakkari district (Rhea 1880).

Kashka is the curds from buttermilk dried and kept for the winter among the neo-Aramaic-speakers from Iraqi Kurdistan (Krotkoff 1982: 83). As the word is borrowed from Kurdish, we may wonder if the product too is borrowed.

Kashk is very common among the Azarbayjani Turks, who dry *shur* in the sun and form it into small balls or flat cakes (Bazin and Bromberger 1982: 35).

A black dried product used as a condiment in Iran, Afghanistan and some parts of Turkey.

Kishk babli, '*kishk* of Babylon', comes in the form of black pieces, according to Ibn Baytar in the 12th century (1877–83, I: 445), who compares it to *ḥalq,* an unknown plant, whose leaves they dry in the oven, obtaining irregular black pieces. This seems to be the first mention of the black *kashk,* a speciality of Babylon at that time.

Kashk siyah 'black *kashk*' is *furfur* and *panir siyah* 'black curded cheese', three Classical Persian terms equivalent to the Turkish *qara qurut,* according to the *Borhan-e qate'* (Vullers 1855, II: 662, 723; Steingass 1975: 962). It would seem that the term *kashk siyah* is no longer known in Iran, but the product is still in use and known by the Turkish name *qara qurut.*

Qara qurut, a dark paste used as a condiment among the Azarbayjanis today, is obtained by cooking and drying out *kashk* (Bazin and Bromberger 1982: 35). *Krut* is well known and very much appreciated as a 'hot' condiment for winter use among the rural Afghans, as is *qurut* among urban Iranians (Tehran), who prepare it from sour milk which has cooked slowly for a long time.

Tarf, tarp or *tarf siyah,* another Persian word given by Zamakhshari (12th century) as an equivalent to Arabic *rakhbin* (p 353), is defined as 'black dried curdled milk' that is to say 'black *kashk*' (Vullers 1855, I: 436). Of *rakhbin* (also a Persian word), Vullers says that it is a dish made of cheese, flour and milk acid, turned black just like cheese from dry and black curds.[8]

Tarf may be white and similar to *kashk sefid,* 'white *kashk*'; it is then 'sour clotted milk strained and dried in the sun for winter use' (Steingass 1975). In Turan today, *tarf* is the dried, boiled liquid residue of *qorut* (Martin 1980: 24).

In the 19th century Turkish *kesh* corresponded to the Persian *kashk siyah,* and *tarp* (*tarf*) (Zenker 1866).

A soft product: cheese, curd, sour milk, among the Kurds and the Turks.

Keshk is 'soft cheese' among the Kurds (Jaba 1879); *kesk* (variant) is 'fresh cheese' (Jaba) or simply 'cheese' (Soane 1913).

Kesh in Turkish is a 'kind of cheese' (Zenker 1866), a 'low-fat cheese' (Kelekian 1911), a 'cheese made from skimmed milk or yoghurt' (*Türkçe Sözlük* 1983) and finally a 'kind of curd sour milk' (Kelekian).

Quacheq in Macedonia is a ewe's-milk cheese. It may be eaten while fresh or after it has ripened (Doane et al 1969: 99).

Whey is *kishk* in 11th-century Iraqi Arabic, equivalent to the Arabic *masl* and Syriac *tarhaqa* (Bar Bahlul 1891–1901: 2088).

The similarity of the terms and products as between populations speaking Iranian languages (except Pashto and Baluchi) and those speaking Turkish languages indicates the region-wide linguistic influence and diffusion of the terms and products. Nevertheless some differences can be discerned: *keshk* designates a soft product among Kurds and Turks, and a dry product among peoples of other Iranian languages and the Azarbayjani Turks.

By-products from cereals

Barley infusion. *Kishk, kishka* or *kishkab*, is the barley preparation of which all the medieval medical scholars speak. They were clearly under the influence of Greek medicine which considered *ptisana*, 'barley water', as a true panacea.

Kashk al-sha'ir, 'barley *kashk*', was a medical recipe in 12th-century Egypt, as given by Maimonides (1964: 39), and in 12th-century Andalusia, as given by Ibn Zuhr (1992: 11).

Ab kashk (*ab* = water) was used in the 12th century as a synonym for the Persian *tarina, tarkhina, takhina*,[9] and the Arabic *'awitah*[10] (Zamakhshari 1963: 346). Later, *tarkhina, tarkhwana* designate a thick pottage of cereals (Steingass 1975).

Kashkab is 'barley water, *ptisan*' in classical 16th- to 19th-century Iran (Steingass 1975; Zenker 1866).

Kashk is 'barley water' (Platts 1982: 837) in 19th-century Urdu, influenced by Moghol.

Keshk is 'barley infusion' in 19th-century Turkey (= Persian *keshkab*, Zenker).

Barley gruel or broth – a dish cooked for immediate consumption in 12th- to 19th-century Iran and elsewhere in the Middle East from the 12th century.

Kashkba (*ba* = 'gruel, bouillie') and *ash kashk* (*ash* = 'brouet'), in the 12th century. Both *kashkba* and *ash kashk* were synonyms of *tarfba*, all of them being equivalent to Arabic *masliyya* (Zamakhshari 1963: 344). They can be understood, too, as preparations based on sour milk, or whey (Persian *tarf*, Arabic *masl*).

Kashkow, 'gruel', *kashku*, 'barley broth' (Steingass 1975), variants of *kashkab*.

Table 8.2 By-products from barley (or cereals)

Language, century	Barley infusion	Barley gruel	Barley broth	Barley bread	Bread of barley, wheat, beans and lentils or vetches	Coarse flour	Fermented cereals	Barley	Coarse bran	Cereal infusion
Persian 10th–12th	*āb kashk*	*kashkbā*	*āsh kashk, kashkū, kashkāb, kashkāw*	*kashkin, nān kashkin, nān kashkina*	*kashkin, kashkina*					
Persian 16th–19th	*kashkāb* *kashk*		*kashk*		*kashkin, kashkina*			*kashk*		
Persian 20th	*kashkāb*									
Urdu 19th	*kashk*							*kashk*		
Armenian 5th				*kashkēn*						
Turkish 19th				*kashkina*						

Table 8.2 (continued)

Language, century	Barley infusion	Barley gruel	Barley broth	Barley bread	Bread of barley, wheat, beans and lentils or vetches	Coarse flour	Fermented cereals	Barley	Coarse bran	Cereal infusion
Arabic, Egypt 12th–13th	*kashk al-sha'ir*									
Central Middle East 10th–17th	*kishk, kishka, kashkāb, mā'kishk*		*kishk*			*kishk*		*kashk*		
al-Andalus 9th–13th	*kashk al-sha'ir*	*kashk*								*kashk al-hintah*
Lebanon 20th							*kishk*			
Tunisia									*kashkär*	
Syria 19th–20th		*kishk*								

Kashkab = *ash jow* = 'bouillie d'orge' (Moallem 1926).

Kishk is a 'gruel from wheat or barley', in 12th-century Egypt (Ibn Baytar, sv: *ma' al-sha'ir*), and a 'barley cream' in modern Syriac (Elias Nisibé in P. de Lagarde 1879: 35).

Kashk, among contemporary Pashtuns, is a thick cereal broth (Russian *kashitza*) or a broth made from pieces of bread (Russian *pokhlyebka*) (Arslanov 1966: 680)

Barley bread, bread, in old Armenia, Iran and Turkey. This is the first meaning under which the composite word appears in the historical record.

K'ashken is 'barley bread' in 5th- to 6th-century Armenian (Elishe 1957).

Kashkin, nan kashkin, nan kashkina, 'barley bread' in 10th-century Iran (*Shahnameh*).

Kashkin and *kashkina* also designate a complex bread 'made of barley, millet, beans and lentils'. *Kashkina* may also be a bread 'made of wheat, barley, beans and vetches', in 16th-century Iran (Steingass 1975). The mixing of other constituents with barley is very common because of the bad quality of barley bread in general.

Keshkina is 'barley bread' in Turkish (Zenker 1866).

Coarse flour: in the 13th-century Middle East, *kishk* is a coarse flour (*jashish*) of any grains (Ibn al-Hasha 1941: 63; Ibn al-'Adim 1976: 870).

Fermented (sour) cereals: in 20th-century Lebanon *kishk* is hulled wheat macerated in water for three days, which can then be ground into flour (Khawam 1970: 61, 130).

Barley: *kashk* in 16th- to 17th-century Iran and other parts of the Middle East (Golius in Vullers 1855; Steingass 1975), and in 19th-century Punjab (Platts 1982: 837).

Coarse bran: *kashkar* in 19th-century Tunisia (Beaussier 1887).

Complex products and dishes

A complex preserved food from cereals and a dried sour product. These kinds of preserved foods are recorded in early Arabic literary texts. From the early 10th century, we have records of preparations named *kishk* more complex than those found in present-day Lebanon, Syria, Egypt and Iraq.

Table 8.3 Complex products and dishes

Language and century	Preserved food: wheat, leaven and vegetables	Preserved food: cereals and sour dried milk	Fried wheat, onions, beet, purslain in fish-jelly and dried	Preserved food: fermented cereals with leaven
Persian 10th–12th				
Persian 16th–18th		*kashkīna* *kashkīn*	*kashkīna*	
Moghol 16th				
Persian 20th				
Urdu 19th–20th				
Armenian, Turkey 20th				
Turkish 19th				
Azari				
Turkmen				
Georgian 17th				
Iraq Arab 10th	*kishk shāmī*	*kishk*		*kishk shāmī*
Iraq 13th		*kishk*		
Aleppo 13th		*keshk* *leben*		*keshk* *khamr*
Damasc. 1503				
Hauran 19th		*keshk* *leben*		*keshk* *hammer*
Syria 19th		*kishk*		
Lebanon 20th		*kishik*		
Syriac 19th				
Egypt 17th–20th		*kishk*		

Table 8.3 (continued)

Language and century	Dish of cereals in sour milk	Dish with sour milk	Dishes (meat, vegetables) including kashk/kishk	Dish of cereals and milk
Persian 10th–12th		*kashkbā,* *āsh kashk*		
Persian 16th–18th	*kashkbā* *kashkīna*	*kashkbā*		*kashkāb*
Moghol 16th				
Persian 20th			*kashk bademjūn*	
Urdu 19th–20th				
Armenian, Turkey 20th				
Turkish 19th	*kesh*			*keshk*
Azari				
Turkmen	*keshkīna*			
Georgian 17th				*kashī*
Iraq Arab 10th			*kishkiyya*	
Iraq 13th			*kishkiyya*	
Aleppo 13th				
Damasc. 1503			*kishk*	
Hauran 19th				
Syria 19th			*kishkiyye*	
Lebanon 20th			*kishk bizayt*	
Syriac 19th				
Egypt 17th–20th			*kishk +* *kishik*	

Table 8.3 (continued)

Language and century	Dish of cereals, sheep's-milk and meat	Dish of cereals and meat, cf *herissa*	Drink from powder of cereals and sour milk dried	Sweetmeat of milk, curdled or not, flour, and sugar or honey
Persian 10th–12th				
Persian 16th–18th	*kashk*	*kashkak* *kashka* *kashkek* *keshk*		
Moghol 16th		*kashk*		
Persian 20th				
Urdu 19th–20th	*kashk*			
Armenian, Turkey 20th		*keshkeg* *k'eashkak* *k'eashkèak* *kishk*		
Turkish 19th		*keshkek*		
Azari		*kashkā*		
Turkmen				
Georgian 17th				
Iraq Arab 10th				
Iraq 13th				
Aleppo 13th		*kishkāh*		
Damasc. 1503		*kishkak*		
Hauran 19th				
Syria 19th				
Lebanon 20th			*kishik*	
Syriac 19th		*kashkā* *kashkīna*		
Egypt 17th–20th				*kishk (nīrab, harāsh al-'ajāiz)*

They seem to be unknown in contemporary Iran.

Wheat, leaven and many vegetables. Kishk in this form is first mentioned by the 10th-century Iraqi, al-Warraq, who gives two recipes for it. Later on, the 13th-century Maghrebi, Ibn al-Hasha, gives a similar Middle Eastern recipe (1941). It was then shaped into round flat cakes.

Al-Warraq's recipe for *kishk shami* (1987: 102; ch on acid dishes) proceeds as follows:

> Wheat coarsely cracked, then cleaned and boiled in water, then dried and cleaned again until there is no more bran. Knead with hot water in the right quantity, add a little leaven and put in a large container in the sun for six days, covering it during the night, until it becomes well soured, then add thinly cut vegetables, not chicory or rocket (*jirjir*) since they do not enhance it, but many leeks, fresh coriander, rue (*ruta* sp *sadab*) and, for those who like it, onions cut into small rounds and pieces, aubergines, squash (*qar'*), cabbage, *khaukh ad-dibb* which are acid little plums, and good verjuice. Knead all that together and allow to dry in the sun for five days. Then shape it into round flat cakes.

Wheat, laban or whey and a few vegetables. A variation on *kishk shami* calls for sour milk (*raib*) instead of water and requires no vegetables except mint (*na'na'*) and celery (*kerfes*) (al-Warraq 1987: 102).

Al-Warraq gives another recipe for *kishk* (1987: 103) with variants:

> Take some wheat, crush it coarsely and boil it slightly, then dry and crack it again coarsely; add some chickpea with that wheat and let it ferment; then knead the whole and put in the sun for 15 days; when there is no more humidity, pour on it the whey which flows from very sour *laban raib*. Sprinkle some salt on it when it ferments. Then take mint, Persian celery, purslane, rue, fresh coriander, squash, everything thinly cut, and mix well forming round flat cakes that you dry in the sun. The variants: some like to add garlic, some like to add verjuice (*husram*).

In the 16th century (probably in the maritime provinces of Iran) *kashkina* designated a kind of preserved food made from 'fried wheat which, with onions, beet and purslane seeds, are steeped in fish-jelly and dried in the sun' (Steingass 1975). The *Borhan-e Qate'* gives a similar recipe: 'fried wheat with fish-jelly, mushrooms, beets and purslane, and dried in the sun' (in Vullers 1855).

Cereals and dried sour milk. Kishk as a food made from coarse flour and *laban*, which is then dried (13th century).

The occurrence of the description of *kishk* in Ibn al-Hasha's glossary (1941) suggests that this product was unknown in the Maghreb. It has no vegetables as in the recipe of al-Warraq: 'as for the *kishkiyya* recipe: *kishk* of barley is soaked in sour *laban* till it turns sour, then it is dried, and this meal is thickened; this soured *kishk* is then preserved (*yuddakhara*) in round or other shapes.' Here *kishk* of barley means both a certain preparation of the barley grain (*jashish*, 'coarse flour') and the final product.

The contemporary Aleppo recipe is very similar at the beginning: 'it is coarse flour from grains[11] which are soaked in fresh milk for several days, then dried in the sun on the terrace. There are two kinds: *kishk al-khamir* and *kishk al-laban*. They are used in the preparation of gruels, pastry dishes and omelettes' (Ibn al-'Adim 1976: 870–71).

This kind of preserved food from cereals and dried sour milk was probably known in the Levant continuously from at least the 13th century. Bergrenn (1844) gives a very similar description, and it is attested among 19th- and 20th-century Syrian montagnards, who preserve it for winter use, sometimes cooking it with *qawurma* (minced meat preserved in fat) and garlic (Harfouch 1894: 304).

Kishk was also a very common food prepared from wheat with sour milk in 19th-century Egypt (Freytag 1975). Lane gives a precise description for the same period. It is

> prepared from wheat, first moistened, then dried, trodden in a vessel to separate the husks, and coarsely ground with a hand-mill: the meal is mixed with milk, and about six hours afterwards is spooned out upon a little straw or bran, and then left for two or three days to dry. When required for use, it is either soaked or pounded, and put into a sieve, over a vessel; and then boiling water is poured on it. What remains in the sieve is thrown away (1860: 488–9, n 3).

This *kishk* is surely much less sour than the Lebanese one which ferments for three to five days.

In 16th- to 18th-century Iran both *kashkin* and *kashkina* mean 'wheat soaked in sour milk and dried in the sun' (Steingass 1975). In Iran both words originally (5th to 6th, 10th centuries) designated barley bread. The recipe is not precise enough and we do not know whether or not the wheat is ground coarsely.

Cereals and dried sour milk. Kishk as a meal from *burghul* and *laban* which is then dried.

Aida Kanafani-Zahar gives a very precise description of the making of *kishk* among the villagers of the Beqa' plain in Lebanon today. I quote it first as a model, to illustrate a recipe which is certainly many centuries old. They mix *laban*, *burghul* and salt and let them ferment for three to five days (depending on air temperature) in a great earthen pot (*ma'jan*, 0.75 m. in diameter) with a wide mouth. They refresh it once or twice a day with *laban* and knead it all together. Then they spread it upon a linen cloth on the roof of the house. At this stage the women of the house need the help of other women: six or seven *farraka* 'rubbers' start work and, as soon as the product is dry, they rub it between their hands, making it finer and finer; then they sieve it. After that, it is left drying in the sun for four to five days, covered during the night. For 40 kg of *burghul* (plus two parts of milk: 80 kg) six persons rub for two or three hours and sieve for one hour to obtain 30 kg of *kishk*. It may be very sour, since the fermentation is not always well controlled (Kanafani-Zahar, in press). This *kishk* comes in the form of flour more or less thin, white, sour in flavour, not unpleasant, according to Guigues (1927), though he notes it goes rancid fairly quickly and it is not used after April.

Keshk hammer (should be read as *khamar*, 'leaven') and *keshk laban* were two kinds of *keshk* known at the beginning of the 19th century in the Hawran (south Syria), where there lived a mixture of Turks, Christians (mostly Greek Orthodox), Druzes, bedouin Arabs of small stature and scanty beards, and fellahin of great stature and big beards, and the most common dishes among the fellahin and the lower classes were *burghul* and *keshk*. They distinguished the two kinds of *keshk* according to the ferment. The first was prepared by putting leaven into the *burghul* and pouring water on it; it was then left until almost putrid, and afterwards spread out in the sun to dry; after that it was pounded, and served up with oil or butter when needed. The second was prepared by putting *laban* instead of leaven; in other respects the process was the same (Burckhardt 1822: 293).

We saw both kinds of *kishk* recorded in 13th-century Aleppo, but they were made with coarse flour instead of *burghul*.

Complex dishes for immediate consumption made from cereals and sour milk: in Iran and Turkey and among the Turkmen, 19th to 20th centuries.

Kashkba is a pottage with curds ('caillebotte') in Iran (Moallem 1926).

Kashkina is 'bread soaked in *ab kashk*', 'caillebotte liquide' (presumably not curds), in Iran (ibid).

Keshkina is a dish made from roasted cereals with onions and sour milk, among the 19th-century Turkmen (Zenker 1866). It is very close to the Iranian *keshkina*, a preserved meal, as quoted earlier.

Keshkin was also a Turkmen dish prepared from wheat soaked in curded milk (Bianchi and Kieffer 1871). The word does not appear in modern dictionaries (Baskakova and Khamzaeva 1956). This recipe corresponds better to the Persian pattern, and may have been borrowed a long time ago.

Kesh is a meal made from yoghurt and gruel (from an unspecified cereal) in Turkey (Gaziantep province) today.[12]

Dishes from sour milk in classical Iran.

Kashkba = *ash kashk* = *tarfba* = Arabic *masliyya* in the 12th century. Zamakhshari gives no further explanation. But we know that in Baghdadi cooking of the same period *masliyya* was a complex dish where *masl* (dried buttermilk) was added to meat and vegetables (al-Baghdadi 1964: 26, Arberry 1939: 43). While it is difficult to know precisely what the terms *kashkba* and *ash kashk* referred to in the time of Zamakhshari, we may infer that *kashkba* has some resemblance to the Arab *masliyya*.

On the other hand *tarfba* – 'puls cum opsonio ex oxygala sicca nigra (*qara qurut*)' (*Borhan-e Qate'*, in Vullers 1855) – is a cereal meal made from *kashk siyah*. It is also a 'food made from clotted cream' (Steingass 1975).

Dishes in which kashk *or* kishk *are added to vegetables and/or meat.* In 10th-century Iraq *kishkiyya* is a dish prepared with meat, vegetables and fresh condiment and left to boil. When it is nearly cooked, finely ground *kishk* is added (four kinds of *kishk* are quoted, which we shall explain later), then verjuice; when the *kishk* is cooked, cinnamon and sliced onions, or cloves and sunbul are added, and it is left on a low fire (al-Warraq 1987: 165, after Muhammad b. Harun).

Kashk badamjan is very popular in Iran (Tehran) today: egg-plants cooked [fried] with onions, peas and tomatoes. Before serving, crushed garlic is lightly grilled, and dry mint is added to it. Then the dish is taken out of the oven and half a glass of dissolved *kashk* is thrown on it with the garlic and the mint, dissolved saffron and nuts. In Gilan *kashk badamjan* is prepared with meat.[13]

The last two recipes, from 10th-century Iraq and modern Tehran, concur on adding *kashk* at the end of the process.

Kishk is a 15th-century Syrian dish consisting of *kishk* boiled with meat, beets, cabbage, turnip, chick-peas, cauliflower, egg-plant, leek, parsley, rue (*sadab*), mint, garlic (Damascus manuscript of 1503).

In 20th-century Syria, Lebanon and Palestine, *kishkiyya* is a dish including *kishk* (quoted, with no further detail, from 'Frayha', by Denizeau 1960: 454).

In 20th-century Lebanon, *lahm bi-kishik* is 'soaked and soured wheat cooked with meat, fat, garlic, pepper' (Khawam 1970: 61).

Kishik bi-zayt: *kishik* in powder form is diluted in cold water to make a paste to which is added olive oil, minced onions, parsley, mint, and chopped nuts. This salad is eaten in the morning among the villagers of the Beqa' in Lebanon (Kanafani-Zahar in press). Khawam gives a similar recipe (1970: 130).

Kishik is also used as a cool summer beverage in rural Lebanon today, by diluting a little powder in cold water (Kanafani-Zahar).

A 19th-century Egyptian dish called *kishk* (see above) is prepared from wheat and milk.

When required for use, it is either soaked or pounded, and put in a sieve, over a vessel; and then boiling water is poured on it. What remains in the sieve is thrown away: what passes through is generally poured into a saucepan of boiled meat or fowl, over the fire. Some leaves of white beet, fried in butter, are usually added to each plate of it (Lane 1860: 489, n 3).

This *kishk* is not sour.

Kishk sa'idi in Egypt today is chicken broth thickened with flour, with *kishk* added. It is eaten with bread (Benghiat 1985: 62). *Khaltah* in 19th-century Egypt was a dish containing *kishk*, *ful nabit* (sprouted broad beans), lentils, rice and onions. It was eaten on Good Friday (Lane 1860: 488–9).

A dish made from cereals and milk, in Iran, Turkey, Georgia. In 19th-century Iran *keshkab*, and 19th-century Turkey *keshk*, are made from wheat cooked in milk (Zenker 1866).

In 17th-century Georgia *kashi* is broth of millet (*pet'vi*) with milk, or a kind of *bulghur* cooked with milk or with water. Tchoubinoff (1840) defines *kashi* as 'gruau de lait' 'moloshneya kasha'. As stated earlier, the Georgian word, though borrowed from the Persian *kaji*, has the meaning of *kashk*.

A dish of cereals, sheep's milk and meat. Kashk in 16th- to 18th-century Iran was a dish of wheat and barley flour with sheep's milk, in which were put one part of wheat and one part of meat (*Borhan-e Qate'* in Vullers 1855). In 19th-century northern India, it was a thick pottage made of wheat flour or barley meal with sheep's milk, to which meat or wheat were added (Platts 1982: 837).

Dishes prepared from cereals and meat

A dish from rice and meat, as prepared in the imperial kitchens of the Mughal Shahs, in 16th-century northern India, where *kashk* entered the class of dishes mainly composed of meat and rice: 10 sir meat, 5 sir crushed wheat (*kashk*), 3 sir ghee, 1 sir *gram* (peas), half sir salt, 1.5 sir onions, half sir ginger – 1 dam cinnamon, 2 mithqal saffron, 2 mithqal cloves, 2 mithqal cardamums, 2 mithqal cumin seed. Those quantities were suitable for 5 servings. The rice is cooked separately (Abu'l-Fazl 'Allami 1927: 63).

We know how much the Mughal culture borrowed from the Iranians, especially in luxury living.

A dish made into a paste (*like* harissa); in which *kashkak* dominates; originally an Iranian meal. The oldest references are for classical Iran and 15th- to 16th-century Syria. Today it seems known only in Turkey and northern Iraq,[14] but no longer in Iran or Lebanon.

Kishkak was meat boiled with wheat (*qamh*) in Syrian bourgeois cooking of the 15th to 16th centuries (Damascus manuscript of 1503).

Kashkak/kashkek (Persian diminutive of *kashk*) was still known in 19th-century Iran, a thick gruel of cereals with meat broth *rish* (*Borhan-e Qate'*; Zenker 1866). More precisely it was 'barley or wheat especially boiled whole with meat till it has become soft' (Steingass 1975). This explanation gives the pattern of the dish as we shall see.

In 19th-century Turkey, *keskek* was a 'soupe de gruau et de viande bouillie dans le genre de la *herissa*' (Barbier de Meynard 1881); 'like *herissa*' suggests a dish similar to the Iranian product. The other definitions are slightly different or less precise: 'soup or gruel made from barley or wheat and broth' (Zenker), 'gruel boiled with meat cut into small pieces' (Kelekian 1911). Today *keskek* is designated as a 'gastronomic speciality' (Gürün nd). The *Söz Derleme Dergisi* (1941) specifies that this food, made from crushed wheat with meat, is in use in the provinces of Kırşehir, Bursa, Samsun, Sinop, Ordu, Kütahya, Kayseri, Ankara, Bilecik, Konya.[15]

Keshkeg is found among the Armenians today, but only among those living in Turkey.[16] To wheat soaked overnight, add minced chicken or turkey meat, one litre of boiling water and half a litre of chicken broth, and cook this on a slow fire until the wheat is tender and the water absorbed (add more water if necessary); add seasonings, salt, pepper, and beat it to a smooth paste. Melt butter (60 gr) with paprika and pour it on the dish before serving, sprinkling cumin as much as you like. Turkey meat may be replaced by lamb or beef. This dish is said to be a kind of *herissa* (*La cuisine arménienne* nd).

Keshkeg, *k'eashkak*, *k'eashkèak* – the phonetic variants in the different Armenian dialects in the 19th century – designate a simpler dish made with crushed wheat or barley (*qorqut* wheat or husked barley) upon which melted fat is poured. It can also be called *herissa*. Here again the Armenians reproduce an old Persian dish. The modern Armenian recipe is very similar to the one given by Steingass – 'like *herissa*' – and may be a persistence of the original Persian recipe borrowed by the Turks.

From the comparison with *herissa* we can conclude that the original *kashkak* is made from crushed cereals cooked with meat to a smooth paste.

In the court cuisine of 13th-century Aleppo, *kishkah* was meat cooked with crushed wheat and flavourings: mastic, *dar sini*, adding at the end *qurfa*,[17] olive oil or sesame oil. It appears in Ibn al-'Adim's chapter on wheat-based foods (1976: 595).

In modern, 19th-century Syriac *kashka* is 'meat and corn boiled together', an Azari-Turkish loan-word (MacLean 1901: 141). From this author, we can conclude that the word *kashka* exists among the Azar-bayjanis from the Turkish side, and that it designates a dish in the same genre. *Kashkina* designates something very similar: 'pounded wheat and meat' (ibid).

A sweetmeat made from milk (curdled or not), flour and sugar – only in Egypt.

Among the Egyptian fellahin of the 17th century *kishk* was 'a meal of curdled milk with flour and honey', a kind of *halwah*, a popular food (Mehren 1872: 34). There were other kinds of *kishk*: *nirab* and *harash al-'ajaiz* (ibid: 36–7), but we do not know if they were sweet or not.

CULTURAL ASPECTS OF *KASHK* OR *KISHK*

As a preserved food for winter use

Among villagers in Lebanon, food conservation is extremely important and regulates not only the food but also the domestic division of labour, especially women's work. For example, they bake bread once every 10 or 15 days according to the season, in contrast to Yemenis or Moroccan Berbers who bake every day. *Kishik* (from *bulghur* and *laban*, dried and powdered) is a staple and one of the most valued preserved foods for year-round consumption, but especially for winter, when people sometimes cannot move from the house. 'The wheat heart is inside it, the best of the milk is in it.' It may be eaten in various ways – cold beverages, soups, stews, with thin pancakes. They stock it in earthenware jars corked at the top, but with an opening lower down from where they take the *kishik*. This *kishik* is unknown to the city-dwellers, for example in Beirut (Kanafani-Zahar, in press).

We have noted the antiquity and continuity of the complex preparation in the Levant from the 10th century until the present.

Furugh Afnan Hourani gives a similar description for various regions of the Middle East and Turkey without specifying exact locations (1984: 58–9). In Egypt, there is a preparation similar to the Lebanese, but it does not seem to be widely known.

Among pastoralists in Iran, Afghanistan and other parts of the Middle East, the milk product is an important preserved food for winter use. It is also valued by city-dwellers, who regard it as a strong condiment – 'it is hot, good in winter' – and use it as a thickening agent. *Kashk siyah* among Iranians, Afghans and some Pakistanis, and *kashk* or *kishik*, are used both as condiments and as staples, being dried sour milk or *bulghur* and *laban*, dried and powdered.

Forming part of festive meals

Though a popular and everyday meal, it also plays an important part in religious feasts. In this way *kashkba* was, in classical Iran, 'a kind of milk-diet dressed in Muharram' (Steingass 1975); it was synonymous with *ash halim*, 'a kind of gruel' made of meat, wheat and *kashk*, after *Borhan-e Qate*' (Vullers 1855).[18]

In 19th-century Egypt, where many Muslims observed some of the Coptic religious feast days and customs, on Good Friday a dish of *khalta* was eaten (see above), 'composed of kishk, with fool nábit, lentils, rice, onions &c'[19] (Lane 1860: 488–9). In social celebrations at the birth of a child, several dishes were prepared by the women of the house, whether of the middle or the wealthier classes, and sent to friends and female relations on the fourth or fifth day after the birth. Those dishes were *mufattaqa*, *libabeh*, *hilbeh* (with fenugreek) and *kishk* (Lane 1860: 504). The first three were based on or sweetened with honey, and we may suppose that the *kishk* was sweetened too.

As a cold medicine

The medical scholars all speak of the barley preparation and use the words *kashk/kishk*, or *kashkab/kishkab*, terms derived from Persian whose Arabic equivalent is *ma' kishk*. The barley broth is the *ptisana* of the Greeks and a panacea of great antiquity. Arab medicine adopted it all the more since barley bread and barley preparations were widely used in Arab lands.

But medical opinion varied. Ibn Sina in the *Qanun* (sv *sha'ir*, II: 440) recommends *kishka* for putting on hot tumours (*awram*); it is good for urine (*bul*); *ma' kishk* gives firmness to the marrow (*rar*). Al-Razi (10th century) is firmly opposed to the use of *kishkiyye*, to which he attributes inflammations of all kinds (nd: 29). Al-Warraq (10th century) recommends a broth of *kishk* against coughs, tiredness and pleurisy, and considers it useful against scabies (*majrabat*) (1987: 269); this *kishk* is cooked in water to which are added ginger, long pepper, cumin and some sheep fat. Ghazali (1975: 1058–1111) refers to *kashkab* in his comparison between the physician and the wise man, and the necessity for prescribing the exact treatment: 'the treatment for fever and for jaundice is to take *skanjabin* [oxymel] and *kashkab* [barley broth]. Only those two medicines can assure recovery' (1959: 10–11). The Andalusian 'Abd al-Malik ibn Zuhr (d. 1162) considers *kashk al-sha'ir* to be refreshing, internally humidifying, evacuating and cleansing, and very good for fever. Externally it opens the pores and is used to wash the face or the body after exertion. For Ibn Baytar (12th century), *kishk al-hintah* is 'wheat infusion'; *kishka*, as we have seen, more usually refers to barley preparations, like the Greek *ptisana*. Maimonides in his *Treatise on Accidents* (1964: 39) recommends, in hot weather, the use of *kashk al-sha'ir*, for which he gives a recipe: polished barley, seed of fumitory, of endive and ox-tongue, Iraqi poppy, white sandalwood, nard, dill flower, olive oil, much water; reduce it to three-quarters, add wine vinegar until the liquid is coloured red, finally filter. Al-Samarqandi (early 13th century) considers barley *kishk* prepared with dill as a good emetic to eliminate phlegm (1967: 106). For Da'ud al-Antaki (16th century) *kishk* is still an infusion: 'the water in which wheat or barley has been soaked and boiled or both' (1979: sv *kishk*). He adds that it is a well-known preparation.

THE ORIGINAL MEANING OF THE TERM
AND THE DIFFUSION OF THE PRODUCTS

The geographical distribution of the products and methods of preservation

The dry curdled milk product is present in many countries under different names. We have good examples showing the distribution of the techniques. We must not forget that similar techniques can be found with different names: in Afghanistan *qurut* is exactly the same as the Persian *kashk*, dry curdled milk (Balland 1985); in Greece *trahana* or *tarhonya* is exactly the same as the Lebanese *kishk* (A. Boxer, quoted by Conran 1983). It seems that the eastern limit of this kind of curdled milk is in Pakistan. Further east, people do not use curdled milk but the sour milk equivalent to *laban*. To the west, in Mediterranean countries, curds are generally converted into cheese.

Kishk is a product based on cereals and curdled milk, and as such originated in areas where sedentary agriculturists co-exist with nomadic pastoralists.

In certain Arabic-speaking countries, *aqit* 'is made from curdled milk, dried in irregular pieces and then pounded for use' (Kazimirski 1860).

In certain Turkish-speaking regions *qarut/qurut* (Anatolian Turkish *kurut*) is synonymous with *kishk* and means 'dried curdled milk' (Zenker 1866). This meaning is so far the only one attested in old Western Turkish, in Mahmud al-Kashgari's 11th-century dictionary. Morteza Moallem (1926) gives a similar meaning 'petit lait condensé, caillebotte'. And in Barbier de Meynard (1881, II: 558) *qurut* is a kind of dried cheese made from whey that is left to dry after having been boiled. The term comes from *qurumak* 'to dry'. In Central Asia *qurut* is a preserve obtained by drying yoghurt made from skimmed sheep's milk, with no salt added. The skimming is necessary for long conservation. The product comes in the form of small blocks, sour, very hard, kept for winter use. Kazakh and Kirghiz shepherds like to suck it. It is also used as a condiment, rich in calorific value. They sometimes add it to a paste of flour and milk, to which may be added minced mutton.[20]

Qurut is present among certain peoples speaking Iranian languages who borrowed the Turkish word, as in the case of the Pashtuns living in Afghanistan and Pakistan (where it is *krut*), the Brahui of Pakistan (oral information from Gérard Dufourcq), and the Baluch. They also appreciate *qara qurut*, a very strong condiment in use with the same valuation and same name in Iran. At present this Turkish term *qara qurut*, as mentioned earlier, is today used only in Persian to designate the black dried curdled milk, a valued condiment among the Iranians and Afghans while it is almost unknown in Turkey.

As a preserving technique, in parts of the 13th-century Middle East, *masl* seems equivalent to *kishk*: 'small balls of barley flour which they soak in sour *laban* till they become very sour, then they dry them and use them to thicken the meal which is called *al-masliyya*' (Ibn al-Hasha 1941: no. 687).

In Anatolia, *tarhana* is a preserved food based on cooked and sieved vegetables, to which they add *lebne*, salt, yeast and flour. The paste is left for leavening for three days, then cut into small pieces, which are dried and rubbed between the hands to the shape of small grains, which are then stored (Afnan Hourani 1984: 59). In Greek cooking, *trahana* or *tarhonya* seems to be very close to *kishk* of the Lebanese type. It thickens the soup, giving it a sour and nutty taste (Conran 1983). People chew it, just as people of northern Egypt chew the small dried milky balls (Benghiat 1985: 62), or the Turkish populations of northern Iran chew their version of the product (information from L. Bazin).

What is the original meaning of the word?
Today the word refers to complex dishes produced with sophisticated techniques among peasants and townsmen of Lebanon, Iran, Egypt and elsewhere in the region, so well adapted among them that it indicates a continuity of practices from much earlier times. The name, however, as we have seen, is borrowed from the Persian. This raises some questions.

Let us review the different possible theses regarding the original meaning of the word. It may seem at first that the dual reference of *kashk*, to by-products of both cereals and milk, is a coincidence: two products of a very different nature, and two words of different meanings and origins which may have 'telescoped'. But this formulation is not supported by the evidence.

Let us examine three propositions on the original nature of the product: the word first designated a by-product of milk; the word first designated a by-product of barley; and the word first designated a complex preparation. What is the evidence for, and the consequences of, each proposition?

The word first designated a by-product of milk. We notice a rather homogeneous geographical and linguistic incidence of *kashk*: it is a staple among pastoralists speaking Iranian languages, or those speaking Turkish languages in contact with Iranian-speaking pastoralists; they only have one word, one use. And we know that Turkish borrowed the word from Persian.

It is a by-product of cereals. We find many relations with the Sanskrit root *kasha*, 'to trace a furrow', Persian *kisht*, 'sown field', and with Sanskrit *kashaya*, 'medicinal drink', as we saw earlier. In this semantic field, we can observe an important derivation in the Persian terms to indicate distinct products: the derivation is precise: *kashkba, kashkak, kashkin*. Finally, if the product originally meant 'dry sour milk', it is not possible to give a semantic explanation for the derived meaning, 'barley water'.

The word originally designated a complex preparation. We can consider the chronology of loan-words: the 5th- to 6th-century Armenian *k'ashken* borrows from Persian a derived term meaning barley bread. It is, at the same time, the most ancient occurrence of the word. The 10th-century Arabic *kashk/kishk* borrows from Persian a term meaning among the Middle Eastern Arabs 'preserved food from cereals and milk' (al-Warraq 1987). The 16th-century Turkish *keshk* borrows from Persian a term meaning cheese. The Damascus manuscript of 1503 borrows from Persian *kashkak* meaning *herissa*. If we consider the earliest occurrences of the words, we find that they are all derived terms designating dishes with cereals, *kashkin, kashkina, kashkak, kashkba, kashkab, keshkiyya*. From that, the hypothesis of an original meaning of a 'complex preparation from cereals' is confirmed by the precision of the derived terms which, in Persian, from the appearance of the word, cover a semantic field which gives evidence of various uses of cereals, principally of barley. Moreover, the early borrowings in other languages (Armenian and Arabic) also testify to a complex preparation based on cereals. Though the word is absent in Ancient and Middle Persian, we saw that we could relate it to a root containing the idea of agriculture, which indicates a preparation from cereals.

How, then, does this meaning of the word, as 'preparations from barley', pass on to indicate 'sour-milk preparations'? The answer may be found in the similarities and analogies in the properties of the two ranges of products, and ultimately their combination.

Similarity of texture: barley makes a poor, heavy, damp bread, a crumbly product. It makes a better gruel (with coarsely pounded grains) cooked in broth, or in a coarse bread. Moreover, it is a cereal which it is necessary to mix with other cereals or legumes in order to make a more digestible bread; which is also what happens with the *kashkina* made from barley, vetch, beans and lentils. The granular consistency of the barley preparations recalls the granular consistency of the dry sour milk, and the term designating prepared barley can be applied by analogy to the milk preparation. This was probably one of the most important similarities. Historically, moreover, barley or barley bread in central Europe, just as in the Middle East, was often eaten with milk to make it more palatable and more digestible (Maurizio 1932).

Similarity in the sour flavour: when barley flour is boiled to a gruel, then left to cool, then heated again, it develops a sour flavour, because it contains lactic acid (Maurizio 1932: 232–3). This was probably the second most important similarity: sour barley gruel and gruels made from soured milk.

Similarity in the form of round flat cakes: the early descriptions by al-Warraq and Ibn al-Hasha of the complex preserved food *kishk* indicate that it was in the form of round flat cakes, which was also the form of the barley bread.[21]

Similarity in colour: barley bread is generally of a dark-brownish colour, which is similar to *kashk siyah*, black *kashk*.

Another approach is to consider how milk is related to barley gruel at different levels: by analogy of appearance and flavour; by being added in the cooking of barley gruel; by soaking the dry barley preparation. On the other hand we saw that Persian has *tarf* to designate the dry sour milk, and *jow* to designate the barley.

CONCLUSION

From the foregoing discussion we can propose the hypothesis that Persian *kashk* originally designated a *barley preparation*, a *barley gruel*, which corresponds to the oldest alimentary preparations recorded under that name. From that gruel, after adding leaven, two products are obtained which can be preserved: first, with the addition of a little water, bread: *kashkina*, *nan kashkina*; secondly, with the addition of much more water, a fermented gruel, which can then be dried.

If fermented milk is used instead of leaven, two things follow. We may suppose that Iranian-speaking pastoralists, for whom dried sour milk is a staple, and who have no easy access to barley, applied the word *kashk* by analogy to the dry sour milk. Then the word passed to the rest of the

Middle East, and among the agriculturists *kishk* came to designate complex preserved foods made from cereal and a ferment, whether leaven or sour milk. But was the technique also borrowed? Unfortunately the available data do not allow a firm answer. Nevertheless the existence of Syriac words to designate the preparation would suggest that the technique was known in other parts of the Middle East at an early stage.

By an evolution of vocabulary and by analogy, *kishk* acquired a wide polysemy, which is the sign of frequent use: plain barley, a preserved food from cereals and sour milk, a preparation with *kishk*, a barley broth, fermented cereals, a cheese, whey, etc. Some of the qualifying terms and adjectives were probably lost following the 'principle of economy': *nan kashkin* in the 10th-century *Shahnameh* came to be *kashkin* later on.

Finally we can say that the study of the diffusion of such a humble cultural artefact may throw new light on social relations between culturally different populations: Zoroastrians of Sassanian Iran and Christian Armenians; Muslim Persians, Kurds and Arabs; Persians and Turks. In fact the Persian *kashk* of the pastoral tribes was diffused as far as the prestigious dishes of the Baghdad court, itself derived from Persian cooking: *faludhaj*, *sikbaj* ... This humble dish was first adopted by princely cooking in 10th-century Iraq, though it is absent from the 12th-century book of al-Baghdadi. It is present in the 13th-century kitchens of the princes of Aleppo, in those of the 14th- to 15th-century Mamluk sultans of Cairo, and in those of the 16th-century Mughal shahs of Kashmir, as well as in the cooking of all the villagers of the Muslim and Christian Middle East, with few exceptions. It is sometimes a good cultural marker, as in Lebanon, where the Circassians neither name it nor use it, nor do Armenians from Armenia, while Armenians from Turkey do.

We can see that *kishk* occupies a prominent place in the diffusion of cultural objects in the Middle East, through the prestige of Persian culture spread in those countries by the Arabs since the beginning of their expansion, and some of the effects remain with us today.

Terms	Meanings	Sources

Indo-European languages

New Persian (5th to 6th centuries)

kashk		*Shahnameh* (10th C)
Derived terms:		
k'ashkēn	'barley bread'	Elishe (5th–6th C) (1957: 144)
kashkīn	'barley bread'	*Shahnameh*
kashkbā	'barley gruel'	Zamakhshari (12th C) (1963: 344)
Composite terms:		
nān-e kashk	'barley bread'	*Shahnameh*
nān-e kashkin	'barley bread'	*Shahnameh*
nān kashkinah	'barley bread'	*Shahnameh*
āb kashk	'barley water'	Zamakhshari (1963: 346)
āsh kashk	'barley broth'	Zamakhshari (344)

Classical Persian (from 16th century)

kashk		Abu'l-Fazl (16th C)
Derived terms:		
kashkāb	'barley water, ptisan'	Steingass (19th C) (1975)
kashku	'barley broth'	Steingass
kashkak	complex dish	Steingass
kashkin	bread / dry preserve	Steingass
kashkina	bread / dry preserve	Steingass
Composite terms:		
kashk siyah	'black *kashk*'	Vullers (1855); Zenker (1866)
kashk sefid	'white *kashk*'	note in Zamakhshari (1963: 344)

Contemporary Persian

kashk	dry yoghurt (*māst*)	Ramazani (1974)
Composite terms:		
kashk bademjān	*kashk* with egg-plants	

Armenian

Derived terms only:		
k'ashkēn	'barley bread'	Elishe (5th–6th C)
keshkeg, k'eashkak,		
k'eashkèak	complex dishes	19th–20th C

Urdu

kashk	'barley', 'b. water', 'thick pottage', 'dried sour milk'	Platts (1884: 837)

Terms	Meanings	Sources

Indo-European languages (continued)

Pashto
kshk — 'cereal broth', 'bread soup' — *Dict Afghan-russe* (1966: 680)

Pastoralists speaking Iranian languages
North-western dialects:

Talish
kashk — dried casein — Bazin (1980, II: 49)

Gilan
kashk — id — Bazin & Bromberger (1982: 35)

Kurdish
keshk, kashk (Hakkari) — id — Rhea (1880); Jaba (1879)
kesk — Soane (1913)
keshka — 20th C

South-western dialect:

Bakhtyari
kashk, āw kashk — id — Digard (1981: 198)

Greek
Macedonian
quacheq — cheese — Doane et al. (1969: 99)

Semitic languages

Arabic:
Iraq
kishk / kishik — al-Warraq (10th C); Ibn Sina, II, sv *sha'īr*; Bar Bahlul (9th C); al-Samarqandi (13th C); 20th C

Derived terms:
kishkiyya — complex dish — al-Warraq, al-Razi (10th C); 20th C
kashkāb — 'barley infusion' — Ghazali (end of 9th C)

Composite terms:
kishk shāmī — 'Syrian *kishk*' — al-Warraq
kishk mosūlī — '*kishk* of Mosul' — al-Warraq
kishk hamīd — 'sour *kishk*' — al-Warraq
kishk babkī — ?[22] — al-Warraq
kishk bushūl — ? — al-Warraq
kishk bāblī — '*kishk* of Babylon' — Ibn Baytar (1877–83, no 683, I: 445)

Terms	Meanings	Sources

Semitic languages (continued)

Middle East: Syria, Lebanon, Palestine

Terms	Meanings	Sources
kishk / kishik	dry preserve	[23]
Derived terms:		
kishkāh	complex dish	Ibn al-'Adim (13th C) (1976: 595)
kishkak	complex dish	Damascus MS (1503)
kishkiyye	complex dish	Frayha (in Denizeau 1960: 454)
Composite terms:		
keshk hamr	with 'leaven'	Ibn al-'Adim; Burckhardt (1822: 293)
keshk laban	with 'curd milk'	Ibn al-'Adim; Burckhardt (ibid)

Egypt

Terms	Meanings	Sources
kishk		17th C Mehren (1872: 34); Freytag (1975); Lane (1866: 488–9, 504)
Composite terms:		
kashk al-sha'īr	'of barley'	Maimonides (12th C) (1964: 39)
kishk musbba'un	'of 7 components'	Khalil al-Zahiri (14th–15th C) (1894: 125)
kishk sa'idī	chicken *kishk*	Benghiat (1985)

Tunisia

Terms	Meanings	Sources
kashkār	'coarse bran'	Beaussier (1958)

Al-Andalus

Terms	Meanings	Sources
kishk	barley paste	Ibn Habib (d 853)
kishk al-sha'īr	'*kishk* of barley'	Ibn Zuhr (d 1162) (1992: 11)
kishk al-hintah	'*kishk* of wheat'	Ibn Baytar (12th C) (1877–83, sv *sha'īr*)

Syriac (dialects of north-west Iran, Mosul plain, east Syrians of Kurdistan)

Terms	Meanings	Sources
kishk	barley gruel	Elias Nisibé in P. de Lagarde (1879: 35)
Derived terms:		
kashkā	complex dish	MacLean (19th C) (1901: 141)
kashkīnā		MacLean

Neo-Aramaic (dialect of Kurdistan)

Terms	Meanings	Sources
kashkā		Krotkoff (19th C) (1982: 83, 130)

Terms	Meanings	Sources
Altaic languages		
Turkish		
kesh		Tanıklariyle (16th C) (1957, IV: 503)
keshk		Zenker (1866); Kelekian (1911)
Derived terms:		
keshkek	complex dish	Zenker; Barbier de Meynard (1881), Kelekian; Gürün (nd)
keshkīna	'barley bread'	Zenker
Azarbayjani		
kashk		Bazin and Bromberger (1982: 35)
kashkā		MacLean (1901: 141)
Turkmen		
keshkīna		Zenker
keshkīn		Bianchi and Kieffer (1871)
Caucasic languages		
Georgian (17th century)		
kashī	'cereals cooked with milk'	Tchoubinoff (1840)

Notes

1. I want to thank all those who have supported and helped me in this research: Dominique Gauthier of CNRS (Georgian), M. Mahé of EPHE 4e section (Armenian), J. P. Lecoq of EPHE 4e section (Iranian), Annie Berthier of BN (Turkish), Françoise Kotobi of CNRS (Iranian), Louis Bazin of CNRS (Turkish), A. G. Haudricourt of CNRS, Gérard Dufourcq (Afghanistan), P. N. Boratav (Turkish). See Appendix (above) for detailed linguistic material and the sources used.
2. The asterisk indicates a word of which no instances exist, but which is presumed, on philological grounds, to have existed.
3. Hübschmann (1895: 238) says from the New Persian *kashkin*.
4. In the 10th century, that is at the same time as the appearance of the Persian word. Again we have a clear demonstration of the gap of perhaps several centuries between the literary evidence and the reality that we may never know.
5. I exclude the sweetmeat *kishkül fiqra* or *fuqara* since it is a loan-word from Persian *kashkul*, 'beggar's cup', from *kash* + *kul* 'carried on the shoulder' (*Borhan-e Qate'*).

6. Today, after contact with Russian, it is *kasha*.
7. The Russian *kasha*, 'buckwheat gruel', is probably also related to Sanskrit *kashaya*.
8. *Rakhbin* is 'sour milk, buttermilk or anything dressed with it; a dish made of sour and fresh milk with flour; new cheese' (Steingass 1975).
9. The word is probably of Greek origin.
10. I could not find *'awitah* (Dozy 1957; Kazimirski 1860; Steingass).
11. The definition 'coarse flour made from any grain', identical to Ibn al-Hasha's, is probably taken from al-Razi's *al-Mansuri*, but I could not verify this.
12. *Söz Derleme Dergisi* 1941, mentioned in correspondence from L. Bazin.
13. Personal information from Françoise Kotobi, 1992. [Normally *kashk badamjan* is without meat; when prepared with meat it is known as *halim-badamjan*; information from Ziba Mir-Hosseini – Eds.]
14. Personal letter, 2 April 1992, from L. Bazin.
15. Personal letter, 2 April 1992, from L. Bazin.
16. They borrowed it from Turkish; Armenians from Armenia know neither the name nor the product. [Also, it exists at the present time in Anatolia and in the Mosul province of Iraq – Eds.]
17. Both cinnamons often appear in the same recipe: *qurfa* is *cinnamonum zeylanicum* from Ceylon, thinner and finer than *dar-sini*, *cinnamonum cassia* from China.
18. As *halim* is still eaten today [Eds].
19. *Ful nabit* are fava beans which begin to sprout.
20. Personal correspondence, 2 April 1992, from L. Bazin.
21. Note the technical similarity with 17th-century Switzerland, a region absolutely out of contact with our countries: 'l'orge ... donne un pain doux de goût, agréable qui, à vrai dire, est un peu humide et devient dur rapidement. C'est pourquoi, dans les populations des Alpes ... on cuisait une ou deux fois par an cette sorte de pains d'orge. On les coupait en disques plats et minces que l'on enfilait sur des cordes et qui pendaient au dessus du foyer, et, selon les besoins, ils les mangeaient l'hiver, ramollis sur du bouillon de viande ou du lait' (A. von Haller 1782, in Maurizio 1932: 504).
22. Persian *babak*, diminutive of *bab*, means 'little father', or 'turquoise'; it is also the name of a famous medieval Iranian rebel leader, but the reference here is not clear.
23. 13th C: Ibn al-Hasha (1941); Ibn al-'Adim (1976: 870).
    14-15th C: *1001 Nights* (Breslau 7: 300) but it is impossible to define it.
    16th C: Damascus MS of 1503; Da'ud al-Antaki.
    18th C: *Lisan al-'arab* vocalizes *kashk* in Arabic as in Persian, but it seems the only case.
    19th C: Bergrenn (1844); Harfouch (1894: 304).
    20th C: Dalman (1928–39, VI: 295, 28; in Denizeau 1960: 454); Khawam (1970); Kanafani-Zahar (in press).

Part II

Food and the Social Order

9. The Revival of Traditional Cooking in Modern Arab Cookbooks

Peter Heine

Dealing with modern Arab cookbooks is quite an adventure, because there are reasons for asking: what is an Arab cookbook? Are books on Arab cuisine Arab cookbooks, whether their language is English, French or even German? A negative answer to this question could be a little hasty. Perhaps cookbooks in a foreign language addressed to a non-Arab public could not be so designated. But there are some cookbooks on Arab cuisine, especially in French, which are clearly intended for Arab users.

Let me give only two examples: first, *L'Art culinaire libanais* by George N. Rayes (1957). It is very clear that this book was written for Lebanese or perhaps other Arab readers.[1] The recipes show an unmistakably Lebanese programme, with all those dishes for which Lebanese cuisine is famous. In certain cases we find both the French and the Arabic names of a dish like *Kibbe au four sur plateau*, which is *Kibbe bi'l-siniya*. In other cases there is an addition like *méthode arabe*. The way the Arabic terms are transliterated will please all those philological purists who insist on the correct spelling of sun- and moon-letters. The traditional character of *L'Art culinaire libanais* is also shown by a chapter headed: 'Les lapins et les gazelles'. Consciousness of the existence of a specific Lebanese cuisine can also be seen from the special indication of European recipes – the book finishes with 'Quelques desserts européens'. Unfortunately we are not informed for whom the book was written. Rayes gives no explanation at all. His 'author's note' indicates that the original text was in Arabic, because he says: 'En Arabe, on emploie le même mot, qali:, pour designer les diverses opérations de passer au beurre, faire revenir et frire, qui en français sont exprimées par des termes différents' (p 2). Perhaps *L'Art culinaire libanais* was addressed to Lebanese who had a strictly French or European schooling, who could speak Arabic, but could not read it well enough to understand an Arabic cookbook. Furthermore I have the strong impression that the book was written as a kind of promotion for a shop selling household supplies. There are at least 36 pages with advertisements: among those for airlines or frozen food are some for Rayes Shop, advertising washing machines, kitchen equipment and so on.

Another, more recent book, is also clearly written for local use: *La Cuisine algérienne*, by Fatima Zohra Bouayed (1983). The only book on Algerian cuisine I have found, it was written for the Algerian public and is therefore a good indicator of the knowledge of Arabic in Algeria up to the mid-1980s. The author says in her presentation that in writing the book she wanted to show her fellow-countrymen and women the wealth of Algerian cuisine, and the varieties of cooking in different regions of the country, and she speaks of preserving the culinary heritage of Algeria with her collection of recipes.

I will come back to this book later. For the moment let us state that the Arabic language is not the only criterion of an Arab cookbook. I think we have to consider the audience for whom the book is intended. There are books on Arab cuisine written especially for Western readers by Western and oriental writers, which differ in quality, size and price. We all know some of them. The most famous include: Claudia Roden's *A Book of Middle Eastern Food* (1968); Mina El Glaoui's *Ma Cuisine marocaine* (nd), a book that is clearly written for better-off Western tourists; Robert Carrier's *A Taste of Morocco* (1987), which can be called a coffee-table book, a beautiful book that nobody, I think, ever uses in the kitchen; Mary Laird's *Lebanese Mountain Cookery* (1987), a book perhaps intended for the US-Arab community. These I do not consider Arab cookbooks – though it would be interesting to know which countries of the Arab world are more and which are less covered by this type of cookbook. In Germany, with which I am familiar, most books deal with Morocco, Tunisia and also with non-Arab Turkey, countries with high numbers of tourists from Europe. So let me repeat that I define an Arab cookbook as one which is written for an Arab reader.

Some books are difficult to classify. For example, the Arabic translation of Tess Mallos's *The Complete Middle East Cookbook* (1987) is clearly intended for an Arab public. Even more complicated is the case of Fatouma Benkirane's *al-Tabkh al-Maghribi al-Mu'asir* (1984), that was published also in English, French and German, with one foreword by Paul Bocuse and another by Maurice Messegué. The German edition at least appeared in 1981, before the Arabic one. The book tries to modernize traditional Moroccan cuisine, which Madame Benkirane sees as too complicated and time-consuming. She also deplores the high calorie count of a normal

Moroccan dish. From the fact that one foreword is written by Bocuse we will understand that she reduces cooking times, quantities of fat, and so on. The book is written in the first place for Moroccan readers, at least so she states in her introduction. But its publication in European languages first, and the forewords by two well-known French specialists in cooking and dietetics, indicate that it was written mainly for Westerners. In her introduction, even in the Arabic version, Madame Benkirane does not address Moroccans.

In the Moroccan context two more books should be mentioned, although they are not written by or for Moroccans or Arabs: first, Zette Guinaudeau-Franc's *Fes vu par sa cuisine* (1957), which was enlivened with photographs and coloured drawings and given a new title: *Les Secrets des cuisines en terre marocaine* (1981). The book is an important contribution to the description of the culinary culture of Morocco. The other book is Viviane and Nina Moryoussef's *La Cuisine juive marocaine* (1983), a book that tries to keep the special cuisine of Jewish Moroccans alive.

ARAB COOKBOOKS OF AN INTERNATIONAL TYPE

Cookbooks written for an Arab public are normally addressed to women – though I could trace only one, S. al-Kuhayli's *al-Tabkh al-'Arabi al-Asil* (1990) that explicitly and consistently used verbs in the second person singular or imperative in the feminine form. They often have introductions that can be compared with the *muqaddimat* we find in medieval Arab cookbooks. Most of the modern books I have seen start with invocations to God and citations of the appropriate Ayat from the Qur'an; some also have quotations from Hadith literature, such as *Kitab al-Wusla ila 'l-Habib* or al-Warraq's *Kitab al-Tabikh*. It goes without saying that none of these books, old or new, even mentions pork.

Among modern Arab cookbooks we can distinguish two different types. The first deals with modern international cuisine and has no special concern for Arab cooking, although several Arab dishes are mentioned; for example, Saduf Kamal and Sima 'Uthman's *Alifba' al-Tabkh* (1980), which states that it contains more than 460 recipes from Lebanon, from other Arab countries and from the rest of the world. This book could perhaps be used as an indicator of social change, at least in Lebanon. The introduction says that young women today do not learn cooking any more. They are busy with their studies at the university, and later on have to earn their living and provide for their families, so they are not able to learn how to cook just by watching and imitating their mothers or other older women of the household. They are not able to prepare food, which is why so many of them buy canned or frozen food, or the family goes out to restaurants. This practice is seen as no good for the health of the family. Often out of these problems of the kitchen result problems between the spouses (p 7). The book should be a remedy for these dangers. In reading the book, I had the strong impression that it was influenced by European models. The layout and the pictures, the structure and the very pedagogic tone are all to be found in cookbooks for beginners from Britain, France, Germany or wherever.

I was interested in the recipes of *Alifba' al-Tabkh* for several reasons. Of course we are confronted with the same problem of definition, if we say that a certain dish is either Arab/oriental or European. If we count only strictly European recipes like *afukadu ma'a 'l-mayunayz, kuktayl gambari, salatat 'l-batata, hasa' al-basl bi'l-krim, al-kunsumih, al-aruzz al-amriki al-matbukh*, all pasta dishes like *lazaniya, rafiyuli, kanniluni* and so on, *krukit al-dajjaj, batata krukit, shara'ih al-lahm (istik)* or *jatu al-shukulata*, to name only a few, about one-third of the book's recipes are of European style.

The same can be said of Batul Shara al-Din's *Fann al-Tabkh* (n. d., but before 1985); the author prides herself on having collected the best and healthiest Lebanese and Arabic recipes. Here we find recipes for *salata franjiyya*, comprising lettuce, parsley, peppermint, green onions, tomatoes, potatoes and cucumbers, or *al-salata al-rusiyya* made from potatoes, mayonnaise and some spices. What is very European in this book is the permanent concern with dietetic questions. The author starts her introduction with the sentence: 'It is important that your food be healthy and nourishing' (*sihhiyan wa mufidan*) (p 7).

The influence of European cooking on the Arab kitchen is deplored by S. al-Kuhayli, who criticizes the use of tinned food and pre-cooked dishes in restaurants, which has nothing to do with the high tradition of Middle Eastern cooking (1990: 7). This is the reason she has written her book, which indeed contains mostly Arab recipes. She also tries to distinguish it from earlier cookbooks by a different arrangement of the various chapters, starting with drinks, and leaving meat recipes for the very end of the book.

DETECTING THE ARAB REGIONS

The last point is also stressed in the *Qamus al-Tabkh al-Sahih* (1980), written by a group of professional cooks and housewives (*asatidha al-tabkh wa-rabbat al-buyut*). Nevertheless this is quite a different book from those mentioned before. Perhaps it can be called a turning-point in the writing of modern Arab cookbooks. In the introduction, the Imam al-Shafi'i is cited and special stress is laid on the importance of a healthy diet (p 7). The book is a compendium of more than 2000 recipes of Lebanese, other Arab and foreign origins, and also 160 old Arab recipes. It is something special, because for the first time, to my knowledge, it distinguishes different modes of preparation of the same dish in different Arab countries while at the same time clearly distinguishing Arab recipes from European ones. Thus, it gives the methods for making *fata'ir* in Syria (*tariqa shamiyya*), Lebanon, Iraq and Egypt (pp 338–45). In the same way, the use of certain ingredients in different Arabic countries is described. This is very interesting concerning an American plant, the potato; we find here many recipes for potatoes indicated as *tariqa shamiyya* or *tariqa 'iraqiyya*, and so on. This shows that potatoes are widely used in this part of the Arab world, although they were introduced into Iraq, for example, only in the 1880s.

Another point concerning the structure of the book and the way the recipes are arranged in an alphabetical and at the same time a regional order is that quite different recipes are put together. So we find under the entry *al-qamh* different recipes for using wheat. For Syria it is *al-saliqa*, which is made from 250 grams of wheat, sugar, walnut, sweet pomegranate, aniseed and orange-flower essence. Under the same entry we find the Iraqi way of making *harisa* and the old Arabic *hintiyya* (pp 378–81), which are savoury dishes. This is a traditional way of ordering recipes according to their structure or texture, which we know from the classical Arab cook-books. As far as I can see, there is no European model for this arrangement of recipes, with one exception, south German and Austrian recipes for dumplings. Even in the *Larousse gastronomique* I could not find this combination of sweet and savoury recipes.

The old Arab recipes are listed in alphabetical order. The book starts with *abazir*, which is explained as *khubz 'arabi qadim*, followed by the famous *ibrahimiyya* (p 9). The recipes are taken from old Arab cookbooks without any modification or explanation, just in their traditional form; this means that there is no information about the quantities of the ingredients or the duration of the cooking. Even the few lines of poetry which accompany the old recipes are reproduced, with no indication of the source from which they are taken. What is strange about this book on Arab cooking is that it contains no recipes from North Africa or the Arab peninsula at all; which sheds an interesting light on the understanding of culinary provinces in the Arab world.

NATIONAL COOKBOOKS IN THE ARAB WORLD

Starting from the *Qamus al-Tabkh al-Sahih* we find many books which have a clearly regional character, with a strong inclination for the revival of traditional Arab ways of cooking. So let us again consider the books on Algerian and modern Moroccan cuisine.

The Algerian book was originally written in French, and I know of no translation into Arabic. Madame Bouayed (1983) says in her introduction that there exists an Algerian cuisine, composed of the ancient, pre-Islamic ways of cooking, the secrets of the cuisine of Baghdad, Cairo and Córdoba, with a final influence from Ottoman cuisine. The slight influence of French cuisine is explained by the fact that Islamic food taboos have interfered with the acceptance of this great tradition of cooking. Madame Bouayed encountered a problem not mentioned in any other modern cookbook I have seen. She found that in different parts of Algeria the same name is applied to different dishes, or the same dish is known in different regions by different names. She deals with this problem by giving all the different names known to her. This again is an interesting observation concerning the situation of language in Algeria.

Other cookbooks in Arabic follow the same line in defining national cuisine. Fatima Husayn's *al-Akalat al-Kuwaytiyya* (1985)[2] tried to establish a Kuwaiti cuisine and at the same time to give the impression that this cuisine is very old. This is done, for example, by borrowing a classical Arab cooking technique. We know from the old Arab cookbooks that the *tanur* was used for cooking chicken and fish. These foods were put on spits and inserted into the heated oven. Fatima Husayn includes recipes of this type in her book. Being unsure whether her readers will understand what she is talking about, she adds small sketches to show the outline of the *tanur* with skewered fish or meat inside. Even though the book includes photographs of some cooking techniques, it is interesting that none can be found showing the *tanur* used in the way described in the recipes. This technique of *tanur* cooking can also be found in a modern Baghdad cookbook, as we will describe soon.

The tendency to revive old techniques is an interesting development, even if these recipes will only rarely be realized. It is, however, still difficult to see what is Kuwaiti about this cuisine. Perhaps a kebab of shrimps with rice flour is a special Kuwaiti dish (p 83). The word 'kebab' is also rendered in the Kuwaiti pronunciation as *chebab*. *Akalat Kuwaytiyya* seems to be sponsored by the Kuwaiti government; as much is hinted at in the foreword to the second printing, which states that the book was given to Kuwaiti embassies for use at receptions and dinners. The book is also used in

Kuwaiti schools (pp 7, 9).

The changing contents of Arab cookbooks after 1980 can also be seen from a book written by Naziha Adib and Firdaws al-Mukhtar (1990), two Iraqi teachers at the Madrasat al-funun al-baitiyya in al-A'zamiyya, a quarter of Baghdad. The Arabic title is *Dalil al-tabkh wa'l-aghdhiya*. On the back of the volume, however, is the English title: *Guide for Iraqi Cooking and Baghdadi Dishes*. The idea of a specifically Iraqi cuisine dates back at least to the 1960s. I remember that in 1966–7 the Baghdadi newspaper *Baghdad News* ran a series on the wives of foreign ambassadors in Iraq. One standard question in these articles was: 'How do you like Iraqi food?' The answer was of course always positive and *dolma* was especially mentioned. *Dolma*, however, comes from the Turkish *yaprak dolması*, stuffed vine leaves, so this typical Iraqi dish did not even have an Arabic name.

The book by the two lady teachers has a large introductory section about the nutritional aspects of different kinds of food, the physiological and medical consequences of eating, the appropriate diets for pregnant women, children from one to five, elderly people, tables on the quantities of vitamins in different vegetables, weight-watcher programmes and so on. Furthermore it describes the utensils needed in the kitchen, including the traditional Iraqi ones, and goes on to specify the correct tablecloth and tableware and how they should be laid according to the (Western) rules.[3] The book contains about 1000 recipes, mostly Arab but some Western.

Leaving aside the question of why the Arabic and English titles of this book should be so completely different, let me turn to the related question of why this is an Iraqi cookbook and not an Arab one. In addition to the fact that rice is seen as the most important food, together with bread, there are also some recipes which we find to be specifically Iraqi. I will mention here only two of them. The first is *baja* (*bacha* or *pacha*), prepared from a sheep's head, trotters and tripe, rice, more mutton, crushed almonds, spices and salt, bread and *laban* with garlic (p 118). The other dish is said to be a speciality of the Shi'ite Iraqi population: *fazanjun*.[4] In this book it is prepared with chicken, walnut, sour pomegranate juice, fat, salt, sugar and water, though I know it also with wild duck instead of chicken. From an Iraqi point of view these are truly Iraqi dishes, although *fazanjun* is originally from Iran.[5]

Although it was known from books on the Arabic dialects of Saudi Arabia that there exists a special cuisine of the Arabian peninsula, information about this cuisine was very scarce for many years. Muna Qaburi has published *Atayib munawwa'a* (1990), in the foreword to which she speaks of 'our Saudi cuisine (*matbakhna al-sa 'udi*)'. But what is typically Saudi in her recipes is difficult to see. The book has some interesting adaptations of European recipes to the Saudi situation, such as a recipe for Swiss roll with dates, while the recipes for sweets are nearly all borrowed from European cuisine. Looking through these and other cookbooks from Saudi Arabia, one has to bear in mind that there are different culinary traditions in the kingdom, especially those from Hijaz and from Najd. So the publication of these 'Saudi' cookbooks indicates a tendency to create a national cuisine that did not exist before.[6] This culinary development has, of course, some political connotations: for example, the reasoning that, if there is a nation, then there must be a homogeneous national culture; cuisine being part of the national culture, it must be homogeneous too.[7]

Typical Saudi cuisine is documented in Zubayda Mawsili, Safiyya al-Sulayman and Samiyya al-Harakan's *Min Fann al-Tabkh al-Sa 'udi* (1990). This book was published in co-operation with the cultural section of the Jam'iyya al-nahda al-nisa'iyya al-khayriyya. Profits from sales of the book are reserved for the poor of the kingdom. As explained in the foreword, the idea of collecting Saudi recipes was introduced by Amira Muda bint al-Khalid ibn Abd al-'Aziz, a member of the royal family. The reason for this book was that the great number of foreign workers in the kingdom had brought with them their cooking traditions and techniques and exotic dishes which had become quite popular with the Saudis. Social and economic change in Saudi Arabia has also had gastronomic consequences. Many restaurants serving international food are to be found in the big cities of the kingdom, and there are many special restaurants for Indian, Chinese, Italian or French cuisine. From advertisements in Saudi news-papers, one gets the impression that there are no Saudi restaurants at all. The amira and the ladies of the Jam'iyya al-nahda saw a danger that the cooking traditions of Saudi Arabia would be forgotten, so they decided to collect all the traditional recipes they could find. Older housewives were asked to reveal the secrets of their cuisine and many of them responded positively. Fear of the loss of cultural traditions has also moved Saudi newspapers to publish articles on everyday culture. The Riyadh-based *Arab News*, for example, in Ramadan 1992 had numerous pieces on the preparation of tea, Ramadan lanterns, the smoking of waterpipes, and so on.

In the Saudi cookbook, the index of recipes for each dish gives the names of the ladies who contributed to the book. All the recipes come from the kitchens of the traditional Saudi households. The editors of this collection fear that most of the traditional cooking techniques are already forgotten, which is why they give very detailed information about the preparation of the ingredients. Of course, it is not easy to explain why *kusa mahshi* is a Saudi dish. But I compared texts collected in Omar Al Sasi's *Sprichwörter und andere volkskundliche Texte aus Mekka* (1972), which contains 14 recipes given to the author by a 70-year-old lady of his family, and I found all these recipes, with slight differences, in *Min Fann al-Tabkh al-Saʿudi*. The book contains very few recipes with European connotations; for example, a recipe called *rida al-walidayn* has an addition, *krima kramila* (p 502). But it also has chapters which I could only rarely find in other Arab cookbooks, such as one on mixed pickles (*mukhallal*) and traditional preserves. This book is a very valuable document on traditional Saudi cuisine.[8]

At a book fair during Ramadan 1992 in the Emirates and Oman, I saw many cookbooks on Gulf cuisine, for example H. and K. ʿAbid's *Sawani Khalijiyya* (n.d.), or a book called *Asnaf al-Tabkh al-Khaliji*, written by a group of Arab cooks ('Majmuʿa min al-tabbakhin al-ʿArab'), which has recipes from Saudi Arabia, Kuwait, Qatar and Iraq. Until now I have not found an Omani cookbook in Arabic, though there is a small booklet in English by M. S. Dorr, *A Taste of Oman. Traditional Omani Food. Authentic Recipes and How to Prepare Them*. We may hope that in the near future a book will be published on Omani cuisine too.

CONCLUSION

Arab cookbooks have changed in many ways during the past 40 years. They are nearly all addressed to working women, who have no time or opportunity to learn cooking from an older woman of their families. At least until the mid-1950s, and in a country like Algeria even longer, command of modern written Arabic may not have been so well developed that Arabic cookbooks could be sold. With a growing number of literate women, there has developed a market for cookbooks in Arabic. These books tried to be modern, Western and international. From the 1980s on, there has been a tendency in these books that could be called revivalistic. They no longer deal with an international cuisine, but concentrate on Arab food. They emphasize that the different traditional cuisines of different Arab countries and within these countries cannot be ignored, and they stress these differences. The authors hope to help in the search for an Arab identity and for an Iraqi, Saudi or Moroccan identity. So there is the same ideological development taking place in cookbooks that can be found within all aspects of Arab society.

Notes

1. I saw a cookbook in Arabic by the same author, entitled *Fann al-tabkh* (Rayes 1981), a reprint of a 1951 edition, but I had no opportunity to read it.
2. Alan Davidson informs me that an English version was published before the Arabic.
3. Perhaps this book has the same function as that of Nazira Nikola and Bahiya Othman, *Usul al-Tahi* (1988), mentioned by Sami Zubaida in this volume.
4. al-'Alawi (1990: 41) writes that the Shi'a in Iraq used to be called *Ahl al-mut'a wa'l-fazanjun*, 'people of temporary marriage and *fesenjan*'.
5. [On *fesenjan* in Iran, see Bromberger, and Fragner, 'Caucasus', in this volume. *Pacha* is presumably related to the Iranian and Turkish dish *kalleh-pacheh* (Eds.)]
6. The same could be said about the creation of a national Saudi costume.
7. See Zubaida in this volume.
8. For a more detailed interpretation of this book, see Mai Yamani's chapter in this volume. Mr L. Maunz, DAAD-lecturer in German at the University of Riyadh, informed me by letter (17 May 1992) about the recent publication of two more cookbooks in Saudi Arabia: Hafiz (1411) and 'Ali (1989).

10. Jewish Food in the Middle East

Claudia Roden

Jewish food in the Middle East is Sephardi cooking. I use the term in the broad sense of today, meaning not only the Jews whose ancestors lived in the Iberian peninsula but all those whose roots are around the Mediterranean and in the Middle East, including the Iraqi and Yemeni Jews.

Since the exodus of Jews from the Middle East and North Africa which began in the 1950s, the Sephardim have been in a majority in Israel and the West. French Jewry has taken a North African character since Algerian, Tunisian and Moroccan Jews have flooded in and Jewish restaurants and groceries in France are now full of Middle Eastern goodies. While the culture of Sephardi Jews is belittled in Israel, their cooking predominates. Almost all the caterers and professional cooks are oriental Jews, and public or institutional food and street food become more oriental every year. A few years ago I received a telephone call from my Hebrew publishers asking if I had a fish couscous recipe easy to make for 500 people. I asked if it was for a wedding and was told it was for the army: 'They refuse to continue with gefilte fish.'

This orientalization of the food is a reality which has not quite become accepted. At school children are taught in their textbooks that on Friday night the family meal is gefilte fish and chicken soup, when most are eating couscous or fish with egg and lemon sauce and rice. These are still called 'ethnic'. Some years ago I was told that children were so ashamed of their ethnic food that, when they were asked what they ate, they only admitted to *falafel* and 'steakim' and 'chipsim' and, when their mothers sent food for the harvest festival, the variety was extraordinary.

Dishes brought by immigrants change in a new environment. Sephardi cooking has not yet become standardized in the way the cooking of Ashkenazi Jews with roots in Eastern Europe has, because the last generations of Sephardi Jews have only recently left the old homelands, and the need to preserve family identity and the memory of parents and an old life that was happy is still strong. The Sephardim have not had two or three generations of integration like the Ashkenazim and their identity is still tied to a particular spot. Because of this, their cooking is regional.

Cooking is always that part of culture and tradition which survives the longest. The variable process of integration and 'modernization' of Sephardi cooking can be seen in France where the well-to-do urban North African Jews have adapted their recipes to suit fashionable French tastes (they make things lighter with less fat, use veal instead of mutton and not too much hot pepper) while others are still eating as they did when they lived in Berber mountain villages, buying offal and looking for cardoons in the markets.

In Israel standardization has occurred through mass production of food. Certain types of *kibbeh*, *borekas* (pies) and relishes, for instance, have become fast foods. In cafeterias and army kitchens a general mish-mash has evolved with young men from Iraq, Morocco, Yemen and elsewhere pooling the knowledge learnt from their mothers.

Compared to the cooking of Ashkenazi Jews, the home cooking of the Sephardim is immensely rich and varied, elaborate and sophisticated. Ashkenazi cooking had its roots in medieval Germany and it developed in the enclosed environment of the ghettos of Europe, the *shtetl*s (villages) of Poland, and the Pale of Settlement in Russia. It was the cooking of poverty and of a relentlessly persecuted people closed in on itself, with little contact with the non-Jewish population and the outside world. In contrast Sephardi Jews had an intimate contact and were deeply influenced by the world they lived in, which was the Islamic world.

With the exception of Christian Italy and Christian Spain all the lands where the Sephardim lived before the 17th century were under Islamic rule. Even the Jews of Spain came for the most part with the Arabs and were descended from Jews from countries which had been part of the Muslim conquests in the 8th century. In the 13th century the major concentrations of Jewish life moved to the Christian areas of the Iberian peninsula, and for almost 300 years most of Spanish Jewry developed within a Christian society. But when the Jews were expelled from Spain in 1492 most of them returned to the Islamic world, to North Africa and the lands of the Ottoman Empire.

Their range of dishes reflects the Sephardic experience in large urban communities as well as in backwaters, both very modest and very grand, in almost every country in the Middle East. Their very great culinary repertoire reflects the special symbiosis of the Jews with the Islamic world and with the complex environment of different ethnic and religious groups that existed in the area. Jews adopted local customs and ways of life. Like their neighbours, they entertained warmly, graciously and constantly. To honour a guest on a Jewish holiday or family celebration was the ultimate joy.

Festivities went on for ever. In Morocco, for instance, there were seven days of celebration for a birth or circumcision, seven days for a Barmitzvah, two weeks for a wedding; there was the day of showing the trousseau, the henna day, the day of the *mikvah* (bath), the day of the presents, the day of the fish. And after the week of celebrations, for an entire week the wife returned with her husband to visit different members of the family. Different specialities were made to mark each of these events.

Living as they did in a warm and sunny world with their lives orientated towards the outdoors, and much less fear of persecution, the Sephardim were the opposite of the Ashkenazim. Compared to their brethren, the Sephardim had a sunnier, more sensual, hedonistic personality, and that had a bearing on their eating and cooking. Good eating was a part of traditional Jewish life in the Middle East.

The cooking of the Sephardi Jews was that of the countries they lived in, but there were differences. The observance of the Jewish dietary laws or the laws of *Kashrut*, and the adaptation of certain dishes in accordance with them, meant that Jewish cooking had distinctive characteristics. Because of the prohibition on combining meat and dairy foods, the Jews used oil instead of butter or clarified butter for cooking (olive, corn, peanut, cotton-seed, argan and sesame oil were used). I was told that you could smell a Jewish home from the cooking fat.

Certain foods like pork, rabbit, hare, molluscs, crustaceans and fish without scales were forbidden, so substitutes were used. At Passover (*Pesach*), which commemorates the Exodus of the Jews from Egypt, Jews could not eat any grain, including wheat, that can be leavened. Instead, they used ground almonds, potato flour, ground rice, matzo meal and sheets of matzos, to make all kinds of cakes, pancakes, pies, dumplings and fritters. *Kibbeh*, usually made with cracked wheat and lamb, for instance, was prepared with ground rice, mashed potato or matzo meal. Among the ritual foods of Passover was a date and raisin paste called *harrosset*, which symbolized the Nile mud supposedly used by the Jews to build the pyramids. Only the Jews made this.

In Jewish families cooking revolved around *Shabbat* (Saturday), the day of rest, and religious festivals (*Yomim Tovim*) when special ritual and symbolic foods were prepared to glorify the occasions. Dishes adopted to mark the festive calendar acquired a few embellishments. During the *Shabbat*, which began 18 minutes before sunset on Friday and ended the following evening after dark when three stars could be seen, 'work', including cooking and baking, was prohibited. Before the *Shabbat* began, all preparations had to be completed for two rich festive meals, one for Friday evening, the other for Saturday lunch, and for a third simpler meal which was served before sunset on Saturday.

So that a dish could be eaten hot for the Saturday lunch, it was partly cooked and left to continue cooking on the lowest possible flame overnight. Traditionally it was cooked in the ashes of a fire, the pot covered with a blanket, or it was brought to the public oven, sealed with a flour and water paste. In North Africa, the *dafina* or *skhina*, as the dish was called, was composed of different foods cooked in the same large pot. Every community had its own special recipe using meat (often meat loaf), chicken, stuffed intestine, calf's foot, potatoes, sweet potatoes, chick-peas, beans, broad beans, rice and hard-boiled eggs in their shells. Some very original dishes resulted: for example, in Morocco a chicken stuffed with dates and marzipan, or with quince.

Jews also had some dishes which were different from the local cuisines. There was always something from another land. The Jews were particularly mobile. They moved westward with the Arabs from the 8th century then eastward in the 16th. Their cooking acquired an Iberian character as Spanish Jewry came to the fore between the 11th and 15th centuries and when Jewish exiles, expelled from Spain in the 15th century and from Portugal soon after, poured into North Africa and into the Ottoman Empire. When the empire became the centre of the Sephardic world, Ottoman dishes were adopted by the communities in all its outposts. The Jews had freedom of movement in the empire and they travelled from one corner to the other for trade. They had their own networks of communication, which helped to spread dishes and brought a kind of unity to the cooking of the communities in different countries.

In a way these dishes are a record and memory of the moments of glory in Sephardi history – of the centuries in Spain, when a synthesis of Muslim, Christian and Jewish cultures produced great and sophisticated styles of cooking, and of life in the Ottoman Empire, when many Jews attained high social positions, some of them attached to the court. There were court physicians and advisers, finance ministers and wealthy merchants, so that high standards of culinary refinement became part of Jewish traditions. While Ashkenazi culture came out of poverty-stricken village life, Sephardi culture was shaped by an elite that was grand, even aristocratic.

In the general Sephardi repertoire there are many Judaeo-Spanish specialities, but identifying medieval Spanish roots is difficult because the Ladino-speaking Jews gave Judaeo-Spanish names to everything. In parts of Turkey, like the city of Salonika, where the Jews from Spain were so numerous that their culture swamped that of the local Jews, even Jews who did not originate in Spain adopted Spanish-sounding names for their local dishes.

Among these dishes are the famous *huevos haminados* which are made by all oriental communities and which are now sold in the street in Israel as *hamine*; *borekitas*, *boyos* and *bulemas* which are made with various flaky, puff and paper-thin pastry and filled with spinach, cheese, onion and meat or with *gomo de berenjana*, aubergine and cheese, or *handrajo*, a mixture of aubergine, onion and tomato. *Marunchinos* and *almendrada* are little pastries made with ground almonds and egg white, *sansaticos* are nut-filled triangles flavoured with cinnamon and sprinkled with sesame seeds, *travados* are deep-fried turnovers filled with walnuts and soaked in syrup, *pinonate* are shreds of dough cooked in syrup with nuts, *dulce de naranja* are little rolls of orange peel threaded on a string and cooked in syrup, *dulce de bimbrio* quince paste.

Morocco is an example of a country with distinctive Jewish dishes, which are different in every city. Jewish cooking there is considered one of the four important cuisines, comparable to those of Marrakesh, Tetouan and Fez. But in many countries throughout the Mediterranean the Jewish communities were subdivided and the cooking reflected the various origins of their members. A long tradition among Sephardim allowed Jews leaving one area to establish their own unique congregation in their new community. These separate congregations persisted for centuries. Under these conditions different styles of cooking were also kept up.

In Egypt, for example, the old Arabized community, established early in the 'Hara' or Harat al-Yahud, which was built in 389, and the Suk al-Samak (the fish market) in Alexandria, and in a number of small towns and villages, was joined by several waves of immigrants. Jews came from the Yemen as early as the Middle Ages. The Spanish and Portuguese began to arrive in the 15th century by way of Turkey. They continued to speak old Castilian and their dialect, Ladino, into the 20th century. Immigrants came from Salonika, Smyrna and Istanbul, from Syria and Palestine, the Balkans, Corfu, Italy (mainly from Leghorn), Morocco, Tunisia and Algeria. There were also Ashkenazim from Eastern Europe. To the pool of dishes from all these countries was added a French touch. In Egypt, French had become one of the languages of the Sephardim during the 19th century when the Jewish community of France, with the financial assistance of the Rothschilds, installed and subsidized French secular schools, the Alliance Israélite Universelle, in the far corners of the Ottoman Empire.

The development of a Europeanized Jewish middle-class bourgeoisie, educated first by Jewish then by Christian and secular missions, which began with the building of the Suez Canal by the French, brought more European styles of cooking. But while all kinds of dishes appeared on the family everyday table, the same things always appeared at receptions and tea parties. There were always vine leaves, *sambusak*, *fila*, *kahk*, *konafa*, baklava, *ghorayebah*, *ma'moul* – and everything was beautifully crafted in the traditional time-honoured rolls, balls, triangles, cigars, coils and half-moons. Even though they were typically Middle Eastern, they were prepared with a special Jewish touch which, apart from the fat, had to do with flavouring and shape, thinness of pastry, and proportion of filling.

People often ask me if there is such a thing as Jewish food. Because these dishes have such a powerful hold on the emotions of Jews, are so much part of their ancestral memories and so tied to their culture and identity, I believe that they should be considered Jewish.

11. Food and Gender in a Yemeni Community

Ianthe Maclagan

This chapter looks at food as a way of exploring gender relations. It looks at male–female relations in themselves and in comparison and contrast to two other groups of relations: women's to each other and those between the two main endogamous groups, butchers and tribesmen. It concerns a town with a population of about 1000 in the western highlands of North Yemen; what I say is specific to that place, although there may well be similarities with other areas of Yemen. My fieldwork was carried out in 1981–3, and the present tense refers to that time.

Food is one of the main idioms through which gender relations are expressed. The women's world and the men's world meet at food. Men buy it, women prepare it. Men and women eat it but often separately: men in contexts of public display and women privately. They also eat together as a family group. Women's relation to food – what they are able to eat, how much of their time must be spent preparing it – is defined by their relation to men. Men's relation to food is also delimited by women, through whose labour the food must pass after purchase (or production) and before consumption.

Food is a focus of inter-gender tensions and conflicts. Women constantly use food in the struggle to keep or improve their positions. At the same time food expresses symbolic oppositions between the sexes.

MALE AND FEMALE OBLIGATIONS

Food is a key idiom and instrument for the definition and maintenance of gender obligations. This is reflected in the fact that when I asked a group of women what they quarrelled with their husbands about most they unanimously chorused 'Ghada'!' – 'Lunch!'

Men's and women's obligations to each other are defined largely in terms of food. Men owe women their subsistence. A woman has the theoretical right to be kept by men all her life: her father or, in his absence, her brother or nearest male relative if she is not married, and her husband if she is. If a woman complains to her father about her husband, he may tell her to put up with him on the grounds that he provides for her, gives her all that is necessary. This, from the father's point of view, is the defining feature of a satisfactory husband. The only possible ground on which women said a woman has the right to approach the *hakim* (Islamic judge) to seek a divorce is failure of the husband to maintain her.

Women's relation to food is defined by their relation to men. This applies both to what they are able to eat and to how much of their time must be spent preparing meals. Women who have no man in the household, or whose men are away, say they eat badly. They have no one to buy luxuries like fruit. Above all they do not usually eat meat. Meat is associated with men; women and children eating alone often eat meatless meals. Women's comments on the presence or absence of men (for example, those away working in Saudi Arabia) usually centre on food, and women often express the absence of a man in terms of eating poorly.

Food is so imbued with social meaning, so important in indicating who is providing for a woman, that it was difficult to talk about it in other terms. I tried to discuss food as nutrition with a pregnant friend. I suggested she ought to be eating some meat or chicken and greens. She replied by saying there was no one to buy her these things. She was staying in her room in her brother's house during her husband's absence. My attempt to discuss 'nutrition', as I saw it, met with no response in those terms, but with a description of whose protection she came under and of men's obligations to women as regards food. Food, and its type and where it came from, was seen in terms of social relationships between men and women, not her physical health.

Women's obligations towards men also centre round food. A woman's day is structured by obligations towards men concerning food preparation. Women get up in the morning before men to prepare tea and breakfast. After that the early part of the morning is a relatively unstructured period, when women do household chores as needed and sometimes visit neighbours. By 11 or so they start to prepare the main meal to be eaten in the middle of the day. If I was out visiting at this time of the morning, women would ask me where my husband's dinner was.

When my husband was away, women's attitude towards me in the later part of the morning changed dramatically, and, instead of asking where his dinner was, they would say: 'You haven't got any work to do in your house, come and sit and talk to me while I get the meal ready.' Thus women impose control on other women in terms of men; because they saw me as freer when my husband was away, I was freer. A man's presence structures the day and necessitates work at certain times.

It is taken for granted in the town that women prepare food for men; even men who have learned to cook during a bachelor existence while working in Saudi Arabia never do so at home. Cooking for a man is so defined as a woman's obligation that men continue to see it as one even if the woman is ill. Women emphasize how a husband will make them get up and cook him a meal however ill they are; they can lie down and rest once his belly is full.

FORMAL FOOD

Both the context and sequence of a formal meal and the quality and type of the ingredients need to be right. The most important meal of the day, the one to which guests are invited and round which expectations and obligations centre, is the midday meal *ghada'*. This is also the most predictable in content, with relatively little variation in the dishes served, particularly when male guests are present. The more formal and ceremonial the occasion, the more the dishes conform to a fixed pattern. The less formal a meal is, the less predictable the dishes offered; breakfast and supper are much more varied, depending on what is available, and snacks make use of the most varied range of foods of all. Breakfast and supper can be elaborated by the addition of extra foods and delicacies to make them special for guests, but *ghada'* is most special and most suitable for guests in its most typical form, with its established, predictable, necessary succession of dishes.

The first of these is *bint* (for *bint al-sahn*, 'daughter of the dish'), which consists of layered flaky pastry with melted clarified butter and honey. It offers the opportunity of honouring the guests by using real butter (instead of tinned vegetable ghee) and, less often because of its rarity and cost, Yemeni honey. *Bint* is rarely served except on special occasions when there are guests, and so helps to define a meal as ceremonial. This is followed by *shfut*, a dish made up of *luhuh* (a pancake-like bread from sorghum) soaked in buttermilk, eaten with onion greens or quarters of onions and tomatoes, or with a relish made by grinding garlic, chilli, tomato and spices together (*sahawiq*). Heated bread and milk with clarified butter (*dafi*) optionally follows, or – more rural and traditional – a porridge made with wheat. Then there is a dish of rice, plain or cooked with onion and tomato, often served with relish. Yemenis eat rice alone as a dish in itself rather than a background to other dishes. Then comes the *hulba*, the central dish of the meal which leads up to the meat. This is the dish called *silta* in some parts of Yemen. It consists of a froth of ground, soaked, whipped-up fenugreek seeds served poured over a meat-stock base with a few vegetables in it.

For a ceremonial meal, the dishes may be laid out ready in a room into which the men go to eat, but the *hulba* is always brought in bubbling hot. The host stirs in relish and extra meat stock with a piece of bread before the *hulba* is eaten by dipping bread into the dish. Before the *hulba* is finished, the meat is distributed by the host, who chooses one or more pieces to place in front of each guest. The quantity of meat expresses the host's generosity and status, and honours the guests. In this way it is the climax and the most important part of the meal, while the *hulba* is central as being the precursor of the meat and a much-loved national dish, essential to a proper dinner. They are linked by the *hulba*'s containing the stock from cooking the meat. Some of this stock (*maraq*) may also be served separately in glasses for adding to the *hulba* or offering to honoured guests.

It is noteworthy that it is a man who makes the final adjustment to the main dish, not the women who prepared it. It is as if he appropriates the dish in order to give it. Men also often shout peremptorily for the *hulba* to be brought, another way of claiming ownership of it. Male control, especially over the meat element, masks the fact that women do the work and emphasizes the male as host offering the meal.

After the meat, orange and apple quarters are usually served, and later, with the meal cleared away or in another room, *qahwa* (coffee-husk infusion, spoken of as *qufl al-ghada'*, 'the lock of the meal') to round it off.

Men eat a formal meal extremely fast. Each course, laid out on the floor with the men all squatting round, disappears in a few minutes during which all attention is focused on eating, with no pausing for conversation or any comments on the food. Perhaps this helps the illusion that the food is offered by the host from nowhere, whereas comment on how it tastes, who made it and how, would shift attention to what has been kept hidden. One dish is barely finished before the next is called for. The main dish, especially, is demanded with shouts of '*hulba!*'. The more ceremonial the meal, the faster it is eaten. If there is a large number of guests, they may be served in shifts. A celebratory meal attended by men may be over, with the guests dispersed, in 15 minutes, so the significance of the hospitality offered for the occasion is concentrated very directly into the food, without conversation or companionability.

Formal meals are offered by men to men, but prepared by women for men. During all this time, women are busy behind the scenes, while only men publicly consume the display the women have produced. Women work out of sight, giving dishes to boys or men of the household to take in or bringing them to the door in answer to shouts for the next dish. The male appearance of independence and dignified self-sufficiency is maintained by the food's appearing as if the man was not dependent on a butcher to kill the meat and a woman to cook it – handed in from nowhere.

For a big meal, women have friends and neighbours in to help, and the kitchen is all bustle and rush. The women have no time to sit down or eat, and will eat what they want later, if they still feel like it. This does not necessarily mean they eat only the men's leavings; they can put whole dishes aside for themselves. But what the women eat often misses out a course or two of the men's meal, and is not served with the same formality and whisking on and off of dishes in strict succession. They eat calmly, almost casually, without the same intensity of concentration.

Men's ceremonial meals mark occasions such as weddings, visits by important men or officials from other areas, and the return of pilgrims from the Hajj. They are a form of display, a public show of hospitality linked to the expression of maleness. Hospitality is a kind of display of maleness, of male power and generosity and success. Women do not eat publicly and their meals are not a vehicle for the display of male hospitality; men do not provide expensive ingredients for women to offer each other. Female hospitality, enacted by women for women, has a different basis, depending on women's allocation of resources over which they have some control, and is exemplified by snacks, small gifts and reciprocal exchanges.

BALADI FOOD

Another aspect of what constitutes proper food, besides the content and sequence of meals, is the value placed upon locally produced food. This *baladi* food is greatly esteemed and is always considered to taste better than imported substitutes. It is much more expensive. It is also scarcer; most *baladi* food is not sold on the market. Local eggs and bananas are smaller but sold at the same price as their imported counterparts. Yemeni honey sells at £40 (YR300) for a whisky-bottle full. It is so normal for *baladi* produce to cost more that when Yemen finally started oil production, filling-station staff joked, 'It'll cost you more for *baladi* petrol, of course.'

Local foods are also imbued with a value besides taste. They are mandatory in some ritual situations: a woman after childbirth should have *baladi* honey and clarified butter (*samn*) to strengthen her, while newborn babies have clarified butter smeared in their mouths and on their noses, supposedly to get them used to it. These foods are considered almost magical, or at least, in many cases, ritually efficacious. *Baladi* clarified butter is considered healing and purifying, has many ritual uses, and is regarded as something of a cure-all.

The aesthetic and symbolic weight carried by *baladi* foods affects the demands men make upon women. Many ingredients for the proper meal are difficult to get in their traditional, *baladi* form except as part of household production. Valued food depends on women to produce or process it. Imported substitutes – tinned vegetable ghee and powdered milk – can be bought, but the taste is not as good. It is possible to buy local buttermilk and clarified butter, but only in small quantities and at considerable expense. Similarly, women's labour improves the quality of *luhuh* over that made with machine-milled sorghum (women say it has less tendency to fall apart). Hand-milled wheat was also preferable, but that particular choice between the products of female labour and shop-bought substitutes has finally been settled in favour of bought and electrically milled grain.

Women vary in how much of the household's food they produce and prepare, and how much is bought. Some households have a more rural type of economy, getting agricultural produce from lands outside the town worked by sharecroppers or men of the family. Women may do some processing of produce for consumption, for example picking over and cleaning sorghum in preparation for grinding.

Patterns of production and consumption are changing very rapidly. The list of imported foods available in the town is almost endless. Some which more obviously replace or supplement local produce are eggs and frozen chickens. But the changes are not yet complete, and the products of women's labour, offered as part of male hospitality, enhance male prestige.

FOOD AND FEMALE PROTEST

Men depend on women both for everyday food and for the ability to play host, to receive guests and offer them food in suitable fashion. This gives women an opportunity for leverage. Food is not only definitional of expectations of women, it is also the area where they can most effectively express protest. Accounts of quarrels often involved incidents where women had failed to fulfil male expectations in this regard; they had not provided appropriate food on time or had expressed their feelings by the way they served food, particularly to guests: slopping it down in front of them or spilling it over them.

The clearest example of protest is when women return to their fathers out of anger or dissatisfaction with their husbands. This is an everyday occurrence; almost every woman leaves at least once in a marriage, and many lose count of how many times they have done so. It is a woman's right. It is inconvenient and embarrassing for her husband: he cannot so much as get a glass of tea for himself. Depending on what other female labour is available to him, he may be quite helpless, may have to take his meals in the public restaurant, and cannot offer hospitality to guests. The fact that women are the sole preparers of food gives them this possibility.

WOMEN'S RELATIONS WITH EACH OTHER

The preparation of food for men can be a source of great effort and anxiety, when women join forces and work as a team to produce the required display for men, or activate their networks of friends and neighbours to help in a crisis. Surprised by unexpected visitors, a woman will borrow extra pots from neighbours, or send over a chicken to cook quickly on a gas ring if she has only a clay oven herself. Teams of women co-operate to produce a big feast for several successive sittings of men.

Besides co-operating in producing food for men, women give food to each other. A large part of women's friendship with one another, their hospitality, and the networks of exchange and obligation they are involved in are expressed through food. The ways in which this is done contrast with the expression of women's relations with men. Friendship and neighbourly relations are maintained by women giving or sending rounds of bread to each other. A woman eating alone, without a man, may be sent small bowls of food ready to eat. Women tie bread in a cloth and throw it from rooftop to rooftop, or hand it across from window to window. Gifts of bread help maintain neighbourly relations, and are reciprocated on the day when the recipient bakes.

Women who produce food, those with a cow or those just outside the town who have space to cultivate vegetable gardens, will give small presents to a departing visitor – a few white radishes with their leaves, herbs, some buttermilk, or eggs, for example. Others give bread, particularly the special kinds made from various grains. When women visit others after childbirth the standard present is a couple of tins of fruit, a luxury item which may be served to guests. Poor women save the tins of fruit and recycle them as gifts when they in turn visit others. So the same actual tins circulate as tokens of reciprocity: food symbolizing women's support for each other at the commonest life-crisis.

Like all visiting and hospitality, women's visiting among themselves is closely bound up with food and drinks. Women make tea or *qahwa* or both when they get up in the morning, and fill a vacuum flask so it is always ready to be offered to any visitor who may drop in. It would seem awkward and inhospitable to have to start making it from scratch. The earlier equivalent of the now ubiquitous vacuum flask was a kettle kept warm in the corner of a charcoal brazier. *Qahwa* (literally 'coffee') is the drink known in many parts of Yemen as *qishr*, prepared from coffee husks, with or without some of the coffee beans. In this area dried ginger, cinnamon and sugar are added. Tea is made with sugar in the pot and is often spiced with cloves and cardamom. Other spices are sometimes added to tea and *qahwa* according to individual taste. A guest, whether male or female, is always offered tea, *qahwa* or a choice on arrival.

When women make the prescribed visits at life-crises, going to sit with a woman who is sick or after childbirth or bereavement, they carry vacuum flasks of tea and *qahwa* with them. Groups of veiled women going to such an occasion, carrying flasks, are a familiar sight in the town. This eases the burden on the women of the host household, who are receiving large numbers of visitors, and expresses women's concern and solidarity. Women support each other in helping to provide hospitality for social occasions among women, as they do in preparing big meals for serving to men.

SNACKS

In the earlier part of the morning, when women visit each other more casually and often drop in on neighbours, or go for a walk and drop in on friends or acquaintances along the way, tea and *qahwa* are always offered, and very often a snack, called *ksu'*, which may be served any time between breakfast and the midday meal. Men are usually out of the house at this time. Women's hospitality towards each other is typically expressed in the serving of this informal snack. It contrasts with the formal dinner described above, which is characteristic of men's hospitality towards men. It is easy to miss the significance of women's snacks. Compared to main meals, they are unobtrusive and seem casual, almost incidental. Yet they are important, both in nutritional terms and because of women's control of certain foodstuffs and use of them to offer hospitality and enjoyment to other women.

Snacks contrast with main meals prepared for men and offered by men to their guests in their unpredictability of both content and timing. Whereas the dishes of a formal lunch are predetermined, the range of possible snack food is very wide. It includes a number of foods only occasionally eaten or only seasonally available, such as lentils cooked in their pods, raw peas, pumpkin and sweet potatoes, which have no place in formal meals and which women eat as treats. Produce which the woman has acquired as part of her rights over land, such as various boiled pulses in their pods or boiled heads of sorghum, may be served. Women with gas ovens bake little fancy shiny *ka'k* from enriched dough to offer to visitors.

Snacks often consist of foods over which women have particular control: the produce of their labour such as *luhuh* and buttermilk, home-made cottage cheese, foods they have grown in a vegetable garden, or fancy baking. Sometimes the food may come from or through men, but women own and give it, as men do meals. Snacks rarely include meat, though one woman offered me a large quantity for a morning snack, explaining with pride: 'We slaughter.' Bought luxury foods such as oranges may be offered, but again more rarely. Snacks typically use the foods women produce for the household, plus any interesting extras available. These snacks will be eaten by women of the house, their children and any women visitors, sitting round without moving to another room.

The contrasts between snacks and meals reflect those between women's relations to men and to each other. Snacks are served by women to women and children and women visitors; they include a wide variety of foods; they are eaten informally in the room where the women were sitting anyway. The atmosphere is relaxed and informal and may include chatting; only one food may be served, or several dishes at once. Formal meals are prepared by women but offered by male hosts to male guests, consist of a limited variety of foods including, most importantly, meat, and are served in a different room, with a formal atmosphere and no talking; and the dishes are served in an established sequence. Formal meals happen at a set time of day, while snacks are fitted in round women's work. Snacks happen in the morning when men are out of the house; men return home for the midday meal, which may be held up till they appear. Men provide, or should provide, the ingredients for ceremonial and family meals. If women obtain other food, from men, from gifts, from their families, from their gardens, by baking, or by spending their own money, they can use it for female hospitality.

Women choose their friendships. Although considerably constrained by geographical proximity, they do choose some rather than others for close associates from among available neighbours, and also have quarrels, break off relations and re-establish them, according to wish. Women's relationships of friendship and support, which are freely chosen (within limits), are expressed by fluid and variable food-giving. Women's obligations to men, more rigidly defined by economic and legal dependence, are expressed in the more rigid food patterns of set meals.

Women control bread production, deciding when to bake, getting into patterns of exchange with neighbours to save everybody baking every day, using bread to make and keep links with others, giving it away as charity, circulating it from woman to woman across their own territory of adjacent windows and roofs. I speak of 'bread', but a large vocabulary distinguishes dozens of different types according to the grains used (wheat, barley, sorghum, millet, maize, lentils and combinations); whether leavened with yeast, fermented, or not; and the method of cooking – as a pancake on a griddle, spread by hand on the inside of the cylindrical oven, or preformed and applied there on a cushion. It could be said that male giving and hospitality is symbolized and exemplified by meat, female by bread.

FOOD, TRIBESMEN, BUTCHERS, WOMEN

Relations between the two main endogamous groups in the town, tribesmen and butchers, show parallels to those between men and women. This has been argued by Gerholm (1980), who suggests that in terms of the idiom of traditional relations between groups, tribesmen are to butchers as men are to women. Gerholm elaborates his argument using the idiom of the *janbiyya*, the dagger which tribesmen carried upright in the middle of their belts, and which, as he says, Westerners inevitably perceive as a phallic symbol. The fact that butchers were not allowed to wear these daggers reflected their status as people who were not able to defend themselves. They were considered weak and deficient and were traditionally protected by the tribesmen and served them. As Gerholm points out, this has similarities with the position of women, who are considered weaker, are explicitly under the protection of men, and serve them. Gerholm suggests that the butcher is symbolically seen as physically, socially and sexually weaker than the tribesman.

I shall use the symbolic and practical connotations of food, instead of weapons, to develop Gerholm's argument further and to explore more parallels between male/female relations and tribesman/butcher relations. In both cases food plays a major part in the way the difference between the two groups is defined and expressed.

'Butchers' is the commonest designation in the town for the group which includes those who slaughter and sell meat and do other dirty or polluting work such as tanning leather, besides serving others as barbers and wedding attendants, and selling bread and food, which it is honourable to provide free as part of hospitality. As proper hospitality is associated with and confers 'maleness', so the shameful selling of the basics of hospitality is associated with the symbolically unmanned 'deficient' group. In this town, butchers are seen as the typical members of this group, which numbers about a third of the town's population. The word for butchers is that most often used to designate the group as a whole, while both butchers and tribespeople explain by reference to slaughtering why they could not marry each other.

Buying meat is also associated with maleness. On market day, butchers set up tripods and hang up freshly slaughtered animals, then cut off the meat and sell it till it is all gone, before going on to slaughter the next animal. This all happens very fast, while a crowd of customers presses round, competing for the butcher's attention; the less successful see the whole animal disappear before their turn comes. All the meat is the same price (in 1982, YR40 [£5] a kilo for beef, YR60 for mutton) and the composition of each portion is a matter for negotiation; the customer has to reject bad bits and demand others. The butcher slaps chunks of meat from various parts of the animal on to his scales, and then holds them up to balance suspended on a chain. Sometimes it was not clear, at least to me, which customer's portion was being made up, and I watched eagerly only to see it handed to someone else. The butcher, low status by definition, has it in his power to decide the quality of every man's dinner.

Buying meat needs manly firmness. The whole market is a male arena, but the huddle shouting and arguing, pushing and competing for attention around each butcher's tripod is even more so. Arguing and bargaining, holding one's own and standing up for oneself, embody manliness. The need to be able to defend oneself is not only symbolic; butchers and their customers have been known to come to blows.

There is a contradiction in the cultural emphasis and high value given to meat, while those who sell, profit from and control the distribution of this most valued food are thereby defined as low status – even while they grow rich, eat well together with their families, and have 20 people hanging on their next cut of the knife on market day.

Tribesmen still despise the butchers, almost never intermarry with them, and consider that they are there to serve. They see this as a universal natural order: 'The butchers serve the tribesmen all over the world,' asserted a tribal informant. The suggestion that tribesmen see butchers as like women is borne out by accusations heard from tribesmen that, in disputes, butchers take refuge behind their womenfolk and on rooftops, women's territory.

However, the reality in the town is now somewhat different. The butchers are a prosperous, powerful group. With increased wealth in the town and its hinterland, butchers have done well out of high meat consumption. On market days, as many as 15 slaughter. Butchering is very profitable, and many butchers are prosperous. Their status as 'deficient' is not borne out by their prosperity. They are growing rich off their despised occupation. The most luxurious and expensive new house belongs to a butcher family. In a society where display of wealth has become increasingly important, they are well placed to compete.

They are also strong in the town in that they are strongly interconnected by marriage and kin ties, more closely so than the tribesmen. This directly results from their being prohibited from marrying outside their own group, whereas the tribesmen are linked in marriage with villages in the rest of the mountain as well as further afield. The butchers have less far-flung, more concentrated networks.

Disadvantaged in status within the traditional framework, they have been quick to turn to new sources of wealth and advancement, such as the ownership of the town's electricity supply. Their strength arises from their very disadvantages, combined with the opportunities offered by the recent influx of wealth, of which they have been able to take full advantage.

WOMEN AND BUTCHERS COMPARED

Butchers and women are similar in that both groups are seen as weak and serving a more powerful group. Men see women, and tribesmen see butchers, as there to serve them. Some of the services provided by butchers are, like women's, connected with food; others are analogous to the tasks of women because they are personal services.

Women are frequently described as 'weak' in comparison to men. This implies a social rather than physical weakness; women's traditional workload in fact involves heavy labour and requires strength and stamina for load carrying and grinding of grain. Women are defined as socially incapacitated, unable to do certain things for themselves, dependent on male protection and male representatives. Their weakness is especially defined in terms of lack of mobility, having to sit at home. The physical restrictions on women's mobility are paralleled by the restrictions on marriage and social mobility for butchers.

Both women and butchers have avenues of action open to them because they are supposed to be 'weak' and in the position of servers. In different ways, women and butchers do gain power through their special positions with regard to food. By their code of shame, men and tribesmen create a monopoly of work and therefore give some power to butchers and women, by making themselves dependent. The supposedly subservient position of butchers gives them new economic opportunities which are allowing them to escape from their subservience.

Food is a source of women's power because they prepare it. It would be as unthinkable for a man to prepare a meal as for a tribesman to slaughter. This power is expressed at the extreme by men's fear of being poisoned; this is not a common occurrence but is a threat women make as an ultimatum – for example, to try to prevent a husband taking a second wife. In parallel, the antagonized tribal neighbours of the butcher woman who runs the restaurant claimed she poisoned the customers, perhaps expressing some of the threat they felt from this shameful, very profitable enterprise.

In more everyday terms, women's control over food preparation means they control men's ability to offer hospitality. Men's hospitality is closely linked with ideas of manhood. Thus women, by refusing to enable men's hospitality, or by doing it in a shameful way, such as slopping food over a guest, have power to undermine the manhood of men. Because women enable men to be hosts, men are vulnerable through women's control over food.

Butchers control the quality of meat each man eats, where meat is the food which expresses maleness and male hospitality. Butchers, like women, have power over men's ability to be hosts, a power also associated with maleness. They also are the controlling centre of a scene of public confrontation and competition where men's masculinity, their manly ability to stand up for themselves, is at stake. In this situation, butchers embody a threat to the manhood of tribesmen. To be manly, not to need protection, being one's own representative, is the antithesis of women's position, and also of the traditional position of butchers when, in the past, they were not allowed to wear daggers and were seen as unable to defend themselves.

The relation between the women of the different status groups is very different from that of the men. This is symbolized by their different relation to bread: whereas men can get bread only by buying it from butchers or having it made by women of their family, women can exchange bread among themselves, across the boundaries of the tribesman/butcher dichotomy. In day-to-day life, the distinctions between women are blurred. Butcher women visit tribeswomen and are visited by them. Neighbour relations and proximity are all-important for women and override status-group considerations in social situations. The food exchanges described also link tribal and butcher women.

The butchers have power to undermine or validate the manhood of the group which is held to be identified with the manhood denied to the butcher group. Women are absent from this scene, and among themselves blur these distinctions. Their relations are typified by the reciprocity of bread-giving rather than the competitive struggle for meat.

The 'strong' say they protect the 'weak' who serve them. However far this is true, they are also dependent on the weak because they need their services. This gives the weak certain kinds of power – not equal power, because different in kind. This is true of both butchers and women: in both cases the group culturally defined as superior depends on the other group for essential services. In the case of the butchers, the power of the servers has got out of hand, as it were, and escaped the boundaries of the traditional situation, because of new economic opportunities which they have been free to take up, having no ideology of 'shame' to debar them. For women this is not so, and their power remains relative and limited, the power of the weak who can withdraw their labour and subvert the services they provide, but cannot escape altogether from the boundaries which constrain them.

For butchers, some of the restrictions, most importantly the marriage bar, have remained in place, but material and economic power relations are no longer in line with the symbolic structures. Butchers can get rich either by exploiting their traditional disadvantage and selling meat, or by investing their capital and taking up new opportunities. Women's position does not give them that material, economic base for a subversion which is not only within the system but partly transcends and escapes from it.

Economic change will not necessarily be to the advantage of women as it has been to that of butchers. It does not offer them a route to economic power; rather the reverse. The tendency is for the products of women's labour to be replaced with bought commodities. If female labour can more easily be replaced with money, this may give women less of the leverage which depends on their indispensable hard work.

Gaining more leisure may lead to women having less of the scope to manoeuvre which comes from being indispensable servers. Yet women place a very high value on leisure and rest from exhausting labour. Their leisure goes into enjoyable female socializing and the creation and maintenance of networks exchanging information, support and services. How these changes will work out for women remains to be seen.

12. You Are What You Cook: cuisine and class in Mecca

Mai Yamani

Mecca, being the holiest city of Islam and the direction, *Qibla*, towards which all Muslims turn to pray, has throughout Islamic history attracted pilgrims from different countries. And some of these pilgrims have, for various reasons, settled in the city after the performance of the Hajj – the fifth and last of the Islamic 'pillars' or duties. These multi-racial settlers have obviously brought with them a variety of customs and traditions, including culinary traditions; with time, these have been adapted to the local taste, gradually adding to the collection of what may be termed 'Meccan' food. Thus, dishes became no longer labelled Indian, Indonesian, Egyptian or Turkish; the rich variety of cuisine is now proudly referred to as 'Meccan'. Some names of dishes remained unchanged from the original language, for example, *laddu*, a sweet of Indian origin. Others were modified in order to sound Meccan-Arabic: e.g. *zurbiyan* (buryani, an Indian rice dish). Yet others are known by the name of their country of origin, for instance *ruz Bukhari* (Bukhara rice). Although Meccan culture, like its food, is distinctly heterogeneous, the various ethnic groups all identify with the local Arab tribe of Quraish and with the local Sunni doctrine (specifically the Shafi'i and Hanafi schools of Islamic law) as a focus of identity.

Throughout history, Mecca has been a focal point for the whole Muslim world. And this was perhaps even more the case during the 1980s, with the Islamic revival and the increase in consciousness of Islamic identity. Nevertheless, Meccans have also been conscious of their own multi-ethnic origin and heterogeneous culture, especially when compared with the homogeneous, isolated, tribal desert culture of the interior of the peninsula, the Najd. Their multi-ethnic background is reflected in music, architecture, patterns of dress and the cuisine; this latter is distinguished by relatively complex recipes in comparison with the pure desert cuisine.

The social background, education and outlook of Meccans was urban
in character and their way of life has always been subject to the influence
of other cultures. Not only did the pilgrimage bring Muslims from different
countries, but also Meccans have travelled extensively since the 19th
century and sent their children to study in other Islamic countries. This
open and urban character distinguishes Meccan cuisine from its bedouin
tribal counterpart. It is noteworthy that only since the late 1930s, and
more especially since the beginning of the 1950s, have Meccans begun to
develop contacts with non-Muslim cultures. This is as a result of the
discovery of oil and the consequent development of the Saudi economy
which, in turn, led both to an increase in travel to Western countries and
to the influx of large numbers of Westerners working within Saudi Arabia.
But such contact comes about only when Meccans are outside their city,
since Mecca continues to retain the unique quality of being reserved solely
for Muslims. Non-Muslims can neither visit the city nor live there. This
is, Meccans explain, in order to preserve the sanctity of the place.

Economically, Mecca (together with its neighbouring cities, Jeddah
and Medina) being a centre of trade and benefiting from the pilgrimage,
was always more prosperous than the other regions in the peninsula (today's
Saudi Arabia) until the discovery of oil in the eastern region (in the 1930s).
Prior to the discovery of oil, the western province, the Hijaz, earned
relatively substantial revenues from the tax paid by every pilgrim, from
other income from pilgrims, and from international trading centred on
the Red Sea ports.

Until the discovery of oil, Mecca and Jeddah were the richest cities in
Arabia, and until the late 1930s the Hijaz region was an international
marketplace with a tradition of international trade. From the beginning of
the century until the 1930s, commerce was almost entirely based on imports
from India. Other imports came from Singapore, Indonesia or Ethiopia
(coffee), from Red Sea ports and from the Gulf – for example dates from
Basra. Trade was entirely within the Eastern world, from other Muslim
countries. Mecca exported nothing. However, following the 1930s,
specifically after the Second World War, most imports originated in the
West. Even those commodities previously bought from the East and still
available there (such as rice) began to come from the West, e.g. Holland
and the USA.

Aside from its economic background, Mecca has been viewed by
Muslims as being 'otherworldly', not quite of this earth. It is referred to
as *Makka al-mukarrama*, 'the honourable Mecca'. Everything that happens
there is viewed as special. Good deeds are multiplied when performed in

that place, and one prayer in the Great Mosque equals 1000 prayers at any other mosque except at the Prophet's Mosque in Medina. (This is according to a hadith.) Meccans believe that it is as a chosen people that they have been born in the Holy Places; Muslims from other countries, according to this belief, come to receive its blessing and some have settled there. Thus, Mecca today confers a strong symbolic significance.

Following the unification of Saudi Arabia and the foundation of the modern state in 1932, the barriers between the provinces (of which there were previously four) were to be eliminated. But inevitably the distinction between people on the basis of their city of origin has remained. Being Meccan today symbolizes the identity of a people who view themselves as distinct from others. But Meccans also exist in the context of their country, Saudi Arabia; for this is how they generally perceive themselves, how they speak of themselves, and how they are understood. Meccan culture, or specifically Meccan food, generally merges with their national identity, for example when with expatriates. In this situation Meccan food would be referred to as Saudi food. This is because the Saudis internally and externally need to assert their distinctiveness from the non–Saudi, namely outsiders. People are conscious that their mode of conduct is specific to them as Saudi Arabians as opposed to Westerners. Thus, there is since the 1980s a nationalistic side to food and behaviour coexisting alongside regional consciousness. This regional consciousness is based and expressed through 'ways of belonging' to individual cities. Meccan food comprises one of the 'ways of belonging' to the symbolic identity of Mecca.

This chapter examines the significance of food to an elite group, most of whom, although originally from Mecca, are for economic and social reasons no longer resident in the city. The big, successful merchant families, the families of 'ulema' (religious teachers) or of pilgrim guides (mutawwifin), have left Mecca for Jeddah, the commercial centre of the Hijaz and indeed of Saudi Arabia (as distinct from the political centre, Riyadh). The group studied are for the most part a merchant elite, although a few hold government posts. Since the 1960s Jeddah has been the main residential centre for the elite of Mecca. Thus Mecca is today inhabited by foreign Muslims together with indigenous people who maintain the community. An informant explained to me that throughout history, since the days of the Prophet, Mecca has exported its own people. Hence, the group studied are Meccans who are no longer resident in the Holy City; nevertheless, they increasingly desire to be identified with it. For those who have left Mecca during the past two or three decades or for those of the generation that has never lived in the Holy City, the mere past identification with it conveys a sense of pride, of group identity and group cohesion.

Food for the larger group originating from Mecca – 'Meccans', as they are called – presents a symbolic expression of a sense of identity and belonging. Food, the way it is cooked, presented and consumed, serves to distinguish and identify a group of people who have a clear consciousness of factors which make them different from others. Furthermore, food distinguishes the elite from those in other sections of society; it serves as a status indicator. For this group of Meccans, who are described as 'the families' (al-'awa'il), 'the face of the people' (wujaha'), or 'the example of the people' (a'yan), the consumption, quality, quantity and presentation of food is significant. Minutest details to distinguish their status are observed especially when in public, at formal events. As their public image is defined, so their status and social boundary are also defined. Status is closely connected to the concept of tajammul which means 'seemliness', appearing comme il faut, 'honouring', 'adding credit', 'whitening the face' of the family. One way of exhibiting tajammul is through food; a well-defined code of behaviour, which is known and shared by the elite studied therein providing a sense of togetherness.

There are 'refined' and elegant ways of presenting food, for example: Meccan meat and vegetables are cut into very small pieces, nothing is presented in large chunks except when the whole lamb is used for special occasions. This is again a contrast between the urban and the bedouin cuisine – the latter is presented in larger pieces.

There are specific rules for serving the guest, al-mubashara, the appropriate formal language, set expressions and set compliments exchanged, for example, between the host and his guest to thank for a meal or to invite the guests to the dining table. An elaborate vocabulary of words and phrases exists to describe the presentation of food; known only to members of this elite social group, who pride themselves on knowing these things. The Meccan families are conscious of following the rules of 'good taste', which are closely connected to the demonstration of the prevalent standards of generosity.

The significance of food as a demonstrator of status and cultural distinctiveness has become much more important since the beginning of the 1980s; this is a consequence of a situation of rapid increase in social and geographical mobility due to an economic upheaval that started in the 1960s and gained momentum with the oil boom in 1973 and the greater boom in 1979. Additional changes have come about as a result of contact with Western cultures. During the 1980s, as a reaction to the events of previous years, people became relatively less receptive to change and more preoccupied with consolidating their position, defining their identity more clearly, and sharpening their sense of belonging. The 1980s was a period of competition leading to status consciousness, allied with re-emphasis on identity through religious and traditional practices.

There is a consciousness of their identity in its different forms or levels: Islamic, Saudi Arabian, or at the level of cities – for example, Meccan. During the 1980s, many 'traditions' were revived, some modified, others even invented. As one informant explained: 'If we do not hold on now to our traditions, to our roots, they will be lost!'

Following the situation of rapid and bewildering changes in the social, political, economic and religious contexts of the larger society, the social group studied seeks continuity, legitimacy and cohesion of the group through the observance of strict 'traditional' and religious practices. And so, in the context of food, they also derive and express a sense of identity through specific dishes, a special combination of spices, the manner of presentation, the consumption of food and in the timing of a meal.

Ceremonies have been re-created from the past, distinguished through traditional objects and traditional food. Certain ceremonies that had disappeared during the past three decades or so have returned, sometimes in a modified form – for example, the *ghumra* henna ceremony during the event of marriage, the party held for the naming of a child on the seventh day (*al- sabu'*) or the annual commemoration of a death (*hawl*). In these and other ceremonies, food is a central object of the rituals. In the henna ceremony, special silver trays called *al-ma'ashir* carry the traditional Meccan sweets, namely *laddu* and *labaniyya*, which are milk-based, *halawa tahiniyya* (sesame-based), *harissa* (puréed meat and wheat served with sugar), *mahjamiyya* and traditional Meccan breads *shurayk* and *ka'k* – as well as Meccan goat cheese and olives. These are served at room temperature and displayed in a prominent place. The combination of sweets, bread and cheese is ordinary food in everyday life, but during the henna ceremony it acquires a symbolic significance: it symbolizes the past, days when such foods were luxuries.

The re-emphasis on tradition is nowadays closely linked to conspicuous consumption. A well-presented meal is very large and costly. With wealth, people are able to organize social occasions at which they display grand meals and demonstrate the rules of generosity and propriety. However, it is important to note that wealth does not on its own determine or establish status; traditionally acknowledged criteria for status are also significant. Perhaps at the beginning of the oil boom, wealth freely available became something of a social leveller. Now, however, people are returning to traditional themes in order to be distinguished. In the 1980s, people began to move from the field of quantity to that of quality. Hence, for example, a plate consisting of fava beans, *ful midammas*, prepared with a sauce of clarified butter, cumin and lemon juice, stands out in a grand meal from many other Eastern and Western dishes. This traditional Meccan dish and others are special because they either comprise or symbolize a creation linked to the past and therefore convey a sense of continuity to the social group. The revival during the 1980s of traditional Meccan food (food that had almost disappeared during the previous two decades) also legitimized new activities: the new way of life that these Meccans began to experience which required structure and definition in order to be controllable by the people themselves.

Food distinguishes events in the life of this community for both those in Mecca and those outside it. Thus there is a traditional Meccan dish or a combination of dishes for every different event. Shared collectively by the social group, the food becomes a strong symbol of unity for them. In this manner, the people are distinguished, the events are also defined: people clearly identify themselves as Meccans in a period of increased consciousness. With the general re-emphasis and strengthening of religious practices, numerous religious events or gatherings have been revived and are distinguished, in addition to prayer, by food. For example, a traditional meal of a whole roast lamb (or several lambs) on rice with the accompanying side dishes, which is served to mark the end of the celebration of the birth of the Prophet, the *mawlid*; a special sweet dish (*'ashuriyya*), made from ten different kinds of grain, which is prepared to commemorate the 10th of Muharram (*'ashur*). There is special food prepared only during Ramadan. The latter consists mainly of a dish of barley soup, *ful midammas*, cheese and meat pastries (*sambusak*), and meat on a bed of bread immersed in stock flavoured with cardamom and covered with yoghurt (*fatta*). Particular to Ramadan are sweet dishes such as filo pastries filled with almonds and immersed in honey (*gatayyif*). Special food is used to celebrate the Hijri Muslim New Year. Milk, fruit and a particular local goat cheese are considered best to start the New Year since these represent purity. Of course, today these products are abundant all over the country, where every common or exotic fruit is flown in from various parts of the world, but still they remain significant in order to celebrate the event. A special dish marking the feast at the end of Ramadan (*'id al-fitr*) is a sweet dish (*dubyaza*) made from whole, dried, cooked dates, dried apricots, dried figs, sultanas and almonds. A roast lamb is also cooked (*al-minazzala*) for this occasion; it is cut into pieces (prior to cooking) rather than presented whole. The other feast following the pilgrimage (*'id al-hajj*) is distinguished by a local variety of pastries filled either with dates or with almonds (*ma'mul*), and shortbread flavoured with cardamom (*ghurayyiba*). (Dates grow in Medina and almonds grow in Taif, the mountainous town south of Mecca.) On the 15th of Sha'ban, the month preceding Ramadan, Meccans prepare another pastry dish (*mishabbak*). At Mina, the final place to visit during the performance of the pilgrimage, a very fine layer of pastry covered with powdered sugar (*zallabiyya*) is prepared. Meccans who are not performing the Hajj during that particular year still prepare this sweet to mark the event. For the event of death a specific meal is cooked and served to mark the end of formal condolence (*gat'aza*) on the third day. The central dish for this occasion is rice with chickpeas and meat (*ruz bihummus*), an aromatic dish of finely chopped tripe and liver (*sagat*), and sometimes squash stew with meat and split peas – squash is a vegetable considered to have been the favourite of the Prophet Muhammad.

A meal consisting of whole lamb on rice (*mandi*), with accompanying dishes such as sesame-seed paste with cucumber salad (*salatat tahina*), is served at the ceremony commemorating a death anniversary (*hawl*). Likewise, special food is cooked for the events of birth or marriage. In addition, other meals are cooked and shared on special occasions – for example, on a cloudy day to welcome 'the sugary clouds' (*al-ghaym al-sukkari*). This meal consists of rice with lentils (*ruz bi-'adas*), salad of tamarind (*salatat huma*) and fried fish, fresh from the Red Sea. It is interesting to note that during the more religious traditional ceremonies such as the celebration of the birth of the Prophet (*mawlid*) or the death anniversary (*hawl*), the meal is always served on a white plastic tablecloth placed on the floor. Plastic has been used since it became available in the country to prevent staining of the carpets underneath. Before the introduction of plastic, people used a circular mat made of palm leaves (*misaffa*), about one metre in diameter. For everyday meals, as well as at other less traditional events such as a wedding party at a hotel, food is served at Western-style dining-tables, and varieties of dishes from different countries, Arab, Western and oriental are cooked. At the more traditional religious events, forks and knives are not used; instead the right hand or a spoon is used.

In addition to the events above described, this group of Meccan families, wherever they happen to be, hold 'Meccan nights' with Meccan themes, objects and food, some of which are re-created from the past. Special combinations of typically Meccan dishes, small grilled meatballs heavily spiked with garlic (*mabshur*), won ton-like steamed pastry filled with minced meat (*mantu*), and *mittabbag*, a fine layer of pastry filled with eggs, minced meat and chives, and sweet *mittabbag* made with honey and bananas or with local cheese and honey, are served by men dressed in old-style Meccan dress and consumed by guests seated on high-backed Meccan benches. Since this item of furniture has come back into fashion, a brisk trade has developed in reproducing benches, the originals having practically disappeared among this elite social group. Rosewater and water with other flavours such as the plant *kadi* are drunk from special Meccan water containers and bowls.

The return or revival of 'tradition' is apparent in the conduct of both men and women. The sexes are segregated at most formal gatherings, as they have been in the past. Food at the women's parties is nearly always more elaborate than at the men's. For example, a hotel manager in Jeddah informed me that at the men's wedding ceremony the dinner always follows the same menu, a simple and traditional choice of 'Meccan' food: several whole roast lambs, rice, salad made of sesame sauce and cucumber, and *turumba*, little fingers of pastry soaked in honey. At the women's ceremony, however, the food is much more varied and elaborate. Not only Hijazi food (from Mecca, Jeddah or Medina), but also Lebanese, Egyptian and other Arab dishes and even Western delicacies such as avocados and smoked salmon are presented, though not necessarily consumed. The whole lamb remains a central part of the meal, but for the women it is pre-carved and 'off the bone'. The reason for this is that no woman would consider carving the lamb on such an occasion; this would be considered neither delicate nor chic. Several men explained to me that the difference between men's and women's food, dress, and the elaborate manners of formal greeting and speech, is that women are more concerned than men about 'appearances' (*mazahir*) and that they like variety which is not in the nature of men.

Extending hospitality and showing generosity to the guest is one way of establishing or maintaining status and respectability. By generosity and hospitality is implied that, from the beginning of a party until the last guest leaves, the host or hostess should stand throughout, showing courtesy (*mujamala*) and recognition (*tagdir*) for their guests. Serving the guest (*al-mubashara*) is described by Meccans as chivalry and a sense of honour and generosity (*muru'wa*). In Islam, even when the host has higher status than the guest, he should serve him and eat later. Members of the social group studied admire this behaviour and attempt to observe it. They repeat the hadith: 'He who loves Allah and his messenger should be generous to his guest.' Even with the ostentatiously large number of domestic staff (mostly Filipinos) it is the 'people of the house' (*ahl al-bayt*) who actually serve the guests. The servants only bring the food from the kitchen while the host or hostess and their extended family offer it in the appropriate manner to the guests. The guest is not left for a moment without being offered food: juices, nuts, dates, coffees (Najdi, Arabic, Turkish), mint tea and Lipton tea, then dinner which is delayed for as long as possible since the rule is that the guest leaves immediately after, and again teas, coffees and a mixture of 'digestive' spices, betel-nut, cardamom, cloves and peppermints (a particularly Meccan combination). Incense (*'uda*) is burned and passed around before and especially after food as another sign of hospitality, as well as oil-based sandalwood, amber or rose perfumes. Throughout the party the host or hostess and their extended family implore the guest, by Allah, to eat. However much the guest is eating the host or hostess repeats 'You have not eaten ... By Allah, you have not eaten.' The guest replies with one of the many set compliments in acknowledgement of the generosity, such as 'May Allah make your house always prosperous', to which the host replies, 'With your presence only', or 'May Allah make you more generous'; to this the guest replies, 'We only follow your generosity.'

Some older informants told me that, in their day, hospitality and generosity meant feeding the guest directly, from the host's hand to the guest's mouth. A very honoured guest was not allowed to eat with her own hand: from the moment she was seated at the meal she was fed. 'If members of the house, for example, number eight, each would offer her at least one morsel.' The custom of direct feeding has died out. Nowadays, the host only helps the guest eat by perhaps shelling pistachios, or cutting meat or chicken into smaller pieces for them, or by adding food to their plates – even if these are already full. The rules for serving the guest (*al-mubashara*) express social stratification. Among this social group, who eats with whom, who is served by whom, are indications of social status and age; for example, at a dinner party, the more honoured guests are seated at 'the head of the table' and are served by the more senior of the family, while the younger or less important guests are seated at the opposite end and are still served, but only by the younger family members.

Although food is a central preoccupation at every social gathering, I have noticed that no one mentions the word 'food', for to do this in public is considered bad manners. Thus, although the hostess and her family have gone to the trouble of preparing more than 30 dishes to cover their table for a 'tea invitation', when she asks the guests to proceed to the table she will say: 'Please oblige us, come and drink some tea.' This reflects the good taste or *savoir faire* of the hostess, who does not wish to embarrass her guests by openly alluding to food. From my observations the sense of embarrassment or shame is more acute for the women than for the men.

Generosity is expressed and measured by the quantity of food offered to the guests. A sign of honouring the guest is by the presentation of a whole lamb. There is nearly always at the table, at a formal event, considerably more food than can possibly be consumed by the guests and household. So what happens to the leftovers from such lavish banquets? They are usually distributed to friends and relatives, and to poorer families by way of alms (*sadaqa*). Every family of high economic and social status has several poor families to whom they regularly offer charity – charity in food as well as in clothes, money and so forth. Thus, the same evening or the morning after a big dinner or a religious event, the chauffeurs go around from house to house, distributing the food. Most relatives get their share of the leftovers. The type of food keeps well; indeed, it improves in flavour overnight. People explain that by the following day, the spices and flavours mingling well in one dish become more subtle. Meat is a traditional form of alms (*sadaqa*). Members of the group studied regularly slaughter lamb in their own courtyards; they keep part of the meat for their own household's consumption and send the rest to those in need. Sometimes the lamb is slaughtered for a specific intention (*niyya*) – for example, the recovery of a family member who has been ill – but the slaughter is usually in order to protect the family and maintain prosperity. Meccans eat *harri* (lamb) meat only from a region south of Mecca; they do not like imported lamb, they consider beef to be inferior, and they never eat pork. Hence, other than lamb, chicken and varieties of fish from the Red Sea are everyday food.

Food is traditionally offered to people as gifts; *tu'ma* consisting of food are very often exchanged today. Most days at one's table at mealtime, there is at least one plate that is *tu'ma*, sent by a relative or friend. One should never return this plate empty; it must be returned full, if not with food then just with sugar. However, food should be sent to the house and never brought by the guest (as an immediate appreciation of a dinner). This can only be done by a close relative because between family members there is no formality or embarrassment. The *dakhla* is another gift of food, but is often in the form of a feast given in honour of a person who has returned from a trip. Sometimes this gift of food is sent to the home. Furthermore, food is offered to an extended family afflicted with a death. Distant relatives and close friends send cooked food, especially during the first three days of formal condolence. This practice is based on a hadith.

Despite all the conspicuous consumption in connection with food, there is a constant fear of the evil eye attached to it. Food being connected with basic beliefs and values, a sense of identity and belonging, and with social status, but primarily food being essential to life, makes it appear particularly susceptible to the evil eye (*hassad*). Anyone, whether consciously or unconsciously, could cast the evil eye. The fear is more for certain types of food, and especially so if the person who is to consume the food is either vulnerable or in a position to be envied. Hence, for example, the special chicken broth (*masluga*) consumed by the new mother is especially prone to the evil eye, as is the milk for an infant. These vulnerable foods are always covered by a cloth or opaque paper for protection. Fruits are also vulnerable; baskets of fruit are always covered until the moment they are to be eaten. All food that was formerly a rarity or considered a delicacy is considered more prone to the evil eye.

Polite guests would always use the expression *Masha'llah*, 'Whatever Allah wishes', in a stage whisper, upon seeing a banquet – both to express their goodwill and also their admiration. It is customary for women to eat a light meal (*talbiba* or *tasbira* – appeasement of hunger) at home, prior to attending a formal 'tea' or dinner party. This is partly to look elegant and refined (since appearing hungry in front of others is not considered dignified) and partly because of the evil eye, since eating heartily in front of a large group is risking exposure to this.

It is customary in Mecca to seat all guests at a meal at the same time. However, the rule is that when a guest finishes eating he or she should leave the table and not wait for others who are still eating. This is according to the Qur'anic verse: 'And if you have eaten, disperse, even if you are enjoying conversation'; people explain that it is bad manners for those who have finished eating to sit 'counting the morsels'. This could cause the evil eye. Although people do exchange a few words at mealtimes, there is no tradition of formal conversation at table as in other societies. Furthermore, all dishes are presented together to be consumed at the same time, there is no sequence of courses to be waited for. Hence, the time spent at a meal depends on how much and how quickly an individual eats.

There are various preventative measures against the evil eye, other than covering the food. One should not mention the name of a particular dish, such as meat (*laham*), but instead call it something else such as *kuku* or *hayla*. The latter is taught to children, for they are most vulnerable. When a person is suspected of having got the evil eye while eating, a condition people describe as 'receiving a morsel' (*jatu lugma*), a Sayyid (religious man) is sought to remove the morsel. The stomach is rid of the evil eye by

the application of a piece of wet cotton wool to the afflicted part which, by
the power of the Sayyid's prayers, removes the bad morsel. Not many
people engage in this type of remedy today; other procedures against the
evil eye are taken. The only measure universally acknowledged as being
sound is the repetition of a particular sura from the Qur'an.

The place where food is served and cooked is in the home. All
innovation, all tradition occurs here. Hence the home contributes to
guarding and developing the local or the national identity of cuisine. There
were traditionally no restaurants in Saudi Arabia, except for popular public
eating places called *gahawi* (cafés), where men eat outdoors seated on high
benches, rounding off their meals with tea and a water-pipe (*shisha*). No
woman would ever eat in a public place. Even for men of this social group,
it is considered shameful (*'ayb*) to eat in the souks, i.e. in a public place.
Today Western-style restaurants have opened. Most are part of the
international chains of hotels offering Chinese, Japanese, various European
and Middle Eastern food. These cater to expatriates living in Saudi Arabia,
although some Saudi Arabians of other sections of the society have started
to patronize them.

Food in the home has always been cooked by women – Meccan men
rarely if ever cook. Recipes are visually and orally transmitted from mother
to daughter. Formerly female slaves who lived as part of the family helped
in cooking the family recipes. Today, women among the elite social group
do not cook the food themselves. Meccan food is cooked by male foreign
cooks. The latter are usually Filipino, Lebanese, Sudanese, Egyptian or
Moroccan. The male cook is never Saudi Arabian. The professional cook
is taught the recipes of Meccan food by the lady of the house or by a
knowledgeable female member of the maternal or paternal family. Although
a woman may pride herself on not having to cook herself (since having a
cook is a status indicator), she still prides herself on knowing traditional
Meccan cuisine.

The first national Saudi cookbook was published in Saudi Arabia in
1984. It was written jointly by six Saudi women of high-status patronymic
groups from different parts of the country, and recipes are from various
cities and regions, though these are not identified in the text (see Heine,
this volume).

And so it can be seen that after so much change – internal and external,
political, economic and social – perhaps the final bastion of personal
expression remains with food, which may be used, whether consciously
or unconsciously, to express so much about people's beliefs, identity and
consciousness. As the Arab saying goes, 'Eat what you like and dress as
others would like you to.'

13. Eating Habits and Cultural Boundaries in Northern Iran

Christian Bromberger

Food and the ways it is prepared often bear the signs of their supposed local or ethnic origin: Brussels sprouts, Brazil nuts, *salade niçoise*, spaghetti bolognese, steak tartare, *kofteh tabrizi* (balls of minced meat mixed with crushed chick-peas). At the same time, peoples and ethnic groups are just as frequently referred to in association with culinary habits which are regarded as peculiarly loathsome: for the English the French are 'frog eaters', the latter reciprocate with 'rosbifs', while both call the Italians 'macaronis'. In Afghanistan Uzbeks are called 'noodle eaters' by their neighbours and, in Iran, Arabs from Khuzestan are stigmatized as 'lizard eaters' (*susmar-khor*).[1]

Local parochialism draws on much the same references. In France, for instance, terms such as 'slug eaters', 'fly eaters', 'refuse' or 'rubbish eaters' and the like are common nicknames used by fellow-countrymen to designate and disparage people from neighbouring villages. Comparisons and metaphors further demonstrate this transcultural propensity to frame other people's identity in that alimentary mode. The reason may be that the individual or the group bears some affinities with the item of food. For instance a fat chap will be called 'roly-poly', or a woman be depicted as 'as flat as a pancake'. Or else the other's qualities may be appreciated in terms of savour. Thus, in France, a bread-eating country, a kind fellow will be said to be 'as good as fresh bread', and in many countries a girl may be 'as sweet as sugar', or 'all honey'; *ba-namak* (or *bi-namak*), with (or without) salt, as it is said in Persian of a girl with (or without) charm.

How does this perception of otherness through food work in northern Iran? What is the logical frame of this popular perception? These are some of the questions to be discussed in this chapter.

BREAD EATERS VERSUS RICE EATERS

The Elborz range forms a natural and cultural boundary between two worlds that are radically distinct because of their climate and landscape and the production activities and ways of life of their inhabitants. To the north, the province of Gilan benefits from a damp, subtropical climate and displays a richly carpeted landscape of rice fields, citrus and mulberry orchards and tea plantations at the foot of the mountains, or else glaucous ponds by the Caspian Sea.[2] To the west and south, the arid neighbouring provinces of Azarbayjan and Tehran have founded their rural economy on the farming of barley and wheat in association with sheep pastoralism. A major discrepancy exists between the ways of life of the people of the plateau (called 'Araqi'[3] by their Caspian neighbours) and the rural people of Gilan (called 'Rashti' by the Tehranis after the name of the provincial capital Rasht). A careful inventory of people's practices, behaviours, customs and ways of life on either side of the boundary line set by the summits of the Elborz shows so many differences with such great contrasts that some authors have felt entitled to define Gilan as a sort of reverse of Iran (Bazin and Bromberger 1982: 95–7). In that respect, culinary habits are highly revealing.

On the plateau, bread remains the basic food, at least for the poorest classes of society; in the 1970s it provided about 40 per cent of daily food intake (Bazin 1973). People eat it at the three meals, along with dairy products (yoghurt, cheese), mutton and/or vegetable stews, or else with mutton stock (*abgusht*) or vegetable soup (*ash*). Domestic rituals emphasize the importance of that basic item of food: when one lays the table the correct procedure consists of putting down first in front of each plate a few pieces of the thin, soft bread (*lavash*) that forms the essential part of the meal. Bread is by no means a mere accompaniment to other dishes, but is closely associated with all of the dishes that are consumed: yoghurt, cheese, stew patties, eggs, etc. Every item of food is brought to the mouth with pieces of bread, then swallowed.

It goes without saying that daily nourishment among the poorer classes is only distantly related to the general image of Iranian cuisine. White rice served with grilled lamb (*chelow kabab*), or rice dishes to which various ingredients (including vegetables, fruit, lamb, poultry, spices) previously stir-fried in a pan are added during the cooking (*polow*), remain exceptional, conspicuously marking special commensal occasions such as feasts, parties, reception of guests, restaurant dinners. It is true, however, that the consumption of rice, which was formerly limited to wealthy urban circles within central Iran, has spread to the poorer social classes these past 30 years, one of the results of the trend in modern Iran towards the levelling of social behaviour and difference by the copying of prevailing urban models.

In spite of this homogenizing process, a huge gap remains between the eating habits of the Araqi and those of the Rashti.[4] In the central plain of Gilan, where rice growing is practically a monoculture, an adult man used to eat about two pounds (uncooked) of husked and polished rice a day, which represented in the 1970s from 40 to 65 per cent of his daily diet. The custom of eating rice at the main meals, once general in Caspian Iran, is not so firmly grounded now, except in southern Talish, a 'conservation zone' for traditional customs and practices situated to the west of the central plain (see Figure 13.1).

For breakfast or a morning snack (qelyeh-nahar), rice is either served cold (from the leftovers of the previous day's meals), enriched with cheese, cloves of garlic that have been soaked in vinegar or else with fish roe (mainly from surmullet, mahi-sefid), fresh string beans or broad beans that have been soaked in water, onions, walnuts; or it is served hot, soaked in sweetened milk, mixed with the syrup of a fruit of the lotus family (Diospyros lotus), or simply a little morello cherry or citron (badrang) jam. The morning rice is thus associated with salty and sour preparations when cold, and sweet ingredients when hot.

For lunch – the most substantial meal of the day – and for dinner, stews (mainly prepared with green or dried vegetables, according to the season, herbs, meat and more particularly with poultry and wildfowl), vegetable or cheese omelettes, fried eggs,[5] stir-fried fish, yoghurt, fresh fruit, according to circumstances, make up the meal with the rice dish. This daily rice (kateh) does not claim the aesthetic look nor the aromatic savour of polow, which here, as in central Iran, though with some special variations, remains the 'must' for special occasions. The kateh is in fact a quick, simple preparation, using only a few ingredients: the rice grains, often of a short type, are dipped into cold water, then cooked until the water is fully absorbed. Then a little clarified butter may be added and the whole dish is left to steam. The result is a compacted mixture, whose grains stick together and which, once it has been turned out, must be cut with a knife before being shaped into patties ready to eat. Completely different are the procedures used for the preparation of polow and chelow: for these the rice, generally of a long-grain type, must be soaked for many hours, then dipped into boiling water and strained halfway through the cooking, which will be carried out by slowly steaming it, so that, at the end of the cooking, the grains are firm, dry and separate.

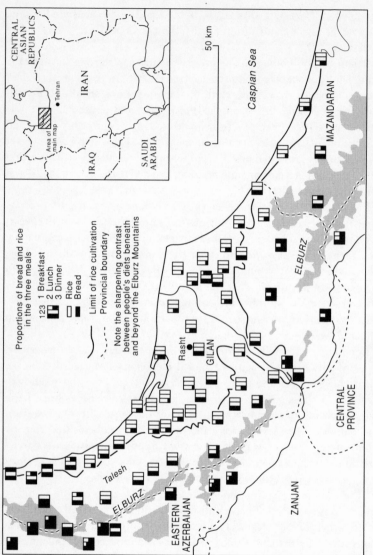

Fig. 1. Proportions of bread and rice in the three meals

While everyday and special cooking on the plateau are opposed by the very nature of the basic foods involved (bread versus rice), in Gilan the distinction is made through the different cooking processes used for the same food (*kateh* as against *polow* and *chelow*). Rice, which is omnipresent on Gilak tables, provides the basic ingredient for innumerable pastries that are made for special family or religious occasions.

Intake of animal protein comes mainly from the consumption of poultry and wildfowl from the ponds, fish, and to a minor extent mutton and beef. The Gilanis are very fond of the scaled fish which are numerous in the river mouths, lagoons and shore waters of the Caspian Sea, such as carp, catfish, bream, and especially the 'white-fleshed fish' (*mahi sefid*, a variety of surmullet). The association of rice and fish yields the famous Gilani dish *polow-mahi*, one of the region's culinary markers for strangers. It is remarkable that Gilanis used not to eat those well-known Caspian specialities, the sturgeon and its caviar, whose consumption, like that of all fish without scales, was considered *haram* (against the law of Islam) until 1983, when Ayatollah Khomeini issued a fatwa lifting the ban and declaring sturgeon and caviar *halal* (religiously permitted).

The importance of beef in the region should be underlined: consumption of 4 pounds a person per year out of a total of 18 pounds of meat. This specific feature already struck Chodzko in the mid-19th century. 'Among all the regions of Persia,' he wrote, 'Gilan is the only place where beef is eaten and even sold in bazaars,' adding: 'As for the Persians who live beyond the Caspian Mounts [i.e. the Araqi], they loathe beef' (1850: 203).

As for bread, it seems to be quite a newcomer in the Caspian region, as shown by the following comment by countrymen of the Talish plain: 'If you had mentioned bread some 30 years ago, we would have said: "What is it?"' (Bazin 1980, II: 57). As rare as rice traditionally is on the plateau, bread remained until very recently a food displayed among the well-off during feasts, to show the wealth and ease of the house. Such a concern for ostentation would prevail over people's aversion to that food. 'The Gilani landlord eats and thinks like his sharecroppers,' notes Chodzko, 'but he would fear to be misjudged by his peers for his lack of decorum if he did not offer his guests some wheat bread' (1850: 204).

From this short survey, we can see that Rashti and Araqi diets are distinguished by a whole set of oppositions based on the basic foods, such as rice and bread, on the accompanying ingredients (fish and meat), on the status a simple food is endowed with (rice as a daily food versus rice as a prestige ingredient for feasts, and inversely for bread), on the importance of the item in the diet (beef), or finally on the endless subtleties that distinguish similar preparations – for instance the ingredients used for *polow* (generally agreed to be the royal dish of Iranian cuisine), or the consumption of tea, which the Gilanis like to drink *kam-rang* (i.e. light-coloured) whereas the people of the plateau prefer it *por-rang* (i.e. dark-coloured, strong). These contrasts in cooking, food preparation and food associations work out as regional markers providing particularly rich materials for defining otherness.

KALLEH-MAHI-KHOR VERSUS DAHAN-GOSHAD

Is it necessary to underline that the consciousness of one's cultural identity cannot be reduced to mere acknowledgement of the differences between oneself and others? Among the materials provided by the experience of otherness, some features are perceived as emblematic while others are overlooked. Thus one may oppose the open paradigm of indicators (the features of differentiation revealed by a substantivist and contrastive analysis of data) to a more limited paradigm of markers (the features acknowledged and retained as symbolic of otherness).

Among the culinary habits of their neighbours, the countrymen of Gilan particularly take note of their predilection for bread, which they view sometimes with amusement, sometimes with pity. They call the people of Tehran *dahan-goshad* ('large-mouth'), because they keep chewing bread, displaying their large teeth. According to traditional stereotypes, the Araqi are nothing but poor 'barley-bread eaters' for whom rice from Gilan remains an enviable luxury. At a time when the daily culinary habits of the plateau people and the Gilanis still formed two entirely distinct systems, the consumption of bread represented, for the countrymen of the Caspian plain, both an object of derision and the supreme threat: 'The Guilek,' reported Rabino and Lafont at the beginning of the century, 'doesn't eat any bread but he considers it as a food that does not suit his constitution, and this to such a point that an angry man will tell his wife: "Go and eat some bread then die!"' Quoted by the latter authors, Captain A. Conolly remarked, towards 1830, that Gilak parents, when they scolded one of their children, would threaten to send him to Irak (Araq), where he would suffer the odious punishment of having to eat some bread (Rabino and Lafont 1910: 139–40). It should come as no surprise to find that, by contrast, many Araqi proverbs praise the excellence of that same food, and that the sight and smell of it, far from making them flee, attract them and keep them at home. '*Nan inja, ab inja, koja ravam beh az inja?*' ('There's bread here, there's water here, where could I find a better place than here?')

Among the foods that Gilani people are most fond of, olives (prepared with pomegranate juice and ground walnut), beef and particularly fish arouse a deep sense of revulsion in Araqi people, so much so that the mere mention of the name of these foods causes many of them to mimic nausea. For the plateau people, the Gilanis are *kalleh-e mahi-khor* ('fish-head eaters'), a nickname combining aversion and derision. The Caspian countrymen are occasional fish-head eaters when they eat fish head lightly fried with crushed garlic or with *fesenjan* (a stew prepared with pomegranate juice and ground walnuts). They are well aware of the amused scorn with which their neighbours view that fringe of their gastronomy: so they dissimulate in front of a stranger, taking care not to allow him to see it, mentioning it only *a mezza voce* and with an appearance of unwillingness if not displeasure. However, any praise for their regional cooking will soon disperse this passing cloud of culinary shame; after all, the Gilanis will comment, when can the people of the plateau ever eat fresh fish (which, as we have seen, would disgust most of them) and rice in abundance (which would, to tell the truth, please most of them)?

This construction of the other, even (perhaps especially) if he is close, in terms of derision – differentiating him and separating him from me by identifying him as the eater of foods that are taboo to me, marking him as the negative and repulsive pole of my own identity – represents a general mechanism, a 'normal' mode of constructing differences (cf Lévi-Strauss 1983: 15). 'Gastrophobia' for 'exo-cooking' (cf Fischler 1979) is a privileged declaration of ethnic identity and superiority.

How can one be a Rashti?

Connected to these culinary representations of cultural otherness are a whole set of ethnic stereotypes, that is, Gilani and Araqi value judgements of each other as handed down by tradition. At first sight, culinary representations and ethnic stereotypes form two independent, semantically unrelated textual series. I shall examine the major features of the Rashti ethnotype as pictured by the man of the plateau and more particularly the inhabitant of Tehran, through anecdotes and jokes (*jok* in Persian!).

The Caspian region is portrayed by the Araqi as a home of stupid people. A large minority of *jok-e rashti* (Rashti ethnic jokes) mock the naivety and silliness of the men of that province. Most of all, Rashti jokes[6] focus on their reputed sexual indolence. Many portray a complacent deceived husband, rejoicing that his son looks like the local butcher rather than the one from a neighbouring place, or cowardly in refusing any confrontation with his wife's lover. This reputation earns the Rashti the second nickname given them by the people of the plateau: *kamarsost* (impotent). A whole set of phrases stressing their lack of manliness is used to characterize them: they are said to be *bi rag* (lacking vein, that is, phlegmatic), *bi bokhar* (lacking heat, that is, cold), *bi ghayrat* (without honour). Being anaemic, how could they be virile, since, according to the still strongly rooted belief – and not only among the uneducated classes – that semen is nothing but the froth of blood? Each drop of semen is said to correspond to forty drops of blood.

These stereotypes lead us a priori far from the domain of food and seem to refer to an indigenous ethnology which amplifies differences in social behaviour to the extreme, and a popular ethology which interprets these differences according to theories more or less inherited from learned traditions, such as those of physiognomy or climatology. But if we examine this question further, especially through 'meta-folklore' (i.e. indigenous theories), we can see that culinary representations and ethnic stereotypes form parts of the same system, as two equivalent – though not independent – series according to modalities we have now to establish.

THE HOT AND THE COLD

The categories hot (*garm*) and cold (*sard*), completed by the secondary categories wet (*martub*) and dry (*khoshk*), are first of all basic principles for classifying foods and diseases, primarily because these represent the two main fields of application of the system.[7] Everyone in Iranian society knows the classification of diseases and nutriments into hot and cold, while the same categories are more diffusely and less consciously, though equally firmly, applied to life-cycle stages, social relations and ethnic qualities. These classifications, as we shall see, derive from theories of health and diet that form a hard, stable, resistant core to the system as a whole.

Hot and cold here are not measures of temperature but of qualities of energy potential; hot foods, according to the principles of humoral medicine that form the basis of the system, are those that regenerate the hot and fundamental humour that is blood. Conversely, cold foods, reputed to have a low energy value, are thought to conflict over the excess of blood and induce phlegm, a cold humour. All foods (except salt, some fungi, some types of water, which are considered neutral) are classified into one or the other category. For instance, for the Araqi, all dry vegetables and fruits, some varieties of fresh vegetables and fruits, wheat, sugar, animal fat, most poultries, mutton are classified as hot. By contrast, most fresh vegetables and fruits, rice, beef, fish and dairy products are cold (see Table 13.1). Tastes are also classified according to this dichotomy: the sweet and the piquant are hot, the salty is neutral, the sour cold. Along the scale

Table 13.1. Classification of hot and cold foods according to 'Araqi' people (from Tehran and Isfahan)

HOT	COLD
Dry fruits: walnut, hazel, almond, pistachio, date, sultana coconut, banana, fig, quince, pear, apple melon grapes, black mulberry, apricot (after *sahayl*[1]), chestnut, olive	**Fresh fruits:** pomegranate, peach, nectarine, plum, cherry, morello cherry, orange, lemon watermelon grapes, black mulberry, apricot (before *sahayl*), sour grapes
Vegetables, herbs, spices: garlic, onion egg-plant, leek, radish, parsley, fenugreek, coriander red pumpkin (vetch, hemp seed) chick-pea, broad bean pepper, saffron, curcuma	**Vegetables, herbs, spices:** potato haricot bean, carrot, lettuce, tomato, cucumber yellow pumpkin lentil
Cereals: barley, millet, wheat, maize	**Cereals:** rice
Meat: camel, ewe, sheep,[2] lamb,[2] goat,[2] pigeon, cock,[2] hen, turkey, duck, wildfowl	**Meat:** beef, veal, chicken[2]
	Fish (except sturgeon and caviar)
Animal and vegetable fats: yolk of egg	white of egg
	Dairy products: milk, cream, yoghurt, buttermilk, cheese, casein
honey sugar water from Khorasan, well-water	water from Isfahan, spring-water

1. After *sahayl*: after Canopus, i.e. during summer, when fruits ripen. Thus some fruits are considered cold when unripe and hot when ripe or dried (for instance sour grapes are considered very cold and sultanas very hot, see Table 13.2).
2. Uncertain status, depending on individual variations. Nevertheless, people usually ascribe different status (hot or cold) to male or female animals of the same species.

of food classifications, tastes act as modifiers, tempering or strengthening the qualities of foods, and helping to discriminate between two that are close to each other: thus sweet lemon is not as cold as sour lemon, ordinary melon is hotter than water melon, and so on.

If hot and cold form two discontinuous sets, there is a gradation within each of these categories; among hot foods, people will at once identify the hottest (dates, sugar and sweets, coconut, garlic, nuts, raisins, pepper): *atesh, misuzeh* (it is like fire, it burns) they say. This sub-category of the hot is the only one to be distinguished with a name. Further down the scale, markers are not so obvious and the order of foods seems to form a continuum. Closer investigation, having recourse in cases of uncertainty to the triad test,[8] reveals three other sub-categories of 'hot' which are not related to any lexical term: 'covert categories', in the language of ethnoscience, which remain implicit in contrast with overt, explicit categories.

The question becomes complicated when one tries to establish the principles of classification of cold foods. Two criteria interact here, the degree of coldness and the degree of wetness, with the result that foods will be classified along two axes depending on whether they are cold and dry (*khonak*) or cold and wet (*martub*). Besides dairy products, beef and veal, wet foods include vegetables and cereals containing a high proportion of starch (*neshasteh*). Investigation of the distribution of foods along the cold axis reveals four sub-categories, none of them given linguistic terms apart from the quantifying adverbs 'little' or 'much'; moreover, the boundaries between them seem even more blurred than in the case of the hot. Yet sour grapes and cucumbers are definitely singled out, the former at the top of the cold and dry, the latter at the top of the cold and wet (see Table 13.2).

What sense does this taxonomy make? One might be tempted to see here an empirical classification of food based on its nutritive qualities; after all, it is the way people having something to do with food often present and assert it; for them the gradation from hot to cold records first of all the energetic input of the items of food. A quick survey of the classification could support this argument: the items at the head of the hierarchy (dry fruit, sweets, etc.) have a high food value, the ones at the bottom (like cucumbers) have particularly low food value. This nutritionalist and substantialist explanation of the system, however, comes up against two major problems: first, the extent to which the classification varies according to individuals and regions; second, the fact that nutritional criteria are irrelevant to the classification of a large number of items.

In a synthetic article dealing with the categorization of food into hot and cold in various countries, Anderson noted 'the incredible amount of variability in the system' (1984: 759). It is true – and the Iranian experience confirms it – that the same individual during a single conversation may express contradictory opinions on the qualities of some food. From one individual to another, and still more from one region to another, classificatory variations are numerous, and sometimes disconcerting. Most of them affect the weaker parts of the system; that is, groups of foods that are a little hot or a little cold: thus mutton (ram or ewe) and lamb, goat meat, cock have an uncertain status. Some variations are even more radical: for the Araqis, beef, milk and haricot beans are cold, whereas the Gilanis consider them hot.

A nutritional explanation of the whole system rapidly shows its limits. It makes sense that sweets and some dried fruits appear at the head of the honours list for hot, but it is harder to understand the position given by the Araqis to lentils, haricot beans, rice, butter made of yoghurt and beef, all classified as cold despite their much higher food value than that of

Table 13.2 'Araqi' food ranking

From least cold to coldest, from least hot to hottest, from least dry to driest, from least wet to wettest (the last opposition, between dry and wet, is relevant in daily use only for cold foods). Within each category (A, B, C, D) there is a gradation: each line represents a distinct step along the scale cold or hot.

Cold Foods

Wet	Dry
A1: butter,[1] casein tomato, potato	A: egg white, fish, lentil, cockerel, grapes, black mulberry (before *sahayl*), Isfahan water, wine
B1: milk, cream, buttermilk, cheese, yoghurt	B: pomegranate, carrot, lettuce, nectarine, peach, cherry, sweet lemon
rice,[2] beef, veal	yellow pumpkin, beans orange, bitter orange, mandarin
C1: watermelon	C: morello cherry, sour lemon
D1: cucumber	D: sour grapes

Table 13.2 (continued)

Neutral Foods

tea, mushrooms, salt

Hot Foods

a: ewe, lamb, hen, egg yolk, chestnut, curcuma, duck
b: turkey, cock, wildfowl, coleseed, hazelnut, animal or vegetable fat (ghee, oil)
    wheat, broad bean, vetch, pistachio, black grapes, black mulberry (after *sahayl*),
    apricot (very ripe)
    almond
    olive, parsley, apple
    fenugreek
    hemp seed
    barley, chick-pea
    millet
c: saffron, coriander, vinegar
    red pumpkin, aubergine
    quince, pear
    Khorasan water
    radish, leek
    white grapes, white mulberry (after *sahayl*)
    pigeon
    banana, melon, fig, onion
d: pepper
    walnut, sultana
    coconut, garlic
    chocolate, syrup, pastries
    sugar,
    dates

---

1.   Depending on origin: butter from ewes is considered hotter than cow's butter.
2.   Depending on type: short, round-grained rice, including a high proportion of starch, is considered colder and wetter than long, thin-grained rice.

apples, aubergines, leeks, radishes, pumpkins or water from Khorasan, which are considered hot. Further, gradations within the same category are far from reproducing the hierarchy based on calorie inputs: onions, aubergines and radishes are considered hotter than almonds, pistachios or hazelnuts, beef is colder than cockerel or potatoes. Clearly, a single criterion – in this case energetic input – cannot account for the logic of a system which, after thorough study, reveals its multidimensional character.

In fact, several criteria, some obvious, others latent, interact in assigning a quality to a food:

Wetness: this either marks as cold (remember that, in this classificatory system, wetness is nowadays only found in combination with coldness) foods of high nutritional value: for instance, for the Araqis, rice, beef and veal, dairy products; or else it opposes fruits of a similar food–value quality (the watermelon, which is wet, is considered cold, whereas the melon, which is dry, is classified as hot).

Taste: sweet and piquant foods are, on the whole, considered hot, and sour foods cold, thus reinforcing the contrast between melons and watermelons which are simultaneously opposed as dry versus wet and sweeter versus less sweet. This largely explains the difference of status between bananas, pears and apples on the one hand, and pomegranates, oranges and lemons on the other.

Colour, when the same item has distinctly coloured varieties: thus red pumpkins are classed as hot, yellow pumpkins as cold, and white mulberries and white grapes are considered hotter than blackberries and blue grapes. Inverted examples can also be found, confirming the flexibility of some marginal ones within the system. For instance, black mulberries and black grapes can be considered as hotter than white mulberries and white grapes.

Sex, for animals, often appears as a discriminating element; thus cocks and hens, sheep and ewes are respectively classed as either cold or hot but never the same.

Age: slight differences of age in animals to be consumed are sometimes invoked: young animals are reputed to be colder than adults.

Other oppositions may also intervene, making the process of classification even more complicated, for example the natural or artificial quality of the food: sweets made of chemical components (colourings, etc.) are reckoned to be hotter than totally natural sweets, and so on and so forth.

Thus, as we can see, the system of hot and cold rests on several conscious or subconscious dimensions that interact so that it is hard to distinguish the interdependent taxonomic principles. Everything works as if some oppositions (consistency, taste, colour, etc.) had been reinterpreted according to a more generic and integrative opposition. This reassignment of criteria devoid of hierarchy – which at times can prove very flexible, as with colours – largely explains the adaptability of the system: an item of food can present 'mixed signals', to use Anderson's felicitous phrase (1984: 760), slightly wet but very sweet, both sour and sweet – all the ingredients for generating taxonomic fuzziness!

This classificatory system is not a mere grid used for the analysis of 'the eatable' but a practical model offering individuals coherent answers to the various problems they will have to cope with during the course of daily life. It is first and foremost in the field of illness and health that the categories of the hot and the cold operate. In fact, this system as a whole rests on the theories of humoral medicine, descended from Hippocrates and Galen, which, until last century, shaped 'the most widespread medical belief system in the world' (Anderson 1984: 755), and according to which health was governed by the balance of the four chief humours, which can each be defined as a combination of the hot or the cold and of the dry or the wet (blood is hot and wet, yellow bile is hot and dry, phlegm is cold and wet, black bile is cold and dry). Any disease results from a lack of balance of the four cardinal humours and therefore must be treated by the addition or the subtraction of hot, cold, wet or dry.

In the popular classifications used in Iran, each disease is thus qualified as 'cold' or 'hot' (the opposition dry versus wet is only subsidiary, as we have already seen with food) and consequently is treated, by traditional medicine, according to an allopathetic cure. Thus, eruptive diseases are generally classified as hot and as such need to be countered by a cold diet: watermelon juice, for example, for typhoid fever;[9] conversely, illnesses without any visible exterior symptoms are often considered cold, thus requiring a contrary treatment (sugar-candy and honey, for example, for stomach-ache). In his everyday life, the individual makes sure of a good body balance by practising vigilant control over the colour of his urine (darkness indicates an excess of heat, lightness an excess of cold) and over the state of his skin (skin eruptions draw attention to an excess of heat).

The art of good cooking consists of preparing well-balanced meals by harmoniously determining the right proportions of hot and cold foods, according to the seasons, the time of day and the qualities of the guests. Cold periods (winter, night-time) require hot meals, warm periods (summer, daytime) cold meals. A particular diet should correspond to each stage in life, and the cycle of life is conceived as an ascending then descending graph that accompanies the individual from cold (infancy) to hot (youth), then from hot (middle age) to cold (old age). Some critical periods of life are treated with closer care: mothers will simmer cold preparations (that is, using no garlic, onions, pepper or any other heating ingredients) for their sons when they are highly pubescent, while, in the opposite direction, before the wedding night they offer dates and walnuts (that is, heating products) to the bridegroom, but not to the bride, who should remain passive.

If the ideal daily diet is made of moderation, can one say that excesses of hot or cold will be considered equally harmful? In fact, a hierarchy forms between wet, cold and hot, in which considerations of diet and symbolism interact, sometimes in opposition to each other. Among cold foods, the man of the Iranian plateau prefers the cool and dry (*khonak*) and avoids, and may even dread, those which are wet (*martub*), for he believes them to generate illnesses. If cool connotes healthy food, hot evokes festive food, material wealth and ease, high cuisine: hot *polows*, savoury, piquant or sweet stews (like *fesenjan*), valued meat, confectioneries, pastries prepared for family or religious feasts or events. So the opposition between the cool and the hot shapes and symbolizes the division between daily diet and *grande cuisine*.

THE HOT, THE COLD, THE SEX AND THE REST

As a simple and obvious means for coping with health and food problems, the system of hot and cold also stands – though in a more implicit mode – as an anthropological model for comprehending and classifying others and for managing interpersonal and interethnic relations.

According to this system, individuals and peoples owe their qualities to the climate as much as to diet; it is commonly said that a hot diet will breed a sanguine, expansive temperament, supporting sturdiness, strength and virility, and connoting wealth and abundance; hot ingredients are, on the whole, more expensive than cold or neutral products and are essential in the preparation of the most glamorous dishes. By contrast, cold and wet food corresponds to a phlegmatic, introverted temperament, feebleness and sexual impotence, culinary and economic poverty.[10] In everyday life, different attitudes will be displayed towards a hot eater and a cold eater. Garrulousness and aggressiveness will be feared from the former, so to mollify him he will be offered some yoghurt or any other cooling sort of food; the latter one will try to shake out of his apathy by treating him with some heating sort of food, dry fruit for instance.

We can see now how this trip among culinary classifications takes us back to the very core of problems of ethnic perceptions and differentiations. The Gilanis owe their reputation for indolence and impotence largely to their qualities of cold and wet eaters. According to this system, how could they be virile when they consume so much rice, fish, wet vegetables and fruits? Thus culinary markers appear both as emblems of ethnic differences and, subsumed by the categories of hot, cold and wet, as major elements discriminating the content of these differences in people's minds. Far from constituting an independent paradigm, culinary nicknames and ethnic stereotypes form part of a larger system of representations in which varieties of food and varieties of temperaments respond and correspond to each other.[11]

Notes

1. An earlier version of this paper was published in French (see Bromberger 1985). I am very grateful to J. L. Alberti and R. L. Tapper for their crucial help in translating and editing the present English version.

2. For a description of Gilan and ways of life in the Caspian world, see Bromberger (1988, 1989).

3. Literally Iraqi; this term is a remnant of ancient 'Abbasid territorial divisions. 'Iraq of the Arabs' (lower Mesopotamia) was then opposed to 'foreign Iraq' (the lands to the east, from Azarbayjan to the Great Salt Desert: see Le Strange 1966: 24-5 and 185-6). Gilanis still use the term Araq for the latter and, more extensively, all the Iranian territory located beyond the Elborz range.

4. Nevertheless, Gilani cooking processes and culturally valued tastes partake of the same general system as those of the Iranian plateau: predilection for a long cooking, facilitating the development of flavours; association of opposed tastes (sweet and sour) in stews; deep repulsion for the strongest flavours; and a paradigmatic pattern in eating habits: all dishes are served at once and associated for consumption.

5. Eggs play an important part in Gilani cooking. Two dishes which symbolize inner identity are *mirza-qasemi*, a kind of omelette of eggplants, and *baqela-qatoq*, a stew made of fresh string beans or broad beans, both prepared with eggs. *Baqela-qatoq / bi-morghaneh / haft ta olaq / ti mehmaneh* – 'A *baqela-qatoq* without egg, your guests are seven donkeys!' In relation to these emblematic dishes, controversies often arise over cooking orthodoxy and what the *true* recipe is.

6. For a detailed analysis of the meanings and functions of these ethnic slurs, see Bromberger (1986).

7. On the historical background to these food and disease classifications, see Lloyd (1964), Nasr (1976), Ullmann (1978), Anderson (1984), Foucault

(1984), Tilsley Benham (1986). Contemporary studies include, on Afghanistan, Centlivres (1985), Tapper and Tapper (1986); on central America, Currier (1966).

8. The triad test consists of submitting three items or groups of items (A, B, C) to somebody, asking him which ones are closest (A to B, A to C, or B to C). Using this technique one can assess the actual ranking and classificatory process when categories are not distinguished by name.

9. Several examples of allopathic treatments are mentioned by Colliver-Rice (1923: 259) and by Massé (1938: 337-8).

10. Significantly, in traditional Iran as well as in the Mediterranean and the Middle East, fatness is a conspicuous sign of wealth, power and success. Conversely, to be thin usually means low social status.

11. The flexibility of this system allows every group to provide itself with a positive self-image through food and eating habits. Thus the Gilanis, who consider beef, cow's milk, beans and rice as hot or very slightly cold, feel no doubt about their own virility and hot temperament.

Part III

The Language of Food

14. Beyond Taste: the complements of colour and smell in the medieval Arab culinary tradition

Manuela Marín

In the introduction to his cookery book, Muhammad b. Hasan al-Baghdadi, who wrote in the 13th century, divides pleasures into six classes: 'to wit, food, drink, clothes, sex, scent and sound'. Food was, for al-Baghdadi, the 'noblest and most consequential' of these pleasures, and he states clearly that his own personal preference for eating as a source of delight was the reason that inspired him to compile his book.[1]

This was far from being an exceptional viewpoint, as is attested by the number of extant Arabic cookbooks from the medieval period, out of a considerable literature written on the subject, an important part of which is unfortunately lost.[2] This interest in food and cooking reflects the existence of an urban leisured class which adopted an earlier tradition of Persian and Arab origin and gave it a distinct and original character, according to different geographical settings and historical periods. Moreover, these culinary texts, while offering a detailed view of eating habits and preferences in medieval Islamic societies, suggest that food alone was not an exclusive source of pleasure. My intention in this paper is to survey and examine how other senses, besides that of taste, were stimulated to participate in the pleasure-seeking goal portrayed in the classical Arabic cookbooks.

For this study I have selected three texts which cover a wide geographical and chronological range. First, there is Ibn Sayyar al-Warraq's *Kitab Tabikh* (1987), written during the 10th century in Iraq. The book is one of the most comprehensive recipe compilations still preserved and the author collected much of his material from earlier sources. The *Kitab Tabikh* is an interesting instance of culinary standards in Abbasid society, while the frequent use of culinary poems reflects in an illuminating way the kind of public to whom the book was addressed: literati and well-off persons who were interested in food delicacies as well as in other bodily and spiritual pleasures.

The second text emanates from a slightly different tradition, that of the Islamic West. It was written in the first half of the 14th century by Ibn Razin al-Tujibi, a native of Murcia in Spain. Entitled *Fadalat al-khiwan fi tayyibat al-ta'am wa'l-alwan*, Ibn Razin's book contains a number of recipes of 'eastern' origin, but, as the author himself states in its introduction, the *Fadala* is based upon the Andalusian and Maghrebi cooking traditions, which have in some cases a distinct character, as may be appreciated in the fish recipes recorded by Ibn Razin.[3]

Finally, the third text I have examined for this chapter is the anonymous compilation entitled *Kanz al-fawa'id fi tanwi' al-fawa'id*. Of possible Egyptian origin, the *Kanz* has an encyclopaedic character; it contains more than 800 recipes, many of them closely connected to the 'extended family' of eastern cookbooks written around the 13th and 14th centuries, to which belong al-Baghdadi's *Kitab Tabikh*, and the *Kitab al-Wusla ila'l-Habib* and *Wasf al-at'ima*.[4] As the longest representative of this tradition, the *Kanz* is a useful complement to the works by both al-Warraq and Ibn Razin. These three cookbooks provide a broad basis for the subject under study, in terms of both space and time.

Part of the pleasure of good food lies in the anticipation of it. The sight of a good dish suggests to the table companions the imminent enjoyment to be derived from its consumption. But there is, too, a sense of aesthetic pleasure in the way a dish is arranged, decorated and coloured. Al-Warraq frequently uses the word *zayn* and verbal forms of the same root ('to decorate, to adorn') when, at the end of a recipe, he recommends the final touch to a dish. This last stage in cooking preparations was felt in some cases to be something exceptional, pertaining to grand occasions, such as banquets and public ceremonies; in a recipe for *sanbusaj* (a puff-pastry pie), the author says: 'If you like, you can decorate it with eggs, as is done in banquets and important meals' (al-Warraq 1987: 89). At the same time, the frequency and abundance of information on dish garnishes suggest that this was also a common practice.

The elements used for decoration in al-Warraq's book are spread over the surface of the dish and, although their own flavour may add a distinct character to it, it is obvious that these elements are intended for the pleasure of the eye. The combination of two or more elements for decoration is a common feature of these recipes, where we find a meat dish adorned with rue and a boiled egg cut in four pieces (p 107), or a chicken recipe with a cold sauce decorated with boiled egg yolks and pomegranate seeds (p 70). More substantial decoration is given for another meat dish, adorned with sausages, eggs, cheese, olives and vegetables (p 108); in a recipe for *narjisiya*, the garnish is made of sausages, puff-pastry pies and fried loaves of bread (p 183).[5] Generally speaking, however, Ibn Sayyar's recipes are more delicately decorated, with things such as pomegranate seeds (p 69), fresh coriander (p 187), pieces of cucumber (p 70) or chopped rue, widely used for this purpose, alone or with pieces of celery (pp 116, 117, 119, 122, 137). These decorations were used for both meat and vegetable dishes, in some cases providing interesting colour combinations, as in a recipe crowned with rue, pomegranate seeds, sumac and almonds (p 112). Mint as a decorating element is used together with walnuts or celery (pp 71, 173), but it is not as common as rue.

Some recipes from al-Warraq's book show a more elaborate decoration. In a recipe for a kind of bean pastry fried with spices and spread on a platter, saffron-coloured almonds are arranged in a star design (p 118). Another good example is found in a recipe for *narjisiya* (p 182), served in a stone frying-pan placed on a bamboo tray. The frying-pan, blackened by fire, is 'dressed' on a round bread loaf. On the surface of the dish, boiled egg yolks are arranged, each one bearing a small sprig of rue.

A constant interest in colour may be appreciated in many of these examples of decorated dishes. Almonds were dyed red or yellow to adorn sweet preparations, such as *khabis* (p 251), and they were mixed happily with green pistachio nuts over the dome-like structure of this confection (p 246). In fact, colours were used specifically as an important element in sweet preparations, and al-Warraq gives a short list of the different dyes to be employed in this respect (p 15).[6] Although not so widely used as in later works, saffron is the main colouring element in al-Warraq's recipes for sweets (pp 242, 246, 248, 253, 262), and in some other dishes, like *zirbaja* and *'adasiya* (pp 152, 167: given as an option for those who like it).

As in other recipe collections, colour is the dominant factor in the confection of some recipes which are called 'white', 'green' or 'black'. Thus we have, in al-Warraq's cookbook, recipes for white and green *zirbaja* or for white and green *isfidhabaja* (pp 152, 159, 160). Green was obtained, in the first case, through the use of fresh celery, rue and pistachio, while the green *isfidhabaja* was made with coriander and celery juices and a liberal use of fresh coriander. Other instances of white dishes are the *baqliya*, the *tharida* (a kind of omelette) and *khabis* (pp 161, 196, 207, 246). No indication is given as to how the whiteness of these particular dishes is obtained; in the case of *zirbaja* and *isfidhabaja*, when the green and white recipes are compared, the significant point in the white recipes is the absence of fresh green celery or coriander. So it may be assumed that whiteness meant the absence of a dominant colour in the preparation of a given dish. On the other hand, black is used only for three recipes of the same dish, the *qaliya*, and the colour is obtained by the addition of sumac or *kamakh* juice (pp 212, 213).

The use of different colours or coloured elements seems then to be the main aesthetic value in the cookbook of al-Warraq. References to the actual shape of confections are rare and mostly restricted to sweets, as in the already mentioned *khabis*, to which we may add pieces of bread shaped as half-moons or in a sweet confection with a design on its surface (pp 272, 277).

Needless to say, the flavour of a dish is as important as its appearance. I shall not deal here with the aromatics incorporated in the process of cooking itself, which have given Arab food a distinct character from medieval times to our day. What I intend to examine now is the role of perfumes in culinary texts, either when they are added to any dish as a part of its final preparation or when they are used for other purposes.

Al-Warraq makes a clear distinction between *tib* (perfume) and *abazir* (spices), both used to give fragrance to a dish (p 48). The first category corresponds to what Ibn Masawayh calls *al-usul* ('basic perfumes'), namely musk, amber, aloes, camphor and saffron (Sbath 1937).[7] In his classification, al-Warraq adds to this list other aromatic substances like cloves, spikenard, nutmeg, cubeb pepper and rosewater. As will be shown below, sprinkling dishes with rosewater as a final touch, a common feature of later cookbooks, is not so evident in al-Warraq's. Nor does he give many indications of the use of the other perfumes he mentions in the introductory chapters of his book.

These basic perfumes were, of course, expensive, but they were also accessible to the leisure class. Their appearance in al-Warraq's book is related to dishes for kings and grandees, like a kind of *lawzinaj* (almond sweets) made for kings while travelling, to which musk, amber and mastic are added (p 265).[8] Al-Warraq also gives a recipe for *khashkananaj*, a sweet dish perfumed with camphor or musk (pp 265, 271). It is interesting to note that musk is recommended to perfume a beverage (*nabidh*) made from sugar in winter, while camphor was used in summer for the same purpose. Pots in which food is to be stored are scented with aloes and amber (p 329). One of the most significant uses of perfumes in al-Warraq's cookbook is related to the preparation of a kind of *sikbaj* by a slave girl of Ibrahim b. al-Mahdi, called Bid'a, who made it for the Caliph al-Amin. Bid'a asked Ibn al-Mahdi's chief cook to bring all the necessary ingredients, among them a *mithqal* of amber and two *mithqal* of Indian aloes. These were used to perfume the different kinds of meat, already cleaned, before placing them in the pot to be cooked (p 133).

The need to achieve purity of smells is stressed throughout al-Warraq's book, in which he requires the use of new pots for the preparation of many dishes, in order to prevent the intrusion of previous flavours. If a new pot is not available, the old one should be cleaned very carefully, first with mud and then with celery (p 9). The concern for cleanliness and purity, so evident in other aspects of Islamic culture, also finds its way into the culinary texts and al-Warraq is no exception to this broader pattern. His book contains chapters devoted to recipes for different kinds of soap, toothpicks and perfumes. These recipes are put into the context of eating habits and uses; table companions should clean their mouths and hands and perfume themselves before sitting together. Clean and scented, they are then ready to partake of food that has also benefited from the use of perfumes.

Turning now to the Islamic West, the cookbook by Ibn Razin al-Tujibi provides an interesting development in the culinary tradition. Some dishes are embellished, as in al-Warraq, when prepared for banquets and special occasions (Ibn Razin 1981: 109–10, 122). But we do not find in Ibn Razin fresh vegetables like cucumber or celery used for decoration. Rue, so common in al-Warraq, is absent in Ibn Razin, who uses only mint for this purpose (pp 154, 158, 159, 185). In fact, decoration of dishes in the *Fadala* is of two kinds. In the first, sugar or spices (mainly cinnamon, pepper and ginger) are sprinkled over the surface of the dish, usually all together or in combinations such as cinnamon/ginger, cinnamon/pepper, sugar/cinnamon and ginger/pepper. These coatings apply to meat dishes; fish, eggs or vegetable dishes have no decoration and sweets are simply covered with sugar.[9]

A second kind of garnish corresponds to the 'heavy' decorations already noted in al-Warraq's *Kitab Tabikh*. They are, however, much more frequent and complicated. Boiled eggs used for this end are very common, by themselves or in combination with olives (p 45), almonds, walnuts and grated cheese (p 46) or with mint (pp 96, 159). A further step is taken when boiled eggs are used for decoration, together with meatballs (p 175) or with another meat preparation called *isfariya* (p 152). The most elaborate embellishment of all is found in a recipe for a chicken *tharida*, involving a process of three different stages. First, boiled eggs are cut into four pieces with a thread. Secondly, chicken livers and gizzards are made into a paste with salt, spices and egg whites. After being shaped into small pastilles, the paste is fried and cut into oblong pieces. And thirdly, four boiled egg yolks are also fried. All these elements are left aside to decorate the *tharida*, over which cinnamon and ginger are also sprinkled (p 47).[10]

The decorative patterns followed by Ibn Razin seem to give less importance to colour than those used by al-Warraq. This is confirmed by the specific references to the colouring of dishes found in the *Fadalat al-khiwan*. The Andalusian author recommends only the use of saffron as a dyeing agent. This he does much more frequently than his Eastern predecessor; alone or dissolved in rosewater, saffron is present in the great majority of Ibn Razin's recipes. Saffron is used for meat, fish, vegetables, eggs or sweets in a way that suggests the abundant availability of this product in the Islamic West. Ibn Razin recommends, in some cases, not to put too much saffron in some dishes (e.g. pp 47, 129), because, as he explains, it may spoil the dish; however, his consistent and generous use of saffron implies the existence of a general taste for this condiment. It has to be remembered here that saffron has a distinct scent that goes together with its colouring qualities, but these are stressed in some recipes, in which saffron is used to colour pieces of pumpkin, eggplants, boiled eggs and so on.

This uniformity of colouring is broken, in Ibn Razin's cookbook, only by the presence of two kinds of *tafaya*, green and white (p 103). The *tafaya* is the Western Islamic counterpart of the *isfidhabaja* mentioned by al-Warraq and is held to have been introduced into al-Andalus in the ninth century by the famous Iraqi musician Ziryab.[11] As in the Islamic East, fresh coriander, together with the juice of chard, is used to give the dish its green colouring.

Spikenard and rosewater are the favourite scents in Ibn Razin's *Fadala*. Expensive perfumes like musk or camphor may be dissolved, in small quantities, in rosewater (pp 167, 250, 251) to scent meat or sweet dishes. But Ibn Razin seems to be cautious over the use of these kinds of perfume. Aloes, for instance, are only found once in his book, to perfume a container in which sweets are to be stored (pp 63–4), and amber is totally absent from it. Perhaps the general use of saffron may be explained as a replacement for other and possibly much more expensive perfumes, whose use was restricted to high social circles. In his chapter on soaps and other hygiene preparations, Ibn Razin includes these scents, but in one of the recipes he states clearly that this kind of soap is used by kings and grandees after a meal (pp 277–9, no 5). And he also gives the recipe for the common kind of soap, which is made only from chick-peas (no 8).[12]

Thus it appears that Ibn Razin's cookbook is less concerned than al-Warraq's with the aesthetic aspects of a meal. Perfumes are also of lesser importance and it is significant that Ibn Razin does not include a chapter on them, as is the case in the Eastern Islamic culinary books. On the other hand, Ibn Razin's recipes are rich and varied, with a great part of the book dedicated to meat dishes. Geographical and economic reasons may explain the restricted use of costly perfumes in the culinary culture of Western Islamic lands, but the taste for substantial and rich dishes which can be appreciated in Ibn Razin's book reflects, I think, their use by a well-off urban middle class. Extravagance has never been among the virtues of that class.

We arrive finally at the third and last of the cookbooks selected for this exercise in the history of taste. I have already mentioned the problems relating to the authorship and geographical origin of the *Kanz al-fawa'id*. Its encyclopaedic character is, however, evidence enough of the intentions of its unknown author; he was trying to collect as many recipes as possible. This poses some problems when trying to analyse its contents, probably drawn from many different sources which are never quoted, contrary to the procedure followed by al-Warraq. We do not know therefore to what extent the recipes collected in the *Kanz* reflect the culinary habits of a social group or whether they simply betray the interest of the author in compiling as much material as possible from all the sources available to him.

Keeping that in mind, we shall proceed to examine the data provided by this anonymous treatise. As to what concerns the decoration of dishes, the *Kanz* shows a marked preference for herbs, spices and sugar; we do not find here the 'heavy' decorations used by al-Warraq and Ibn Razin. Dishes are embellished in the *Kanz* with chopped mint (nos 16, 19, 23, 24), chopped rue (nos 202, 203), jasmine (no 116), cinnamon (nos 22, 25, 30), sumac (no 212), pistachio (no 259) or sugar (nos 64, 132). Possible combinations include boiled eggs with cinnamon (nos 28, 35), pistachios with hazelnuts and sugar (no 34), roast hazelnuts with sugar (no 115), cinnamon with spikenard (no 172) and, finally, dry coriander with caraway, pepper and mastic (no 148). All these things are used on meat and vegetable dishes, while sweets are decorated with hazelnuts, pistachio and sugar (nos 303, 305, 309, 316, 319, 322, 329, 332, 338, 343). On one occasion, saffron-coloured almonds are used for a sweet made of dates (no 344).

More elaborate decorations are not very common in the *Kanz*, where in only two cases have I been able to find something similar to al-Warraq's concern with the visual aspect of dishes. There is a recipe for chicken in the *Kanz*, in which the meat is placed over a bed of sweet basil. Sauce is poured over the chicken, which is then decorated with pieces of cucumber, chopped boiled eggs and tarragon leaves (no 473). The other example is a dish of chick-peas, decorated with black olives, roast hazelnuts, a prepared mixture of spices (*atraf al-tib*), rue and mint (p 616).

Colour as an element of decoration is present in the *Kanz* in all kinds of dishes. Saffron is again the basic ingredient and it can be dissolved in rosewater, vinegar or honey, or mixed with flour. A dish of meat is accompanied by saffron-coloured rice (no 110). Saffron is also used to dye almonds or hazelnuts which decorate sweets (nos 333, 338, 345) or other preparations (nos 497, 564, 593). In contrast to the other cookbooks, limited to the use of saffron to obtain the orange-yellow colour, the *Kanz* suggests the possibility of using turmeric (*kurkum*), if only on one occasion (for a dish of birds; no 148). Another dyeing agent peculiar to the *Kanz* is safflower (*'usfur*), recommended to obtain a red colour (nos 175, 535, 543, 552). Both turmeric and safflower are significantly less expensive than saffron; although they lack its scent, they could be used as substitutes for its colouring qualities. The market-regulation books indicate that fraud was common in the sale of saffron (Ibn al-Ukhuwwa 1938: 123), which speaks eloquently of its high price. Using other colouring agents was then not only a matter of choice but also of economy.

White as a distinct colour is also present in the *Kanz* in the names of some recipes, like *faludhajiya* (no 317) or *hintiya* (no 50), which is made with almond water and almond oil. The colour black is to be avoided and the *Kanz* recommends caution in the use of sumac, which in great quantities may blacken a dish (no 259).

As in al-Warraq's text, the *Kanz* restricts its indications for different shapes to the chapter on sweets. There we find recipes for confections such as the *mushabbaka* (no 276), the finger-shaped *sha'biya* (no 279) or the sweet figures (*tamathil*) of *mashash* (no 284). But the most interesting text included in the *Kanz* on the pleasure of sight associated with food is connected with a recipe for fowl. This is a very interesting piece of culinary information, presented by the author as being of Andalusian origin. The basic point in an otherwise long and complicated recipe is that the birds have to be cooked in glass containers, to allow the table companions the pleasure of viewing the process of cooking. In the words of the *Kanz*, 'watching the movement of the birds with their heads up and down, together with white and black chick-peas and green fennel, is one of the most marvellous and good things [to be seen]' (no 149). It should perhaps be noted that this is a recipe intended for a drinking session in the winter season and it is said to be favoured by kings and grandees in al-Andalus and the Maghreb.[13]

The most common scent used in the *Kanz* is rosewater, to which stronger perfumes like camphor or musk are frequently added. A distinctive character of the *Kanz* is its preference for rose scent, reflected in the extensive use of rosewater as a perfume, as well as other rose confections such as rose jam and dry or fresh rosebuds, included in the preparation of many dishes. But rose perfume is far from being the only scent present in the *Kanz*, which makes liberal use of a wide variety of perfumes.

Camphor by itself is employed in a number of dishes (nos 12, 33, 49, 50, 51, 52, 66, 67, 68, 108, 111), as is the case with musk (nos 51, 61, 62, 63, 67, 135, 262, 287, 290). Both these perfumes were felt to have different qualities according to the seasons; as in al-Warraq, camphor is recommended for hot weather, musk for the winter (no 340: a sweet recipe made of dates and honey). According to the author of the *Kanz*, camphor should be employed with caution, because in great quantities it may impart a bitter taste to the dish (no 68). Saffron is appreciated as a perfuming agent, as well as for its colouring qualities (nos 226, 379). Amber and aloes are not so frequent, but they appear occasionally (no 354).

The use of perfumes, general throughout the *Kanz*, is intensified in the chapters devoted to sweets, drinks and pickles. Sweets are usually perfumed with rosewater, musk and more rarely with camphor, but suggestions for a particular kind of sweet also include nutmeg, cubeb pepper, cloves, saffron, aloes and musk (no 286). Drinks and pickles are stored in containers carefully scented with amber and aloes (nos 432, 437, 438, 439, 489, 587–8, 599). And, as was the case with al-Warraq, the *Kanz* includes at the end of the book specific chapters devoted to the preparation of perfumes, soaps, scented waters and perfumed pastilles.

Perfumes are thus a marked characteristic of food preparation and presentation in the *Kanz*. The aesthetic aspect is also important, but it is perhaps less emphasized. If we consider the *Kanz* as a later stage in the historical evolution of Arab culinary tradition, it would seem that, at least in the Islamic East, the sense of smell had become the most important one for accompanying a good meal. The visual appeal is not lost and colours continue to play a role in the decoration of dishes, but decoration in the *Kanz* has not the touch of originality found in al-Warraq's cookbook. Pomegranate seeds, for instance, are widely used for cooking in the *Kanz*, but not for the embellishment of dishes.

The interest in making food more appetizing through the combination of different colours and decorations is not exclusive to Arab culinary tradition (see Wilson 1991). Through the cookbooks analysed in this chapter it is nevertheless possible to appreciate a marked preference for

'golden' meals, dyed with saffron or other colouring agents (ibid). Dishes
are sometimes compared to a garden (al-Warraq 1987: 105), where nature
combines its different products and varieties in a beautiful and organized
way. This aesthetic aspect is enhanced, in Arabic cookbooks, by the use of
perfumes.

Combining the pleasures of taste and smell in a joint gustatory
experience is, in my opinion, one of the most characteristic aspects of
Arab culinary tradition. Perfumes are closely related to the care and
appearance of the body in Islamic culture, for both men and women.[14]
They are also recommended for health purposes; to avoid the 'foulness of
the air', rooms should contain cooling aromatics or perfumes.[15] Scents are
held to be among the good things of the earth, things to be enjoyed and
appreciated, as al-Baghdadi so wisely explained in the introduction to his
cookbook. It is therefore not surprising to see how the culinary tradition
incorporated the use of perfumes as a necessary complement to the pleasure
of eating and drinking.

Notes

1. See Arberry's translation (1939: 32). The Arabic text was first edited by D.
   Chelebi (Mosul, 1934); see also al-Baghdadi (1934).
2. See the editorial introduction to al-Warraq's *Kitab Tabikh*, in which early
   texts are mentioned. For an overall view of culinary texts in Islamic culture,
   see Rodinson (1949) and Waines (1989).
3. The *Fadala* has been edited twice by Benchekroun (1981 and 1984).
   Translation of some recipes, with an introduction, in de la Granja (1960).
4. See the introduction to the edition of *Kanz al-fawa'id* by Marín and Waines
   (in press).
5. For other examples of this kind of 'heavy' decoration, see pp 201, 204 and
   205 (recipes for *thara'id* of meat).
6. See also ch 103 (pp 276-7).
7. For another interesting example of medical literature on perfumes, see Sbath
   (1944).
8. Camphor and musk are present in two other recipes for *lawzinaj* on this
   same page.
9. In one case (p 77), the sweet is decorated with roasted pine nuts.
10. A similar recipe is on pp 50-51.
11. See Dozy (1957 sv).
12. Nos 1 and 5 may correspond to 'middle-class' preparations.
13. For another example of this combination of drinking and a dish of birds, see
    Marín (1991).
14. See Kanafani (1983). A collection of prophetic traditions about perfumes is
    in Ibn Muhammad (1990).
15. See the text by Ibn Ridwan, trans by Dols (1984: 131f).

15. Blood, Wine and Water: social and symbolic aspects of drinks and drinking in the Islamic Middle East

Richard Tapper

'You are what you eat,' as the saying goes, though it is not always appreciated that there are at least two senses in which it is true. Apart from the biological, there is the cultural component of identity, according to which food customs are very prominent as subjective markers of class, gender, ethnicity or other social categorization.[1]

Equally true, in the same senses, would be, 'You are what you drink.' There are several cultural senses to this, at least in the Middle East. First, while 'bread and salt' are proverbially the medium of hospitality, with attendant implications of shared substance and hence identity, and consequent obligations of mutual help and protection, in practice day-to-day hospitality and conviviality are expressed through drinks, notably tea and coffee. Secondly, some drinks take on a relatively non-political differentiating meaning as ethnic, class or regional markers; in the Middle East this is commonly the case with water, as discussed below. Thirdly, in extreme political and ideological confrontations, certain liquids can become heavily loaded metaphors.

This chapter was originally written as a paper for a seminar series on the theme of 'drink and drinking'.[2] The anthropological literature normally assumes 'drink' to be 'alcoholic'.[3] Indeed, earlier papers in the series established a tradition of presenting a detailed analysis of the ceremonial role of alcoholic beverages in a particular cultural context (*sake* in Japan, *kava* in Fiji, palm-wine in East Africa, wine in rural France). Such an equation of 'drink' with 'alcohol' probably reflects normal English-language usage, though 'drink' clearly has wider meanings, notably in its opposition to and association with 'food'.

My own first two field studies were of totally 'dry' cultures: Shahsevan nomads in Iran and Pashtun tribespeople in Afghanistan. More recently I worked in a Turkish provincial town which, though by no means dry, could hardly be said to put an important cultural emphasis on the consumption of alcohol. To an extent my brief in 'representing' the Middle East at the seminar was to discuss the implications of the Islamic prohibition of alcohol.

This prohibition is one of the better-known, even stereotyped, attributes of Islam – through images of the smashing of whisky bottles at the peak of the Islamic Revolution in Iran, the penalties for illegal distillation among expatriate workers in Saudi Arabia, and so on. But this attitude of strict condemnation is, of course, part of a cultural complex, in which other 'drinks' are prominent: most obviously water, but also tea, coffee and other beverages; while in some Middle Eastern languages tobacco smoking is closely linked with 'drinking', as, in cultural terms, is the taking of drugs.

Clearly in Middle Eastern languages, too, there is a problem of categories. It is not at all clear what we should translate as 'drinking': what substances it covers, whether it is distinct from 'eating', or linked with other processes. Thus, the Turkish *içmek*, the Pashto *tsakil*, the Arabic *shariba* are standard terms for both 'drinking' and 'smoking',[4] much in the English sense of 'drawing', taking a 'draught' of a pipe or a drink; that is, taking a flowing substance into the body. In Tehrani Persian, however, while you 'draw on' (*kashidan*) a cigarette or a pipe, a single verb (*khordan*) covers 'eating' and 'drinking' and a whole range of other activities and ideas, including 'taking' bribes or oaths; *nushidan* is used only for 'to drink' with the connotation 'for pleasure'. In Arabic (*'akala/shariba*), Turkish (*yemek/içmek*) and Afghan Persian (*khordan/nushidan*) 'eating' and 'drinking' are differentiated, and in Turkish the same verb (*içmek*) is used for 'smoking', 'taking' an oath, and 'drinking'. In Arabic and Persian, the noun *mashrub*, like the English 'drink', implies 'alcoholic'; so also does *içki* in Turkish.

How do the various substances that one 'drinks', and constructions of them, relate to each other? And just as important, how do they relate, as ethnic or religious markers, to Middle Eastern constructions of drink in other cultures? I have chosen to focus on three liquids which are full of metaphorical resonances, not just in the Islamic Middle East but elsewhere: blood, wine and water.

Although several other chapters in this book, and a small literature elsewhere, refer to 'drinks' and 'liquids', I know of no comprehensive study or survey. It is potentially a large field, and a chapter of this length on such a subject cannot be comprehensive or conclusive; it can only be suggestive. For context, I shall first touch on the place of tea and coffee, the most common beverages in Middle Eastern cultures; then move to consider how water, wine and blood are treated in the Qur'an and Muslim tradition generally. Then I examine contexts and meanings of drinking in Turkey, focusing particularly on attitudes to water. Finally I briefly consider some metaphorical constructions of water, wine and blood in the Islamic Revolution in Iran.

Tea and coffee

Coffee and tea were not found in early Islamic times (Hattox 1985). Tea is a recent introduction to the Middle East, in most parts dating back no earlier than the 19th century, but tea drinking is now a regular, ceremonial and central activity, and has been described fairly often, if in rather pedestrian terms, in the ethnographic and other literature. Coffee is considerably older, having been discovered in Yemen in perhaps the 13th century, and gradually introduced in Egypt, Anatolia and Iran in the 16th century. There were prolonged debates among Islamic scholars about whether coffee was lawful. Some held it to be intoxicating and therefore unlawful, others contended that it had the virtue of keeping drinkers awake and therefore was a valuable aid to the pious in their nocturnal devotions. It was eventually widely adopted, even among Wahhabi fundamentalists, and became associated with bedouin nomads, of whom there are endless ethnographic accounts of the preparation and serving of coffee as an important routine and ritual, in terms comparable, for example, to the Japanese tea ceremony.

Some writers applaud the introduction of coffee as a replacement for the earlier addiction to wine. The term *qahwa*, from which the English 'coffee' probably derives, was an earlier Arabic word for wine. Another substance credited with the same virtue is tobacco, introduced to the Middle East soon after coffee, around 1600. Tobacco too was for a time subject to debate among scholars: were its effects such as to render it unlawful? Generally it was accepted, though not by stricter Muslims such as Wahhabis.[5]

Already in 17th-century Iran we can read that visitors were offered tobacco (the water pipe) and coffee, served in small cups and sipped, as today.[6] This was standard practice, according to later reports such as Lane's excellent *Manners and Customs of the Modern Egyptians* (1860: 134f), dating from the early 19th century. Since then, however, in much of the Middle East tea has replaced coffee as the most common beverage. Coffee, where it is still to be found, tends to be reserved for special occasions, while tea is drunk throughout the day.

Beyond the generalization that everywhere guests continue to be offered tea (or coffee) and tobacco, and that these substances are closely related in people's attitudes, there is, of course, a very wide range of difference in the ceremonies of hospitality in which they are involved, a matter which could provide scope for an intriguing comparative investigation but can be only briefly addressed here.

SERVING THE GUESTS: SOME VARIATIONS IN CUSTOM

Among Shahsevan nomads in north-western Iran,[7] the main drink is black tea. Most families have their own samovars, and status rivalry is associated with either genuine old Russian brass *nigalay* or modern oil-burners. A single teapot is constantly refilled from the simmering samovar and poured into a set of Russian-style tea glasses, each with its saucer or metal holder (silver in wealthier families). When the tea is about ready for serving, a sugar loaf is brought in and a son of the household breaks it up in front of the guests – a ceremony echoing an important event in the rites of betrothal. The tea glasses are passed round among the guests, starting with the most honoured; each of the first batch of guests to be served consumes two or three glasses, then refuses more, whereupon the glasses are rinsed and the next batch are served. In classier tribal society, guests take lumps of sugar, put them in the glass, stir and drink from the glass. In poorer families, or informal situations, each sugar lump is put straight in the mouth and tea is decanted from the glass on to the saucer and slurped from the saucer through the sugar; this practice has the effect, if not the purpose, of cooling the drink more quickly.[8] Tea and sugar are major expenses in each household budget – indeed, in the 1960s among the poorest families consumption was still both new and infrequent. Tea-houses in surrounding villages and towns are known as *qahva*, though coffee has not been served in them for many years.

In rural northern Afghanistan,[9] by contrast, green and black tea are differentiated and offered according to the season of the year or the preference of the individual. Each guest receives not only his own bowl but his own small china teapot, containing enough for four to five bowls, and drinks at his own speed. Usually, in tea-houses or well-to-do family homes, a large quantity of powdered sugar is poured into the bowl before it is handed to the guest, though sometimes lump sugar is offered, which again involves a different drinking technique. Large samovars are found in tea-houses, which are generally known as *samawar* as a result, while families in much of the country own and use copper *chayjush* tea kettles.

In western Turkish provincial towns,[10] as in Iran, only black tea is known, though coffee here is also highly valued and kept by every family for special occasions. Tea-houses (*çayhane*) are places where men meet, usually to drink coffee. Family guests, male or female, are likely to be offered either tea or coffee; or they may be served a swift single cup of coffee while the tea is brewing. Only among family or very close friends is the teapot brought out from the kitchen in front of the guests. Usually, guests see only the tray of tea glasses, with separate bowls of sugar-lumps (usually from shop-bought boxes); and the sugar is stirred into the glasses.

These three examples illustrate something of the range of variation across the Middle East in the logistics and etiquette of offering drink to guests, and the extent to which there is a sharing of cups, pots, implements and so forth (Desmet-Grégoire 1991). These variations clearly relate to social constructions of identity and difference, but examination of these is beyond the scope of the present discussion.

DRINKS AND LIQUIDS IN THE QUR'AN AND ISLAMIC LAW

What of the attitude to drinks and drinking purveyed in the Qur'an? In the Prophet's time, the drinking of wine was apparently common and associated with gambling. In early revelations, indeed, wine seems to be approved as a sign of God's grace: 'of the fruits of palm-trees, and of grapes, ye obtain an inebriating liquor, and also good nourishment',[11] though the latter may be meant as a contrast with the liquor. The wine of paradise, moreover, is associated with both milk and honey. Muhammad appears to have changed his attitude. There is a succession of revelations, first declaring that the benefits of drinking wine and gambling are outweighed by their sin, then later prohibiting wine, idols, gambling and divination as the works of Satan, particularly, it seems, because prayer was seen to suffer when people became drunk.[12]

Wine came to be condemned as *haram*, an unclean substance akin to blood and urine; drinking it became one of the greatest sins. This condemnation is supported by numerous traditions, including one to the effect that an increase in drinking will be a sign of the Last Days. Prohibition of wine and spirits came to be a distinctive marker of the Muslim world, by contrast with Christians and Jews, though consumption has been common in much of society.

That said, there has been protracted debate on what wine is. Probably in Muhammad's experience there was only date wine; later, any alcoholic beverages made from grapes, dates, honey, wheat or barley were classed as wine (*khamr*), in so far as they intoxicate and obscure the faculty of reason (*'aql*) and self-control – this was the basis of later debates concerning the nature of and proper attitudes to coffee, tea, tobacco, *qat* and harder drugs. Non-fermented sweet drinks – *sharbat* – made from fruits diluted with water are, however, allowed and much prized.[13]

Water figures in the law mainly in terms of its purifying capacities. Without going into detail, according to most schools the main impurities include the acts and conditions of coition, menstruation and childbirth, and things such as wine, pigs, dogs and their products, dead bodies and some human body products. These impurities can be removed by water, which must be running, or from a still pool of a certain size, or at least with unimpaired colour, taste and smell. In extremis, if no water is available, dust, sand and stones may be used.[14]

Among other liquid substances, milk and honey are prominently mentioned, both of them crossing the boundary between drink and food; milk is the archetypical white substance, while honey can be white, yellow, red or black, according to the plants on which the bees have fed.[15] In some passages, human beings are said to be created of congealed blood; in one passage, from seed 'poured forth', 'issuing' from the loins of man and the breast of woman respectively.[16]

When the Qur'an turns to describing paradise, as it does frequently, attitudes to water and wine become clearer. Not only do copious fountains of delicious water beckon the believer from almost every other page, but wine, or at least a special kind (non-intoxicating? non-bitter?), is the reward of the faithful, no longer forbidden. More precisely, 'rivers of incorruptible water; and rivers of milk, the taste whereof changeth not; and rivers of wine, pleasant unto those who drink; and rivers of clarified honey'.[17] Other substances that pollute or intoxicate on earth do not exist in paradise. According to some traditions, there will be no urination or defecation, but all excretions from the body will emerge in the form of perspiration which will diffuse an odour like that of musk (Lane 1860: 67). At the same time, one of the chief horrors of hell is boiling water, both as the drink of the damned and as a regular shower poured over the body.

Blood, in the Qur'an and Islamic law, is one of the most polluting substances, in association with food: it is absolutely forbidden to eat or drink fluid blood. The blood of menstruation and birth is also highly polluting. Yet in other contexts – sacrifice and martyrdom – blood can be especially sacred.

DRINKS AND LIQUIDS IN THE HUMORAL SYSTEM

Islamic constructions of blood, and its relation to water and wine, can be seen more clearly as parts of the humoral system of natural philosophy which pervaded the Middle East (and Europe) until recently. The origins of some aspects of this tradition are Greek/Hellenic, but the cosmology and symbolism of the classical tradition were modified by Islamic scientists, philosophers and theologians from the earliest period of Islam. Elaborations of the tradition are both complex and diverse; for our present purpose a brief and simplified outline must suffice.

In the temporal realm, form and matter are seen as ever-changing relations between four elements (fire, air, water and earth) and their associated qualities (paired combinations of hot or cold, and moist or dry). All beings and objects of the material world are compounds of these elements and are ranked according to their composition. There are three types of soul, each associated with particular faculties and located in particular organs of the body: the vegetative or natural soul, located in the liver; the animal or vital, located in the heart; and the rational, located in the brain. Only humans, among living creatures, possess the rational faculty (*'aql*). Humans were created of congealed blood, but the body is made up of four humours (blood, yellow bile, phlegm and black bile) which result from processes of digestion of food and are essential to bodily functions. The humours combine with the primary elements and their associated qualities, and interact with both natural and supernatural environments, to form the temperament of the individual, which locates that individual cosmologically.

Good health is a function of an operational balance between environment, human faculties and humours; sympathetic action is the main mechanism by which changes in the circumstances of an individual can be effected. In this system, blood is understood as the prime agent of nutrition, while all food is classified by its qualities (hot/cold, moist/dry) and its strength. Transformations effected by cooking, or conversely by rotting, are used to explain virtually all physiological processes. Islamic idioms of purity and pollution are intrinsic to such explanations of nutrition and disease.[18]

Blood and water are starkly contrasted in this system of ideas, with ramifying resonances in contemporary Muslim cultures. Blood is one of the four humours, associated with the heart and with the element of fire as hot and dry; in the heart it is linked with emotion and passion (*nafs*), with youth and women. In contrast, water is one of the four elements, associated with the moist and cold humour of phlegm, with the brain, and with reason or self-control (*'aql*), the capacities of maturity and maleness. Blood is the basis of birth, lineage, identity, commensality among kin; water is linked with individuality within the wider community. More generally, blood is associated with both this world and hell, with temporal and material existence, with sadness, bitterness, passion, sexual love; water is associated with heaven and eternity, with deity and spiritual values, with happiness, sweetness, self-control, divine love.

Drinks such as coffee and tea play no part in this imagery or in its local applications; but milk, wine and sherbet do. Milk is generally regarded as more of a food than a drink: unlike water, before consumption it should have stopped flowing and become a solid – it is not drunk raw, but must be 'cooked' in various ways. It is commonly placed in a serial relation to blood: it is the food of the very young, which builds up their blood. 'Milk siblings', who have no blood tie but are nursed from the same breast, are forbidden in marriage to each other – they have acquired common substance (blood) after birth. 'Blood siblings' are those who have no tie of substance through birth or nurture, but choose to 'share blood' in order to incur the obligations of common substance.

Wine and sherbet are combinations of fruit juice, sugar and water that are respectively sour and intoxicating, and sweet and non-intoxicating. The ambiguities between them (the Persian/Turkish terms for them share the same Arabic root *sh-r-b*) are resolved in scholarly religious circles by a ban on wine and the elevation of sherbet; in common practice the former becomes the drink of men and the latter of women.[19]

What is clear from the above survey is that blood, wine and water are powerful symbols in Islamic tradition, closely related to each other, multivocal and highly ambiguous, characteristics which are strongly developed both in Sufi imagery and in local constructions and practices. The following two sections exemplify this by examining further the role of drinks and liquids in two contrasting social contexts.

Water in a Turkish town

In Eğirdir, a Turkish provincial town I visited regularly between 1979 and 1984 (including most of 1983), the commonest drink, as elsewhere, was tea, although coffee was more highly valued: both more expensive and more traditional, and less easy to obtain (especially when the government banned the import of coffee in 1979). Guests at home, or in a shop or office, are offered coffee or tea, or simply served a single cup of Turkish coffee soon after arrival, to be followed later by sweets, fruits, cakes and more prolonged glasses of tea, almost always with sugar. As for alcohol, all but the most religious men learn to drink *rakı* (arrack: aniseed-flavoured spirit) in the army, and may continue at home: it is very much a national drink. Beer, wine and other liquors are manufactured in Turkey and freely available, but they are expensive and not so favoured or common as *rakı* in most homes, being foreign in associations. All such drinks should be consumed with food, with *mezze* titbits at least. Women do not drink alcohol, and smoke only in private. There is alcohol, however, in the ubiquitous *kolonya*, with which everybody allows their hands to be drenched at regular intervals, except during Ramazan and on other religious occasions.

Water plays a major role in Turkish folklore (İnan 1968; Gönüllü 1985). In Eğirdir it is an obsession, which might seem surprising. In the desert, or at least in the stereotypic arid Middle Eastern environment, one expects a concern with water as the very source of survival, leading perhaps to such idealizations as those in Qur'anic depictions of paradise. Here, however, the environment is the opposite of a desert: Eğirdir sits on a spit of land almost surrounded by one of the largest lakes in Turkey, the quality of whose water is a source of local pride and satisfaction, despite growing pollution from town sewage. Everyone believes there to be scientific proof of the absence of *mikrob*; experts are said to know the location of the 181 underwater springs that feed the lake. The topic of water is as common in daily intercourse as the weather is in Britain. In fact Eğirdir people are not unusual in this: when Turks from different parts of the country meet, they compare claims to the quality of their local water, claims expressed in stereotyped terms referring to sweetness, coolness and aperitif powers: 'the spring in our village has water as cold as ice, sweet as sherbet, you can drink gallons of it without feeling full; and if you drink, you'll be able to eat huge meals ...'.

Picnics are common spring and summer pastimes in all classes of Turkish society. The objective almost invariably is a spring, even among Eğirdir people, who, on summer days when tourists make pilgrimages to their lake, themselves go up-country to one of the local mountain springs. At the spring, one relaxes in comfort and serenity, cooking and eating large and complex meals, and playing games; playing, indeed, at 'paradise', the word on everyone's lips. Very similar are pilgrimages to local shrines, which, like mosques, all have some sort of fresh water supply.[20]

Another dimension of this focus on water and sweetness among the Turkish townspeople (and *mutatis mutandis* among other Muslims in the Middle East) is revealed in the text used in the Mevlud, one of the most important religious rituals in the town, now as in the past.

Süleyman Çelebi's poem, the *Mevlid-i Şerif*, was written in 1409 in a language which is simple and direct, an effect likened by the translator Edmonds to that of the first chapters of the Gospels of Matthew or Luke or some Christmas carols for Christians, though it is very much a poem for all seasons.[21] Recitals occur frequently throughout the year. Mevlud gatherings are held separately for men and women: men's most often in the mosque, especially during the major Islamic feasts, while women's recitals are almost always held at home.

The *Mevlid* is a long poem, divided into a number of sections, describing the miracles and teachings of the Prophet. It has two climaxes, textually and emotionally related to each other: the Prophet's birth, and his miraculous visit to heaven. The first climax is related in the first person by the Prophet's mother, Emine Hanım: just before giving birth, she cries out with thirst and is at once offered a glass brimming with sherbet, whiter and colder than snow and sweeter than any sugar; it is offered by houris, who tell her that it comes from Allah; she drinks, and feels her being transformed, so that she can no longer distinguish herself from Light (*nur*). At that moment, a white bird descends, Emine gives birth to Muhammad, and heaven and earth are then bathed with Light.

At the second climax, the Prophet makes his miraculous Night Journey to Jerusalem and thence to heaven. It is said by Gabriel, who guides him, that heaven and earth that night are filled with the water of Zamzam, the holy well in the precinct at Mecca. When this is mentioned, the sponsor of the recital has rosewater (which is always associated with Muhammad – and his sweat) sprinkled on all the participants; or, at the commemoration of a recent death, the commonest occasion for Mevluds, each participant is given a glass of sherbet – sweet and dilute lemonade; or, most often among men, no drink but boiled fruit sweets. Informants make an explicit link between sherbet (sweet fruit drink), rosewater, and Zamzam water (which pilgrims bring back from Mecca by the gallon). Further, a sweet, religious, virtuous smell is described as 'like musk', again associated with rosewater: for example, in the mortuary preparations, after the corpse has been washed it is drenched in rosewater, to 'make the grave smell like musk'. Rosewater, finally, is the proper replacement for *kolonya* on religious occasions, when welcoming guests to one's home.

In the context of conservative rural Turkey, water is thus all-important, mainly for its divine resonances with Zamzam and sherbet – coolness, sweetness and light. Wine and blood, and milk and honey, figure in the background, subject to the standard taboos, but treated more pragmatically than ceremonially.[22]

BLOOD, WINE AND WATER IN IRAN

In the context of urban Iran, particularly in the Islamic Republic, wine and blood join water in the foreground of experience and imagery.

Wine (*mey*) pervades Persian civilization, literary, social and spiritual. Sufi mystical imagery and poetry use the intoxication of wine as a metaphor for the joy of losing personal identity and achieving union with God. Blood, in direct contrast, symbolizes the pain and sorrow of separation from God; but this sorrow itself is necessary for achieving reunion; a more direct and final way to God is to shed the blood of martyrdom. The Sufi's tears are of blood. In other contexts water figures strongly: the Sufi must drink water to cool the heat generated by his devotions; but the waters in the various fountains in the gardens through which he progresses towards Knowledge and Truth are pure Light (*nur*), the Light without fire, both the essence of divinity and the vehicle and means of prophetic succession. Significantly the Persian (*cheshmeh*), Arabic (*'ayn*), and Turkish (*pınar*, *göz*) words for 'spring' or 'fountain' also mean 'eye', and are linked with light, as well as with tears of both blood and water.

An unsympathetic observer in the 17th century, Père Raphaël du Mans, superior of the Capuchin mission at Isfahan, commented scathingly on both the water and the wine which were drunk in Persia. The water in Isfahan was disgustingly polluted, he said, and he found the wine (compared to French ones) strong, dry, cold, heavy, earthy, bitter to the taste, and liable to cause hangovers. Moreover, his hosts drank wine with muttered excuses and facial grimaces; and they drank it not (as presumably he felt they should) for its taste nor for its digestive properties, but simply in order to achieve intoxication, to forget the cares of the world (du Mans 1890: 100, 136f). Other visitors have been more sympathetic, more in tune with the effects of wine, water pipe and music found at a typical Persian dinner party, combining to induce a state of wellbeing and subdued ecstasy.[23]

The morality and legitimacy of wine drinking have been a constant subject for religious debate in Iran. Fischer, in his study of the education of modern Iranian Shi'ite clergy, records the variant opinions expressed, for example, that Avicenna held that wine was permitted for intelligent people (those with *'aql*) but forbidden for the fool; while tradition records that 'Ali, the most prominent Shi'ite imam, said that if a drop of wine were to fall in a well, and if then a sheep were to drink from the well and rejoin the flock, he would not eat the meat of any sheep of that flock. Generally, Shi'ite divines are united in condemning any substance or activity (including music and dancing, wine, gambling, drugs, even love and poetry) considered capable of intoxication, that is, of overpowering the *'aql* and causing the release of passions and emotions (Fischer 1980: 129, 161).

Blood and water are central to 'the Karbala paradigm', which Fischer considers to have been the driving force of the Islamic Revolution. That is, the annual commemoration of the martyrdom of Hoseyn, 'Ali's son and the third imam, on 'Ashura, the tenth day of the month of Muharram. The events commemorated are those of the historical battle of Karbala in Iraq, when Hoseyn and a small band of followers fought the armed forces of the Caliph Yazid. Having watched his family die of thirst in the desert, Hoseyn and his supporters were slain. To the Shi'ites, the martyrdom is the most heartrending, pitiful – yet glorious – tragedy in history. One of the most heinous acts of Yazid's tyranny was to refuse access to water – an elementary human need that by the desert code of honour is never refused to thirsty individuals – not only to his warrior opponents, but to women and children. The Muharram *ta'ziyeh* passion plays and *rowzeh* orations make this a central part of the drama.[24] Shedding tears through weeping, and blood through self-flagellation, bring promise of redemption for the audience.

As revolutions do, the Islamic Revolution turned many meanings upside down: especially those of blood, wine and water. The drama of Karbala was brought from history into the present, from Iraq to the streets of Tehran; after the revolution had succeeded, the scene moved to the American Embassy, and then back to the frontier with Iraq, where it remained until 1988. Slogans of the revolution, chanted or displayed on marchers' banners, played up blood, wine (alcohol) and water as central Islamic (Shi'ite) metaphors, defining the character of the revolutionary, Islamic community and establishing the distance from and contrast with the corrupt Pahlavi regime.[25] Some of the imagery has Sufi origins and orientations.

'Does he pray gladly in Karbala, or does he drink wine with the Chinese leader?'

'Shahanshah's regime – fount of every corruption (*tabahi*).'

'Life in the refuge of this oppressor is wrong,
Whoever becomes man of truth, his life is in death (annihilation).
Drunken sleep, enough! Idol worship, enough!
Death to this shah! Death to this shah!
You pretended to advocate Muslim leadership,
Then why did you chop at the roots of religion?'

The reference here, unlike in Sufi poetry, is to actual self-annihilation in a march facing the real guns of the enemy; a real prospect, an incredible act of existential definition. Mere self-preservation is likened to 'drunken sleep' and idol worship; by dying, being killed, submitting to annihilation, one awakens to Truth and becomes an authentic Muslim.

To march into gunfire requires an act of self-control, but it is more easily accomplished in a state of dissociation, that is, intoxication, loss of self, again a Sufi objective; but it is intoxication with the 'sherbet of martyrdom' (*sharbat-e shahadat*). Both 'dissociation' and 'self-control' are concepts subject to interpretation. Thus, if control equals purity and lack of control leads to pollution, the revolutionary forces of Khomeini and the *'umma* are characterized as pure, by their performance of ablutions and avoidance of alcohol. Drinking is opposed to urination: self-controlled man exerts strict control on both. Muslims are defined by the ban on alcohol (and drunkenness and corruption), and by preceding worship with ablution, cleaning the body with water from all traces of urine, blood, dirt and so forth. The shah and his followers, and the corrupt regime, are wine-bibbers and pissers, drunks, the 'fount of corruption'. The Hezbollahis, a strongly controlled group, with strong control of the body (cf. Douglas 1973), emerge from the corruption of the old regime.

In 'The shah has become a Muslim – the water of his ablutions is the blood of Muslim youth!' the ultimate antithesis – the purity of water ablutions and the pollution of blood – exposes the hypocrisy of the shah. Other slogans accuse the shah not only of washing in blood but of drinking it: the metaphor of the leech, sucking blood and draining life without causing a wound.

'Khomeini – God is your Keeper; he slays your bloodsucker (*khunkhor*) enemy.'

'Name: Reza; surname: Pahlavi; food: blood of the youth.'

'The leech – he learnt how to suck blood from the executioner shah!'

'America, America, shame on your trickery (*neyrang*)!
The blood of our youth drips from your claws!'

During the war with Iraq, stories circulated of Khomeini, too, as 'blood-sucker', allowing the bodies of executed and soon-to-be-executed Mujahidin opponents of the regime to be drained of blood for war-front transfusions, even for the wounded among Khomeini supporters on the streets of Tehran.

Eating, drinking, and washing in blood are signs of the shah's lack of self-control, his corruption, evil dissociation or madness. But the blood of Muslims is also associated with life and allegiance, as a positive force. One slogan ran: 'As long as the blood runs in our veins, Khomeini is our leader'; another: 'The blood of Hoseyn runs in our veins.' The Hezbollahis were able to swear on the blood of the martyrs, smearing handprints of blood on the walls, on faces and so on, while it continued to flow during the riots. This blood is not polluting or profane, but sacred, even the ultimate purity: the power released in blood. As blood is ambiguous in this Shi'i revolutionary imagery, so also are tears: signs of exertion in the jihad, and of sympathy for Hoseyn, they are sometimes said to be the blood of Hoseyn.

In sum, liquid images are central to the formation of the new, revolutionary community. Intoxication with 'wine' creates cowards, incapable of fighting or working, destroys inhibitions on sexual and other passions, and leads to hell, or an illusory 'heaven' on this earth. It stands in opposition to the 'intoxication' of the hero-martyr whose religious zeal and patriotism remove his inhibition on self-sacrifice, and bring him to the real heaven. Both kinds of intoxication, the good and the bad, are in turn opposed to the sobriety and coolness of water and reason, the normal earthly life of work.[26] Water is the proper drink and medium of ablution of a controlled ('aqil) Muslim; wine, once the central metaphor of a Sufi approach to God (individual and 'selfish'), is now constructed literally in its capacity to destroy self-control, the sin of the corrupt regime; while blood is both the ultimate impurity (as the food and ablution of the hated tyrant) and the ultimate purity (the martyr's self-sacrifice in the jihad to restore the purity of Islam).[27]

CONCLUSION

In the Middle East, I suggest, even so simple an act as drinking a glass of water is symbolically complex. What are the resonances? The main theme of this chapter has been to suggest that the most important, at least for men, concern the conceptual relations between water, wine and blood as dominant symbols. This triadic relation has its roots in religious prescriptions and texts. In certain specific ways, each of the three substances has direct links with the supernatural world and divine power. These links are constructed in an idiom involving time and movement: the purity and power of water and blood depend on their flowing, and flowing at the right rate. Somewhat differently, the purity and power of wine are associated with an evocation of a changeless, timeless eternity, while it pollutes in an emerging, literally temporal world.

All three substances, as symbols or metaphors, are essentially multi-vocal, and attitudes to them and constructions of them are highly ambivalent. The relation between them is not fixed, but rather the imagery associated with them can be systematically configured in numerous ways. Each community constructs its own configuration of the liquids, through which it both depicts and sanctions proper morality, and denigrates the values of its prime 'others'. Each liquid has the power as a dominant symbol to transform individuals and to impel them to action; the power comes both from its multivocality and from its complex relations within a cultural configuration of all three substances.

I suggest that the possibility of combining and recombining the images into different configurations accounts for the sustained use of the imagery throughout Islamic history, and that the multivocality of the three and the power of their resonances may be one of the mainsprings of Islamic belief and practice. Not least, the particular configuration in a given local culture will both reflect and determine experiences of how 'others', both Muslim and non-Muslim, configure the same substances. Most obvious examples are the way in which the prohibition on wine distinguishes Muslims from Jews and Christians (more powerfully than that on pork, which distinguishes Muslims from Christians but not Jews), while constructions of blood, particularly in sacrifice, distinguish all three Semitic religions from each other, and from many non-Muslim neighbouring cultures.[28]

Notes

1. As discussed in several other chapters.
2. Early drafts of this chapter were presented at seminars at SOAS, the University of Texas at Austin, the University of Pennsylvania, and the University of St Andrews, and at the 1988 Middle East Studies Association Annual Conference. I am grateful for comments received on those occasions, as well as from participants in the SOAS conference. I am much indebted to Nancy Lindisfarne-Tapper for suggestions, comments and field materials. I have also benefited from discussions with colleagues and present and former graduate students. M. A. S. Abdel-Haleem, David Brooks, Carol Delaney, Erika Friedl, Ziba Mir-Hosseini, Ilsa Schumacher and Nazif Shahrani offered particularly illuminating comments.
3. For example, all but one of the papers in a recent collection (Douglas ed. 1987) concern alcohol, and attempt to correct the view of 'drinking' (namely 'alcohol abuse') as a 'problem'. The exception is Hazan's paper on tea drinking

in a London day-centre. Another contributor (Gusfield) finds coffee opposed to alcohol in American cultural constructions.

4. In Egypt at least; in Jordan and Syria *dakhkhana* is used for smoking.
5. Cf the debates over the mild stimulant *qat* (*Catha edulis*), as described by Weir (1986).
6. See e.g. Chardin (1988); du Mans (1890: 100).
7. I did ethnographic field research among the Shahsevan of Moghan between 1963 and 1966, the period to which the 'ethnographic present' of the text refers.
8. The above description (like that for rural Afghanistan below) applies to male guests, who are clearly segregated from women guests or hosts. Among women and their guests, the same procedures operate in attenuated form.
9. Field research between 1968 and 1972.
10. Field research between 1979 and 1984.
11. Qur'an, 16: 67 (Sale nd: 262).
12. Wensinck (1960); see also Heine (1982: 44f); McAuliffe (1984); Hattox (1985: 46f).
13. For more details, see references in previous note.
14. In arid areas, the life-giving qualities of water came to have a cultural importance equal to its purifying capacities; though contradictions are apparent in such terminology as the Afghan Persian *ab* (water) or *ab-e mani* (seed-water) for semen, a polluting substance (brought to my attention by Nazif Shahrani).
15. As Sale notes (nd: 263, n1).
16. Qur'an, Sura 86 (Sale nd: 577).
17. Qur'an, Sura 47 (Sale nd: 490).
18. Cf Bromberger (this volume). See also Good's account (1977: 172f); and Tapper and Tapper (1986: 70). The foregoing account of the role of liquids in Qur'anic and humoral cosmologies and physiologies is, of course, both schematic and over-generalized. In Middle Eastern communities, alternative – but not necessarily contradictory – theories abound; see, for example, both Good (1977) and Delaney (1986).
19. See also below, the role of sherbet in Turkish and Iranian religious imagery. *Shurba*, a term in general use in Arabic, Persian and Turkish for 'broth', comes from the same root; see above.
20. On picnics and pilgrimages, see Nancy Tapper (1990).
21. See Tapper and Tapper (1987); and Edmonds (1969).
22. In this, as in much, there is a contrast with the Greeks, among whom wine is valued both as drink and as body-washing medium; see, for example, Hirschon (1983: 123).
23. For example, Browne (1950: 119f). Other drinks have become more popular in 20th-century Iran: *'arak*, vodka and recently (before the Islamic Revolution) beer and spirits, locally made as well as the more prestigious foreign imports.
24. See also the *sa'y* rite during the Hajj in Mecca, commemorating Hagar's search for water, and the creation of the well of Zamzam.
25. The following paragraphs owe much to some notes passed to me by Michael Bland, who has been studying the use of metaphor in the discourses of the

revolution.

26. These oppositions were suggested to me by Erika Friedl.
27. In the spilling of martyrs' blood (and the prototype of Hoseyn) there are echoes of the Christian notion of Jesus' blood washing away the sins of the world; but otherwise the configuration in the slogans of the revolution does not make the same circular connections as are present in the classic Christian model: water transformed into wine (in the feast at Canaa); wine transformed into blood (in the Last Supper and communion); and blood transformed into water (in washing away the sins of the world). It would be interesting to pursue further – but not here – the metaphoric relations between these three liquids and the three main foods (meat, fruit and cereal/staples), and their transformations in different European-Middle Eastern traditions.
28. For some other comments on blood and sacrifice, see Tapper and Tapper (1986). Considerable detail on beliefs and practices in relation to blood, wine and water among Jews, various Christian sects and other non-Muslims of the Middle East is to be found in Drower (1956).

16. Of Leaven Foods: Ramadan in Morocco

Abdelhai Diouri

Food in the month of Ramadan has never been the subject of a specialized study. To glean information, we have to resort to works on Ramadan or on Islam in general (see Bibliography), as well as cookery books, particularly the classic *Fadalat al-khiwan* of Ibn Razin (1981), but also current ones.[1] It seemed better therefore to resort to field observations (some 30 case studies) among various urban and rural areas of Morocco (Tangier, Fez, Rabat, Casablanca, Marrakesh; the Souss, the Tafilalet, the Doukkala and the Zemmour).

The material collected, although initially appearing uneven, can be shown, when analysed, to exhibit certain regularities. A dual system of analysis is employed: according to the order of succession of meals, and according to a possible paradigm for the two special meals of Ramadan, *s'hur* and *ftur*, where systematic examination reveals the mechanisms involved in their preparation and function. The substructure is a very simple pattern of food based on cereals (*qutniya*), whether ground or unground, and linked to the use of yeast, showing signs of ancient agricultural rites. This suggests the hypothesis that the prescriptions of the sacred fast are articulated through a framework controlled by symbolic principles.

REVERSALS: NIGHT AND DAY

In Morocco, people eat three meals a day during the month of Ramadan, as throughout the rest of the year. The only difference seems to be a variation in the timing of meals during the day: during Ramadan, all meals are taken at night: first, at sundown (*al-maghrib*), the *ftur* (literary Arabic: *iftar*, breaking the fast); second, somewhat later at a time set by family tradition, the *'asha* (*al-'isha'*, dinner); third, at dead of night, just before dawn, the *s'hur* (*al-sahur*). From daybreak until nightfall, people do not eat, they fast. During the remainder of the year, the reverse is the case: people sleep at night and eat during the day: first, on waking, the *ftur* (*futur*, breakfast); second, at midday, the *ghda'* (*al-ghida'*, lunch); third, in the evening, the *'asha* (*al-'isha'*, dinner).

This difference in the timing of meals, in so far as it consists throughout the month of Ramadan of eating at night rather than sleeping, and fasting during the day rather than eating, suggests that we are dealing with an antonymic inversion of the habitual rhythm of sleeping and eating. However, as we shall see, several irregularities create an asymmetry in this antonymic pattern. Furthermore, the new rhythm created by the fasting–feeding pattern will also impose a rhythm proper to Ramadan on the daily life of both the individual and the group, a rhythm which will also require new adaptive mechanisms, inasmuch as it is nothing less than an articulation of the sacred.

THE ORDER OF MEALS

If people are asked if they are preparing something special in terms of food for Ramadan, they first mention the foods of the *s'hur* (different kinds of *rghaif*, or pancakes), then those of the *ftur* (*harira*, or soup) which are used to break the fast. When pressed, they describe the preparation, on the eve of Ramadan, of *halwa* (honeycake which accompanies the soup), *sellou* or *zammita* (ground sugared cereals)[2] and other dry cakes eaten as after-dinner snacks. Stocks of these sweet foods are replenished during the third or fourth week of the month. The real dinner (*'asha*) is hardly ever mentioned: it consists of a meat-and-vegetable dish, as in normal times, in other words the stew called *tagine*. Dinner is therefore not a special meal during Ramadan, whereas *s'hur* and *ftur* are.

The order in which these two meals are mentioned – first *s'hur* and then *ftur*, not the reverse[3] – is significant: *s'hur* marks the start of something (the fast) whereas *ftur* ends it. This pattern of *s'hur* → *ftur* reveals the basic set of conditions and the justification for the fast: the *niyya* or 'intention' to fast, in other words the decision to abide by the absolute prohibition on food, drink and sexual relations from the moment when dawn makes it possible to distingush 'a white thread from a black thread' until nightfall (Qur'an 2: 187).

There is clearly an ascetic aspect in the multiple dimensions of the practice of the Ramadan fast: to savour the poverty of the poor, their hunger, to share with them, to expiate one's own sins, to forgive others theirs, to renew contact with one's nearest and dearest, to tame one's passions, to counter Satan at every turn. This aspect, however, rather than opposing Ramadan with not-Ramadan, prefigures what should be man's normal, albeit ideal, behaviour throughout life. Even more, it attempts to define man's absolute status: between the beasts and the angels.[4]

In other words, it is not food which is the focus of Ramadan, but rather the fast whose sacred nature is established by a strict system of sanctions and prohibitions. Food as such is not regulated by any legal prescription. People refer to the famous Tradition of the frugality of the Prophet (water and dates, Bukhari nd, III: 37, 47) which was scrupulously observed by mystics (Hallaj used to break his fast with a date and a mouthful of water). In effect, everything seems to make eating food an act which defines the limits of the fast, as suggested by the Tradition: 'Hasten the *iftar* and delay the *sahur*' (Bukhari nd, III: 47). The fast is sacred, food symbolic.

Ramadan can thus be seen to determine a specific mental, psychic and physical attitude towards the body, the group and spiritual values, which further implies a different experience, both internal and social. Hunger, supplemented by the prohibition on decorating the body and applying perfume and cosmetics, brings it back every year to a 'state of nature', shown externally through the skin colour and breath odour by which those who fast recognize each other as if reflected in a multiple mirror. Generalized daytime tension, animated night-time visits at which one discusses everything and nothing and which are stimulated by overtures of forgiveness, manage to free relationships from their strong and rigid bondage to institutions, to let them roam free in a mystery which belongs to the realm of play.

EXCESS

If individuals held to the alimentary Tradition of the Prophet during Ramadan, their body weight would certainly show evidence of it by the end of the month. Indeed, this is still true for those believers, their ranks swollen by young adolescents, who invest Ramadan with the sense of mystical crisis typical of their age group. In fact, today, particularly in the towns, the exact reverse occurs: many people experience a substantial weight increase. It is as if the use of the two traditional basic elements – sugar (dates) and flour (*raghif*) – is expanded to excess. Forty years ago, the *ftur* consisted of a bowl of soup preceded by 'a sweet fruit, a small amount of honey or even just a mouthful of water: that alone gave strength ... [and the *s'hur* consisted] of a light meal: toast smeared with butter or bread soaked in beaten eggs and lightly cooked in butter ... [or, according to] an old custom ... a hot loaf, just taken from the oven; that was typical of the old peasants' (Ben Talha 1950: 7–8). Today, with what appears to be a self-generated indulgence, the traditional sweet fruit – the dates of *ftur* – are supplemented by other sweet fruits, dried figs and *halwa*; and the *s'hur* loaf (or *rghifa*) is supplemented by eggs or 'French toast'. Moreover, eggs are now eaten at both meals, as is milk, which older people mention only occasionally as having been eaten formerly at the *s'hur* in the form of sour milk. Besides, there are now snacks eaten between meals, such as *sellou* and/or *zammita*, as well as various biscuits, accompanied by tea and/or coffee or coffee with cream (Table 16.1).

Table 16.1 Menus in the 1950s and 1980s

	Ftur	Dinner	Snacks	*S'hur*
1950s	dates + *harira*, or honey or water	dinner		*rghaif* + tea? + *sellou* + sour milk or French toast
1980s	water + milk + egg *halwa* + *harira*	dinner	tea, coffee milk + *sellou* + *zammita* + biscuits	egg + *rghaif* + tea + *sellou* + sour milk

We should ask about the causes and significance of such a shift in emphasis. So far, we only have one element of a solution, even if it is hidden behind the argument – only of apparent value – of an unexpected compensation for the fasting, hitherto considered as a privation. We have here a functional problem linked to the labelling of meals, particularly to the meaning of *ghda'*. In fact, the succession of meals during Ramadan does not represent just a simple reordering – by displacement or inversion (in the rhetorical sense) – of the chain *ftur* → *ghda'* → *'asha* typical of normal times. The fact that the *'asha* (both the word and the timing) is preserved during Ramadan apparently leads to the elision of the *ghda'*, which is not, thereby, adequately replaced by the *s'hur* (because of the difference in timing and in content). Thus:

Normal periods:	*ftur*	*ghda'*	*'asha*
Ramadan:	*ftur*	*'asha*	*s'hur*

The *ghda'*, the main course in normal periods, is transferred here to the *'asha*, providing the same content and the same order (second) in the chain, with only the name changing. Thus the *'asha*, normally characterized by frugality since it is followed by sleep, during Ramadan becomes a *ghda'* which carries neither its own name nor one specific to the sacred month (on the model of the *s'hur*), which could have saved the situation. It is a *ghda'* hidden behind another name, which, moreover, lays it open to confusion because it is already known – *'asha*. This term is probably used here to divert attention from the taboo name (*ghda'*), and creates that disturbance of categories which properly belongs to the symbolic arena. As we shall see, this is a valuable hint at an explanation. However, even though it identifies the arena where we must seek the basic reasons for the excess typical of Ramadan, this disturbance cannot by itself provide the explanation for it.

PARADOXES

A similarly important dissymmetry affects social life. For the inversion of sleeping-and-eating to be symmetrical, the situation would have to be:

Normal time:	eating (day)	sleeping (night)
Ramadan:	sleeping (day)	eating (night)

This is not, however, the case, because a third element must be included, namely work. In normal time, work is interrupted by eating during the day, which, it would seem, could not be the case in Ramadan.

The time taken for eating, and the rescheduling caused by the fast, make the temporal organization of Ramadan a practical problem because it affects and disturbs three basic life-functions – eating, sleeping and working (not to mention reproduction). There appear to be only three solutions: declare the month of Ramadan to be a public holiday, paid for by the state; work at night; or work during the day without interruption. The first solution must be rejected from the start, since it would paralyse whole sectors of the national economy. The second is retained by the traditional sector, but at a relaxed rhythm. The third poses a problem as to whether work should be done in the morning or the afternoon. Work in the morning has the advantage that the worker is still alert, and this is the solution adopted by the modern sector (increasingly important in Morocco). However, it assumes that workers have not stayed up the night before – which is not the case, since people do stay awake most of the night. The idea of working in the afternoon must be rejected, too, because it assumes that people are fit enough to work then – which cannot be the

case, given the fatigue accumulated during the day as a result of the fast.
Indeed, with this third proposal, we are faced with a kind of double bind
which would be transposed from discourse on to the social. It follows that
the intolerable can only be tolerated at the price of a new masquerade
played out around the signifier, work.

The specific nature of the experience of Ramadan conceals three
oppositions: productivity and production falling to near-zero, versus
maximal increase in consumption; fasting and abstinence versus
extravagant feasting; and fasting and continence versus erotic exhilaration
(this particular opposition, obvious enough in the wakes, will be re-
examined below). The second element in each of these oppositions, taken
all together, gives the impression of defining the specific nature of Ramadan
as a type of feast (Rios 1990). We shall see that this is more than mere
impression.

PARADIGMS

The terms mentioned earlier, *rghaïf*, *harira* and *halwa*, are generic terms
which, because of the variety of foods that they each cover, provide the
menus of *s'hur* and *ftur* with a potentially rich paradigmatic depth, without
extending beyond a very narrow range of foodstuffs (Table 16.2).

An overall view of this table suggests two important generalizations.
First, none of these foods comes from the traditional cuisine, which is
considered as purely Moroccan in origin. Second, apart from mint tea,
which is sometimes prepared by men, everything is produced exclusively
by women. Thus, food at Ramadan sanctions culinary traditions of taste
as well as the division of space (and power) between men and women.
From this follows a complete ambience and a complete culture. If we
examine the recipes for these foods, we can propose a third generalization:
their basis in starch and leavening.

S'HUR

The various forms of *rghaïf* and its substitutes in the meal of *s'hur* (see
Table 16.3) are invariably and exclusively made from three components –
flour, water and salt (and sometimes also yeast). The distinction between
them arises solely from the mode of preparation, where 'to knead the dough
[is to] massage meaning' (Virolle-Souibes 1989: 73). Working of the dough,
in two stages (kneading and shaping), comes first; second is the cooking.
If there is stuffing involved, it plays a role only at the level of taste and not
at the structural level of classification (for example, *rghaïf* stuffed with
liver, brains or almond paste, or *briouate* stuffed with rice, *kefta* or almond

Table 16.2 Menus for *s'hur*, *ftur* and snacks

S'hur

mint tea	French toast	milk	cheese	*sellou*	liver
	mtlu'	sour milk	salted cheese	*zammita*	brains
	rghaïf mkhtemrine				
	rghaïf dial ferran				
	stuffed *rghaïf*				
	rghaïf oudnine el qadi				
	rghaïf dial megla				
	mlaoui				
	rezet el qadi				
	trid				
	briouate				
	beghrir				

Ftur

water	dates	milky coffee	lentil *harira*	*halwa* – *rghifa*	eggs
	figs	(cream)	*harira* with chick-	*halwa* – *mkharrga*	
		milkshake	peas		
		with fruits,	*harira* with chick-	*halwa chebbakia*	
		almonds	peas and beans		
			harira bidawiya		
			harira marrakchia	almond *briouate*	
			wheat *dchicha*		
			belboula		
			vegetable soup		

After-dinner snack

mint tea	various dry cakes	*sellou*	almond
coffee with or w/out cream	(particularly *feggas*)	*zammita*	*briouates*

paste). On the other hand, to serve these foods hot and almost systematically sweetened (with sugar, cinnamon, honey or butter) is a constitutive element of these recipes (not shown in the table).

We are concerned only with the first line of the table, that involving

Table 16.3 Types of *rghaïf*, *mlaoui* and so forth

food name	preparation – initial kneading (flour + water + salt)			shaping				cooking	page ref. (Bennani 1987)
	yeast or not	consistency	moistening agent	form	thickness	stuffing	final form		
1 fried bread (French toast)	yeast	rigid	dry, on flour	sliced	15mm	dipped in egg	slices	oven	22
2 *mtlu'*	,,	rigid	,,	rolled flat	4–5mm	–	round discs	clay pot	189
3 (*rghaïf*) *mkhmrine*	,,	,,	,,	cut up	1mm	–	,,	crisped	188
4 *rghaïf dial ferrane*	little or no yeast	soft elastic malleable	little oil	flattened, stretched square by hand	paper thin	fat and *khli'*	folded flat and square	oven	15, 77–80
5 stuffed *rghaïf*	,,	,,	,,	,,	,,	onion, parsley and pepper / liver, brains	,,	lightly oiled pot	187
6 *rghaïf oudnine l qadi*	,,	,,	,,	,,	,,	almond paste	,,	,,	185
7 *rghaïf dial m'qla*	,,	,,	,,	,,	,,	–	,,	fried	187

Table 16.3 (continued)

food name	preparation – initial kneading (flour + water + salt)			shaping				cooking	page ref. (Bennani 1987)
	yeast or not	consistency	moistening agent	form	thickness	stuffing	final form		
8 *mlaoui*	little or no yeast	elastic	oil	rolled	paper thin	–	round and flat	lightly oiled pot	186
9 *mlaoui au khli'*	,,	,,	,,	stretched	,,	*khli'* dried meat	,,	,,	187
10 *rezzet l'qadi*	,,	,,	,,	... to a thread	,,	–	,,	,,	–
11 *trid*	none	soft	soaked in oil	flat	,,	chicken *qadra*	square	over oiled pot	75
12 *briouate*	none	very soft	water	rough surface	thin skin	*kefta*, rice, almond	folded triangle	fried	14, 73–5
13 *bghrir*	much yeast	lightly runny	–	–	poured from ladle	–	round	oiled pot	16, 190

French toast. A round loaf from the previous day is cut in two, then each half is cut into slices 15 mm thick, which are smeared with egg beaten in a little milk and a pinch of salt, then fried in butter and oil. French toast is a happy if paradoxical conjunction of the major characteristics of *s'hur*, which are separated and opposed to each other in other variations of the menu. The first two are already contained within it, in the nature of the bread.

Kneading. The principle involved here is common to all kinds of dough. The process lasts 30 minutes on average. The act of kneading in itself is complex and rich in meaning. It begins with the mixing of water and flour: the water absorbs and swells the fine particles, which 'burst' and stick to each other, restoring them to life by starting the process of fermentation. Mixing alone is insufficient; the mixture must be kneaded, rubbed, crushed and worked over again and again. A simple semantic analysis of the word *'ark* (to knead) is enough to isolate the element of violence (Virolle-Souibes 1989: 78). In fact, *ma'raka* (battle) is derived from the same root, *'rk*, and indeed it is a question here of beating, subduing, rendering obedient and malleable the dough which is being kneaded. For kinds of *briouate*, for example (line 12 in Table 16.3), after the first phase of preparation is over, 'take a little of the dough between the fingers, let it begin to fall and catch it while falling ... work this dough again, lift it with both hands held flat above it and bang it several times hard against the table' (Bennani 1987: 15). From another point of view, the violence thus exercised on the dough has already been assimilated by the young girls, who 'experience this initiation as a kind of torture deploying the tyrannical authority of the teacher ... she who kneads the future kneaders'. In sum, the basic principle consists of 'controlling the delicate balance between dryness and dampness' (Virolle-Souibes 1989: 81, 95), which is doubly illustrated in our material: it is expressed in the gradation in consistency of the dough, from *baghrir* to bread, from semi-liquid to stiff; further, bread dough (like *mtlu'* and *mkhtmrine*) is rolled out dry on a board dusted with flour, whereas all kinds of *rghaïf*, *mlaoui* and *trid* are stretched and compressed on an oiled surface by hands also soaked in oil.

Khmira (yeast, leaven). Failed bread is bread without leaven, or where the leaven has not taken; it is *fière* bread, it connotes a negative sense of bread which contaminates the mistress of the house. A woman who cannot master her dough, that is, who cannot keep one day's leaven alive for the next, is a bad mistress of the household. A successful loaf is well-risen and light. In the column 'yeast/no yeast' in Table 16.3, the *rghaïf* group (lines 4–10) is given by Bennani as prepared with 'a little yeast'. Women from various regions almost always replied negatively to this question, although they were more responsive about *mlaoui* (lines 8–10). Only *trid* is always prepared without leavening. The link between 'leavening' and 'moistening with oil' in the shaping stage suggests a hypothesis based on the opposition of leaven to oil.

leaven →   dry shaping   → dry cooking (oven)
no leaven →   shaping with oil → roasting/frying with oil

Cooking. Here French toast brings together the two modes; being dry-shaped, it is dry-cooked in the oven, like *mtlu*' and *mkhtmrine*, then, cut into slices, it is fried in oil (and butter) like the fried *rghaïf* and the varieties of *briouate*. Frying is also symbolically present in those types of cooking inside a pot lightly smeared with oil or butter.

Coating. It should also be noted that French toast is soaked in eggs beaten with milk and that it is served with sugar or honey and with tea. The last three elements (egg, milk and sugar) linked to the three preceding components (kneaded dough, yeast and oil) provide a complete model of *s'hur*. Indeed, it is often served with nothing else but sour milk, a redundancy characteristic of the whole Ramadan dietary structure.

FTUR

There are many different types of *harira*, several of which are linked to special rituals. For example, on the morning of the *aid sghir*, a semolina *harira* flavoured with aniseed is served; a caraway-flavoured *harira* is served hot with steamed sheep's head on the 'Feast of the Sheep';[5] *'asida*, which is very similar to *harira*, is served on the morning of the *mawlid*; *herrbel* (or *herrberr*) for the *haguza* (the feast of *Ennair*, see below); *dadffi*, or *harira* flavoured with wild mint (*fliu*) and thyme is served to women just after childbirth (it is also served on winter nights, as is a *harira* made with okra); and *illan harira* is served to a mother who is breast-feeding.

In every Moroccan cookery book there are at least three or four recipes for *harira*. It is always mentioned as being used to break the fast every evening in Ramadan. Although each recipe starts from the same point, all are different. The recipes we have gathered during fieldwork are also varied. Indeed, *harira* is probably the one Moroccan dish for which no two regions, families or even individuals give the same recipe. One can always recognize a dish as *harira*, but it never tastes the same. It really belongs to a familial idiolect (Barthes 1964: 96). Differences are often in trivial details, sometimes changes of ingredients and occasionally more important elements.

Harira is cooked in two stages, in different pots: *tqata'*, the making of broth based on diced meat, and *tadwira*, literally the 'action of turning', which involves using a ladle to 'turn' some flour, scattered into the soup gently so as to mix it well without forming lumps.

Tqata' is the plural of *tqti'a*, a cut, a morsel of chopped (*qt'a*) meat: generally the fatty parts of mutton or other meats (scraps of chicken, wings, *kefta*), or simply fat (in some regions steeped in salt); it could also be *idam* or the fat of *khli'* (preserved meat); and sometimes *smen* (butter) or a spoonful of oil – for meat is often unavailable to the poor. These *tqata'* are cooked according to the *qadra* principle, in a light-yellow sauce made from pepper and saffron, onions and parsley. Chick-peas are added. This recipe is identical to that for *tagine qadra* with chick-peas (or with almonds, with or without rice) (Bennani 1987: 147).

Tadwira, by a purely metonymic process, deals with all of the contents of the second pot, primarily legumes such as lentils and beans. However, its essential component is the flour scattered over and 'turned' into the pot, which has the function of 'binding' the *harira*. The dissolved flour is itself mixed with freshly crushed tomatoes (or tomato paste), which deepens the yellow colour of the *harira* towards a bronze tint; and with coriander steeped in salt, which improves the taste and ends up obscuring the browner tones. This mixture, known as *ta'lika* (viscosity), is brought to the boil, and into it are put the *tqata'* stock, already cooked and set aside for this purpose, and some rice (or vermicelli), which gives the soup its grainy rather than velvety nature.

The *tadwira* is very probably the basis of the *harira*; certainly according to general opinion: 'the *harira* depends on the *tadwira*; without the *tadwira* there is no *harira*'. A *harira* could be formed without *tqata'* and probably originally was (Ibn Manzur 1910: entry for *harara*). Indeed, it still is today, in the cases of *hasuwa* and *belbula*. Are we then dealing with two separate recipes added together? Were the *tqata'* merely an addition resulting from some fantasy of refined, decadent taste in an Andalusia given over to bucolic pleasure? Or are they an enrichment, attributable to the need for strengthening foods because of the fast? In practice, the soup is prepared in two pots, and outside the Ramadan period the contents of each pot are kept separate.

The principal variations in *harira* arise from the different ways in which the two components are brought together. The legumes may be cooked in the stock of the *tqata'* or they may be cooked in fresh water; the elements of the *tadwira* may be mixed together in a *ta'lika* or added one at a time. The greatest difference is in the permutation of elements of the second and first components of the soup; for example, in the initial procedure for cooking the meat with onions and tomatoes (Moryoussef and Moryoussef 1983: 43). In all cases, the order in which the elements are introduced into the pot is decisive for the ultimate taste, because of the temporal principle of contamination by earlier elements. If salt and pepper are added at the end (ibid), this will certainly give a salty and seasoned taste but against the background taste of blander foods such as meat and chick-peas; and vice versa.

SNACKS

Halwa. A sign of the approach of Ramadan, criss-crossing the commercial arteries of the medina, is the transformation of the shops of doughnut merchants into *halwa* makers. However, home preparation of *halwa* is still a widespread family practice.

Halwa is served with *harira*; it is served again with *zammita*, along with tea, milk or coffee (with or without cream), as a snack before dinner; and it may be served again after dinner, while waiting for *s'hur*, along with many other cakes – always dry, based on pastry, sometimes mixed with almond or peanut pastes. This is the time of day when families stay up together and friends meet.

Halwa consists of wheat flour, eggs, ground sesame, saffron, olive oil, butter, orange-flower water, vinegar, yeast and a pinch of salt. These ingredients are mixed, energetically kneaded, allowed to rise, shaped, fried in oil and then soaked in warm honey for several minutes before being drained and dusted with sesame seeds.

The recipe brings together flour, yeast, and honey, just as is the case with *rghaïf*, but they are worked quite differently. The preparation is surrounded by specific concerns; one sets aside a day, a heated space for kneading the dough, and a special place for the container. The activity requires at least two people, and is usually the occasion for meeting and social exchange between young girls. Some knead the dough continuously while others take off small balls of dough which they then flatten with rolling-pins, addressing themselves to a truly skilled operation: 'cut the roll of dough into ten cm. squares, draw out from each square five strands, each two cm. wide. Pass the index finger of the left hand over the odd-numbered strands while grasping the two right-hand corners of the square with the other hand and pressing them together until they adhere. Then carefully put down the cake formed by twisting the strands together without breaking them, and cover it' (Bennani 1987: 195). Once the kneading starts, the aroma fills the entire house; as cooking begins, it releases the mingled smells of honey and oil, which linger in the atmosphere for several days.

Sellou-zammita. This is made from wheat flour browned in the pan, browned and crushed sesame seeds, almonds, cinnamon, aniseed, a little honey, salted butter and oil. These are mixed and presented as a mound covered with icing sugar and decorated with vertical lines of peeled grilled almonds.

For many people the only difference between *sellou* and *zammita* is one of consistency. *Sellou* is more sandy in texture, with plenty of sugar and little or no honey. In fact, *zammita* contains, in addition to the above ingredients, chick-peas, melon seeds and linseed, all similarly browned and crushed. Further, unlike the *zammita* used in trance rituals (Diouri 1991), the version eaten during Ramadan is mixed with butter, salted butter and honey.

In effect, even if yeast is not used here, unlike *halwa* and other dry cakes, it does involve fortifying foods which are still within the general category of 'cereals', and derived, basic constituents, in the last analysis, from all the foods of Ramadan.

It is worth noting that, contrary to what one might expect of food during a month of sacred fasting, the menu is rather heavy and difficult to digest. From the breaking of the fast until the small hours, people are constantly eating and/or drinking something. The table laid for *harira* is only cleared for something else to be served, and so on to the dawn call to prayer. There is a tendency among certain social groups to cram all meals into the period between dusk and midnight; then, suddenly, there is nothing more until the following dusk. Medical consultations over stomach upsets reach their annual maximum, and ulcer sufferers have crises that are sometimes fatal. Those who die during Ramadan become martyrs whose memory is engraved on the minds of all during this sacred month. Thus, even if stomach upsets are only rarely so serious, they still constitute an organic basis for the upsetting of temporal categories and the ensuing disturbances (see above).

There is a general acceptance of the theory of symbolism according to which the appearance of a phenomenon is merely its most superficial manifestation which hides its essence elsewhere, like an iceberg. The foodstuffs of Ramadan clearly provide nourishment, but they are too stereotyped and repetitive not to be concealing traces of a hidden code, itself probably anchored in some mythical material which gives it meaning.

Harira

The literal sense of the word is, for most purposes, submerged beneath the thick brown mixture which is the dish itself. The dish stifles the word so that the word in itself cannot give meaning to the dish except at a lower level of connotation, inextricable from the mixture and irredeemably contaminated by other elements which bind together into a compact and forbidding whole, far removed from the clarity of logic. To tell someone, '*Hrirtk hrira*,' means 'You're in a nasty mess,' or 'What a mess!'

We must resort to the etymology of the word and to the evidence of ancient literature.

Etymology (Ibn Manzur 1910). *Harira*: root *h.r.r.* – heat, to warm, hot. This passes, through semantic ramifications, to 'thirst'; 'piquant' (hot pepper which attacks and burns the throat); 'burned' (ground covered with black rocks); 'to level' (the ground); 'fine' or 'pure' (sand free of stones, etc); 'free' (men); 'silk' (soft and warm); then '*harira*: *hasuwwa* made from fatty matter (*dasam*) and flour'.

An analysis of entries within the lexical field of *harira* (Ibn Manzur 1910: svv *harira*, *khazara*, *nakhara* and *hasa*) allows a more precise definition of its characteristics. The first is a basic distinction between *harira* based on flour and *khazira* based on bran. The second demonstrates a progression: '*asida*, then *nakhira*, then *harira* and finally *hasuwwa*'. This progression probably relates to the manner of 'drinking', which is determined by the consistency of the food. *Asida* is a *khazira* without meat; *nakhira* comes from the root *n.kh.r.* – to make a noise with the nose (*minkhar*) while drinking; *hasuwwa* comes from the root *h.s.w.* and means 'drinking like the bird which takes small mouthfuls of water through its beak'. The third characteristic relates to the definition of *khazira* and how it is different from *harira*: '*khazira*: meat from the day before cut into small pieces in a pot and cooked in water and salt until soft; flour is then added until the broth begins to thicken ('*usida bihi*); finally any kind of fat (*adam*) is added: there can be no *khazira* without meat; if it contains none, then it is an *asida*'.

The slot left for *harira* can now be determined. The Arabic *Larousse* provides this definition: '*hasa*' based on flour cooked in milk' – without meat, with no other condiments, but with milk (which falls into the family of *samn*, *dasam*, etc) and, above all, a soup thick and smooth and based on flour.

Traditionally, a 'soup' with 'seven ingredients' was part of the culinary knowledge which played an important role in the education of gentlemen at the Sasanid and Abbasid courts (Rodinson 1949: 100). Elsewhere, when discussing pre-Islamic foods, Rodinson (1960) mentions broth as a 'habitual food of agricultural peoples'. Relying on al-Bukhari and Ibn Hanbal, he gives the example of '*harira* made of flour cooked with milk' and 'the *khazir* (or *khazira*), broth generally made with bran and meat cut into small pieces and boiled in water'. Bukhari himself simply defines '*khazira* based on bran and *harira* based on milk' (III: 93) and '*khatifa* made from crushed barley with milk and *samn*' (III: 105).

Recipes are described in more detail in the culinary literature of the Middle Ages. In the Muslim East, Baghdadi's *Kitab at-Tabikh* gives recipes for meat and flour dishes (ch 4). Under the name *rista*, it gives a recipe for diced meat with peeled chick-peas and lentils to which is added, at the end of the cooking period, a kind of vermicelli, *rista*, made from flour kneaded into fine strands (Arberry 1939: 45).[6] In the Muslim West, Ibn Razin gives nine recipes for 'soups' (1981: 24, 29), and eight for *hasw*, based on bread reduced to fine crumbs, or on moistened flour or leavening (recipes 3 and 4), slowly poured and 'turned' into a broth of plain water and salt or with added oil, egg or chicken, with or without other condiments such as coriander, ginger, cinnamon, onions or garlic. Another three are for *jashisha*, based on crushed wheat, barley or millet cooked in salted water (and/or milk). Finally, an anonymous manuscript on the cuisine of Marrakesh (Anon, *Al-tabkh al-Maghribi*: 182–3) gives three recipes for *jashisha*, the first of which is very close to the modern version of *harira* in that it is prepared in two stages, but with chicken instead of meat.

From this mass of material a simple piece of information emerges: nowhere does the description of *harira* match that found in modern recipes. It is basically made from *flour*, milk and fat. The recipes which come closest have different names (such as *khazira* or *hasw*). The word in current use is, in short, an archaism, whose traces are to be found in the process of making the 'broth' of moistened flour (*tadwira*) and in the general claim that '*harira* depends on the *tadwira*'. It is an archaic synecdoche. In the absence of decisive proof, this evidence reinforces the credibility of the hypothesis that the current recipe is the result of combining two separate dishes. This is particularly evident in the recipe given by the anonymous author of the manuscript on the cuisine of Marrakesh.

Boufertuna

The true, the authentic *harira*, it is repeatedly said, is *boufertuna*, at least in Fez and Rabat. I have examined the recipe, and it is the same and I am assured that the true character of *boufertuna*, its secret, lies in the preparation of the flour broth which is stirred into the pot during the last phase of boiling and which gives it its unique flavour. Rarely described in modern cookery books (Guinaudeau 1976: 29), the information on the secret which comes to us from grandmothers is to the effect that the broth is prepared with leavening taken from yesterday's bread dough.

Now leavening (yeast), which has cropped up repeatedly throughout our examination of Ramadan dishes, is their ultimate feature, critical to both *s'hur* and *ftur*. It could well be that here we have identified the essential ritual element in these foods.

What does leavening signify? Let us not hasten to reduce the symbolic dimension of leavening to a 'process of transmutation dear to the Arabs' (Chelhod 1955: 129). According to one deep-seated and widespread popular belief, leavening represents abundance and prosperity. Leavening supplies the language with metaphors for richness – 'crumbs of leaven bread', 'the good and leaven' (*l'khir wl'khmir*), 'may God make the leavening overflow'; metaphors for procreation – a young girl ready for marriage is 'risen' (*khmret*), and at her marriage she is told, 'may God make you as leavening (*khmira*) in the house'; metaphors for growth – a child grows 'like a loaf'; metaphors for sacred values, *baraka* – to inherit the loaf (*al-khobza*), he has his loaf (*b-khbiztu*). The positive values articulated through leavening in these metaphors are perfectly comprehensible: leavening alters, raises, increases volume and offers an image of growth due to an invisible, internal force, sufficiently mysterious to suggest the hidden supernatural.

Leavening thus resembles a good omen. *Boufertuna*, 'from the Spanish *buena fortuna*' (Dinya 1990: 80, n 1) is neither more nor less than a ritual practice designed to 'bring luck'. If we recall that, outside Ramadan, it is served the day after wedding nights, births, circumcisions and also funerals, it is clear that it accompanies important life crises, every rite of passage which marks, essentially, death and rebirth to a new life, with a youthful vigour. In Morocco – as in Algeria (Virolle-Souibes 1989: 96) – on the third day after the wedding, the new wife 'touches the dough' (*'l-khmira*), and the same on the third day after giving birth. This ritual is clearly linked to procreation and offers the basic model where the meaning of abundance blends with the renewal of strength by fecundity. Society operates a thousand and one means of isolating sterile women.

In that case, what fecundity or fertility is involved in the *boufertuna* at Ramadan? The more one examines it, the less one can think of anything other than the cereals, or 'seeds' in general (*qutniya*), which this rite as a celebration involves – preceded, as we recall, by a ritual fast, just as in simpler societies where major events (hunting, fishing, war, gathering, harvesting, for example) were preceded by fasts and other prohibitions as a rite of entry into the sacred arenas, to make the contact initiated by these actions.

Belbula

Explicitly, *belbula* is a simpler form of the cereal-based soup. Based on crushed barley or millet, it is cooked in water and milk with salt and olive oil. According to informants, it is being displaced in popularity by *harira*, but remains unchallenged as the food for breaking the fast in rural regions, particularly in the mountains, in the Souss and the south where barley, whose cultivation is less demanding, continues as the major cereal crop. What is remarkable here is that the people prepare the soup in this way from barley they have themselves cultivated on their own land. In this, one can discern a recurrence of the festival of *Ennayir* (or *Haguza*, depending on the region), the start of the Julian year, which, as we shall see, is repeated in *Ashura*.

In fact at New Year people eat *herr-berr*, which is similar to *belbula*: hard wheat separated from the bran (rather than crushed barley), cooked in water and milk, usually with sugar in place of salt and oil, and a little moistened flour added at the end of the cooking 'to whiten it'! This is called *ydiru 'l-khmira del-'am* – 'Start with the yeast of the year.' Many proverbs rhyme *Ennayir* and *khmayer* (the plural of *khmira*, leavening) and make *'l-khmira* the reference for the month's activities. Thus *Ennayir* – the 1st of Ennayer – is New Year's Day and falls on the 20th of the days called *liali* – the 40 coldest nights of the year, between the winter solstice and the end of January. Housewives always recall the proverb *Ennayer qttal 'l-khmayer* ('Ennayer kills the leavening') and redouble their vigilance in order to keep theirs safe; 'In Ennayer eat leavening' (*F-nnayer kulu 'l-khmayer*).[7]

This period lasts for three, five or seven days, depending on the region. *Herr-berr* is the first meal in a programme of ritual foods, with each day a special dish of *qutniya* (dried beans, chick-peas, lentils, etc) and of leavened *rghaif*. A couscous with seven fresh vegetables and meat concludes the ritual on the seventh day and marks the passage to products of the New Year; no meat is eaten during the ritual (Doutté 1909: 551). The principle is to feast in case *Haguza* comes at night to fill the stomach with straw or stones etc (according to region; Doutté 1909: 530, 532). 'Make the year's leavening' refers to feasting the stomach to fill the year, but everyone realizes that it also refers elliptically to the ferment that strengthens the land. Man must put as much *qutniya* in his stomach as will swell it so that he has a maximum in reserve for the year to come, enough to grow and produce a good harvest.

This exchange between man and land recurs in 'the tradition that a ball of leavening is buried at the end of the first furrow' (Benhadji-Serradj 1950: 247, n3). It recurs once more in metaphors using agricultural terms to describe human fecundity. When a wife is told, 'May God make you leavening for the house' (*khmira f-dar*), the husband is told, 'May God make you wheat and seed for sowing' (*zra' w-zrri'a*). He is the sown seed, she – in whom the seed is sown – the yeast, that is to say, fertile soil, a prosperous ferment for the seed.

At some level, coupling is in the image of sowing and, inversely, sowing is an example of impregnation. Fermentation does not occur without the decomposition of matter, a corruption which can only recall death, a corpse. There is no doubt that it is at this point, in the representation of this 'segment' – understood, anyway, as a trouble zone, dark, at the limit of what can be represented and understood – that it becomes necessary to resort to ritual for mediation; a 'segment' surrounded by the mists of sacredness and based on a regulation mark of the functions of life in a properly symbolic fashion. It must be left alone; and many precautions (rituals) are taken over what is derived from it, in this case cereals and their consumption.

Imagine death, then, or represent it and the after-life, to start with: the double death – that of the grain which decomposes underground, and that of the cut ear at the surface; and the double life – that of the wheat-germ from which emerges the sheaf, and of the development of future sheaves from which man obtains nourishment. Such appears to be the objective of the double ritual of *Haguza* and *Ashura*, with the figure of Byanno, *Boubennani* (*bonus annus?*) or even the eve of the New Year and its replicate in the *shaïb-'Ashura* (Frazer 1983: 25, 145–57; Doutté 1909: 515, 545ff; Destaing 1905: 64, n7): to kill, to destroy death; to resuscitate, to give life, to copulate – a function which has not yet been discussed.

THE 27TH NIGHT

The first fast is always marked by a special ritual which is different for girls and for boys. With a boy, a coin is placed under his tongue when the fast is broken, then he is given milk to drink and a date to eat. For a girl, a silver ring is placed under her tongue, and in some regions she is made to climb a ladder and adopt a special position before receiving the date and the bowl of milk from her mother's hand, or she has to sit on the edge of a well with a thimble and a needle in her hand (Chemoul 1936: 415). The symbolism of these elements is obvious; money and the power of money for the man, versus the fiancée's ring, the hole; the step up to marriage; needle and thimble are obvious; the bowl of milk and the date are inseparable from the first ceremonial contact of a newly married couple.

In their way, these rituals constitute the codes of a rite of passage from childhood to adulthood through the attractions of marriage – typically stylized on the night of the 27th of Ramadan. Parents take children old enough to have undertaken their first fast – about seven or even much younger – on a pilgrimage to the marabout's shrine in the town centre. The boys wear the traditional bridegroom's costume: white jellaba, red tarbush and yellow *belgha* (babush), all new; the girls made up with high pomp, their hair styled, dressed up, decked out in the jewellery appropriate for the traditional bridal costume (involving *neggafa* and hairdresser). The children are laden down with presents and delicacies.

Many things happen that night and contribute to giving it a special atmosphere of general excitement. On the basis of the quasi-mythical belief that heaven opens its gates that night (Belyazid 1987), there is an intense, invisible to-and-fro between men and God (requests to be fulfilled, fortunes arranged for the year to come), with the descent of angels among men and the ascent from the depths of the earth, via sewers and other openings, of the jinn trapped there since the very first Ramadan, all in the evening rituals of the Gnawa. Incense and perfume fill the town, in a to-and-fro no less intense but almost visible in the streets. A heightening of all the senses marks this 'night of destiny', in a final assault of praying, feasting and seductive hunting which have been brewing throughout the month, as though in regret at its ending.

This is not the 'night of error' which struck the imagination of so many because of the unhindered promiscuity it seemed to introduce.[8] This symbolic marriage of children – the youth of tomorrow – is light years away from that, and very much alive, even though not mentioned in the texts. If one does not lose sight of the preceding elements, it probably represents coitus symbolically in the general ritual seen as a fertility rite, where this notable 'night' illustrates the principle of the 'fertilizing influence of sexual relations on vegetation' (Doutté 1909: 559; after Frazer 1983: 122).

Think of the egg, always present on the table prepared for breaking the fast – the egg, development principle of the germ, of life, birth and rebirth, found again in funeral meals and in the naming ceremony (*'aqiqa*). Think of the date – the fertilizing gland, benediction. Think of milk – maternity nourishing purity. Think of the *zakat al-fitr* or *fetra* – four *mud* of wheat from each member of the family given as an obligatory sacred alms to the needy – the remnant of some ancient bloodless sacrifice of the first-fruits, in the guise of a rite to guarantee survival between the 27th and dawn on the morning of *'Id al-Fitr*.

ANTECEDENTS

Could there be a religious antecedent for Ramadan? Some have tried to locate it in Judaism. To me, it seems highly questionable to put forward any kind of hypothesis over its origin.

Even if the comparison between Exodus 24: 18 and Sura 7 (Surat al-A'raf), both of which mention the institution of a fast of 30 then 40 nights by Moses and Muhammad respectively, is provoking; even if Muhammad is known first to have instituted the 'Ashura fast (which corresponds to the Jewish Yom Kippur) and then to have abandoned it in the second year of the Hijra to put Ramadan in its place (Tabari 1980: 135–6), after a dispute with the rabbis of Medina (Wensinck 1925); and after reviewing all the hypotheses of borrowing from the fast in a lunar month of the pre-Islamic Sabaeans and from the Quraysh tradition of spiritual retreat on Mount Hira' during the month of Ramadan,[9] quite apart from these hypotheses and from the search for origins which motivates them and which itself smells more of metaphysics than of scientific argument, two unchanged elements of interpretation remain.

(1) Analysis of the food system of Ramadan in the Maghreb offers a model of the age-old fertility rite linked to the agrarian cycle. Within it, we find the rite represented in three acts, reordered and assimilated according to Islamic teaching: fasting, coitus and sacrifice of first-fruits.

We should recall here that Ramadan is the name of the ninth month of the Muslim year, and that, at the time when it was instituted as the fasting month, it fell in the summer. This will be far better understood if it is recalled that the word Ramadan is a corruption of *ramada*, root *r.m.d.*, the exhausting heat of summer, as it would be in the deserts of Arabia (Ibn Manzur 1910: sv *ramada*). This was probably the time of harvest, in particular for gathering the dates. In this connection, it is not inappropriate to recall the Tradition of breaking the fast with a date called *tamr*, that is to say 'ripe' (*tamr = 'amr = khamr*), as opposed to *rutb*, dates which are still yellow.[10]

(2) Whatever may have been the origin of Islam's adoption of the 12-month lunar calendar (before Islam, one year in every two or three had 13 lunar months rather than 12), this calendar (instituted shortly before the Prophet's death) does articulate a certain logic, or perhaps an intention, however unconscious, to lose contact with all rituals previously based on the solar or at least agricultural calendar. Muhammad's struggle was with the *mushrikin* of Arabia, even if he had to take a position on the different claims of the other monotheistic religions. It was a question of eradicating the memory of these rituals and erasing all traces of them, probably because they were nourished by pagan beliefs. This seems completely consistent with the overall logic underlying Islam, detaching the imagination from the image in favour of a view which is ever more abstract and thus directed towards an ever more absolute concept of Being.

If, however, there is some truth in the hypothesis that the agrarian rite has been preserved in the Ramadan food system in the Maghreb, crystallized in the element of leavening, it is an example of tenacity and symbolic force despite sacred decrees over 14 centuries (Diouri 1987: 297). The sacred is ruled by a complex and sometimes strict system of formal prohibitions and sanctions. The symbolic is characterized by a system of internal constraints less acute and more insidious (in terms of margins of tolerance), breach of which opens up a world without limits, without landmarks for the subject's consciousness, and where death and procreation probably represent something.

Notes

1. For example: Benkirane (1983); Carrier (1987); Dinya (1990); Guinaudeau-Franc (1976 and 1981); Moryoussef and Moryoussef (1983); and, particularly, the classic study by Bennani (new edn 1987). I do not know Wensinck's *Arabic New Year and the Fast of Tabernacles* (1925), nor Blair's *Sources of Islam* (1925), which appear to be relevant studies.
2. Also called *s'wuf* (translator's note).
3. As mentioned incidentally by Rutter, for example (1928, I: 74–5).
4. The renowned Ghazali, following many predecessors, defined three stages in the development of the fast towards this ideal state: 'general, particular and exceptional' (1975, III: 38–44).
5. *'ayd al-kabir/bayram* (translator).
6. This is presumably the Persian *reshteh*, 'noodle' (Eds).
7. For other such proverbs, see Benhadji-Serradj (1950: 247, n3).
8. Leo Africanus, cited by Doutté (1909: 557); Mouliéras (1899, I: 100–102 and II: 14, 18, 20, 30); Salmon (1905: 362); Doutté (1909: 558 and n1); Trenga (1915: 40); Laoust (1920: 412 and 1921: 196); Lakhsassi (1992).

9. All these hypotheses are discussed, particularly after the studies by Wensinck and Blair, by Chemoul (1936: 421–5).

10. In the palm groves of the Tafilalet in southern Morocco, the rite that inaugurates the ploughing season is to eat a couscous with a date buried inside it: whoever finds the date is guaranteed a fruitful year.

17. Food as a Semiotic Code in Arabic Literature

Sabry Hafez

This chapter outlines the various manifestations of culinary semiotic codes in Arabic literature. It deals with some of the simple coding of culinary metaphors in proverbs and popular literature before moving to the more elaborate use of culinary codes in modern literature. Then it investigates the uses of food in the titles of novels and collections of short stories. The major part of the chapter is devoted to examining the ways in which narrative writers use culinary codes as signifying tools in their work, through a study of their socio-cultural implications, their interaction with the spatial presentation of narrative, the inversion of their significance by divorcing them from their normal context, the association between the culinary and the erotic, and how this moves certain culinary elements from the realm of the acceptable to that of the taboo. It also investigates the interaction between food and religious practices and between culinary customs and changing social values in what is termed in semiotics 'modelling secondary systems'.

The aim of this chapter is to study culinary semiology with its taste and olfactory signs, not as an anthropological or even a purely semiotic endeavour, but as a revealing literary strategy capable of generating multiplicity of meaning within the text, expanding its hermeneutic possibilities and enhancing its relevance to other social sciences. Culinary semiotic codes pervade Arabic literary expression from pre-Islamic poetry through popular narrative and proverbs, up to the various genres of modern Arabic literature. In a literary text, presence and absence of culinary semiology have equal significance. Literary presentation is a complex process of selection in which the selected elements speak for and on behalf of the discarded ones. For 'reading must always aim at a certain relationship, unperceived by the writer, between what he commands and what he does not command of the schemata of the language that he uses. This relationship is not of a certain quantitative distribution of shadow and light, of weakness and force, but a signifying structure that critical reading must produce' (Derrida 1976: 227).

In the present study these clarifications are necessary because the two subjects of this study, culinary codes and literature, are signifying practices and semiotic systems at the same time. Like literary language, an understanding of the significance of culinary codes in Arabic literature requires the probing of the relationship between what they signify in the literary text and the aspects of their social practice which they unintentionally bring with them into the textual world. The new function of culinary codes as a major constituent of literary language cannot be fully realized without taking into account the autonomous nature of their semiotic system. Like language, the dynamic of the present aspects of a culinary vocabulary emerges from its constant dialectic with the absent ones, in other words from its being a part of a whole semiotic system. The comprehension of culinary codes as such is a prerequisite for the perception of the transformation of their signs within the dynamics of another more complex system, literature.

Before investigating the interaction between these two systems, it is necessary to emphasize that the use of the term semiotics here tends more towards the triadic concept of Peirce and later semiotics than its dyadic Saussurean counterpart. Post-structuralist theory has made it imperative to accommodate Derrida's concepts of *différence*, *trace* and *supplément* into the structuralist semiotics when dealing with literary texts and other verbal activities. Derrida's adjustment of the dyadic Saussurean semiotics had long been anticipated by Peirce's triadic concept of Sign, Object and Interpretant. Peirce's introduction of what he called the Interpretant into the very structure of the sign with its signifier and signified, Sign and Object, attempts to overcome the arbitrariness of the sign, contextualize the generation of meaning and bridge the unbridgeable gap in the Saussurean system. The understanding of the complexity of the process of signification is essential for its deciphering, particularly when used within an elaborate system of codes as is the case with literary texts.

The literary text is itself a semiotic code, but within its elaborate network of relationships and literary strategies other social or cultural codes are operative. The function and the degree of elaboration of these codes vary from one literary text to another. Most of the codes employed in literary works, such as culinary ones, are already formulated in other fields of human interaction, and hence have their distinct semiotic structure. But the displacement of these codes from their original context and their introduction into the autonomous world of the literary text often involves certain transformations in both the sign and its interpretant. In their mimetic endeavour to reproduce reality, literary texts reconstruct within their verbal domain various social codes, while others allude to certain rubrics of these codes either directly or through complex intertextual patterns. It is therefore possible to examine the interpretants and significations of certain social semiotic codes through the study of their configurations in the community of literary texts and how their use within literature illuminates some facets of their structure.

SACRED AND REALISTIC MODES

The manifestation of culinary semiology in modern Arabic literature as an important and highly expressive code is associated with the rise and development of realistic sensibility. The advent of realistic representation is widely acknowledged as a moment of catalytic change that marks the transition from the acceptance of the world as given, to the process of its questioning and rationalization. Jameson considers the 'conception of the moment of novelistic *realism* as the literary equivalent, both on the level of discourse and on that of realistic narrative, of what Deleuze and Guattari (in the *Anti-Oedipus*) call *decoding:* the secularization of the older sacred codes, the systematic dissolution of the remaining traces of the hierarchical structures of life and practices which very unequally and over many centuries characterized the organization of life and practices under the *ancien régime* and even more distantly under feudalism itself' (Jameson 1985: 373).

The secularization of the older outlook is an essential prerequisite for the perception and subsequent presentation of certain aspects of social life as codes capable of illuminating reality and restructuring it, let alone the literary displacement of such codes and the modifications of their role for the benefit of artistic expression. The complexity of the process of transferring reality and encoding its major systems into the very fabric of the literary text necessitates a radical change in the understanding of man's perception of both literature and reality and of his ability to control and manipulate them. This can be demonstrated by the study of the radical difference between the nature of use and presentation of culinary codes in the past and in the modern literature of realism.

Classical Arabic literature used culinary codes in expressing various aspects of reality. Pre-Islamic and classical poetry is packed with culinary allusions and terms. The Qur'an is also full of them and employs food and drink in its narrative of both the present life and the hereafter. The famous apple which led to original sin and caused the expulsion of Adam and Eve from heaven, the abundant food which Zachariah found in Mary's sanctuary (Qur'an 3: 37) or the description of Paradise, which is generally rendered in comestible terms, are different examples of this. But they are generally used as fixed elements in a static context intended mainly to communicate a specific message. This was in harmony with the sacred view of the world in which each element was ordained to perform a predestined role. Thus multiple functions and dynamic significations were curtailed. But with the advent of realistic presentation, culinary elements changed in both form and function in the literary text. They appeared in a more immediate and dynamic form and did not confine themselves to a one-dimensional role. This is demonstrated in the latter part of this chapter; first some of the features of the earlier role will be outlined.

PROVERBIAL CODING

Within the traditional superstitious view of the world, culinary semiology was operative, but only in its crudest and most simplistic form which Umberto Eco terms *overcoding*. 'Overcoding records commonly used ready-made syntagms such as: how are you, I beg your pardon, or closed on Sundays, which work as minimal units, single "signs" endowed with an "atomic" meaning' (Eco 1979: 133).

The Arabic language in its classical and vernacular variations abounds with terms and proverbs concerning food and culinary metaphors. The famous Arab hospitality has always expressed itself in terms of food and *qira al-dayf*, nourishing guests, as well as using food and drink to express generosity and other basic sentiments. The modern shorter two-volume Arabic thesaurus, *al-Ifsah fi Fiqh al-Lugha* by Husayn Musa and 'Abd al-Fattah al-Sa'idi (which is a much-abridged version of the standard Arabic thesaurus, *al-Mukhassas* by Ibn Sida (1898–1903), which runs to 17 volumes), devotes more than 80 pages to terms for food and drink which are currently in literary use (pp 397–479). Apart from the standard names of the three daily meals and other words for quick meals and snacks, there are more than 20 words for special meals for guests, visitors, travellers, weddings, circumcisions, births, travelling, mourning, funerals, pilgrimages, etc.[1] The very existence of these specific terms indicates an elaborate system of culinary codification as part of the major rituals of social life.

This is also enforced in classical Arabic proverbs, which are viewed within the literary canon as pieces of wisdom and social commentary as well as valuable literary works. Proverbs are seen by Ibrahim al-Nazzam as literary gems marked by verbal economy, wisdom, literary allusion and rhetorical competence (al-Maydani nd: 7). Most of the classics of Arabic literature, whether dictionaries, encyclopaedic compositions or literary works, contain large numbers of these proverbs. Most proverbs are perceived not as words of wisdom or pronouncements of insightful sages but as distillations of valuable experience deeply rooted in a realistic or historical context.

The famous *Majma' al-Amthal* (Dictionary of Proverbs) of al-Maydani (d. 518 H/1124), which contains some 6000 proverbs and common phrases, provides a context, historical verification and/or a story for each proverb. The dictionary is full of culinary and olfactory terms which are used to enhance the expressive ability of their composition and to give them an air of authenticity and sound experience. Culinary elements are used as indications of the various aspects of the social practice, which utilizes food both to nurture life and to cure its illness. Hence curative as well as fortifying imagery is brought into the proverb by the mention of a single sign. It is clear from the reading of this dictionary that proverbs using food or drink terms are almost self-explanatory, while the clarification of some of the other proverbs runs for several pages. It is therefore natural that many of the former survived and are still used.

This tradition continues in the various vernaculars of the contemporary Arab world. Ahmad Taymur's *al-Amthal al-'Ammiyya* (Egyptian Colloquial Proverbs, 1949) contains 2696 proverbs, 428 (16 per cent) of which use eating, drinking, food and nutrient metaphors to express a great variety of experience and social wisdom. Some of these proverbs are directly related to eating and drinking conduct, but many use culinary metaphors to distil social and moral principles. The percentage increases dramatically when one deals with the proverbs of the rural sector of the community. In his study of rural Algerian proverbs, Murtad observes that domestic economy occupies a high position on the scale of its values (1982: 45–58). Nearly half of the corpus of his proverbs uses terms of food, drink, cooking or nourishment. This is also the case in other Arab countries. In his encyclopaedic survey of the social life of Baghdad in the past hundred years, al-Hajiyya records hundreds of similar proverbs, prominent among them those using bread and the typical Iraqi small baking oven, *tannur* (al-Hajiyya 1985: V, 146–55). In most of these proverbs, bread is used as a rich metaphor, signifying life from its most basic to its most luxurious.

The use of bread symbolism and metaphors in both daily life and literary and proverbial expressions deserves a study of its own. For if a piece of bread is thrown into the street in any Arab country, it will not be long before someone picks it, utters the name of God and puts it aside so it will not be stepped upon by an unsuspecting passer-by. The bread, though one of the least expensive items of any meal, is taken here as a sign for all God-given provisions. It is a representation of and a substitute for all forms of nutrient, a rough sign that crudely sums up a whole body of signs. But this alone would have made the whole act a sign, were it not for the religious connotation as well as the host of social allusions that such behaviour suggests.

THE USE OF FOOD IN TITLES

The use of bread, as well as bread and salt, as a rite of friendship and as a symbol for the very act of eating together, is a highly developed code in realistic works of modern Arabic literature. A number of modern novels and collections of short stories have availed themselves of its rich signification. Many works use it as a title which conjures up a host of images and associations. *'Aysh wa-Milh* (Bread and Salt) is the title of a collection of short stories that launched a group of talented writers[2] in 1960 with an introduction by the Egyptian pioneer of the genre, Yahya Haqqi. The title expresses not only the strong bond of friendship forged between the writers, most of whom were still students at the Faculty of Fine Arts at the time, but also their intention to make their living from writing and artistic endeavour. It also suggests that they all come from a peasant or lower-middle-class background, for it indicates that they have only just enough to keep the wolf from the door. The use of this title reveals their ideological and socio-realistic leanings and their concern for the questions of the less fortunate strata of society.

Another similar title is *Akl 'Aysh* (Only Living, 1955) by the Egyptian writer, Mustafa Mahmud. The literal translation of the title is actually 'bread-eating', which demonstrates the equation of bread with life and its continuous flow. In fact the term itself involves a case of overcoding, for it is an often-used basic phrase meaning earning one's living or doing something specially for this reason, and not because of conviction or desire. Similar implications are also found in the title of the collection *Qas'ah min al-Khubz* (Sack of Bread, 1965) by the Libyan writer 'Abdullah al-Quwayri, or even in that of his other collection, *Al-Zayt wa'l-Tamr* (Oil and Dates, 1971), in which the oil and the date of the palm tree symbolize the livelihood of the desert folk. Even as *Akl 'Aysh* revealed by its very syntax its Egyptian origin, so *Qas'a min al-Khubz* indicates its Libyan source and *al-Zayt wa'l-Tamr* its desert roots.

When bread is divorced from its customary context and is associated with another value which belongs to a different code, as in the title of the collection of short stories *Al-Khubz wa'l-Samt* (Bread and Silence, 1977) by the Saudi Arabian writer Muhammad 'Ulwan, it becomes a symbol of servility and bondage, for its availability in plenty has been at the price for ordinary Saudis of abandoning their freedom and allowing silence to reign supreme. This inverts the life-giving quality of the bread and turns its sign against itself by divorcing it from its normal semantic field. When associated with oppressive silence, bread the symbol of life becomes an emblem of death. Its affinity with an institution such as the government produces a sarcastic and even comic effect in the title of the collection *Khubz al-Hukuma* (Government Bread, 1961) by the Iraqi writer Edmun Sabri. It becomes a symbol of under-payment and an expression of the conflict between loyalty to a job that provides a pittance and the ever-rising cost of living.

Milh al-Ard (The Salt of the Earth, 1972), by the Syrian writer Salah Duhni, extends the metaphor of salt beyond its normal religious use and gives it a strong socialist connotation. Mustafa Mahmud's third collection, *Qit'at Sukkar* (A Piece of Sugar, 1959), uses sugar as a metaphor for the small, transient and sweet moments of life. But the same metaphor is used to produce the opposite effect in the novel *Sukkar Murr* (Bitter Sugar, 1970), by another Egyptian writer, Mahmud 'Awad 'Abd al-'Al, who succeeds through the juxtaposition of clashing tastes and the extended use of interior monologue in dissociating sugar from its sweetness without completely divorcing it from its taste. The novel interweaves the sweet taste of sugar with the bitter memories conjured up by the act of dissolving the sugar in the cup, in order to demonstrate the conflicting feelings evoked by the narrated events, and to posit the clash of tastes as an analogy for the past and the present.

Similar, though shocking, juxtaposition is used in the title of Muhammad 'Afifi's novel *al-Tuffaha wa'l-Jumjuma* (An Apple and a Skull, 1965), which sets the erotic and sensual associations of the apple against the more sombre ones of the skull. As if it were the title of a still life, the juxtaposition creates a vivid image which is sustained, enriched and developed throughout the novel. Another use of food as a metaphor for both the impossible and the false occurs in the title of the novel *Baydat al-Dik* (The Cock's Egg, 1984), by the Moroccan novelist Muhammad Zifzaf. The heroine of the novel is aware that the realization of her double dream (to marry the owner of a bar and to hope for his quick death so that the bar may be hers) is as impossible as obtaining the proverbial cock's egg. Since the cock's egg cannot exist, it follows that its incarnation in the form of the realized dreams has to be false. But when both her dreams are realized, she seems to forget the initial association of her double dream with the cock's egg. This enables her to live her new life without recognizing its absurdity and deceit, but the title works as a constant reminder that such a condition is preposterous and cannot continue.

A similar use occurs in *al-Burtuqal al-Murr* (Bitter Orange, 1975), by the Syrian novelist Salma al-Haffar al-Kuzbari. But the most effective use of the orange as a richly imaginative and evocative symbol is to be found in the work of Palestinian writers. Ghassan Kanafani gives his second collection of short stories the title *Ard al-Burtuqal al-Hazin* (Land of Sad Oranges, 1963), in which he combines his grief for his lost homeland with the freshness of orange orchards violated by the brutal attack on their integrity and sanctuary. The collection includes many variations on the theme of the violated orange orchards and their longing to be united with their rightful owners. Oranges in his collection are a symbol of purity and childhood, when most of the characters were still united with their Palestinian homeland and had not as yet endured the humiliation of life in refugee camps. The alienation of the extorted orange in the hands of its usurper corresponds to that of its Palestinian owners in foreign and often hostile lands. Other variations on this theme pervade the collection *Habbat al-Burtuqal* (Oranges, 1962) by another Palestinian writer, Ahmad 'Inani. Similar use of the orange as a symbol of childhood and purity was given to the pomegranate in the collection of short stories *Habbat al-Rumman* (Pomegranates, 1935) by the Lebanese writer Ra'if Khuri.

References to food are not confined to bread and fruit. The Syrian writer Iskandar Luqa gives one of his collections the title of *Ra's Samaka* (Fish Head, 1961) and another *al-Walima* (The Banquet, 1971). Drinks are also used as highly effective titles, as in the Syrian writer Nayruz Malik's collection *Kub min al-Shay al-Barid* (A Cold Cup of Tea, 1981), or in Mahmud Taymur's collection *Tamr Hinna 'Ajab* (Tamarind Drink, 1958). Coffee houses also give their names to novels and collections of short stories as in *Fi Qahwat al-Majadhib* (1955) by Sa'd Makkawi, *Qahwat al-Mawardi* (1960) by Muhammad Jalal and *Qushtumur* (1988) by Naguib Mahfuz.

RITUALS AND SOCIAL CODES

The most elaborate use of culinary semiotic codes occurs not in the titles of literary works, where food or drink is only a metaphor or symbol, but in the detailed texture of narrative structure, where a constant process of encoding and decoding is taking place. The longer the gap between the time of the realistic narrative and the present becomes, the greater the need to employ detailed social codes in order to reproduce the socio-cultural milieu and make it vivid, authentic and lively. In Naguib Mahfuz's 'Cairo' trilogy (*Bayn al-Qasrayn*, 1956 [Palace Walk, 1990], *Qasr al-Shawq*, 1957 [Palace of Desire, 1991], and *al-Sukkariyya*, 1957 [Sugar Street, 1992]),[3] life is punctuated by culinary and other social rituals. The early part of the trilogy, which takes place during the First World War, is furthest from the present and as a result richest in social codes. The more the novel progresses, the closer it comes to the present, the more the use of such codes dwindles or assumes different functions.

Throughout the novel, the day starts at dawn with the kneading of the dough in the baking room on the ground floor. At the outset of Palace Walk (pp 15–16), although, chronologically, the kneading of the dough takes place after the mother performs the dawn prayer, narrative order reverses this, making it the marker for the beginning of the day. This is reinforced by describing the kneading and the subsequent baking while mentioning the prayer only in reported narrative. Another indication of its importance in the narrative scale of priority is the fact that, although the allocation of space in the house is hierarchically controlled, where the patriarch occupies the top floor, the children the middle floor, the females the ground floor and the baking room is banished to the courtyard, the temporal arrangement of the narrative brings the baking room forward. This narrative inversion of the realistic order subverts reality and balances the social hierarchy that diminishes the status of women, by giving them narrative precedence over the world of men.

The elaborate description of the baking room, with its active females as the source of life and many of its delicious pleasures, gives it a highly significant role in punctuating the day and marking seasonal events from Ramadan and the two annual feasts to various social occasions. No wonder, for it is also the kitchen and the incontestable kingdom of the mother, where she reigns supreme over the domestic life of her family. The room is presented not only as the internal clock of the house, the source of its nourishment (it backs on to the larder and the storeroom), but also as the testing and initiation ground for its women. It harbours special recipes for fattening birds and animals for domestic consumption and women for prospective suitors. The warmth and intimacy of the room and the delicious meals and drinks that flow from it contrast it with other areas of the house.

Once breakfast is prepared, the mother takes it on a brass tray to the dining-room and oversees its serving and consumption. Here again (p 19) Mahfuz uses the culinary code to communicate a host of significant messages. Breakfast is singled out because it is the only meal at which the boys eat with their father, the nearest thing to a family gathering. The dishes eaten at breakfast reveal the social background of the family and even its national identity. Eggs, *ful mudamas* (brown beans), cheese, pickled limes and peppers and hot loaves of flat round bread for breakfast put the family into the upper stratum of the middle class, while the presence of *ful mudamas* fried in ghee and loaves of flat round bread makes it unmistakably Egyptian, for *ful mudamas* is as Egyptian as bacon and eggs are British. The eating of the meal on a low table, around which cushions are placed for seating, further identifies the social setting as one of a family rising to the upper stratum of the middle class rather than falling into it from a higher one. The latter would cling to a normal dining table and chairs. The interaction between the father and his three boys, the only members of the family allowed to eat with him, reveals further information about the character of the father, his educational and cultural background and his relationship with his children.

Although the mother is not allowed to eat with them, her job does not end with the bringing of the breakfast tray. She stands in the room by the water jug, waiting to obey any command. The mother, who reigns supreme downstairs, is reduced to a voiceless marginal existence upstairs. Yet her silent presence during the ritual confers on her a kind of hieromancy which is not available to the other female members of the family. The three boys, though famished, restrain themselves and wait until their father starts, then they follow in order of seniority: Yasin, Fahmy and then Kamal. This shows their highly formal response to their father's approach and the degree of hierarchical interaction within the family. This is reinforced when the author changes the narrative point of view and describes the progression of the meal from the standpoint of the youngest son, Kamal. He fears his father the most, eats cautiously and nervously and is concerned about his inability to compete for his share of food with his two energetic elder brothers, particularly after the father leaves the table. The departure of the father, followed by the mother, leads to the collapse of the eating order and transforms the formalized hierarchical space into a democratic one. Now the three boys fight for the food in a completely different setting. This very transformation is a further indication of the inner dynamics of the family.

The early departure of the father prepares the reader for the finale of his breakfast, when he goes to his room and the mother follows him with a cup containing three raw eggs mixed with milk and honey. Here the narrative opens on the world of different concoctions and tonics; some are prepared for the father to stimulate his appetite or for their aphrodisiac effect, while others are cooked for the daughters to make them plump and attractive to suitors. It also introduces the reader to the two contrasting concerns of men and women in this domain. While the mother is versed in the dietary aspects of such tonics, the father introduces us, through his train of thought, to the narcotic variations on the theme.

Another significant contrast is that between the family gathering over which the father prevails, the breakfast, and that over which the mother presides, the coffee hour, soon before sunset. In the latter, the oppressive patriarchal order is replaced by a democratic matriarchal one (Palace Walk, 52–7). Unlike breakfast, which takes place on the top floor and is confined to the male members of the family, the coffee hour takes place on the first floor and is open to everyone, bar the absent father who, after work, goes on his nightly exploits. It has an order based on inclusion and not on exclusion and, although not every member of the family is allowed to drink coffee, everyone plays a role in the highly significant social ritual which brings them together and allows for the realization of their different needs. The breakfast scene, with its rigidly hierarchic order, necessitates its presentation from a unitary viewpoint and, when the author changes the narrative perspective to narrate the rest of the scene from Kamal's point of view, this is done mainly to demonstrate the power of the hierarchical control. The coffee-hour scene allows for a polyphony of voices and a multidimensional narrative. Unlike the breakfast scene, the change of narrative perspective is conducted not in a manner that uses one voice to enhance the other but to demonstrate the richness of variety and amplify the relaxed atmosphere of the coffee hour.

CULINARY CODES AND SPATIAL VARIATIONS

Literary texts use a host of semiotic codes and the association between various codes enriches their expressive ability and widens their horizon. We saw how family power-politics in the 'Cairo' trilogy demonstrated itself in the daily rituals of eating and drinking coffee as well as in the symbolism of the distribution of space for each activity. The breakfast took place on the top floor, which was the sole domain of the father. Everyone came to *his* ground and played according to *his* rules. The same can be said about the ground floor, the incontestable kingdom of the mother, and even about the first floor during the coffee hour. But since time and change are the two invisible heroes of the trilogy, all this changed, and with it the significance of meals and refreshments that took place in them. In Palace of Desire, the move of the coffee hour from the first floor to the ground floor after the death of Fahmy and the marriage of the two daughters showed how these two major blows to the mother's world have almost eradicated the main source of her social pleasure.

In Sugar Street, the return of the coffee hour to the first floor is used as an indicator of a major relational change. The series of disasters which have afflicted the beautiful younger daughter, Aisha, gives her certain liberties earned through suffering, including smoking openly and participating fully in the coffee hour like the male members of the family. The coffee hour now brings the women from the ground floor to the first, hence establishing at least a quasi-parity between all members of the family. This is possible because of the deteriorating health of the patriarch, which forces him to come down from the top to the first floor. This is also indicated by the change in his diet and daily routine. Now he eats his supper, which consists of yoghurt and an orange, at home. No longer can he partake of the delights of night parties and the food and drink associated with them. This is part of the narrative technique of substituting showing for telling, to enhance the impact of the change. Later on, the absence of the coffee hour becomes as significant as its presence. Presence/absence is one of the important dimensions of the operational code in narrative.

Another significant spatial marker associated with culinary codes is the difference between what is served in the house and what is served outside it. In the first two parts of the trilogy, the father rarely eats supper at home. His nights are reserved for parties in which alcoholic drinks are served with numerous types of *mazza*, appetizers which are eaten as part of the drinking ritual. The *mazza* illustrates how a single item acquires a different meaning by association with other ones. Each appetizer can be eaten separately at home without bringing in the association with alcoholic drinks. But when served together, they move from the realm of the ordinary to that of the taboo. As a result, the word *mazza* is never uttered, let alone are *mazza* served, in the house. In Sugar Street, the word runs through the father's head as part of the silent craving for his secret life that is no longer attainable. The substitution of the word for the ritual turns the pleasurable occasion into a sorrowful memory. Divorcing the word from its old context, even in the clandestine thoughts of the father, inverts its content and turns it from a reminder of delight to an instrument of suffering.

FOOD OUT OF CONTEXT

The separation between the culinary sign and its context is often used in a manner that creates an unbridgeable gap between the sign and its signifier and develops a revulsion to its culinary content. The trilogy has many examples of this. When Yasin was a little boy, his mother used to send him to the fruiterer, with whom she was having a clandestine affair. The fruiterer in return used to send the child back laden with bags of fruit. The fruit, taken out of its culinary context as food, becomes a conveyor of erotic messages and a symbol of sin and betrayal. The memory of the bags of fruit divorced from their normal signification as delicious items of nutrition becomes a curse and continues to torment Yasin long into his adulthood. His suffering ends only many years later with the death of the fruiterer.

This is not confined to the world of the trilogy, or even to the works of Mahfuz. In the work of another writer, Yusuf Idris, one finds many similar examples. In his novella *Al-Gharib* (The Stranger, 1960),[4] the cake given by the stranger's beautiful wife to the narrator, after her failed attempt to seduce him, has similar connotations. The young narrator loves cake, and even tries to eat it after he has resisted her flirtatious pursuits. But unable to overcome the new meaning which the cake has acquired as a symbol of betrayal, he disgorges the portions that he has eaten and throws the rest away. In the boy's world, the cake was a desirable culinary item, but its association with the act of seduction divorces it from its ordinary context and turns it against its normal nexus, inverting it into an object of revulsion and hate.

FOOD, CLASS AND TIME

Food can clearly indicate social class, cultural background and even temporal changes in modes of behaviour and taste. In the first part of Mahfuz's 'Cairo' trilogy, Yasin marries above him, and his wife Zaynab moves into 'Abd al-Jawad's family home. One day, she suggests cooking for them her father's favourite dish, *sharkasiyya* (Circassian),[5] unknown in her husband's household. The very term *sharkasiyya* reverberates with echoes of upper-class life and its feminine form refers to the Circassian concubines in the Ottoman harems who were known for their beauty and their culinary skills. Introduced by Zaynab, whose maiden family name, Iffat, has a clear Turkish ring to it, the dish created a stir in 'Abd al-Jawad's household. 'It garnered everyone's admiration, and most especially Yasin's. Their mother felt a twinge of jealousy. Khadija became frantic and made fun of it' (Palace Walk, p 302). But beneath her aggressive response, Yasin's sister Khadija reveals her admiration of the dish by her eagerness to master it with her customary proficiency, for this would undoubtedly raise her social standing.

Food is a social marker and Khadija's keenness to master *sharkasiyya* and other dishes of the upper class pays off when she also marries above her station and is able to run the kitchen of the Shawkats (another Turkish name) without letting it down. In another of Mahfuz's novels, *Malhamat al-Harafish* (1977; The Harafish, 1994), the author uses food to mark a change of fortune for one of the characters. The cooking aroma of a rich meat dish, *ra'ihat al-taqliyya*, which emanates from the house, is a sign of improvement in the character's social standing and success in his business pursuits. Literature has often used olfactory signs as a vocabulary capable of generating precise referential values and as a semiotic system. *Ra'ihat al-taqliyya* is merely a smell, but Mahfuz turns it into a sign communicating a much more complex message.

Food is also used as a means of characterization in narrative. In the first chapters of the trilogy, the personality of the father is revealed in his manner of eating.

> Their father devoured his food quickly and in great quantities as though his jaws were a mechanical shredding device working non-stop at full speed. He lumped together into one giant mouthful a wide selection of the available dishes – beans, eggs, cheese, pepper and lemon pickles – which he proceeded to pulverize with dispatch while his fingers prepared the next helping. His sons ate with deliberation and care, no matter what it cost them and how incompatible it was with their fiery temperaments (Palace Walk, 20).

The effectiveness of the description of the father's way of eating is enhanced by directly contrasting it with the sons'. The father's manners give the reader an insight into his intense, sturdy personality and his robust approach to life.

Food plays also the major role in characterization and theme in the novel *al-Raj' al-Ba'id* (Distant Echo, 1980),[6] by the Iraqi writer Fu'ad al-Takarli. Two ageing women, Umm Hasan and Najiya, are left alone on the top floor, neglected and hungry. They demand food and complain that they do not get enough and continually remind the others that they are aware of what is going on. They crave a slice of watermelon in particular, for its soothing effect works wonders in the devilish heat of Baghdad, but also to assure themselves that they still count and will be given their share of such a highly desired item. Beneath their incessant complaints about being deprived of food lies their bitterness about being ignored and left out of the important business of the family. They crave attention, but ironically, by their endless demands and complaints, they turn themselves into a nuisance, thus hindering any attempt to take them seriously. Running through the novel like a persistent leitmotiv, their demand for food articulates one of the main themes of the novel: blindness to the feelings and needs of others.

Apart from characterization and theme, food is used to mark the progression of the plot and the passage of time. In Yusuf Idris's *Bayt min Lahm* (House of Flesh, 1971: 5–14), the dinner, *'asha*, is the only meal the five characters of the story eat together. The author uses this daily gathering like a thermometer, to register any change in the internal harmony and mark the progression of the plot. At first the dinner is dull, four women in mourning eating silently and sadly. After the mother's marriage to the blind man, the bleak silence of grief is dissipated and is replaced by merriment and laughter. The dinner becomes a happy gathering for the family and the blind man reveals beneath his former composure a fun-loving person with a fine sense of humour. But when one of her daughters slips into his bed during his siesta, she falls into silence during the following dinner. The blind man continues his gaiety and jocularity and the other two daughters participate in the fun. But one by one they also become involved in the sinful game of donning the ring and slipping into the blind man's bed, and one by one they fall silent, until silence reigns again. It is a different type of pregnant silence that turns the dinner ritual into a nightmare and the story into a provocative metaphor.

Narrative deals with both fictional and realistic time. Food is used in *Bayt min Lahm* to mark fictional time and the progression of the action, but it is used in other texts to reveal the passage of natural time, and with it changes of taste and values. In Fathi Ghanim's *Sitt al-Husn wa'l-Jamal* (Lady of Good and Beauty, 1991), the diet of the heroine, Dunya, the prospective film star, is carefully measured to keep her healthy but slim. It is rich in protein and fibre but low in fat and starch. Lean meals are the new class marker here, in place of the fattening concoctions of yesteryear. Slimness is a far cry from the desired plumpness of the world of Mahfuz's trilogy, and the food associated with it marks a change in taste and criteria of female beauty. Ghanim's novel takes place in the 1950s, only a few decades after the first book in the trilogy. The change of dietary values speaks of the passage of time, even within the trilogy itself where the standard of beauty changes and with it, of course, the dietary values. In Ghanim's novel, the change of diet denotes a transition from one class to another, and from one period to another. Both protagonists, Dunya and 'Umar, come from a poor Alexandrian background, and the transition to a higher social stratum is marked by their access to plenty of meat in their diet. They measure the change in their fortune with food and are anxious that, if they get used to the new standard of eating, they will not be able to return to their previous state of deprivation. They perceive the new diet as a solid proof of their social ascendency and associate the old diet with a bygone era.

THE CULINARY AND THE EROTIC

Food as one of the main pleasures of life is often used in association with other pleasurable activities, particularly sexual ones. In Mahfuz's trilogy, the food offered during the evenings of pleasure in the courtesan's house is radically different from that offered in the serene and correct domestic atmosphere. Like an early part of a sentence which suggests the rest of its composition through a recognizable pattern of associations, the first plates of *mazza* herald the arrival of drinks, as much as the ensuing singing and dancing adumbrate the subsequent sexual activities. The association between sex and intoxicating drinks is strong in the trilogy, not only in the life of the father, but also in those of his two sons: Yasin and Kamal. Earlier in the novel, Yasin admits that, 'wine and women in his life were inseparable and complementary. It was in the company of a woman that he had first gotten a taste for wine. By force of habit it had become one of the valued ingredients and sources of pleasure for him' (Palace Walk, 75).

The strong affinity between wine and sex in the trilogy stems from the fact that they both involve a violation of the religious and social taboos. When Yasin concedes that wine and women are inseparable in his life, the acknowledgement is based on an implicit understanding that 'women' here refers to those of easy virtue. Once a woman is lawfully attained, she automatically loses a great deal of her charm, challenge and erotic fascination. One after the other, Yasin's wives lose their seductive power after a few weeks of marriage and cease to be desirable or even attractive. Since he cannot drink at home, he is forced to separate lawful sex from wine, and it soon becomes as tasteless as water. The excitement of violating taboos stimulates his sexual impulses, and this makes wine, the forbidden drink, a great stimulus and a necessary ingredient in any exciting sexual adventure. As social and religious taboos constitute systems of conduct, their violation constructs its own system of values. This counter-system is formulated through a varied vocabulary of food, drink and women as well as a rigid moral code based on chivalry and camaraderie between friends.

The co-existence of the two conflicting systems in each of the three male heroes of the trilogy underlines the fact that the two systems have much in common despite their ostensible opposition. This is evident in the discussion between the father and his close friend Muhammad Iffat concerning the divorce of Iffat's daughter, Zaynab, from Yasin, who was caught seducing her black maid. What enrages Iffat is not that his son-in-law has had an extramarital affair, for he himself does this all the time, but that Yasin has violated the counter-system according to which such unlawful acts are conducted. Iffat acknowledges, 'It is true that I get drunk, become rowdy, and take lovers, but I refrain from wallowing in the mud. We all do' (Palace Walk, 406). Here is the clear difference between the father and his friends, including Iffat, who play the game according its rules, and Yasin, who reduces the fine art of adultery, with its counter-system of values, to a monstrous, animal-like act. Breaking the rules is what is held against Yasin, not the act of fornication itself. Separating the physical act from the other elements of its proper system – food, drink, singing and dancing – turns it against itself and exposes Yasin to the harsh criticism of both his father and Iffat.

Food and drink perform other functions in the world of sexuality beside the violation of taboos or the formation of an integral system. Food as an aphrodisiac is encountered at the beginning of the trilogy and in other works by Mahfuz, particularly in *Zuqaq al-Maddaq* (Midaq Alley, 1947), where the daily preparation of Salim 'Ulwan's special lunch earns a wide reputation in the alley, particularly after Husniyyah, the baker's wife, possessed by curiosity, steals a portion of the lunch and tries it on her own husband, Ji'dah. The recipe's magic impact, which lasts for two hours of intense virility and sheer sensual delight, was enough to earn it immediate acclaim. In order to heighten the aphrodisiac significance of the meal, the novel contrasts the deteriorating performance of 'Ulwan (as a result of Husniyyah's persistence in stealing a large portion of the bowl of roasted green wheat, pigeon meat, nutmeg and other spices which was sent to be cooked in her bakery, and replacing the rich concoction with ordinary husked wheat) with the improved virility of Ji'dah.

Another use of the profound interaction between food and sex can be found in Idris's 'Laylat Sayf' ('Summer Night', in 1957: 105–33), where food is offered as a prelude to sex and as analogy to its forthcoming realization. In this powerful short story, Idris uses the technique of a story within a story to develop an elaborate structure of 'internal mediation'[7] in which a number of interesting correspondences are at work throughout the story. This is not confined to the dialogue between the frame and the enframed stories, or between the hero and the group of adolescent villagers, but also operates most effectively at the culinary level, where the story offers the double contrast, first between the food offered by the beautiful woman in the city and that consumed in the village, and second between food and sex.

It is mainly a story about food and sex as two corresponding desires, where the former acts as a mediator for the latter and as a substitute for it. The frame story, which is related in first person plural narrative, tells us about the trials and tribulations of a group of adolescent boys in a poor Egyptian village and their struggle to cope with poverty and sexual deprivation. Their attempt to amuse themselves, after a day of hard labour in the fields and inadequate food at home, leads to the telling of the enframed story when they ask Muhammad to relate to them some of his exciting affairs in the city. Ironically the enframed story is mostly narrated in the third person to distance it from the group of young villagers despite the fact that its hero/narrator, Muhammad, relates it directly to them.

Muhammad is slightly older and a lot more experienced than they are, having worked in the city. This makes him a mediator in a 'triangle of desire' in which the mediator is also a rival and an obstacle between them and the desired objects, which is one of the characteristics of internal mediation.[8] When he starts to tell his story about a beautiful woman who called him into her flat and offered him food and drink before going to bed with him, the group of boys soon become as active in the development of his narrative as he is. In fact they often take over, for what he tells is nothing less than their most cherished desire. Food, drink and the woman are stuff of which the dreams of the young villagers are made and Muhammad is only the mediator of these desires. The boys persuade him to behave in his narrative in a certain manner so as to attain on their behalf the desired objects: food, drink and sex. They even criticize him when he hesitates or shows any sign of shyness. In order to cross the obstacles of fear and hesitation, Muhammad uses drink to fortify his resolve and, despite the boys' apparent ignorance of alcoholic drinks, when the woman offers him a drink they urge him to accept it. Unlike Mahfuz's trilogy, where food and drink are used to enhance the erotic atmosphere, the erotic in Idris's story is presented to strengthen the impact of food and vice versa.

The hunger of the young villagers for good nutritious food is outlined at the outset of the narrative, and when the delicious meal is presented to the hero it is charged with erotic implications and every element of it turns into a highly suggestive vocabulary. The description of the meal – a huge turkey stuffed with pigeons, potato and meat – generates envy and hatred towards him, who has eaten what they have always desired but never managed to attain. This envy turns into hatred when, in addition to all this food and drink, he goes to bed with the beautiful woman and refrains from giving them a blow-by-blow description. By the end of the enframed story, the group turns against Muhammad, whose message of food and sex inflames their desires. They ask him to take them to the woman, and the journey to the city is sustained by more questions soliciting detailed information about the woman and the food she offered. The conflict which develops transforms the trip into a nightmare, and they all go back to their village. Here culinary codes are an integral part of an extended metaphor and harmonious elements in a meaningful composition in which the culinary and the erotic work together to reveal the harshness of poverty and deprivation.

RELIGIOUS CULINARY RITUALS

No religious festival takes place in the complete absence of food or drink. As Christmas is marked by turkey and Easter by its eggs, so the major religious occasions in the Muslim Arab world are associated with certain dishes. The Qur'an is full of references to food and drink, and Ramadan is turned by social practice into a month for celebration through food as the breaking of the daily fast is celebrated each evening. Ironically, food consumption goes up in Ramadan by an average of 50 per cent in most Muslim countries. Because of the difficulties of fasting throughout the daylight hours, children neither fast nor are they allowed to partake in its rituals until they are old enough to endure its rigorous discipline. In his short story 'Ramadan' (in 1956: 34–47), Yusuf Idris reveals how participation in the ritualistic life of Ramadan is seen through the eyes of the child as a significant initiation rite. Waking the boy up to participate in the *suhur* (the meal eaten before the call for the dawn prayer)[9] is therefore not the same as saving his share of the food. He fights and cries to be woken up, not because of the food itself but because of the values ascribed to his admission to the rite of *suhur*. The boy correctly understands the *suhur* as a social ceremony and has no interest in the food itself once it has been separated from the rite.

The two Muslim festivals are strongly associated with food: the first, *'id al-fitr*, celebrates the end of the fasting of Ramadan, and the second, *'id al-adha*, is the sacrificial rite *par excellence*. All other religious occasions, such as Muslim new year, the birthday of the Prophet, the night of *isra'*, mid-Sha'ban and 'Ashura' (the 10th of Muharram) are associated with specific food and drink. Literary references to all these occasions are always made through their culinary aspects.

Celebrating less important religious occasions, such as the annual fair of a local saint (*mawlid*), provides Arabic literature with some of its most significant uses of culinary semiotics as a means of commemorating religious events. *Ayyam al-Insan al-Sab'a* (1969; The Seven Days of Man, 1989) by 'Abd al-Hakim Qasim is entirely devoted to the ritual of the annual celebration of the local saint, al-Sayyid al-Badawi. The novel's ingenious structure spreads the narrative of the days of the celebration over many years, so as to widen the cycle of the ritual to correspond to that of the life of the hero/narrator. The first day, 'Al-Hadra' ('The Evening Gathering'), is seen through the eyes of the child narrator, the second is presented many years later through the eyes of the adolescent, and so on until the seventh day is presented by the mature, cynical old narrator. In the process the story of the narrator's family and his education is inscribed into the texture of the annual religious feast. Since the novel is concerned with the cycle of life, each of its seven days/stages is concerned with one culinary aspect: drinking, baking, preparing food for the journey, setting up lodging, cooking, eating, etc.

The most interesting day in this respect is the second day/chapter, 'Al-Khabiz' ('Baking'), in which the inner life of a middle-class Egyptian farming family is elucidated through the process of baking. In this chapter the baking ritual is presented as a complete social rite whose cycle (kneading, shaping the dough into cookies, heating the oven, baking and tasting the results) is as rich as that of the whole *mawlid*. The first chapter, 'Al-Hadra', introduces the world of men, their tea-drinking ritual, their mundane preoccupations and spiritual yearnings. The second, 'Al-Khabiz', launches the novel into the world of women with its domestic, sensual and life-making activities. In the village, baking is a truly communal rite that brings the village women together to participate in this social and domestic exercise. Baking for the annual *mawlid* is even more of a collective exercise because, unlike any normal baking day where participation is voluntary, the contribution to the *mawlid*'s baking is imperative. Both socially and spiritually every household is obliged to donate whatever it can to the preparation of the bread and cookies which will be taken to the *mawlid* in the local town.

Honey, clotted cream, fermented milk, flour, grain, beans, eggs, butter-fat, sugar, yeast, etc., are brought in in succession in a scene reminiscent of the festive processions of offerings to the temple on the walls of ancient Egyptian monuments. Each item communicates a message about the household from which it comes. The honey indicates certain refined wealth, for, in a small Egyptian village, not every farmer is capable of bee farming. The clotted cream speaks of rich livestock, while the curdled milk discloses a poor household living off its one water buffalo by selling the butter and retaining the fermented milk. Eggs imply an even poorer source that has no livestock, only a few hens. The flour and the grain are provided by the families of large agricultural landowners. The butterfat or ghee imparts a message of a highly organized household, while sugar comes normally from the few non-farming families in the village.

The act of baking here mingles with the rite of sacrificial offering to turn the occasion into an elaborate festivity, and the novel uses this opportunity to demonstrate the collective nature of the event. The baking itself is turned into a lively competition of skills between the women of the village. During the day-long process, the richness of the women's lore is revealed and their views of their menfolk are disclosed. The consuming flames of the oven kindle their sexual fantasies and entice them into sexually explicit talk in a manner which provides the reader with an insight into the inner life of the village.

In the fourth day/chapter, on the lodging, the products of baking, bread and cookies, perform two major functions. First, they form the main sustenance of the large group of village men who go to the local town to celebrate the saint's *mawlid*, a week-long event; second, they form the reverse of the baking-day procession. As soon as the men establish their lodging in the town, the bread, *duqqa* (a rural mixture of herbs, salt and spices) and cookies will be taken out to the houses in the neighbourhood to solicit their help and canvas their support. The townsfolk cherish these rural delicacies and wait or even ask for their share of the treat every year. In their place they send to the lodging implements and utensils such as kerosene burners, knives, pots and pans, or even other food such as onions, oil, sugar and tea. Indeed, the produce of the baking day is the lifeline of the villagers in the town: it nourishes them, facilitates their social life and lubricates their interaction with the otherwise hostile town-dwellers.

MODELLING SECONDARY SYSTEMS

Semiotic research finally shifts its attention to phenomena which it would be difficult to term sign systems, but which are rather behaviour and value systems ... systems of etiquette, hierarchies and the so-called 'modelling secondary systems' – under which heading the Soviets bring in myths, legends, primitive theologies which present in an organized way the world vision of a certain society and finally the typology of cultures which study the codes which define a given cultural model – for example the code of the mentality of medieval chivalry (Eco 1979: 12).

Arab generosity, codes of conduct in birth, marriage and death ceremonies, the need for insistence before accepting an invitation to eat, and equally the need to extend an invitation without actually meaning or fearing that it will be taken seriously, are all part of the coded behaviour in the Arab culture. But like any behavioural codes, they do change constantly and one of the ways of revealing their change is the use of culinary semiotic codes in literature.

Idris's 'Thwid al-'Arusa' ('Bride's Detour', in 1958: 73–83) is one of the stories which deal with a radical change in the behavioural code through its culinary practice. The story selects a rich social practice in which a number of cultural codes are interwoven in a complex ritual and shows how breaking one of these codes exposes the decay of others. It deals with the most extravagant of rural rituals, the celebration of marriage. Like any sensitive observer, Idris realizes that an established cultural code breaks at its weakest link. In certain parts of the Egyptian countryside, when marriage takes place between a couple from two different villages, the bride is taken in a large procession from her village to that of her bridegroom. On their way, they pass by other villages and the old cultural code demands that the villagers go out to invite them and persuade them, by force if necessary, to accept their invitation to celebrate with them and stay overnight, then continue their trip the following morning. The code also ordains that the task of the bride's procession is to get her to her bridegroom as soon as possible, and they must therefore resist the invitation forcefully and fight their way through if necessary. In effect, each part of the code lives by cancelling the other out.

The tension between the two parts of the code is vital for the survival of them both, and with them a host of other cultural doctrines concerning generosity, magnanimity, bravery and dignity. In order to show the dynamics of the subtle interdependence between all these codes, Idris elaborates in the first half of his story the long and colourful history of the social rite of *thwid al-'arusa*. Then he presents his special study of the actual example he uses to expose the radical changes that have turned the old rite into mere verbal courtesy. He selects his bride from a poverty-stricken little village and demonstrates that the wedding meal is the main motivation for participating in the procession, hence the exaggerated size of the procession. Exaggeration is one of the main textual strategies in the story to treat the decay of the code as a comic rather than a tragic event.

To show the spectacular collapse of the code, the story selects, for the first encounter with an inviting village, a group of strong men led by a fearful giant who works for an old farming estate and resists the changes of the new economic realities. The sight of the giant leads the procession to deputize Rajab, its wisest man, to negotiate with him.

The encounter shows the two parties talking at cross-purposes: Rajab is motivated by hunger and the desire to maximize the spoils of the journey while the giant wants to demonstrate his valour and keep up the old appearance of generosity and wealth. The codes which define these two different, even opposed, cultural models do not match and this turns the encounter into a comedy. The members of the procession are motivated by hard economic reality, their opponents by a decaying cultural practice, and it is only natural that the triumph of the laws of economics over those old practices is both easy and ironic. The procession enjoy the spoils of their gullible acceptance of the invitation as well as the subsequent chaos it causes. The difficulty of providing food and shelter for a large number of unexpected guests enforces the new economic mentality, leads the owner of the estate to dismiss his men and more importantly results in the eradication of the old practice of *thwid al-'arusa*.

In 'Tabliyya min al-Sama' ' ('A meal from Heaven', in 1958: 44-57), Idris employs food to expose the dynamics of another cultural code, the folkloric belief among Egyptian peasants that blasphemy puts a curse on the whole community. The protagonist of the story, Shaykh 'Ali, manipulates this fear and selects a day, Friday, encoded in the popular lore of fear (like Friday the 13th in English superstition) to challenge Heaven openly and ask for a meal and cigarettes, for he has had no food for two days and has not smoked for a week. Conducted loudly in the village square, the open defiance awakens the villagers' fears and leads them to provide him with the food he wants. Shaykh 'Ali's dignity and self-respect prevent him from asking his fellow-villagers to provide for him. It is normal to ask God, but the manner in which he makes his demand provokes the villagers to action and even enables him to dictate the type of food he will accept.

From the various sections of this chapter it is clear that culinary semiotic codes penetrate every aspect of literary expression. Food functions as an autonomous code where the separation of its signs from their context necessitates an alteration of their significance. On the thematic plane, it identifies social setting, indicates cultural background, points to class and time, and illuminates religious and folk beliefs. Food also interacts with the spatial dimensions of the presentation and plays a vital part in a large number of human activities, from the religious to the erotic. It demonstrates the change in cultural codes and in taste and standards of beauty. On the textual plane, culinary codes are used in titles with great effectiveness. They identify the setting, mark narrative time and are major elements in characterization.

Notes

1. A meal is called *qira* for a guest, *ma'duba* or *mad'a* for a visitor, *tuhfa* for an unexpected visitor, *walima* for a wedding, *shundakhi* for the bride before the wedding, *khurs* for giving birth, *khursa* for women during the few days after giving birth, *'aqiqa* on the occasion of the first haircut of the new born, *'adhira* and *a'dhar* for circumcision, *naqi'a* for someone returning from a long journey, *wakira* for celebrating a new house, *luhna* or *sulfa* for a small snack between meals, *'ujala* for a quick meal, *qafiya*, *qafy* or *zalla* for honouring someone, *wadima* for mourning or a funeral, *shundakh* for someone returning from pilgrimage, and so on.
2. The writers are 'Izz al-Din Najib, Al-Dasuqi Fahmi, Mahmud Baqshish, Muhammad Jad and Sayyid Khamis.
3. Quotations from the trilogy are taken from the English translation and page references are to the English edition.
4. 'Al-Gharib' ('The Stranger'), which appeared in Idris's collection *Akhir al-Dunya* (1960), was translated into English in the collection *Rings of Burnished Brass*, trans Kathrine Cobham (London, Heinemann, 1984), pp 92–157.
5. *Sharkasiyya* is a dish of meat or chicken cooked with onion, celery and tomato in a rich hazelnut sauce and served with rice.
6. This important novel has not yet been translated into English.
7. For a detailed account of the concept of 'internal mediation', see Girard (1965: 1–52).
8. The concept of the 'triangular desire' – the desiring subject, the mediator and the desire or desired object – is developed by Girard (1965).
9. The Ramadan fast involves abstention from eating, drinking and smoking between dawn and sunset. The first meal after sunset is called *iftar* (breakfast); the second, eaten before dawn, is called *suhur*; cf Diouri, this volume.

Bibliography

'Abīd, H. and K., n.d., *Ṣawānī Khalījiyya*, Bahrain.

Abu'l-Faẓl 'Allāmī (16th century), 1927, *The Ā'īn-i Akbarī*, trans H. Blochman, ed D. C. Phillot, for the Asiatic Society of Bengal, Calcutta.

Adīb, Nazīha, and Firdaws al-Mukhtār, 1990, *Dalīl al-Ṭabkh wa'l-Aghdhiya*, 7th printing, Beirut.

Adjarian, H., 1979, *Hayeren Armatakan Bararan*, 2nd edn, Vol 4, Erevan: Academy Press.

Afnan Hourani, F., 1984, 'Laban, laban: an essay on cooking with yogurt', *Petits Propos Culinaires* 18, pp 54–60.

Afshār, Iraj (ed), 1981/1360, *Āshpazi-ye Dowreh-ye Safavi: Matn-e Du Resāleh az ān Dowreh*, Tehran.

Äkhmädov, Ähmäd-Jabir, 1986, *Azärbayjan Kulinariyası*, Baku.

al-'Alawī, Ḥasan, 1990, *al-Shī'a wa'l-Dawla 'l-Qawmiyya fī'l-'Irāq*, London: Dār al-Zawrā'.

'Alī, Su'ād 'Uthmān, 1989, *Mawsū'āt al-Ṭabkh al-Sa'ūdī wa'l-Sharqī*, Jedda.

Alkhazov, N. K., A. D. Dzhabarov, N. M. Maleev, B. A. Sadykhov, N. M. Khalilov and A. A. Shikhamirov, 1963, *Azerbaydzhanskaya kulinariya*, Baku.

Allan, J. A., 1981, *Libya: the Experience of Oil*, London: Croom Helm.

— 1985, 'Irrigated agriculture in the Middle East: the future', in Peter Beaumont and Keith McLachlan (eds), *Agricultural Development in the Middle East*, London: John Wiley & Sons.

— 1988, 'The Great Man-Made River: progress and prospects of Libya's water carrier', *Libyan Studies* 19, pp 141–6.

— 1989a, 'The effects of the demand for livestock products on natural resources', in J. A. Allan, K. S. McLachlan and M. M. Buru (eds), *Libya: State and Region*, London: SOAS CNMES.

— 1989b, 'Water resource evaluation and development in Libya – 1969–1989', *Libyan Studies* 20, pp 235–42.

— 1991, 'Water in the Middle East', *Proceedings of the 1991 BRISMES Conference*, London: SOAS CNMES.

— 1992, 'Evolving water demands and development options', in P. P. Howell and J. A. Allan (eds), *The Nile*, Cambridge University Press.

Aminov, S. A., 1959, *Taomhoi tojiki*, Stalinabad.

Aminov, S., S. A. Vanukevich, and S. S. Aminov, 1988, *Tadzhikskie Natsional'nye Bliuda*, Dushanbe.

Anderson, Eugene N., 1984, ' "Heating" and "cooling" foods re-examined', *Social Science Information* 23 (4–5), pp 755–73.

Anon (13th century), *Kitāb al-Wuṣla ilā 'l-Ḥabīb*, MS, edn in preparation by Manuela Marín and David Waines.

Anon, 1800/1214, *Borhān-e qāṭe'*, Turkish trans by Aḥmad Asim, Constantinople.

Anon, 1937 (1503), *Kitāb al-Ṭabāḥa*, ed H. Zayyāt, Beirut: Al–Mashreq.

Anon, 1939–1957, *Türkiye'de Halk Ağzından Söz Derleme Dergisi*, 4 vols, Ankara: Türk Dil Kurumu.

Anon, 1965/1334, *Borhān-e qāṭe'*, ed Moḥammad 'Abbās, Tehran.

Anon, 1980, *Qāmūs al-Ṭabkh al-Ṣaḥīḥ*, Beirut.

Anon, 1981, *Tatarskaia Kulinariia*, Kazan: Tatarskoe Knizhnoe Izdatel'stvo.

Anon, 1982, *Türk Mutfağı Sempozyumu Bildirileri*, Ankara: Ankara Üniversitesi Basımevi.

Anon, 1983, *Türkçe Sözlük*, 7th edn, Ankara:Türk Dil Kurumu.

Anon, 1989, *La Cuisine Azerbaidjanaise*, Moscow: Vneshtorgizdat.

Anon, *al-Ṭabkh al-Maghribī fī 'Aṣr al-Muwaḥḥidīn*, Microfilm no. 810, Rabat: Archives de la Bibliothèque Générale, 110f.

Anon, in press, *Kanz al-Fawā'id fī Tanwī' al-Fawā'id*, ed Manuela Marín and David Waines, Beirut.

Anon, n.d., *La Cuisine Arménienne*, Paris: Union Arménienne de Bienfaisance.

al-Antākī, Dā'ūd (16th century), 1979, *Tadkirāt Ūlī 'l-Albāb*, Beirut: al Maktaba al-Shu'biya.

Arberry, A. J., 1939, 'A Baghdad cookery-book', *Islamic Culture* 13, pp 21–47 and 189–214.

Aslanov, M. G. 1966, *Afgansko-Russkiy Slovar* (Pashto-Russian Dictionary), 2 vols, Moscow.

Bagdasarov, A., A. Vanukevich, and T. Khudayshukurov, 1981, *Turkmenskaya Kulinariya*, Ashkhabad.

al-Baghdadi, Muḥammad b. Ḥasan (d 1239), 1934, *Kitāb al-Ṭabīkh*, ed D. Chelebi, Mosul (see also Arberry, 1939).

— 1964, *Kitāb al-Ṭabīkh*, ed Fakhrī al-Bārūrī, Beirut.

Balland, D., 1985, 'Fromages traditionnels et fromages industriels d'Afghanistan', *Production Pastorale et Société* 17, pp 13–26.

Bar Bahlūl (10th century), 1891–1901, *Lexicon Syriacum*, ed Rubens Duval, 3 vols, Paris: Imprimerie Nationale.

Barbier de Meynard, A. C., 1881, *Dictionnaire Turc-Français*, 2 vols, Paris.

Barthes, Roland, 1961, 'Pour une psycho-sociologie de l'alimentation contemporaine', *Annales: Economies, Sociétés, Civilisations*, pp 977–86.

— 1964, 'Eléments de sémiologie', *Communications* 4, pp 91–135.

Baskakova, N. A., and M. P. Khamzaeva, 1956, *Turkmeni-Russka Slovar*, Moscow.

Batmanglij, Najmieh, 1986, *Food of Life, a Book of Ancient Persian and Modern Iranian Cooking and Ceremonies*, Washington DC: Mage.

— 1993, *New Food of Life: Ancient Persian and Modern Iranian Cooking and Ceremonies*, New York: Mage.

Bā'urchi-Baghdādi, Ḥājji Moḥammad 'Ali (early 16th century), n.d., *Kārnāmeh dar Bāb-e Tabbākhi va San'at-e ān*; see Afshar (1981), pp 34–184.

Bazin, Marcel, 1973, 'Quelques données sur l'alimentation dans la région de Qom', *Studia Iranica* 2 (2), pp 243–53.

— 1980, *Le Tâlech, une Région Ethnique au Nord de l'Iran*, 2 vols, Tehran: Institut Français d'Iranologie; Paris: ADPF.

Bazin, Marcel, and Bromberger, Christian, 1979, *Documents pour l'Etude de la Repartition de quelques Traits Culturels dans le Guilan et l'Azerbayjan Oriental*, Paris: CNRS.

— 1982, *Gilân et Âzarbâyjan Oriental. Cartes et Documents Ethnographiques*, Tehran: Institut Français d'Iranologie; Paris: ADPF.

Beaussier, H., 1958 (1887), *Dictionnaire Pratique Arabe-Français*, Algiers: La Maison des Livres.

Belyazid, F., 1987, *Une porte sur le Ciel*, 90-minute film, Paris and Rabat.

Benghiat, S., 1985, 'Kishk', *Petits Propos Culinaires* 19, pp 61–2.

Benhadji-Serradj, M., 1950, 'Fêtes d'Ennayer au Benī Snūs', *IBLA* 51, pp 247–57.

Benkirane, Fatouma, 1983, *Les Meilleures Recettes de la Cuisine Marocaine*. Casablanca: Sochepress; Paris: J. P. Taillandier.

— 1984, *al-Tabkh al-Maghribī al-Mu'āṣir*, Casablanca/Paris.

Bennani, L., 1987, *La Cuisine Marocaine*, new edn, Casablanca: Almadaris.

Ben Talha, A., 1950, 'Coutûmes locales des Musulmans de la ville de Moulay Idriss et de sa région à l'occasion du mois de Ramadan et du mois de Chaâbane', *Bulletin de l'Enseignement Public au Maroc* (Rabat) 211, 2e trimestre, pp 6–21.

Bergrenn, J., 1844, *Guide Français-Arabe Vulgaire*, Uppsala.

Bianchi, T. X., and J. Kieffer, 1871, *Dictionnaire Turc-Français*, 2 vols, Constantinople.

Blair, J. C., 1925, *Sources of Islam: an Enquiry into the Sources of the Faith and Practice of the Muhammadan Religion*, Madras: Christian Literature Society for India.

Bonine, Michael, Peter Beaumont, and Keith McLachlan (eds), 1989, *Qanat, Kariz and Khattara*, Outwell: Menas Press.

Borubaev, T., 1985, *Kirgizskaya Kukhniya*, Frunze.

Bouayed, Fatima Zohra, 1983, *La Cuisine Algérienne*, Algiers: Entreprise Nationale du Livre.

Bourdieu, Pierre, 1984 (1979), *Distinction*, Cambridge, Mass.: Harvard University Press.

— 1977 (1973), *Outline of a Theory of Practice*, Cambridge: Cambridge University Press.

Braudel, Fernand, 1981 (1975), *The Structures of Everyday Life*, vol. I of *Civilization and Capitalism 15th-18th Century*, London: Harper-Collins.

Bromberger, Christian, 1985, 'Identité alimentaire et altérité culturelle dans le nord de l'Iran: le froid, le chaud, le sexe et le reste', in Pierre Centlivres (ed) *Identité Alimentaire et Altérité Culturelle* (Recherches et Travaux de l'Institut d'Ethnologie de Neuchâtel 6), Université de Neuchâtel, Faculté de Lettres, pp 2–34.

— 1986, 'Les blagues ethniques dans le nord de l'Iran. Sens et fonctions d'un corpus de récits facétieux', *Cahiers de Littérature Orale* 20, pp 73–101.

— 1988, 'Comment peut-on être Rashti? Contenues, perceptions et implications du fait ethnique dans le nord de l'Iran', in *Le Fait Ethnique en Iran et en Afghanistan*, ed Jean-Pierre Digard, Paris: CNRS, pp 89–108.

— 1989, *Habitat, Architecture and Rural Society in the Gilân Plain (Northern Iran)* (Bonner Geographische Abhandlungen, Heft 80), Bonn: Ferd Dümmlers Verlag.

Browne, Edward G., 1950 (1893), *A Year among the Persians*, London: A. and C. Black Ltd.

al-Bukhārī, n.d., *Saḥīḥ al-Bukhārī*, 9 parts in 3 vols (copy of Sultanian edition, Cairo 1313 AH), Beirut: Dār al-Jā'il.

Burckhardt, J. L., 1822, *Travels in Syria and the Holy Land*, London.

Carrier, Robert, 1987, *A Taste of Morocco*, London; trans 1988, *Le Gout du Maroc*, Paris: Flammarion.

Centlivres, Pierre, 1972, *Un Bazar d'Asie Centrale: Forme et Organisation du Bazar de Tashqurghân*, Wiesbaden: Reichert.

— 1985, 'Hippocrate dans la cuisine: le chaud et le froid en Afghanistan du nord', in Pierre Centlivres (ed), *Identité Alimentaire et Altérité Culturelle* (Recherches et Travaux de l'Institut d'Ethnologie de Neuchâtel 6), Université de Neuchâtel, Faculté de Lettres, pp 35–58.

Centlivres-Demont, Micheline, 1985, 'Le pain des champs et le pain des villes: changements et identité alimentaires en Turquie', in Pierre Centlivres (ed), *Identité Alimentaire et Altérité Culturelle* (Recherches et Travaux de l'Institut d'Ethnologie 6), Université de Neuchâtel, Faculté de Lettres, pp 121–31.

Chardin, Sir John, 1988, *Travels in Persia 1673–1677*, New York: Dover.

Chelebi, Evliya, 1976, *Evliya Çelebi: Siyahetname*, simplified by Tevfik Temelkuran, Necati Aktaş, ed Mumin Çevik, 6 vols in 3, Istanbul: Ucdal Neşriyatı.

Chelhod, Joseph, 1955, *Le Sacrifice chez les Arabes*, Paris: PUF.

Chemoul, M., 1936, 'Les institutions musulmanes: le jeûne du Ramadan', *Bulletin de l'Enseignment Public au Maroc* (Rabat) 149, pp 403–25.

Chodzko, Alexandre, 1850, 'Le Ghilan ou les marais caspiens', *Nouvelles Annales de Voyage* 1, pp 193–215.

Colliver-Rice, C., 1923, *Persian Women and their Ways*, London: Seeley.

Conran, Lady C., 1983, 'Tracta and trahanas', *Petits Propos Culinaires* 14, pp 76–7.

Currier, Richard L., 1966, 'The hot–cold syndrome and symbolic balance in Mexican and Spanish-American folk-medicine', *Ethnology* 5 (3), pp 252–63.

Dalman, G., 1928–39, *Arbeit und Sitte in Palästina*, 7 vols, Gütersloh.

Dankoff, Robert, 1990, *Evliya Çelebi in Bitlis*, Leiden: Brill.

Delaney, Carol, 1986, 'The meaning of paternity and the virgin birth debate', *Man (N S)* 21, pp 494–513.

Denizeau, C., 1960, *Dictionnaire des Parlers Arabes de Syrie, Liban et Palestine*, Paris: Maisonneuve.

Derrida, Jacques, 1976, *Of Grammatology*, trans Gayatri Chakravorty Spivak, Baltimore: Johns Hopkins University Press.

Desmet-Grégoire, Hélène (ed), 1991, *Contributions au Thème du et des Cafés dans les Sociétés du Proche-Orient* (Cahiers de l'IREMAM), Aix-en-Provence: CNRS.

Destaing, E., 1905, 'L'Ennayer chez les Beni Snûs', *Revue Africaine* 49, pp 51–70.

Digard, Jean-Pierre, 1981, *Techniques des Nomades Baxtyâri d'Iran*, Paris: Maison des Sciences de l'Homme; Cambridge: Cambridge University Press.

Dinya, 1990, *La Cuisine Marocaine de Rabat, un Art et une Tradition*, Rabat:

Publication Ribat-El Bath.

Diouri, Abdelhaï, 1987, ' 'Alā ḍarb al-jadba', *al-Baḥth al-'Ilmī* (Rabat) 38, year 23, pp 285–99.

— 1991, 'Lahlou, nourriture sacrificielle des Gnaoua du Maroc' to appear in *Proceedings of the International Symposium on Food and Society in Islamic Culture*, Xativa.

Doane, C. F., et al, 1969, *Cheese Varieties and Descriptions*, Washington DC: US Department of Agriculture, Dairy Products Laboratory.

Dols, Michael W., 1984, *Medieval Islamic Medicine*, Berkeley: University of California Press.

Dorr, Marcia Stegath, n.d. (1990?), *A Taste of Oman. Traditional Omani Food. Authentic Recipes and how to Prepare them*, n.p. (Muscat: Mazoon Printing Press?)

Douglas, Mary, 1966, *Purity and Danger: an Analysis of Concepts of Pollution and Taboo*, London: Routledge.

— 1973, *Natural Symbols*, Harmondsworth: Penguin.

— 1975 (1972), 'Deciphering a meal', in M. Douglas, *Implicit Meanings*, London: Routledge.

— (ed) 1987, *Constructive Drinking: Perspectives on Drink from Anthropology*, Cambridge: Cambridge University Press; Paris: Maison des Sciences de l'Homme.

Doutté, E., 1909, *Magie et Religion dans l'Afrique du Nord*, Algiers: A. Jourdain.

Dozy, E., 1957 (1881), *Supplément aux Dictionnaires Arabes*, Beirut.

Drower, E. S., 1956, *Water into Wine: a Study of Ritual Idiom in the Middle East*, London: Oxus.

du Mans, Père Raphaël, 1890, *Estat de la Perse en 1660*, Paris.

Eco, Umberto, 1979, *A Theory of Semiotics*, Bloomington: Indiana University Press.

Edmonds, Anne, 1969, 'The Mevlidi Sherif', *Current Turkish Thought* 600.

El Glaoui, Mina, n.d., *Ma Cuisine Marocaine*, n.p.

Elishē (5th–6th century), 1957, *Elishēi vasn Vardanans' ew Hayots' Paterazmin*, ed E. Tēr Minasean, Yerevan.

Emmerick, R. E., and P. O. Skjærvo, 1982, *Studies in the Vocabulary of the Khotanese*, vol 1, Vienna: Verlag der Österreichischen Akademie der Wissenschaften.

Fahriye, Ayşe, 1882–3/1300, *Ev Kadını*, Istanbul.

FAO (Food and Agricultural Organization of the UN), 1965, *The Economic Relationships between Grains and Rice*, Commodity Bulletin Series no 39.

Faroqhi, Suraiya, 1984, *Towns and Townsmen of Ottoman Anatolia: Trades, Crafts and Food Production in an Urban Setting, 1520–1650*, Cambridge: Cambridge University Press.

Fiddes, Nick, 1992, *Meat: a Natural Symbol*, London: Routledge.

Ferdowsi (10th century), 1866–78, *Shahnāmeh*, ed and trans J. Mohl, 7 vols, Paris.

Fischer, Michael M. J., 1980, *Iran: from Religious Dispute to Revolution*, Cambridge, Mass.: Harvard University Press.

Fischler, Claude, 1979, 'Gastro-nomie et gastro-anomie', *Communications* 31, pp 189–210.

Flandrin, Jean-Louis, 1992, *Chronique de Platine: pour une Gastronomie Historique*,

Paris: Odile Jacob.

Foucault, Michel, 1984, *Histoire de la Sexualité*, vol 2: *l'Usage des Plaisirs*, Paris: Gallimard.

Fragner, Bert G., 1984, 'Zur Erforschung der kulinarischen Kultur Irans', *Die Welt des Islams* 23–4, pp 320–60.

Frazer, James, 1983 (1890), *Le Rameau d'Or. Esprit des Blés et des Bois*, Paris: Robert Lafont.

Freytag, G. W., 1975 (1830), *Lexicon Arabico-Latinum*, 4 vols, Beirut: Librairie du Liban.

Gerholm, Tomas, 1980, 'Knives and sheaths: notes on a sexual idiom of social inequality in North Yemen', *Ethnos* 1 (3), pp 82–91.

Ghānim, Fatḥī, 1991, *Sitt al-Husn wa'l-Jamāl*, Cairo: Dār al-Hilāl.

Ghanoonparvar, Mohammad Reza, 1984, *Persian Cuisine*, Book One: *Traditional Foods*, Lexington: Mazda.

al-Ghazālī, A. H. (11th–12th century), 1959, *Ayyuhā'l-walad. Lettre au Disciple*, ed and trans T. Sabbagh, Beirut: Unesco.

— 1975, *Iḥyā' 'Ulūm al-Dīn*, 16 parts in 6 vols, Beirut: Dār al-Fikr.

Girard, René, 1965, *Deceit, Desire and the Novel: Self and Other in Literary Structure*, trans Yvonne Freccero, Baltimore: Johns Hopkins University Press.

Gönüllü, Ali Rıza, 1985, 'Türk inançlarında "su" ', *Türk Folkloru* 73, pp 17–18.

Good, Byron, 1977, 'The heart of what's the matter: the structure of medical discourse in a provincial Iranian town', unpublished PhD thesis, University of Chicago.

Goody, Jack, 1982, *Cooking, Cuisine and Class: a Study in Comparative Sociology*, Cambridge: Cambridge University Press.

Gouin, P., 1990, 'Rapes, jarres, faisselles. La production et l'exportation des produits laitiers dans l'Indus du 3e millénaire', *Paléorient* 16 (2), pp 37–54.

Granja, F. de la, 1960, *La Cocina Arábigoandaluza según un Manuscrito Inédito*, unpublished PhD thesis, Madrid: Faculdad de Filosofia y Letras.

Guigues, P., 1927, 'L'alimentation au Liban. Le bourghoul. Le kichk', *Bulletin des Sciences Pharmacologiques* (May), pp 278–81.

Guinaudeau-Franc, Zette, 1957, *Fes vu par sa Cuisine*, Rabat: Gastronomie Marocaine.

— 1976, *Traditional Moroccan Cooking*, Paris-Saint Cloud: Editions Guinaudeau.

— 1981, *Les Secrets des Cuisines en Terre Marocaine*, Paris: J. P. Taillendier; Casablanca: Sochepress (new edn of Guinaudeau-Franc 1957).

Gurdon, Charles, 1985, 'Livestock in the Middle East', in Peter Beaumont and Keith McLachlan (eds), *Agricultural Development in the Middle East*, London: John Wiley & Sons.

Gürün, O.A., n.d., *Türkçe-Fransizca Sözlük*, Istanbul.

Gusfield, Joseph, 1987, 'Passage to play: rituals of drinking time in American society', in Douglas (ed), 1987, pp 73–90.

Ḥāfiẓ, Rabīha Aḥmad, 1411/1990, *Uṣūl al-Ṭabkh al-Saʿūdī wa'l-Sharqī*, Riyadh.

al-Ḥajiyya, ʿAzīz Jāsim, 1985, *Baghdādiyāt*, vol 5, Baghdad: Dār al-Ḥurriyya.

Halıcı, Nevin, 1989, *Turkish Cookbook*, London: Dorling Kindersley.

Harfouch, J., 1894, *Drogman Arabe*, Beirut.

Hattox, Ralph, 1985, *Coffee and Coffeehouses*, Seattle: University of Washington Press.

Hazan, Haim, 1987, 'Holding time still with cups of tea', in Douglas (ed), 1987, pp 205–19.

Heine, Peter, 1982, *Weinstudien: Untersuchungen zu Anbau, Produktion und Konsum des Weins im arabisch-islamischen Mittelalter*, Wiesbaden: Harrassowitz.

— 1988, *Kulinarische Studien. Untersuchungen zur Kochkunst im arabisch-islamischen Mittelalter*, Wiesbaden: Harrassowitz.

Hirschon, Renée, 1983, 'Women, the aged and religious activity', in A. Lily Macrakis and Peter S. Allen (eds), *Women and Men in Greece: a Society in Transition*, Baltimore: Johns Hopkins University Press, pp 113–29 (also special issue of *Journal of Modern Greek Studies* 1 (1)).

Hübschmann, H., 1883, *Armenische Studien*, Leipzig.

— 1895, *Persische Studien*, Strassburg.

Husayn, Fāṭima, 1985, *al-Akalāt al-Kuwaytiyya*, Kuwait.

Ibn al-'Adīm (13th century), 1976, *Al-Wuṣla ilā'l Ḥabīb fī Waṣf al-Ṭayyibāt wa'l-Ṭīb*, 2 vols, Aleppo: Daryat al-Khaṭīb.

Ibn Baytār, Abū Muḥammad, 1874, *Kitāb Jāmi' al-Mufradāt*, 2 vols, Cairo.

— 1877–83, *Traité des Simples*, trans L. Leclerc, 3 vols, Paris.

Ibn Ḥabīb (d 853), 1992, *Mukhtaṣar fī'l-ṭibb. Compendio de Medicina*, ed and trans C. Alvarez de Morales and F Giron Irueste, Madrid: Consejo Superior de Investigaciones Científicas.

Ibn al-Ḥashā (13th century), 1941, *Glossaire sur le Manṣūrī de Rāzī*, ed G. S. Colin and H. P. J. Renaud, Rabat.

Ibn Manẓūr, 1910, *Lisān al-'Arab*, Beirut.

Ibn Muḥammad, I., 1990, *Tarwīḥ al-Arīb fī'l-Ādāb wa-Aḥkām al-Ṭīb*, Ṭanṭā.

Ibn Razīn al-Tujībī, 1981, *Faḍālāt al-Khiwān fī Ṭayyibāt al-Ṭa'ām wa'l-Alwān*, ed with introduction and notes by M. Benchekroun, Rabat: Imprimerie Alrisala; also Beirut, 1984.

Ibn Sīda (11th century), 1898–1903, *al-Mukhaṣṣaṣ*, 17 vols, Cairo: al-Maṭba' al-Amīriyya bi-Būlāq.

Ibn Sīnā, n.d., *al-Qānūn fī'l-Ṭibb*, 3 vols, Baghdad.

Ibn al-Ukhuwwa, 1938, *Ma'ālim al-Qurba fī Aḥkām al-Ḥisba*, ed R. Levy, London.

Ibn Zuhr, 'Abd al-Malik (d 1162), 1992, *Kitāb al-Aghdhiya*, ed and trans E. García Sánchez, Madrid: Consejo Superior de Investigaciones Científicas.

Idrīs, Yūsuf, 1956, *Jumhūriyyat Farahāt*, Cairo: Dār Rūz al-Yūsuf.

— 1957, *A laysa Kadhalik*, Cairo: Markaz Kutub al-Sharq al-Awsaṭ.

— 1958, *Ḥādithāt Sharafa*, Beirut: Dār al-Ādāb.

— 1960, *Ākhir al-Dunyā*, Cairo: Dār Rūz al-Yūsuf.

— 1971, *Bayt min Laḥm*, Cairo: 'Ālam al-Kutub.

İnan, Abdülkadir, 1968, *Türklerde Su Kültü ile ilgili Gelenekler*, Ankara.

Jaba, A., 1879, *Dictionnaire Kurde-Français*, ed F. Justi, St Petersburg: Imperial Academy of Sciences.

al-Jāhiz, Abū 'Uthmān (9th century), 1960, *Kitāb al-Bukhalā'*, Beirut: Dār Ṣādir.

Jameson, Fredric, 1985, 'The realist floor-plan', in Marshall Blonsky (comp.), *On Signs*, Baltimore: Johns Hopkins University Press.

Janvry, A. de, 1986, 'Food security and the integration of agriculture: options and dilemmas', *Ceres* 109 (Jan/Feb), pp 33–7.

Jaubert, R., 1983, *Sedentary Agriculture in the Drier Areas of Syria*, Aleppo:

ICARDA.

Kamāl, Sadūf, and Sima 'Uthmān, 1980, *Alif bā' al-Ṭabkh*, Beirut.

Kanafani, Aida, S., 1983, *Aesthetics and Ritual in the United Arab Emirates. The Anthropology of Food and Personal Adornment among Arab Women*, Beirut: American University of Beirut.

Kanafani-Zahar, Aida, in press, *Mūne: La Conservation Alimentaire Traditionnelle au Liban*, Paris: Maison des Sciences de l'Homme.

al-Kāshghārī, Mahmūd (Mahmûd Kâshgarlı) (11th century), 1915–17, *Kitāb Dīwān Lughāt al-Turk*, Istanbul: Ahmet Rifat.

— 1985, *Classical Turkish Dictionary*, trans B. Atalay, Ankara.

Kazimirski, A. de B., 1860, *Dictionnaire Arabe-Français*, 2 vols, Paris: Maisonneuve.

Kelekian, D., 1911/1329, *Dictionnaire Turc-Français*, Constantinople.

Khaldi, N., 1984, *Evolving Food Gaps in the Middle East/North Africa: Prospects and Policy Implications*, Washington, DC: International Food Policy Research Institute, pp 1–74.

Khawam, R., 1970, *La Cuisine Arabe*, Paris: Phebus.

Khodzhiev, Vahob, 1988, *Firmennye Bliuda i Napitki Tadzhikistana*, Dushanbe.

— 1989, *Lepeshki Tadzhikskaya Kukhniya*, Dushanbe.

— 1990, *Plovy Tadzhikskaya Kukhniya*, Dushanbe.

— 1990, *Traditionnaya i Sovremennaya Tadzhikskaya Kukhniya*, Dushanbe.

— 1991, *O Kulinarakh i Novykh Retseptakh Bliud i Napitkov*, Dushanbe.

Khosrokhavar, Farhad, 1989, 'La pratique alimentaire', in Yann Richard (ed), *Entre l'Iran et l'Occident: Adaptation et Assimilation des Idées et Techniques Occidentales en Iran*, Paris: Maison des Sciences de l'Homme, pp 143–54.

Koukoules, Phedon, 1952, *Vyzantinon Vios kai Politismos* (*Vie et Civilisation Byzantines*), Athens: Institut Français d'Athènes.

Kristeva, Julia, 1985, 'The speaking subject', in Marshall Blonsky (comp.), *On Signs*, Baltimore: Johns Hopkins University Press.

Krotkoff, G., 1982, *A Neo-Aramaic Dialect of Kurdistan*, New Haven, Conn.: American Oriental Society.

al-Kuhaylī, S. 1990, *al-Ṭabkh al-'Arabī al-Aṣīl*, Beirut.

Lagarde, P. de, 1879, *Praetermissorum Libri Duo*, Göttingen.

Laird, Mary Louise, 1987, *Lebanese Mountain Cookery*, Boston, Mass: D. R. Godine.

Lakhsassi, A., 1992, *Monographie sur l'Ashura*, in press.

Lane, Edward, 1978 (1860), *An Account of the Manners and Customs of the Modern Egyptians Written in Egypt During the Years 1833–1835*, London and The Hague: East-West Publications.

Laoust, E., 1920, *Mots et Choses Berbères. Notes de Linguistique et d'Ethnographie. Dialectes du Maroc*, Paris: Challamel.

— 1921, 'Noms et cérémonies des feux de joie chez les Berbères du Haut et de l'Anti-Atlas', *Hespéris*, pp 3–66, 253–316 and 387–420.

Le Roy Ladurie, Emanuel, 1976 (1966), *The Peasants of the Languedoc*, Urbana: University of Illinois Press.

Le Strange, Guy, 1966 (1905), *The Lands of the Eastern Caliphate*, London: Cass.

Lévi-Strauss, Claude, 1964 (1962), *Totemism*, London: Merlin.

— 1966 (1963), *The Savage Mind*, London: Weidenfeld & Nicolson.

— 1970 (1964), *The Raw and the Cooked*, London: Cape.

— 1973 (1968), *From Honey to Ashes*, London: Cape.

— 1978 (1968), *The Origin of Table Manners*, London: Cape.

— 1983, *Le Regard Eloigné*, Paris: Plon.

Lloyd, G. E. R., 1964, 'The hot and the cold, the dry and the wet in Greek philosophy', *Journal of Hellenic Studies* 84, pp 92–106.

McAuliffe, Jane D., 1984, 'The wines of earth and paradise: Qur'ānic proscriptions and promises', in Roger M. Savory and Dionisius A. Agius (eds), *Logos Islamikos: Studia Islamica in Honorem Georgii Michaelis Wickens* (Papers in Mediaeval Studies 6), Toronto: Pontifical Institute of Mediaeval Studies, pp 159–74.

MacLean, A. J., 1901, *A Dictionary of the Dialects of Vernacular Syriac*, Oxford.

Maḥfūz, Naguib, 1947, *Zuqāq al-Maddaq*, Cairo: Maktabat Miṣr; trans as *Midaq Alley*, London: Heinemann, 1975.

— 1956, *Bayn al-Qaṣrayn*, Cairo: Maktabat Miṣr; trans as *Palace Walk*, London: Doubleday, 1990.

— 1957, *al-Sukkariyya*, Cairo: Maktabat Miṣr; trans as *Sugar Street*, London: Doubleday, 1992.

— 1957, *Qaṣr al-Shawq*, Cairo: Maktabat Miṣr; trans as *Palace of Desire*, London: Doubleday, 1991.

— 1977, *Malhamat al-Ḥarāfīsh*, Cairo: Maktabat Miṣr: trans as *The Harafish*, London: Doubleday, 1994.

Maimonides, M. (12th century), 1964, 'The Treatise on Accidents', in *Moses Maimonides' Two Treatises on the Regimen of Health*, trans A. Bar-Sela et al, Philadelphia: American Philosophical Society.

Majmū'a min al-Ṭabbākhīn al-'Arab, 1990, *Aṣnāf al-Ṭabkh al-Khalījī*, Bahrain: Dār al-Hilāl.

Makhmudov (Mahmudov), Karim, 1962, *Uzbekskie Bliuda*, Tashkent: Uzbekskoi SSR Gosudarstvennoe Izdatel'stvo.

— 1986, *Uzbak tansiq taomlari*, Tashkent.

Makhmudov, K. M., and Kh. A. Ismailova, 1986, *Muchnye bliuda uzbekskoi domashnei kukhni*, Tashkent: Izd. TsK Kompartii Uzbekistana.

Mallos, Tess, 1987, *Mawsū'āt al-Ṭabkh al-Muyassara. Ma'kūlāt al-Sharq al-Awsaṭ* (trans of her *The Complete Middle East Cookbook*), Beirut.

Marcus, Abraham, 1989, *The Middle East on the Eve of Modernity: Aleppo in the Eighteenth Century*, New York: Columbia University Press.

Marín, Manuela, 1991, 'Feast and Food in Muslim Spain', *Proceedings of the Third International Food Congress*, Ankara, pp 127–35.

Martin, Mary, 1980, 'Pastoral production. Milk and firewood in the ecology of Turan', *Expedition* 22–4, pp 24–7.

Massé, Henri, 1938, *Croyances et Coutumes Persanes*, Paris: A. Maisonneuve.

Maurizio, A., 1932, *Histoire de l'Alimentation*, Paris: Payot.

Mawsilī, Zubayda, Safiyya al-Sulaymān and Sāmiyya al-Ḥarakān, 1990, *Min Fann al-Ṭabkh al-Sa'ūdī*, Riyadh.

al-Maydānī, Abu'l-Faḍl Aḥmad, n.d., *Majma' al-Amthāl*, ed Na'īm Ḥasan Zarzūr, Beirut: Dār al-Kutub al-'Ilmiyya.

Mehren, A. F., 1872, *Bedommelse af den nyere Folkelitteratur i Ægypten*, Copenhagen.

Mennell, Stephen, 1985, *All Manners of Food*, London/Oxford: Blackwell.

Mirzā 'Ali Akbar Khān, Āshpaz-Bāshi, 1974/1353 (1883–4), *Sofreh-ye At'ameh* (Popular Culture no 7), Tehran: Cultural Foundation of Iran.

Mo'addeb al-Molk (Yusof Rishār Khān), 1903/1321, *Resāleh-ye Tabbākhi*, Tehran.

Moallem, Morteza, 1926/1345, *Nouveau Dictionnaire Persan-Français*, 2 vols, Tehran.

Mojtahedi, A., 1980, *Rice Growing in Northern Iran*, University of Durham.

Monier-Williams, S. M., 1981 (1899), *Sanskrit-English Dictionary*, New Delhi: Munshiram Manoharlal.

Morier, James, 1895, *The Adventures of Hajji Baba of Ispahan*, London: Macmillan.

Moryoussef, Viviane and Nina, 1983, *La Cuisine Juive Marocaine*, Casablanca: Sochepress; Paris: J. P. Taillandier.

Mouliéras, A., 1892, *Le Maroc Inconnu. Etude Géographique et Sociologique*, 2 vols, Paris: Challamel.

— 1905, *Une Tribu Zénète Anti-Musulmane du Maroc (les Zkara)*, Paris: Challamel.

Murray, G., 1990, 'Livestock in the Middle East', unpublished MSc thesis, London: SOAS, CNMES.

Murtād, 'Abd al-Malik, 1982, *Al-Amthāl al-Sha'biyya al-Jazā'iriyya: Dirāsa fi'l-Amthāl al-Zirā'iyya wa'l-Iqtiṣādiyya bi'l-Gharb al-Jazā'irī*, Algiers: Dīwān al-Maṭbū'āt al-Jāmi'iyya.

Mūsā, Ḥusayn Yūsuf, 1964, *Al-Ifṣāḥ fī Fiqh al-Lugha*, 2 vols, Cairo: Dār al-Fikr al-'Arabī.

Mustafaev, Nazim, 1971, *Azärbayjan Shirniyyati*, Baku: Azärbayjan Dövlät Näshriyyati.

Nashāt al-Dowleh (Joséphine Richard), n.d., *Tabbākhi-ye Nashāt*, Tehran.

Nasr, Seyyed Hossein, 1976, *Islamic Science: an Illustrated Study*, London: World of Islam Festival Publications.

Nikola, Nazira, and Bahiya Othman, 1988, *Uṣūl al-Tahī*, Cairo.

Nurollah, Ostad, 1981 (1594/1003), *Māddat al-ḥayyāt*, in Afshar, pp 185–256.

Orbeliani, S. S., 1928 (1685–1716), *Kartuli Lecsiconi* (A Georgian Dictionary), ed I. Kipshidze and A. Shanidze, Tbilisi.

Peirce, Charles Sanders, 1931–58, *The Collected Papers (1931–5)*, ed Charles Hartshorne and Paul Weiss, 8 vols, Cambridge, Mass.: Harvard University Press.

Perry, Charles, 1988, 'Medieval Near Eastern rotten condiment', in *Proceedings of the Oxford Symposium on Food and Cookery 1987*, London: Prospect Books.

Pitt-Rivers, Julian, 1977, 'The law of hospitality', in his *The Fate of Shechem or the Politics of Sex*, Cambridge: Cambridge University Press.

Planhol, Xavier de, 1985, 'Un vide culturel: le fromage en Turquie', *Production Pastorale et Société* 17, pp 9–12.

Platts, J. T., 1982 (1884), *A Dictionary of Urdū, Classical Hindī, and English*, Oxford University Press.

Pokhlebkin, V. V., 1978, *Natsionalnye Kukhni Nashikh Narodov*, Moscow.

Post, G. E., 1932, *Flora of Syria, Palestine and Sinai*, 2 vols, Beirut: American University of Beirut.

Qaburī, Muna, 1990, *Aṭāyib Munawwa'a*, Al-Jubayl.

Qāsim, 'Abd al-Ḥakīm, 1969, *Ayyām al-Insān al-Sab'a*, Cairo: Dār al-Kātib al-

'Arabī; trans J. N. Bell, *The Seven Days of Man*, Cairo: General Egyptian Book Organization, 1989.

Rabino, H. L., and D. F. Lafont, 1910, 'La culture du riz au Guilân (Perse) et dans les autres provinces du sud de la Caspienne', *Annales de l'Ecole Nationale d'Agriculture de Montpellier* 10, pp 130–63.

Ramazani, N., 1974 (1932), *Persian Cooking*, New York: Quadrangle.

Rayes, George N., 1957, *L'Art Culinaire Libanais*, Beirut.

— 1981 (1951), *Fann al-Ṭabkh*, Beirut.

al-Rāzī, Abū Bakr (10th century), n.d., *Manāfiʿ al-Aghdhiya wa Dafʿa Maḍārihā*, Beirut: Dār Ṣādir.

Rhea, Rev. Samuel Audley, 1880 (1869), 'Brief grammar and vocabulary of the Kurdish language of the Hakari district', *Journal of the American Oriental Society* 10, pp. 118–55.

Richards, Audrey I., 1932, *Hunger and Work in a Savage Tribe: a Functional Study of Nutrition among the Southern Bantu*, London: Routledge & Kegan Paul.

— 1939, *Land, Labour and Diet in Northern Rhodesia: an Economic Study of the Bemba Tribe*, Oxford: Oxford University Press.

Rios, A., 1990, 'The first communion banquet', *Oxford Symposium on Food and Cookery*, London: Prospect Books, pp 175–82.

Roden, Claudia, 1968, *A Book of Middle Eastern Food*, London: Thomas Nelson.

— 1986, *A New Book of Middle Eastern Food*, Harmondsworth: Penguin.

Rodinson, M., 1949, 'Recherches sur les documents arabes relatifs à la cuisine', *Revue des Etudes Islamiques* 17, pp 95–165.

— 1960,'Ghidāʾ ', *Encyclopédie de l'Islam*, 2nd edn, Paris: Maisonneuve; Leiden: Brill, pp 1081–97.

Rutter, E., 1928, *The Holy Cities of Arabia*, 2 vols, London and New York: G. P. Putnam's Sons.

Saberi, Helen, 1986, *Noshe Djan – Afghan Food and Cookery*, London.

al-Saffar, A., A. Charnes and M. Duffua, 1988, *Food Self-sufficiency Investments in the Middle East* (Research Report CCS 493), Center of Cybernetics, College of Business Administration, University of Texas at Austin, pp 1–20.

Sahlins, Marshall D., 1976, *Culture and Practical Reason*, Chicago: University of Chicago Press.

Sale, George (trans), n.d., *The Koran*, London.

Salmon, G., 1905, 'Les Bdadoua,' *Archives Marocaines* 2, pp 358–63.

al-Samarqandī (early 13th century), n.d., *Aqrābādhīn*; trans M. Levey and Noury al-Khaledy as *The Medical Formulary of al-Samarqandī*. Philadelphia: University of Pennsylvania Press, 1967.

Sāmiʿ, Jenerāl al-Seyyed Maḥmud, 1928–9/1337, *Ṭabkh-e Ṭaʿām barā-ye Maktab-e Fonun-e Ḥarbiyeh*, Kabul.

Al Sasi, Omar, 1972, *Sprichwörter und andere volkskundliche Texte aus Mekka*, Münster.

Sbath, P., 1937, '*Kitāb Jawāhir al-Ṭīb al-Mufrada*. Traité sur les Substances Simples Aromatiques par Yohanna ben Massawaîh', *Bulletin de l'Institut d'Egypte* 19, pp 5–27.

— 1944, '*Mukhtaṣar fī 'l-Ṭīb*. Abrégé sur les Arômes par Sahlān ibn Kaissān', *Bulletin de l' Institut d'Egypte* 26, pp 183–213.

Sen, A. K., 1981, *Poverty and Famines: an Essay on Entitlements and Deprivation*,

Oxford: Clarendon Press.

— 1985, 'Food, economics and entitlements', in *Hunger and Poverty: the Poorest Billion* (Working Paper no 1), Helsinki 10, World Institute for Development Economics Research, Annankatu 42, pp 1–30.

Shaida, Margaret, 1992, *The Legendary Cuisine of Persia*, Henley-on-Thames: Lieuse Publications.

Shara al-Dīn, Batūl, n.d., *Fann al-Ṭabkh*, Beirut.

Sheriff, John K., 1989, *The Fate of Meaning: Charles Peirce, Structuralism and Literature*, Princeton, NJ: Princeton University Press.

Sidiqov, D., 1981, *Lazzatli taomlar*, Tashkent.

Simmons, Shirin, 1988, *Entertaining the Persian Way*, London: Lennard.

Soane, E. B., 1913, *Grammar of the Kurmanji or Kurdish Language*, London: Luzac.

Spiegel, F., 1887, *Die arishe Periode*, Leipzig.

Spuler, Bertold, 1952, *Iran in frühislamischer Zeit*, Wiesbaden: Steiner.

Steingass, F., 1975 (1892), *A Comprehensive Persian-English Dictionary*, Beirut: Librairie du Liban.

Stokes, Martin, 1992, *The Arabesk Debate: Music and Musicians in Modern Turkey*, Oxford: Clarendon Press.

Stouff, Louis, 1970, *Revitaillement et Alimentation en Provence aux XIVe et XVe Siècles*, Paris/La Haye: Mouton.

al-Ṭabarī, 1980, *Mohammed, Seau des Prophètes*, Paris: Sindbad.

al-Takarlī, Fu'ād (Fouad), 1980, *al-Raj' al-Ba'īd*, Beirut: Dār Ibn Rushd; trans Martine Faideau and Rachida Turki as *Les Voix de l'Aule*, Paris: Edition J. C. Lattès, 1985.

Tanıklariyle, 1957, *Tarama Sözlüğü*, 4 vols, Istanbul.

Tapper, Nancy, 1990, '*Ziyaret*: gender, movement and exchange in a Turkish community', in Dale Eickelman and James Piscatori (eds), *Muslim Travellers: Pilgrimage, Migration and the Religious Imagination*, London: Routledge.

— 1991, *Bartered Brides: Politics, Gender and Marriage in an Afghan Tribal Society*, Cambridge: Cambridge University Press.

Tapper, Nancy and Richard, 1987, 'The birth of the Prophet: gender and ritual in Turkish Islam', *Man (NS)* 22, pp 69–92.

Tapper, Richard and Nancy, 1986, ' "Eat this, it'll do you a power of good"; food and commensality among Durrani Pashtuns', *American Ethnologist* 13 (1), pp 62–79.

Taymūr, Aḥmad, 1949, *al-Amthāl al-'Āmmiyya*, Cairo: Maṭba'at al-Istiqāma.

Tchoubinoff, D., 1840, *Dictionnaire Géorgien-Russe-Français*, Moscow.

Thalen, D. C. P., 1979, *Ecology and Utilization of Desert Shrub Rangelands in Iraq*, Dordrecht: Dr W. Junk B V Publishers.

Thompson, Stuart (ed), 1993, *Anthropology in Action*, special issue on food.

Tilsley Benham, Jill, 1986, ' "Is that Hippocrates in the kitchen?" A look at sardi/garmi in Iran', in *Proceedings of Oxford Symposium on Food and Cookery 1984 and 1985*, ed T. Jaine, London: Prospect Books, pp 102–14.

Trenga, V., 1915–16. 'Les Branès', *Archives Berbères* I (3), pp 200–18 and (4), pp 293–330.

Turabi, 1987, *Turkish Cookery Book: a Collection of Recipes, Compiled by Turabi Efendi 'from the best Turkish Authorities'*, limited edn, Rottingdean: Cooks Books.

Tursunov, Arif, and Karim Makhmudov, 1982, *Uzbekskie Bliuda*, Tashkent.

Ullman, Manfred, 1978, *Islamic Medicine*, Edinburgh: Edinburgh University Press.

Virolle-Souibes, M., 1989, 'Pétrir la pâte malaxer du sens exemples kabyles', *Techniques et Cultures* 13, pp 73–101.

Vryonis, Speros, 1971, *The Decline of Medieval Hellenism in Asia Minor and the Process of Islamization from the Eleventh through the Fifteenth Centuries*, Berkeley: University of California Press.

Vullers, I. A., 1855, *Lexicon Persico-Latinum*, 2 vols, Bonn.

Waines, David, 1989, *In a Caliph's Kitchen*, London: Riad El-Rayyes.

al-Warrāq, Ibn Sayyār, 1987, *Kitāb Ṭabīkh*, ed K. Ohrnberg and S. Mroueh, Helsinki: Finnish Oriental Society.

Waterbury, John, 1979, *The Hydropolitics of the Nile*, Syracuse University Press.

Weber, Eugene, 1977, *Peasants into Frenchmen*, London: Chatto.

Weinbaum, Marvin G., 1982, *Food, Development and Politics in the Middle East*, Boulder: Westview Press; London: Croom Helm.

Weir, Shelagh, 1986, *Qat in Yemen*, London: British Museum Publications.

Wensinck, A. J., 'Khamr', *Encyclopaedia of Islam*.

— 1925, *Arabic New Year and the Fast of Tabernacles*, Amsterdam.

— 1960, 'Ashura', *Encyclopédie de l'Islam*, 2nd edn, I, pp 72–6.

Wilson, C. A., 1991, 'Ritual, form and colour in the mediaeval food tradition', in C. A. Wilson (ed), *The Appetite and the Eye*, Edinburgh: Edinburgh University Press, pp 5– 27.

Yotopoulos, M., 1983, 'Middle-income classes and food crises: the "new" food-feed competition', *EDC* 33, pp 463–83.

al-Zāhirī, Khalīl (14th–15th century), 1894, *Zubdat Kashf al-Mamālik*, ed P. Ravaisse, Paris.

al-Zamakhsharī, Abu'l-Qāsim Maḥmūd b. 'Umar (12th century), 1963, *Pishrow va Adab*, ed M. Kazem Emam, Tehran.

Zenker, J. T., 1866, *Dictionnaire Turc-Arabe-Persan*, Leipzig.

Zifzāf, Muḥammad, 1984, *Bayḍat al-Dīk*, Casablanca: Manshūrāt al-Jāmi'a.

Zubaida, Sami, 1989, 'Korma and Qavurma', in *Proceedings of the Second International Food Congress*, Konya, pp 470–73.

Index